Gender Concerns in South Asia

Gender Concerns in South Asia

Some Perspectives

Editors
Manjeet Bhatia
Deepali Bhanot
Nirmalya Samanta

Rawat Publications
Jaipur • New Delhi • Bangalore • Mumbai • Hyderabad • Guwahati

ISBN 81-316-0115-3

Published by
Prem Rawat for **Rawat Publications**
Satyam Apts, Sector 3, Jawahar Nagar, Jaipur 302 004 (India)
Phone: 0141 265 1748 / 7006 Fax: 0141 265 1748
E-mail: info@rawatbooks.com
Website: www.rawatbooks.com

New Delhi Office
4858/24, Ansari Road, Daryaganj, New Delhi 110 002
Phone: 011 2326 3290

Also at Bangalore, Mumbai, Hyderabad and Guwahati

Typeset by Rawat Computers, Jaipur
Printed at Chaman Enterprises, New Delhi

Contents

FOREWORD

When Muhammad Yunus received the Nobel Peace Prize for the success of microfinance among the poorest persons in Bangladesh, the attention of the world rested for a while on the paradox of South Asia, the remarkable market growth along with the prevalence of poverty and illiteracy. Concomitant thoughts would turn towards questioning the parameters upon which global discourse has positioned the indicators of "development" and "progress". One is led to seek out alternative models for South Asia, models that may challenge or perhaps even defy conventional measures of civilizational advancement, and even coin new terminologies such the Gross National Happiness (GNH) made popular in Bhutan. In the last half decade international research has tried to enter the cultural corridors of such "Eastern" countries, accepting finally that the oriental gaze that Edward Said decried has indeed to change to become a participative endeavour in cultural understanding and political acumen.

The book *Gender Concerns in South Asia* is a timely entrant in this field of discussion. It presents "perspectives" from established scholars in South Asia, thereby setting up a significant dialogue about nations, identities and marks of globalization. A deeper focus picks out gender issues for elaboration, a subject complex in itself and seldom attempted with the perspicacity found in the present volume. It has always troubled women's studies professionals as to whether "gender" should obtain priority over other affiliations such as citizenship, ethnicity, class or caste. The editors have wisely allowed that question to permeate the texture of the volume and refrained from attempting answers. I find it remarkable that the heterogeneity of South Asia is reflected authentically in the collection, at the same time that issues have been labeled and held cohesively together for analysis. On the subject of the "missing woman" for instance, a term for which we must thank Amartya Sen, several essays give directional tools towards a better understanding of India, yet they also link up with concerns of violence against women, or trafficking, which are manifestations of age-old coercive practices in many countries of South Asia.

The book contextualizes a highly postmodern concern with identity. Gender, as Judith Butler said, is "performative". Essays will directly and indirectly touch upon the shifting paradigms within which "gender" is enacted. In the women's movement in India, in the Beijing PFA, in the Human Rights debates, it is the positioning of the woman in family and community, in the legal system of the country and the region that the change agents of society will enter. This is a book that will be useful for activists and academics alike for it is in the bridges that we erect that the better visions will be found. Politically, SAARC denotes a group identity, socially and culturally layers of "difference" can cause excitement as well as discomfort. Postcoloniality is a lived condition, and the editors of the book successfully hold up that multiplicity before their readers.

It is a pleasure to offer these remarks. I recall with admiration the diligence that went into the making of this volume and I congratulate Manjeet Bhatia, Dipali Bhanot and Nirmalya Samanta for their unflinching belief in the subject they were investigating. I also thank them and the staff at Women's Studies and Development Centre, University of Delhi, for the many wonderful years that I spent as the Director of this vibrant institution.

1 October, 2007

Prof. Malashri Lal
University of Delhi

Acknowledgements

This book would not have been possible without the cooperation of our contributors. Experts in their respective fields they are all engaged in intensive academic research and are also actively involved with issues and causes related to gender and society. We thank all our contributors for their help, cooperation and for being patient with us!

The Women's Studies Development Centre, University of Delhi has been in the real sense the centre from where this work emerged.

We thank Prof. Malashri Lal, Joint Director, South Campus, University of Delhi, and the previous Director of the Women's Studies Development Centre, University of Delhi, for all her support and guidance towards this project. We thank the present Director of the Women's Studies Development Centre, University of Delhi, Prof. Vibha Chaturvedi, for her encouragement and support.

The UGC Refresher Course on *Women in South Asia* that was organized by the Women's Studies Development Centre, University of Delhi and the Centre for Professional Development for Higher Studies, University of Delhi was where the idea of this book germinated. We would like to thank Prof. Gopa Bhardwaj, Director, Centre for Professional Development for Higher Studies, for being a constant source of encouragement.

Contributors

A.R. Nanda is presently working as an Executive Director at the Population Foundation of India. Prior to joining the Foundation, he was serving as the Secretary, Ministry of Health and Family Welfare in the Department of Family Welfare, Government of India.

His contribution to the field of population, development and health, especially reproductive and child health, is widely recognized. Intensification of the reproductive and child health programme, with life cycle approach, is one of his major contributions. Mr Nanda has several publications in important journals and books to his credit.

Anoja Wickramasinghe is presently Senior Professor and Head of Department of Geography, University of Peradeniya, Sri Lanka. Her specialization and teaching areas include Natural Resources Management and Planning, Gender and Development, Gender Analysis and Planning, Community Forestry and Agroforestry, and Environmental Management.

She has published *Deforestation, Women and Forestry: The Case of Sri Lanka* (Intel Books, 1995), and is the author of a number of articles on similar themes.

Anuradha M. Chenoy is Professor in the School of International Studies, Jawaharlal Nehru University, New Delhi. She works on International Relations, Russia, Central Asia and Gender Issues. She has been the Chairperson and Director of the Area Studies Program for Russia and Central Asia, SIS, JNU. Among her notable publications is *Militarism and Women in South Asia* (Kali Books, New Delhi, 2001) and *The Making of New Russia* (Har Anand Publishers, New Delhi, 2001).

Chandni Joshi is the Regional Director of the United Nations Development Fund for Women (UNIFEM) in the South Asia region. Her work in the region involves lobbying with the governments for gender auditing, linking micro voices with macro policies, promoting learning among countries and adding to UNIFEM's knowledge base.

She has been closely involved in the successful mainstreaming of gender in the VI and VII National Development Plans of Nepal, IV Plan of Bangladesh, VII National Development Plan of Pakistan, the Perspective Plan of Maldives, and the IX and X National Development Plans of India. She has in particular been instrumental in putting the issues of women's unaccounted work, peace and violence against women, including trafficking of women in the South Asia region on the map of women's development agenda.

She is the recipient of the SAARC medal in 1988 and has been honoured by His Majesty the King of Nepal, with the Prabal Trishakti Patta, in 1989.

Flavia Agnes is a women's rights advocate, activist and researcher. She has played an important role in bringing women's rights to the forefront within the legal system and in contextualizing issues of gender and identity. Within the premise of 'reforms from within' she has played an important role in reforming the Christian Personal Laws as well as advancing the rights of Muslim women. Her organization, *Majlis* has worked consistently in countering the rising wave of Hindu fundamentalism in the country. Significant among her many publications is her autobiographical book *My Story Our Story ... Of Rebuilding Broken Lives*. Other publications include *Law and Gender Inequality: The Politics of Personal Laws* *in India* and an omnibus, *Women and Law* (co-edited), both published by Oxford University Press.

Indu Agnihotri is currently working as Senior Fellow at the Centre for Women's Development Studies, New Delhi. Prior to this she taught history at the Vivekananda College, University of Delhi. She has a long-term involvement with the women's movement, both as an academic and an activist. She has been writing extensively on the themes of history of the women's movement, violence against women, ecology and environment.

Kamla Bhasin remained in FAO, New Delhi for almost twenty-two years (as an international UN staff) to carry out the FAO-NGO South Asia Programme to provide capacity building, networking and support to NGOs, people's organizations, women's groups and poverty-oriented government programmes.

Since 2001 she has been working as a freelance trainer/ resource person and conducting workshops and Gender Sensitization and Analysis Courses on issues related to gender, women's empowerment and sustainable livelihoods in Africa, Bangladesh, Maldives and Nepal for trainers, policy makers and senior workers of NGOs and senior government servants.

A committed gender activist Bhasin is the founder member of JAGORI, Women's Resource and Training Centre, New Delhi. She writes passionately on gender issues in both Hindi and English and reaches out to a large spectrum of readership including children. Her quick reference books on patriarchy, masculinity and feminism are very popular. She has co-authored along with Ritu Menon *Borders and Boundaries: Women in India's Partition* (Kali for Women, 1997), also published by Rutgers University and Oxford University Press, Karachi.

Lalitendu Jagatdeb is a social scientist specializing in developmental communication. He has worked extensively in the areas of population, development, child survival and safe motherhood, maternal mortality and morbidity, reproductive and sexual health, HIV/AIDS, girl child, gender and rights.

He has worked with various national and international organizations including National Institute of Health and Family

Welfare, ORG Center for Social Research and UNFPA. Currently, he is with Population Foundation of India (PFI), New Delhi.

Lucinda Joy Peach is Associate Professor in the Department of Philosophy and Religion at American University, New York. Her areas of research and teaching include gender and religion, religion and law, women's human rights, and applied ethics (including bioethics, feminist ethics, and legal ethics). She is the author of *Legislating Morality: Religious Identity and Moral Pluralism* (Oxford University Press, 2002). She has edited *Women and World Religions* (Prentice Hall, 2002), *Women in Culture: An Anthology* (Blackwell Publishers 1998), and co-edited (with April Morgan and Colette Mazucelli) *Ethics and Global Affairs: An Active Learning Sourcebook* (New York: Kumarian Press, 2004).

Manjeet Bhatia is in the faculty of the Women's Studies Development Centre, University of Delhi. She is in charge of coordinating a large number of projects that include research work, development of gender studies curriculum and courses, and providing pedagogic tools for students and teachers of the university involved in gender studies. She has recently completed the project *Strategies to Operationalise Legislation on Domestic Violence Against Women: India and the United Kingdom*, sponsored by the British Council of India.

Manzoor Ahmed is Director of BRAC University Institute of Education and Development, Dhaka, Bangladesh. He is also the Convenor of Education Watch Bangladesh – an independent education research and monitoring organization.

He began his professional career in the Institute of Education and Research, Dhaka University and was placed on deputation for a short time with the Ministry of Education of Pakistan as Deputy Education Adviser. He later joined UNICEF in 1978 and served in various senior positions including the Associate Director of the Programme Division, Senior Education Adviser, and UNICEF's Country Director in Ethiopia, China and Japan. He was also for several years the Associate Director of Studies at the International Council for Educational Development in the United States. He is the author of several books and articles on education and development.

Nandita Baruah is presently working with the USAID as the Senior Regional Advisor for the South Asia Anti-Trafficking and Equity Programme. She is a social sector development professional working with both community-based organizations and international bilateral and multilateral agencies on issues related to gender, human rights and community development. She has also worked with the United Nations Development Fund for Women (UNIFEM), as the Regional Coordinator for the South Asia Anti-Trafficking Programme.

She has worked on a number of projects relating to gender equity and justice specific to the rights of women and children in South Asia and on adolescent sexual health, sexual abuse and child rights.

Preet Rustagi is currently working as a Senior Fellow at the Institute for Human Development, New Delhi. She has been working on labour, gender and development issues for the past ten years. Her recent research interests include gender development indicators, work, employment and institutions, crimes against women, and women's equality and empowerment. She has been pursuing intensive sub-state level analysis for India to examine gender inequalities and discrimination against women and has also worked on the South Asia region. She has published several articles on these subjects in various journals and books.

Sheela Saravanan is a researcher with a wide range of experience in India, the United Kingdom and Australia. She is presently working on the project *Maternal and Infant Health in India: The Role and Contribution of Traditional Birth Attendants*. She has coordinated the project *Gender Planning Network* in the South Asia (Bangladesh, India, Nepal, Pakistan and Sri Lanka), funded by IDRC (International Development Research Centre), Canada. The project involved analyzing among other things the gender implications of the micro impact of macro economic policies (MIMAP).

Uma Chakraborty is a historian, who taught at Miranda House, University of Delhi for four decades. She is associated with the women's movement and the movement for democratic rights. She has written on gender, caste and the histories of the underclass and has the distinction of being a pioneer in gender studies. Her writings include *The Social Dimension of Early Buddhism* (Oxford University Press, 1987) and *Rewriting History: The Life and Times of Pandita Ramabai* (Kali for Women, 1998). Her book *Gendering Caste: Through a Feminist Lens* (Stree, 2003) is much acclaimed.

Introduction

The idea of a book like this emerged from the deliberations during a Refresher Course in Women's Studies for college teachers, organized by the Women's Studies and Development Centre, University of Delhi, the central focus of which was *Women in South Asia.* Participants at this course felt that the available literature on the subject was inadequate, and that there was an increasing requirement for more informed analysis about gender issues in this region. This book is an attempt to bring together the thoughts and perspectives of some well-known, serious academics and activists in an anthology that would serve the scholars and teachers working in this area.

In the globalized world of free markets, no area of the world can now remain isolated – economically, politically and socially – from the rest of the international community. The geographical area of South Asia comprising of what is also known as the SAARC (South Asian Association for Regional Cooperation) nations of India, Pakistan, Bangladesh, Sri Lanka, Nepal, Bhutan and the Maldives constitutes one-fourth of the world's population. Dubiously, this region of the world is also the home of more than half of the world's poor people.[1] The enormous implication of just these demographic facts makes this an area of the world that just cannot be ignored.

Though these seven nations of South Asia are distinct from one another and have unique geographical areas, ecological range, political-economic systems and socio-cultural features, they also share many commonalities. During the last century these nations emerged from a colonial past, searching for a post-colonial identity of their own. Saddled with agrarian economics, deep-rooted religiosity and traditional modes of social life that are extremely varied and deeply entrenched in patriarchy, the economies of these South Asian nations have for the past half a century moved slowly towards greater industrialization, modernization and urbanization. Economic development and social uplift have been the central concerns of the governments of these nations. In the past decade this region has seen historic changes in economic growth. The region has the highest ratios of trade to GDP, the largest absolute inflows of foreign direct investment, and an average annual growth rate of 5.3 per cent.[2] The positive effect of this economic upsurge has been an increasing visibility of women in all walks of life as well as decision-making possesses. Yet, there are a number of socio-political and economic issues that are a matter of concern and need to be addressed immediately if sustainable development and the creation of an equitable society are to be achieved. The paradox that characterizes the region of South Asia in terms of developmental parameters is that these nations have very high illiteracy levels, one-third of all maternal deaths occur in this region and almost half of the children in this region below the age of five are malnourished.

Central to many of these issues is the role and position of women. The fact that there are nearly 50 million missing women in this region of the world is a clear indication of the adverse social, political and cultural status of the woman in South Asia. Female foeticide, low levels of education, poor health conditions (more than half of women in India suffer from some form of anaemia), trafficking, unequal job opportunities, an increasing violence against women, the systemic degradation of the environment and the general government apathy all add up to a grim picture of neglect and discrimination against women that cuts across class, caste, religion or regional variations. The region and its population is not homogeneous, diversity and multiplicity are a characteristic of South Asia, and these major concerns related to women manifest themselves differently in different regions of South Asia. The essays in this book evaluate the condition and position of the woman in context of various issues that these nations grapple with in their progress towards development.

Fifteen years after the historic Convention on the Elimination of All Forms of Discrimination Against Women (CEDAW), the Fourth World Conference was held in Beijing in 1995. At this conference it was accepted that a gender perspective was necessary and imperative in all aspects of development, planning and implementation. The resulting Beijing Platform for Action (BPFA) was a commitment by nations towards the advancement of the cause of women's movements across the world as well to address the issue of women's rights through state policies. All the seven South Asian nations are signatories to BFTA and have ratified CEDAW.

In spite of the fact that these nations are signatories to various international treaties and conventions that seek to empower the women, very little is actually done at the grassroots level and centuries old practices of gender discrimination continue to be perpetuated. Alliances with these international treaties, laws and conventions do help in generating stimulating debates and deliberations but the governments of these nations still seem to be groping their way in terms of implementation of professed targets.

Chandni Joshi in her essay looks at the impact of the agendas and decisions that were deliberated and adopted at major United Nations conferences on gender. She traces UNIFEM's role in bringing together NGO and government representatives in the implementation of these decisions. Her essay tracks the progress that the world is making towards gender equality in terms of conscious decisions that are being taken by responsible international agencies. The information that the essay provides helps in making an assessment and evaluation of the strategies and plan inputs that were adopted as resolutions in various summits and conferences by the South Asian nations to empower women and to address the many problems that are gender-specific.

In a complementary analysis *Preet Rustogi* demonstrates the significance of development indicators and their relevance in evaluating the progress of women's developments in this region. Through the use of statistics and data, the essay establishes how the region lags behind in most development indicators and how traditional social ordering along patrilineal-partrilocal families has been a deterrent to the emancipation of women.

The problems related to women and their status can be located in the manner these societies treat their girl child. Discussing the socio-demographic implications of the girl child in terms of education, health and sex ratio, *A.R. Nanda and Lalitendu Jagatdeb* argue that demographic disparity between girls and boys though universal has remained largely invisible because demographers focus on women and not the girl child. An analysis of some of the human development indicators draws a dismal picture. Linking demographic and economic realities with the condition of the girl child in South Asia they suggest an integrated and holistic approach to the girl child's development. The need to integrate the girl child in the mainstream development process is a central concern that must be urgently addressed to by planners and administrators.

In another essay on the girl child *Manzoor Ahmed* voices his concern regarding the denial of the right to education which is an instrument of empowerment. He advocates a 'rights-based approach' to the problem. Evaluating in details the position of South Asia in context of women's education, he points out that policy and recommendation need not necessarily mean action and implementation. An excessively centralized structure, along with rigid bureaucratic tradition, insufficient commitment and inadequate allocation of funds, ensures that the girl child is denied her right to education. In order to address the problem, a politically 'activist' stand needs to be taken.

Demographic analysis reveals startling data regarding the status of women in South Asia, especially in the context to issues of health. *Sheela Saravanan's* assessment of the status of the reproductive health of women in South Asia clearly show that health policies and strategies have often gone wrong and that there is an urgent need to review these policies while it is necessary to strengthen strategies that have produced positive results. Using data regarding the crucial aspects of fertility, contraception and maternal health, the essay points out how nations like Sri Lanka reflect positive indicators while statistics reveal a healthy and remarkable change in patterns of fertility and contraception in Bangladesh.

There is no doubt that economic resources that are controlled by the government of these South Asian nations have to be consciously and systematically diverted towards those sectors that will directly help the women of the region, for example, education, health and self-employment initiatives. The success story of the Gramin Bank in Bangladesh indicates how resource availability at micro levels can be an instrument of vast changes. Yet, the stark reality is that this region, in spite of being one of the poorest in the world is highly militarized and large amount of government funds are diverted towards weapons. It is also a fact that most of the South Asian nations face internal turmoil and disturbance, which also weighs heavy on the government exchequer. Funds for developmental schemes get squeezed and now with globalization and resultant privatization the government is keen to relinquish its welfare activities and depend on market forces and capital investment to fulfil its development priorities.

Anuradha M. Chenoy's essay links the ideology and practice of militarism with patriarchy. She examines historically the construction of the nation and its patriarchal nature and how honour of nation/community/woman is interchangeable categories. Disturbingly, the feminist analysis of international security structures shows stark continuities of traditional ideologies and practice in this period of globalization. She argues that women become the target of violence in any form of conflict be it – national, religious or ethnic – because violence against the women is seen as a violation of the honour or territory of the enemy. Militarism is not restricted to the state alone but is practised by non-state or anti-state movements. Fundamentalist religious movements or groups representing regional or ethnic interests bypass political negotiation and take up arms. The militarist methods of these groups on the one hand seek the agency of women to further their cause and at the same time also seek to control women in many ways that emerge deeply entrenched patriarchal biases.

The South Asian region is in the process of a transformation from agrarian economy to the industrial economy. Inevitably, this transition has affected the individual and society in more than one way. Paradoxically, the economic and social changes have not been able to initiate any alteration in the traditional power structures that control and dominate the social functioning of the region. As issues of education, health, violence and political rights become vital to developmental paradigms, the deeply patriarchal societies of these nations have to consider and reconsider the role and position of women in the family and society. In fact, when it comes to issues of gender, it sometimes seems that the hegemonies of power structures have only got reinforced, rendering the women even more powerless and vulnerable. Apparently, the economic changes in the society make it seem as if women are getting more opportunities and a better deal, but the forces of domination continue to work insidiously and are often not easily identifiable. As the old makes way for the new, various forms of resistances result in conflict situations and it is not surprising that different parts of this region are caught in the throes of immense social upheaval and unrest. The issues of gender must be understood in this context and the woman's vulnerability must be estimated within this hostile space.

Indu Agnihotri reflects on globalization and its effect from the woman's point of view. She sees globalization as an onslaught of free market ideology and feels that the status of women in South Asia can be judged only by an analysis of the macro-level developments and changes that globalization has unleashed. In a countrywise analysis, the situation in each one of these nations, she shows how this region of the world has remained the least gender-sensitive and how gender based disparities not only continue but are accentuated with market liberalization.

The changes unleashed by globalization have affected the environment of South Asian region in a significant manner. *Anoja Wickramasinghe's* essay on women and environment addresses the issues from a gender perspective. The relation of woman with environment is connected with a number of economic, social and cultural factors. The essay seeks to bring the core issues of equity and justice into the environmental debates which so far have been mainly concerned with only the problem of degradation. Since the woman's livelihood and occupational security in South Asia is mainly land-based, the environment becomes central to her well-being. There is thus a need to understand the woman-environment relationship in an integrated manner that includes issues like bio-diversity, land reform, technology, industrialization, and economics so that relevant policies and programmes are created to help change the lives of women in this region.

The social environment in which a woman is South Asia lives is often a hostile space where she is subject to a host of subjugations and is forced to provide forced labour and a number of services. This is more so now with globalization throwing up a large labour force that has no legal safety net and is highly vulnerable to exploitation. *Nandita Baruah,* in her article on trafficking in women and children, describes the various definitional constructs of trafficking. She makes an assessment of the trafficking patterns in the South Asian nations and the legal provisions that have been made by these countries to contain it. The issue of trafficking, like environment, must also be addressed with in the larger spectrum of labour migration, poverty and lack of education and health. The urge to simply enact and enforce a preventive law may not be sufficient.

The societies of South Asian nations are characterized by the co-existence of a number of religious faiths and a high degree of religiosity among the people. Religion is a prime force through which patriarchy operates. Economic changes, which seemingly liberate the women from their traditional roles, threaten patriarchy, which then uses religion to reinforce itself by devising newer methods of exercising control often taking the excuse of morality and ethics and codes of social behaviour. The rise of fundamentalism in this region in the past decade underlines the idea that religion is an effective potent tool of control. Religion works hand in hand with cultural structures to ensure the continuation and perpetuation of power equation in this region.

Flavia Agnes, in her essay on legal pluralism and minority identity, looks at some specific legal cases and brings to light the inherent prejudices that work within the legal frameworks. She also analyzes how the media plays an opinion forming role which is often coloured by social prejudices. In such a scenario, gender justice gets lost in rhetoric. She points out to the positive and encouraging trends that seem to be now emerging.

As the woman becomes more visible in daily life, her image is often subjected to being a projection of male desire. In Laura Mulvey's words 'the determining male gaze projects its fantasy into the female figure'. The media's projection of the image of the woman is the subject of the essay on gender imagery in American and Indian advertisements by *Lucinda Joy Peach.* The essay analyzes how the objectification of the women is done in the media. Drawing parallels as well as distinctions between advertisements in the US and India, she shows how advertisements of both the countries promote negative stereotyping, the beauty myth and 'impossible ideals'. The impact of western images on the indigenous aesthetics of female beauty nevertheless remains an area that needs to be further investigated.

One of the serious concerns of this region is the unrelenting violence against women. These issues are addressed by *Manjeet Bhatia* in her paper. She argues that the definition of violence now includes a number of other violent acts and cannot be simply physical violence alone. The declining sex ratio in many parts of this region clearly indicates that the girl child is not preferred. The son preference in these nations traditionally had its multiple ramifications in early marriage, biased property rights, inadequate nutrition, ill-health and unequal opportunities for education and development. This is the fundamental violence against the females perpetuated in this region which later manifests itself in the many heinous crimes against the women and girls. The declining child sex ratio, acid throwing, rape, early motherhood, unsafe public space and honour killings are visible violence against the women and girls of the region. Focusing on specific cases at the micro level, Bhatia draws the larger grim picture of how well-entrenched patriarchal power structures continue to perpetuate injustice in spite of legal deterrents.

Uma Chakravarti's essay on the role of women involved in women's movements is a questioning of the 'pigeon-holing' of women in stereo-typical roles as a part of the agenda of cultural nationalism. Highlighting specific women's movements in India, she tries to formulate a model for the South Asian situation. She graphs chronologically the trajectory of the women's movements and analyzes the changes. Aware that the movement is not homogenous and its dynamism comes from its interface with other movements and causes both eastern and western, she concludes that today the woman's movements need to look at globalization critically and struggle for developmental strategies that are arrived at through democratic processes and at the same time resist policies that are determined by global centres of power.

Kamla Bhasin's article is characteristic of the passionate intensity with which she involves herself in issues that are close to her heart. She raises some key issues related to women's empowerment and education in the region of South Asia. Drawing our attention to the tragic paradox of affluence and poverty in South Asia, she asserts that poverty is man-made and hence immoral. Looking critically at free market and the paradigms of development, she states that the world has been robbed of its essential feminity and along with it ethics and justice. She emphasizes the need of education for the empowerment of women.

The present twenty-first century is in many ways unfamiliar terrain that the woman steps into for the first time. If agrarian economics and the resultant social and cultural patterns had oppressed and suppressed the woman in a certain way, then the new industrial economic environment which does liberate the woman from many of her traditional identities and provides her with new opportunities, also simultaneously devises its own coercive structures of oppression and discrimination. As editors, we did not want to prioritize the issues and concerns, nor did we want to categorize and group these issues under sub-titles. We believe that all the issues are equally important and are interrelated.

Notes

1. *Progress of South Asian Women 2005*. A Series for the Fifth South Asia Regional Ministerial Conference Celebrating Beijing Plus Ten. UNIFEM, New Delhi. 2005.
2. Ibid.

1

Girl Child

Socio-Demographic Implications for South Asia

A.R. Nanda and Lalitendu Jagatdeb

South Asia is a region of striking socio-economic and cultural diversity with wide variations among countries. It covers seven countries, viz., India, Pakistan, Nepal, Sri Lanka, Bangladesh, Bhutan and Maldives. The region shares about 20 per cent of the global population. Children make up over 40 per cent of the population, constituting a quarter of the children in the world. Population and development situation here is a reflection of the diversity marked by profound variations in demographic and health indicators. The scale and diversity of South Asia present a huge challenge in addressing development issues.

One of the major initiatives for bringing about development among the developing countries is the setting up of the UN Millennium Development Goals. South Asia continues to face challenges, especially in the areas related to Millennium Development Goals. Almost half of the world's poor living at less than a dollar a day live in South Asia. This pervasive poverty contributes to and is exacerbated by low levels of human development (World Bank, 2003).

In terms of health services around 22 per cent of total population is without access to these services. While the best picture is one of Sri Lanka with only 7 per cent population excluded from health services, the other extreme is 55 per cent in the case of Bangladesh (RIS, 2004). The health situation of this region is determined by factors such as geographic distribution of population, poverty, economic development, education and literacy levels, access to safe water, and sanitation as well as functioning and interventions of the health care system (ACHAN, 2000 and South-South Solidarity, 2000).

South Asia remains the centre of discussion because of the poverty condition, magnitude of its health challenges and demographic diversity. The focus has been on children, especially the status of girl child. Urbanization, poverty and breakdown of family structure have left millions of children displaced or forced to fend for themselves in streets where they are especially vulnerable to violence and exploitation. Their experience is not just an important measure of the human rights situation in South Asian countries, but of the state of the children at large. Girl children face particular disadvantages in the South Asian context. Girls figure disproportionately in infant mortality and illiteracy statistics. These factors together with the persistence practices such as dowry and child marriage also feed other cycles of abuse (Amnesty International, 1998).

Human Development: Current Scenario

In this context of the situation of South Asian countries, the status of women, particularly the status of the girl child, has attracted much attention (HDSA, 2000; HDSA, 2002). Discriminatory treatment of the girl child in South Asia deepens the marginalization of women and perpetuates problems from one generation to the next. South Asia has both the lowest literacy rates and the largest gap between the rates of male and female literacy – 66 per cent and 43 per cent respectively in 2001. Three out of every five South Asian women are illiterates, including three-quarters of Pakistani women and nearly four-fifths of

Table 1

Human Development Indicators for South Asia

Indicators	*India*	*Pakistan*	*Bangladesh*	*Nepal*	*Sri Lanka*	*Bhutan*	*Maldives*
Sex ratio (number of females per 1,000 males)	938	937	954	973	1021	981	945
Life expectancy at birth (years) 2001	63	60	61	59	72	63	67
Female life expectancy (as % of male), 2001	102	100	100	99	108	104	98
Female literacy rate (%15 and above) 2001	46	29	31	25	89	34a	97
Maternal mortality ratio (per 100,000 live births), 1985-2001	407	340b	400	540	90	380	350
Seats in parliament held by women, 2003*	9.3	20.6	2.0	7.9	4.4	9.3	6.0
Infant mortality rate, 2001	67	84	51	66	17	74	58
Underweight children (% under 5), 1993-2001	47	38	48	48	29	19	30
Children malnutrition (% of children under 5), 1993-2001	53	38	48	48	33	—	—
Access to safe water (%), 2001	84	90	97	88	77	62	100
Access to sanitation (%), 2001	26	62	48	28	94	70	56
Human Development Index (HDI), 2001	0.590	0.499	0.502	0.499	0.730	0.511	0.751
Gender Development Index (GDI), 2001	0.574	0.469	0.495	0.479	0.726	0.444c	0.739

Notes: a: Year 2000, b: Year 1990-98, c: Year 1998, *: As of March 2003

Source: Human Development in South Asia 2000, 2002 and 2003
Row 1, UN 1999c
Rows 2,3,4,5,7,8,12,13 UNDP 2003; Row 5 (MMR, India, and IMR India) – SRS
Rows 9, 10, 11, World Bank 2002a

Table 2

Gender Disparities: Selected Indicators

Indicators	*India*	*Pakistan*	*Bangladesh*	*Nepal*	*Sri Lanka*	*Bhutan*	*Maldives*
Primary enrolment (gross) M/F	111/92	93/54	100/101	128/108	107/104	—	131/131
Proportion reaching grade 5 M/F	70/65	—	68/76	67/76	—	89/92	53/57
Secondary enrolment (gross)/F	57/40	29/19	45/47	58/43	70/74	—	—
% Illiterate (15 years) M/F	32/55	43/72	51/70	41/76	6/11	—	
HIV prevalence rate (15-24) M/F	0.34/0.71	0.06/0.05	0.01/0.01	0.27/0.28	0.03/0.04	—	
Under 5 mortality M/F	78/90	121/135	85/90	91/106	30/16	82/78	41/56

Source: State of World Population 2003-Investing in Adolescents' Health and Rights, UNFPA, 2003.

Nepalese women. Between 1970 and 2001 the average rate of female literacy in developing countries as a whole rose from 32 to 66 per cent; in South Asia, however, it rose from 17 to 43 per cent.

The vast majority of South Asian women lack even the most rudimentary health facilities, resulting in high maternal and infant mortality rates. Continuous gender-related inequities, in terms of unequal access to land, productive resources, information, skills and education, have already put millions of South Asian women in disadvantaged position and made them extremely vulnerable to any drastic changes in the economy. South Asian women constitute a major workforce in the region. As the majority of them work in the informal sector and as unpaid family helpers, their work goes unrecognized in national system of accounting. They also face various forms of discrimination in employment. Although they often work harder and for longer hours than men, their earnings are significantly lower (UNIFEM, 1996; HDSA, 2003).

Women's political representation is also very poor in South Asia. Only 7 per cent of South Asian parliamentarians are women. The overall picture of gender-related development is grim in South Asia even in comparison to the region's human development levels. In every South Asian country, the gender-related development index (GDI) is lower than the human development index (HDI).

Demographic disparity between girls and boys, and its universality, has remained invisible, especially since demographic studies of the status of women have not focused separately on girls. Only recently analysts have attempted to identify the direct or indirect correlation of the weaker demographic status of the women globally, to the discrimination meted out to girls. In the South Asia region particularly, studies indicate that the major defaulters in recompensing the young female are Bangladesh, India, Nepal and Pakistan (Sohori, 1994).

Status of Girl Child

South Asia has one of the most distorted sex ratios in the world. Excluding South Asia, the ratio of females to males in the world is 106 to 100: in South Asia it is only 94 to 100, a discrepancy suggesting that 79 million women are simply 'missing' – either not allowed to be born, die of chronic malnutrition, or never receive any medical care.

Discrimination against South Asian women begins at, or before, birth. In many countries, gender-selective abortion and infanticide are common. Sex selection before birth and neglect after birth and during childhood result in men outnumbering women. Female feoticide and infanticide, neglect of health, and gender-biased feeding practices combined with heavy work burdens are manifestations of son preference that is sustained by patriarchal structures which prevails across the region.

Traditionally, demographers and planners have focused their concern to the desire for sons and its impact on fertility levels. But, the impact of son preference on the status and development of women has not been given much attention as an area of public policy. The universal desire for sons – an obsession that cuts across all differences of caste, class and religion – determines both the quantity and quality of investments that parents make in their female children. If a malnourished anaemic girl survives the gender biases during childhood is married off in her adolescence, which result in a host of detrimental reproductive outcomes. Child marriages and early pregnancies still continue though the incidence has considerably reduced.

Table 3
Child Sex Ratio in India

Year	*Child Sex Ratio*
1961	976
1971	964
1981	962
1991	945
2001	927

The case of India is a clear pointer to the situation described above. In India, while the improvement in overall sex ratio is noticed in the 2001 census, what is most alarming is the decline in the child sex ratio (CSR), i.e., the sex ratio of children in the age group of 0-6 years. The decline in CSR is not only in respect to the previous census, but it is continuous from 1961 (see Table 3). What is a matter of concern is the points of decline in the last two decades. There has been a decline of 18 points from 945 in 1991 to 927 in census 2001.

The decline in CSR may be due to different factors such as neglect of female children resulting in their higher mortality at younger ages, female infanticide and female foeticide. Female foeticide refers to a practice where the female foetuses are selectively eliminated after pre-natal sex determination, thus avoiding the birth of girls. High incidence of induced abortion and the sharp decline in the CSR in the last decade clearly prove the practice of female foeticide.

The unholy alliance between tradition (son preference) and technology (ultrasound machines) is playing havoc in the so-called developed states. This basically boils down to the misuse of advanced pre-natal sex detection technology (despite the PNDT Act against sex determination) by unscrupulous doctors, who facilitate female foeticide through induced abortions. If we allow things to carry on this way, sex imbalances generated in the juvenile age group will be sustained for a longer duration and have a cascading effect on the country's sex ratio in the coming years (Nanda, 2002).

The states and union territories that have shown large declines in CSR are Punjab (-82), Haryana (-59), Himachal Pradesh (-54), Gujarat (-50), Chandigarh (-54) and Delhi (-50) though they are economically quite developed with high female literacy rates. There are 122 districts spread over 14 states having CSR less than 900.

There are various socio-economic and health implications of declining sex ratio:

- Decreasing number of females in the society is likely to increase sex-related crimes against women.
- This will lead to increase in social problems like rape, abduction, bride selling, forced polyandry etc.

- Such an imbalance will not only lead to growth in crime against women but will also cause various physical, physiological and psychological disorders, particularly among women.
- The health of the woman is affected as she is forced to go for repeated pregnancies and abortions.

As described in the editorial of India Today's issue on Declining Child Sex Ratio, "In the heart of the some of the most prosperous pockets of the country, there is a darkness that has manifested itself in some of the most damning statistics to emerge from the 2001 census. As Independent India has moved ahead, it's attitude towards the girl child has, as the 2001 census suggests, regressed towards the dark ages – India, be it rich or poor, continues to treat its daughters as unwanted citizens. A country that considers half its human resource pool as unworthy of being born can only have a bleak future" (*India Today*, 2003).

In India, the girl child still occupies a position inferior to that of a male child. Despite steady increase in average marriage age, child marriage is still common in rural society. About 17 per cent of births are from mothers in the age group 15-19 years. Every year, 12 million girls are born – three million of whom do not survive to see their fifteenth birthday. About one-third of these deaths occur in the first year of life and it is estimated that every sixth female death is directly due to gender discrimination.

The root cause of malnutrition amongst girls is as much poverty and lack of nutritious food as lack of value attached to girls. Discriminatory feeding practices reveal (DWCD, 2001) that

- girl's nutritional intake is inferior in quality and quantity,
- boys have access to more nutritious food,
- boys are given first priority with the available food within the family, and
- female infants are breastfed less frequently for shorter duration and over a shorter period than boys.

Women in every social stratum face the added disadvantage of gender discrimination which results in a denial of equal opportunities and equal access to resources. Some manifestations of gender discrimination are lower investment in a girl child's education, pressure on girls to marry early, restrictions on women's mobility which constrain their educational and income earning opportunities, and laws which deny women the same rights as men (WHO, 2000).

Positive Steps

Following the United Nations' adoption of the Convention on the Rights of the Child (CRC) in 1989, world leaders and policy makers met at the World Summit for Children (WSC) in 1990 to promise every child a better future. At the summit, world leaders committed themselves to formulating and pursuing goals that would eliminate malnutrition, ensure basic education, water, sanitation, immunization and protect children against exploitation. All countries of South Asia have ratified the CRC, which emphasizes the need to end all discrimination against girls and other disadvantaged children.

The South Asian nations realized that special emphasis had to be given to the girl child in the region – her status, her problems and the persistent negative social perception of the girl child. Highlighting the need for special action to promote equal rights of girls, 1990 was declared "Year of the Girl Child". The objective of the South Asian Association for Regional Cooperation (SAARC) Year of the Girl Child was to sensitize public opinion and to begin the process to evolve a policy on the discriminatory denial of freedom and equity, equality and dignity to the girl child in most part of South Asia. Subsequently, the SAARC announced that 1991-2000 would be the "Decade of Girl Child" with an added commitment to addressing gender-based inequality. South Asia was a leader in highlighting the need for a special focus on girls globally, raising the girl child issue during preparation for the Fourth World Conference on Women held in Beijing during 1995. As a result girl child issues were included in Beijing Platform for Action. The SAARC summit also suggested various programmes to be undertaken to give the girl child the rightful position in the society (Report 2001).

The guiding principles of the Decade of the Girl Child were to:

- ensure equality of status of the girl child,
- formulate and pursue additional goals and strategies, and
- change social attitudes and behaviour practices.

SAARC's additional gender-specific goals and priority areas were to:

- reduce the infant mortality rate and the under-five child mortality rate disparities,
- reduce early marriage and early pregnancies,
- eliminate malnutrition disparities,
- reduce women's and girls' workload related to fetching water and providing sanitary means of excreta disposal,
- provide universal access to basic education for girls,
- reduce adult female illiteracy, and
- protect girls from exploitation.

Despite countries being different in size and stage of material and human development, and therefore in the situation of the girl child, certain common approaches to organized action are necessary to overcome persistent degrees of discrimination which aggravate poverty and degrade life among the non-poor as well (UNICEF, 1996).

The Way Forward

The issue of integrating the girl child into the mainstream development process is a continuing cause of concern to policy planners, administrators and NGOs in the South Asian region. In an attempt to find solutions to the problems of girl child, governments of South Asian countries have adopted numerous policies and programmes. However, the effects of legislations and formulation of these programmes are limited.

Female literacy is considered to be the most sensitive index of social development. There has been a significant growth in numbers enrolled in schools. Nevertheless, the wide gap between male and female literacy reflects the relatively lower enrolment of girls compared to boys. Besides, a major problem has been the high drop-out rates. There are 121 million primary school age children out of school world wide. Sixty-five million of these children are girls. The Millennium Development Goal for gender parity in primary and secondary education is supposed to have been realized by 2005. If specific attention is not paid to the needs of girls, universal primary education will be unattainable (UNICEF, 2004).

Female schooling does seem to increase several aspects of female autonomy. This has a direct impact on fertility decline. At the same time, investments in female schooling should not become an excuse for not investing in other more direct forms of support for benevolent demographic change. A single-minded commitment to the cause of female schooling runs the very risk of placing all the responsibility for fertility and mortality control on the shoulders of women, instead of sharing of such responsibility with other kinds of social and economic development (Basu, 1996).

For the South Asian countries to achieve a brighter future, the social concern for girl children must be brought back to the centre stage of human development. What is required is a comprehensive and above all rights based response. A response that seeks to build an environment where the rights of girl child are protected. Surely, investments in human capital are needed. However, investments will provide the desired results only when an enabling environment is in place. Creating such an enabling environment involves action at legislative, policy and community level. Devising appropriate policies and building enabling institutions can take place only if there is a firm understanding of the needs of each country and the constraints faced by it.

The notion of communication being directly linked to development in a one-way relationship is erroneously perceived. Information and motivational communication are essential but without proper and supportive socio-economic structures they will not provide sufficient conditions for development. Development strategies should incorporate communication policies as a integral part in the diagnosis of needs and in the design and implementation of selected priorities. In such an approach promoting gender equality is a significant challenge. Unless gender inequalities are addressed in communication and development strategies, the social influence on discrimination against girl child will continue (Jagatdeb, 2004).

It needs to be reiterated that understanding of the origin and causes of the girl child problem is imperative as it will facilitate the evolving of effective measures to cope with the problem. Laws and policies are not enough to address the issues of girl child, what is required is a shift in social values and attitudes towards girl child in South Asia. An integrated and holistic approach to the girl child's development is essential for the creation of a new environment in which she can be valued and nurtured.

REFERENCES

ACHAN 2000 (Asian Community Health Action Network), Asian Health Report.

Amnesty International, 1998 "Children South Asia: Securing their Rights", International Secretariat.

Basu, Alaka M., 1996, "Girls Schooling, Autonomy and Fertility Change: What Do These Words Mean in South Asia", in Roger Jeffery and Alaka M. Basu (eds.), *Girl's Schooling, Women's Autonomy and Fertility Change in South Asia*, Sage Publications.

DWCD, 2001 (Department of Women and Child Development), "Convention on the Rights of the Child-India, First Periodic Report, Ministry of Human Resource Development, Government of India.

HDSA, 2000, Human Development in South Asia: The Gender Question, Mahbub ul Haq Human Development Center, Oxford University Press.

HDSA, 2002, Human Development in South Asia: Agriculture and Rural Development, Mahbub ul Haq Human Development Center, Oxford University Press.

HDSA, 2003, Human Development in South Asia: The Employment Challenge, Mahbub ul Haq Human Development Center, Oxford University Press.

India Today, 2003, Unwanted! Girl Child Population Shows a Shocking Decline even in Affluent India, November, 10, 2003.

Jagatdeb Lalitendu, 2004, "Towards Population Stabilization: A Perspective on Communication and Development", *Health for the Millions*, August-September and October-November 2004.

Nanda, A.R., 2002, "Not Just a Numbers Game", *Seminar*, 5-11 March, 2002.

Report, 2001, "South Asia Girl Child Symposium," Rawalpindi, Pakistan, 23-26 July, 2001.

RIS, 2004 (Research and Information System for the Non-Aligned and Other Developing Countries), South Asia Development and Cooperation Report 2004, New Delhi.

Sohori, Neera Kuckreja, 1994, *Status of Girls in Development Strategies*, Har-Anand Publication, 1994.

South-South Solidarity, India, 2000, "Emerging Health Trends in South Asia: Global and National Responses for the 21st Century", Resource Centre for Primary Health Care, Nepal.

UN, 1999c (United Nations), World Population Prospects, The 1998 Revision. Volume II: Sex and Age, New York.

UNFPA, 2003, State of World Population: Investing in Adolescents' Health and Rights.

UNDP, 2002 (United Nations Development Programme), Human Development Report, 2002, New York, Oxford University Report.

UNICEF, 1996 (The United Nations Children's Fund), *Atlas of South Asian Children and Women*, Regional Office for South Asia.

UNICEF, 2004 (The United Nation Children's Fund), *The State of the World's Children, 2004.*

UNIFEM, 1996 (United Nations Development Fund for Women), "Global Trading Practices and Poverty Alleviation in South Asia: Regional Perspectives on Women and Trade", New Delhi.

World Bank, 2002a, *World Development Indicators 2002*, Washington, DC.

World Bank, 2003, "Health Policy Research in South Asia: Building Capacity for Reform", Abdo S. Yazbek and David H. Peters (eds.), August 2003.

WHO 2000 (World Health Organization), "Women of South-East Asia: A Health Profile", Regional Publications SEARO No. 34.

2

Women and Environment in South Asia

Changes and Future Prospects

Anoja Wickramasinghe

The wave of changes that South Asia has gone through in regard to women and environment is reflected in research discourses, achievements, international commitments, national strategies and policy frameworks and also in NGO movement and civil society organizations. Countries in South Asia, primarily Bangladesh, India, Nepal, Pakistan and Sri Lanka that are taken into consideration in this paper, have made a progressive move in these two paradigms – environment and women. In real terms, the integration has occurred either in some special areas, or marginally in various projects and programmes. Future prospects under many circumstances depend heavily on the recognition of environmental rights by which many characteristics structured on social and economic terms, such as hierarchy, class, race, gender, ethnicity, etc., could be discarded. The women-environment nexus, which is featured with diverse and complex issues, consolidates the variation in livelihood, ecology and customary practices.

The contextual conditions affecting both women and the environment in South Asia are demographic, economic and also the trends associated with land and the environment. For instance, despite women's knowledge and concern over environmental and human sustenance, they are affected by the growth of population, reduced per capita land and also the technology that has been promoted for enhancing agriculture production. In the year 2002 Asia has around 1,373 million people accounting for 22 per cent of the world population. Between 1960 and 2002, except for Bhutan and Sri Lanka, in all other countries, population has grown by two to three times. The per capita cultivable land was less than 0.2 hectare in all countries and the lowest of 0.01 has been recorded in Maldives, Nepal and Sri Lanka. While state agency was forced to take the challenges of protecting the environment and enhancing production for food and economic security, the same has resulted in disempowering women in their local environments. One key factor attributed to this throughout Asia has been the lack of a women's agency.

The state agency in almost all the countries in Asia has introduced environmental protection laws, regulatory frameworks/programmes as well as various legislations for land, forests etc. over the last 50 years. Similarly, various measures have been introduced for the enforcement of legislations and also to see the impacts without paying attention to the social domain in which women's status is clearly reflected. As a result, national strategies have not been fully responsive to social issues. Equity, justice and ecological unsustainability are the issues provocating thoughts and demanding solutions in the area of women and environment. Multiple lines link women to their environments in South Asia, and the links reiterated in literature tend to indicate the aspects picked up by various groups, including adacemics and activists. Often, the focus has been on work relations, occupations, women's livelihood sources, tasks and responsibilities within a unit of function, resources utilization, land degradation, food and nutrition, ecological degradation, traditional knowledge, biomass energy, forestry and biodiversity. Similarly, eco-feminism, feminist political ecology etc. reflecting the efforts in conceptualization the relationships has allowed us to furthering analysis of relationships. In this regard, countries like USA have introduced Environmental Justice Strategy in 1995 (see Eady, 2003) calling for enhanced public participation, health and environmental data, research, access to public information, enhanced environmental protection etc. In translating international agendas pertaining to 'sustainable development' and 'women and environment', the most crucial is the framework that is capable of dealing with contextual conditions in South Asia. Interpretation made by Agyeman and others in 2003, in their introduction to the book *Just Sustainabilities: Development in an Unequal World* stimulates thinking for the contextualization. These authors from the perspectives of sustainability emphasize the need to "ensure a better quality of life for all, now, and into the future, in a just and equitable manner while living within the limits of supporting systems".

South Asia as a Platform for Demonstration

South Asia is a case for demonstrating that in a truly sustainable society wider questions of social justice, needs, welfare, and economic opportunity are integrally connected to environmental concerns. Where women were not disempowered and demoralized, the generation-long knowledge-based practices sustained by them have contributed to social sustainability through ecologically sound resource exploitation and management. This endorses Middleton and O'Keefe (2001), who argued that unless analysis of development begins not with symptoms, environmental or economic instability, but with the cause, social injustice, then no development can be sustainable. South Asia is marked with the inadequate participation of women in decision-making in the political hierarchy and their least involvement in securing their own rights. Serious environmental stresses, including land and ecological degradation and resource scarcities, are deepening with multiple adverse effects on women, society and the generations to come. Such situations are associated with the systems that provide greater opportunities for commercial exploitation than for subsistence. The repercussions bear down disproportionately upon women and the poor than on men and the better off who are capable of avoiding the consequences. Social injustice, as a primary cause for women's deprivation and marginalization in their local environments in these circumstances, comes to the core area deviating from the peripheries.

Past experiences reveal that the targets for ensuring environmental sustainability have been taken into consideration by the individual nations focusing on reversing the environmental degradation and loss of resources. Integration of environmental goals into development while safeguarding against degradation has been a widely accepted process. This has been influenced by the global move since 1983, where the World Commission on Environment and Development made a tremendous impact by linking environmental issues with economic and social development. The most widely referred concept and the document throughout in discussing environment and development is the Brundtland Report. We in South Asia were influenced by many subsequent global initiatives that have been established. The first was the 1992 United Nations Conference on Environment and Development, where Agenda 21 was introduced. The second took place ten years later in 2002, where the international community agreed on a plan of implementation at the World Summit on Sustainable Development (WSSD). The Millennium Development Goals (MDGs), set aside at WSSD, focused on the persisting problems including poverty, universal primary education, gender equality, child mortality, maternal health, HIV/AIDS, malaria and other diseases, environmental sustainability and global partnership for development. Similarly, since 1975, with the declaration of Decade for Women (1976-1985) and with the establishment of United Nations Development Fund for Women (UNIFEM), the United Nations has made a move towards the goals of gender equity, through research, policy advocacy and projects and programmes for empowerment, capacity building and mainstreaming. It is quite clear that environment and development on the one hand, and women/ gender and development on the other, have followed two parallel tracts without providing solid merging grounds for these paradigms.

Poverty, inequity and environmental degradation are considered crucial threats to development in South Asia. This global phenomenon is spatial and social, and marked with imbalances in accessing to resources and basic needs. Around 80 per cent of the resources are consumed by 20 per cent of the world population. Similarly, 80 per cent of the poor live in rural areas, depend on natural resources for their livelihood and 70 per cent of the poor are women. In addressing the issues associated with this phenomenon, countries in the South Asian region have to govern and materialize the principles of equality, democracy and equal citizenship rights. The effectiveness of social and economic development measures has not made a progressive change up to our expectations, primarily due to our move on compartmentalized paths. The legal instruments for ensuring women's rights and measures for empowerment and strengthening women's capacity and capabilities to involve in development and sustaining the environments have been advocated throughout during the last three decades. More wider grounds and windows of opportunities are needed for promoting equity, empowerment and environmental sustainability.

The Millennium Development Goals adopted by the United Nations in 2000 and the Plan of Implementation adopted at the World Summit on Sustainable Development in 2002 also recognized the need for furthering our efforts for achieving these goals. The two paradigms – the women and the environment – are not treated equally and simultaneously in the process. Gender mainstreaming for gender equality and empowerment, and the integration of environment into development process for sustainability, need holistic and integrated efforts. In this respect, two critical questions emerge. The first is, are we still moving wide apart advocating to bring these two paradigms together? The second is, have we clearly negotiated for common merging grounds? This chapter suggests that principles of equity, equality and partnership are essentially the issues of citizenship and rights of the citizens.

The Framework

The area of women and environment being one of most complex nexuses of research and development has largely become an experimental territory during the past. Vast arrays of academic discourses have been focused on conceptualizing the linkages using the frameworks such as 'eco-feminism' and 'feminist political ecology' 'livelihood' etc. Yet, the issues of equity and justice have not been taken into the core area of the environmental debate other than degradation. In this respect, the crucial area under investigation is related with the 'environmental citizenship', which is the concern expressed in this chapter. It is considered as a solid basis for negotiation, addressing the issues of inequity and injustice. The basic consideration that needs our attention is not the environmental crisis per se or interconnectedness between women and the environment, but women's citizenship rights. Women's environmental citizenship by which decisions on fair share of resources and their consumption need to be decided, and rights to livelihood and meeting basic needs could be justified. Women's share in environmental space and resources should be determined on their citizenship by which decisions need to be drawn.

The debate on environmental citizenship has been enriched by various researchers. For instance, McLaren (2003) offered the 'environmental space' approach as a framework conceptualizing sustainability in terms of access for all to fair share in the limited environmental resources on which healthy quality of life depends. The basic idea behind this rights-based approach is to draw attention to women's environmental citizenship issues at various levels. This approach from the perspective of women deals with a fair share of the maximum available within given limits, while recognizing the existence of a minimum determined by need and human dignity. The integral incorporation of the equity principles is a distinctive feature. Considering Brazil as an example focusing on uneven land distribution, McLaren showed the importance of economic rights and meeting basic needs as a priority for share in environmental space. As a result of the uneven land distribution, women lost their ability to provide subsistence crops, while men gained opportunities to labouring on plantations. Similarly, Faber and McCarthy (2003) offered 'ecological democracy' approach focusing on sustainability and environmental justice. This has been built upon the argument that environmental justice is the way to protect nature and labour where activists and workers are provided with same access to political decision-making and policy-making processes as are those who control capital. These authors reflected the view that the traditional environmental movement has not been able to institute more sustainable and socially just models of development, therefore, a broad-based movement committed to the principles of ecological democracy becomes essential.

A promising arena has been opened up with the environmental justice movement which is focused on coalition between environmental and social concerns (Agyemen and others, 2003) and the civil rights movement (Taylor, 2000). Social justice perspectives of the environmental issues have been widely demonstrated referring to various concerns in South Asia (Agarwal, 1994; Shiva, 1989 and 1991; Wickramasinghe, 1993a). According to Taylor (2000), environmental justice paradigm is the first paradigm to link environment and race, class, gender and social justice concerns in an explicit framework. Cutter (1995) explained that distinctiveness of this approach is that it focuses on those who are deprived of their environmental rights, such as women, children and the poor. From the perspectives of women and environment in Asia, women's environmental rights are a crucial aspect dealing with the future prospects of social, economic and environmental development holistically.

The academic discourses and ground realities reflected in research on women and environment provide ingredients for this broader debate. What is needed in an acceptable framework to make a transitional move through convincing grounds. Women's environmental rights under these circumstances need reiteration. It is in agreement with 1999 Aarhus Convention on Access to Information, Public Participation in Environmental Decision-Making and Access to Justice in Environmental Matters (UNECE, 1999). It clearly states that, "in order to contribute to the protection of the right of every person of present and future generations to live in an environment adequate to his or her health and well-being, each party shall guarantee the rights of access to information, public participation in decision-making and access to justice in environmental matters in accordance with the provisions of the convention".

ENVIRONMENT AND LIVELIHOOD SECURITY

Environment is central to women's livelihood and occupational security in South Asia due to the land-based nature of the livelihood of majority of women. Despite the reductions in the share labour force engaged in land-based occupations and the share of GDP derived from agriculture, majority of rural dwellers, women in particular, rely heavily on the environment. It is not merely the surrounding that they are concerned with, but also the quality, space, community, management, authorities, resources, safety and distractions. Environment and human security are closely interrelated. The reduced quality of the environment is an indication to the lowering of its capacity to support human communities. The deepening poverty, vulnerability and the increasing risks of depending on land and its resources are experienced more by women than their counterparts. The situation in South Asia is a testimony for insecure livelihood for women, where majority is the de-facto users of land. The de-facto use of land disqualifies women claiming recognition to their livelihood base – the agriculture. Three case studies, conducted under the Collaborative Regional Research Network in South Asia, demonstrate the

Table 1

Women Labouring for Livelihood Security Through Resource Management

Country	*Village*	*Involvement*	*Nature of contribution*
Bangladesh	Khanmohona	62-91%	Labouring for sustaining family-based production, attending to home-based activities in particular for family wellbeing.
Nepal	Chanukhil	78-94%	Labouring for sustaining field production through integrating traditional resource management practices using livestock, forest and family farms for family livelihood.
Sri Lanka	Labunoruwa	68-96%	Labouring for sustaining village ecosystem as a habitat for livelihood security linking multiple elements: forests, farms, home-gardens, water bodies and reservations for the family and community livelihood security.

Source: Wickramasinghe, 1997.

conditions under which women's authority over the environment is marginalized both in privately held and state controlled systems (see Table 1).

The type of work that women perform, their tangible and intangible contribution for their own families, time and energy used in labouring for livelihood have remained unaccounted. As a result, the female economic activity rate is rather low, and exists in the range between 20 and 44. Women in these countries have not reached 100 per cent of the male activity rate. The highest has been recorded in Bangladesh where unpaid female family workers are exclusively high. The women's share of adult labour force varies between 13 and 14 having lowest in Pakistan, and highest in Bangladesh. When compared with many research findings, which emphasize long hours of women's work in subsistence production, the debate on women's works recognition of their livelihood and incentives for their work gets reinstated. The women's labour involvement, as shown in Table 2, where unpaid agricultural labouring is predominant, is a reflection of their dependence on local environment and also the vulnerability to environmental degradation. Their engagement in agriculture as free source rather than as self-employed landowners is a result of their lack of ownership over the livelihood sources.

Table 2

Key Features Related to Women's Labour Involvement

Feature	*India*	*Pakistan*	*Bangladesh*	*Nepal*	*Sri Lanka*
Female activity rate	29	20.8	44.4	37.9	30.5
As a % of male	50.3	40.3	77.2	69.6	55.4
Female economic activity index (1985=100)	95	123.3	107.8	98.3	151.3
Female unpaid family workers (1990-1997)	—	33	71	61	53
Women's share of adult labour force	24	13	41	32	27
% of labour force in agriculture (1990)	64	52	65	94	48

The justice of consistently low share of women's earned income in these countries, where women take the brunt of farm production, is also questionable. It is only 25.1 per cent in Sri Lanka, 19.2 per cent in India, 10.1 per cent in Pakistan, 22.8 per cent in Bangladesh and 26.4 per cent in Nepal. The point reflected here is that the effectiveness of human development made during the past has not improved the economic security for women. Labouring for sustaining land-based production as free source of labour takes place. Issues of free labouring, irregularity of opportunities and unreliability, work for service rather than for remuneration, low wages and also de-facto rights over livelihood sources interrelatedly contribute to women's low share of earned income in South Asia. South Asia being the continent that accounts for nearly half of the population is seriously challenged by the deepening environmental degradation and poverty. The major threat to sustainable development emerges from environmental insecurity stemming from unjust, inequity, overexploitation, pollution, resource extraction, disease, poverty, violence and land degradation. The most outstanding feature in South Asia is not merely the density of population, but the gravity of poverty and resource scarcity. South Asia has to see to the livelihood security seriously because it contains one out of every five people living in poverty in the world today, of which nearly half are women.

Women's citizenship and ecological democracy seems to have more multiple implications than that of any other development issue because matters in hand are not merely a question of mainstreaming but deal with deeper areas than the development agencies have so far dealt with. In the process of globalization and in the market economy women's environmental stewardships have been diluted. Since they have had no ownership authority, their alienation from the resources that they possess takes place. The ground realities that women in contemporary Asia are dealing with highlight some challenges that need to be taken into account for the future. While variation among countries in terms of women's low share of income is predominant, the commonality is that their share of income is extremely low when compared with their male counterparts (see Table 3). Similarities are also noticed in the high percentage of women labour in agriculture, reduced land to labour ratio, actual increase in population in agriculture and also in outstanding increase in cereal imports.

Table 3

Some Vital Statistics Showing Labour Concentration in Agriculture, Inequalities in Income and GDP in Selected Countries

Aspects	*India*	*Pakistan*	*Bangladesh*	*Nepal*	*Sri Lanka*
Employment in agriculture % of total labour force					
1980	69.5	64	72.5	90	51.2
1999	60.6	53.2	55.6	96.6	44.3
Population employed in agriculture ('000)					
1990 male	146363	13861	18729	4891	2291
2000 male	165961	14681	19478	5920	2537
1990 female	83243	6829	16198	3307	1134
2000 female	97730	9839	19254	4189	1349
Cereal imports ('000 metric tonnes)					
1980	417	613	2194	54	883
1999	1779	3249	4765	46	1232
Women's share of earned income	25.7	20.8	23.1	33	34.5
Real GDP per capita (US$)					
Male	2389	2363	1320	1409	3545
Female	902	701	767	763	1452

Source: UNDP, 1999, Oxford University Press, 2003.

Food, water and energy security on the one hand and the amount of produce available for women for satisfying family and community needs on the other, are the pressing problems. Women's roles in safeguarding the environment against degradation and pollution without having authority over decisions cannot be justified on social grounds. Gap between de-facto users, and services focused on labouring, and the de-jure rights to environmental space are wide in Asia.

Environmental Safety and Protection

From the perspectives of women and the environment, the aspects of safety and protection are important for sustaining the environment and human well-being. Environmental safety is determined by two key factors. The first is the environment itself. The second is more complex, and is associated with occupations, types of activities, that people attend to, and the technology that is used. The matters pertaining to protection include two areas. It covers all the aspects related to environmental protection provide for the performers, occupants for which rights over unit of area or a system or resources that one is dealing with becomes important.

The meaning of environment safety and protection to women in the context of South Asia under these circumstances is quite complex. For instance, environmental conditions are a result of management; whereas safety is associated with social determinants – gender roles and ideology; while protection is specific to the governance and policies. Translating these into realities, it could be argued that environment is the most crucial paradigm that could potentially solve development-related repercussions on the grounds of equity, social justice and development. In South Asia, a wide range of environmental issues, such as land degradation, desertification, natural hazards, biodiversity depletion and biomass scarcities, are connected with the inadequacy of policies leading to degradation and depletion of forest cover. Human causation through which such issues are established are associated with the trends in development which in turn cause tremendous impacts on both human society and the environment.

Data given in Table 4 reveals that countries in South Asia have failed to arrest deforestation, irrespective of all the policies and its detrimental effects. Global warming, air pollution, salinization and water scarcities are the strenuous results that people are dealing with. Activities that account for these detrimental consequences are multiple and quite clearly they are stemming from technology, management as well as the work relations with the environment. Soil and nutrient management, water conservation, carbons recycling etc. have become rather isolated from integrated land management efforts so the project-based interventions are becoming more and more prominent. The integrity of management systems is fragmented and it has become extremely destructive for women than that for men, because new interventions are in favour of strengthening men's income and homogeneity of work. The protection of fast depleting ecosystems and the safety of the conditions of the environment for human occupation and contacts in a broader sense have made a progressive move in every country. Throughout South Asia the legislation for the protection of the environment by state agency has discarded the customary rights by which women's connections have been instrumented. As a result, women increasingly have become vulnerable and victims of environmental hostilities due to their continuing engagement in satisfying the basic needs.

Table 4
Deforestation and CO_2 Emission

Country	*Average annual deforestation (%)*			*CO_2 emission (million of tonnes)*	
	1981-85	*1990-95*	*1990-2000*	*1980*	*1999*
Bangladesh	0.9	0.9	1.3	7.6	25.4
India	0.3	0.2	0.1	373.3	1077.0
Nepal	4.0	4.1	1.8	0.5	3.3
Pakistan	0.4	2.9	1.1	31.6	98.9
Sri Lanka	3.5	1.1	1.6	3.4	8.6

Source: World Development Report, 2003.

Taking into account CO_2 emission that has increased significantly it could be argued that development-led degradation would become a serious threat for those who are engaged in various activities in open air so regularly. The meaning of deforestation and CO_2 emission for women in South Asia is much deeper due to their greater dependence over tangible and intangible goods and services.

Environmental safety has become a serious threat to women's health in South Asia due to lack of options for satisfying the requirements for their needs. Increasingly depleting resources like water and biomass fuel, reduced quality of the supply sources and the resources as well as their reduced capacity to support production and regeneration have resulted in increasing women's drudgery of work and their struggle over family well-being. The exhaustive use of women's energy in favour of human well-being no longer confined to matter of gender inequity but a issue of environmental justice.

Environment and Occupational Space

South Asia, being a populous region in the world, is under serious anthropogenic pressures and impacts. The increased population pressure on resources has reduced agricultural space, forests and resources available for women (see Table 5). The most seriously affected are the environment and women's occupations and their sources of livelihood. The progress made over last five decades or so, in South Asian countries, has no bearing on the environment and women's access to and control over resources. The improvements in human development are associated with welfare services guided by the policies pertaining to free education, health and food security that have been adopted. This implies that most of the indicators by which the development effectiveness on women is measured are the result of the process that began prior to the environmental movement and also women's movements that took place since 1970s. Nevertheless, the shift in these two paradigms and the associated academic discourse on women and the environment has made an impact on state agency. Within this context, eco-feminist thoughts are a good example demonstrating the efforts in bridging women and the environment. The globally initiated move towards gender mainstreaming has been picked up by almost all international agencies and also by most of the state agencies that one could think of in each country. The largely neglected area was the environment where mainstreaming has not taken place considering the crucial importance of the environment as the platform for equal opportunities. The contrary here is that the prominent environmental factors such as land, water, biotic resources and soil influence the vast majority of women in South Asia region, whereas the landownership, tenure, technology and resource conservation strategies in the region remained in favour of conventional masculine domain. Women throughout Asia sustained the losses of soil erosion, disasters, resource over exploitation, salinization, deforestation, energy scarcity, biodiversity depletion and environmental degradation. Issues at hand need serious policy attention rather than establishing correlation between women and each area of environmental threats. Women's vulnerability under these circumstances varies spatially in relation to livelihood, ecosystems, occupations, and occupational security of workplaces.

Table 5

Key Features Related to Land and its Distribution in Five Countries in South Asia

Feature	*India*	*Pakistan*	*Bangladesh*	*Nepal*	*Sri Lanka*
Land area ('000 ha.)	297319	77088	13017	13680	6463
Population density (1995) per '000 ha.)	3147	1823	9252	1602	2840
Domesticated land as % of land area	61	34	79	32	36
Land to labour ratio					
1980	0.8	1.1	0.3	0.4	0.7
1990	0.6	0.8	0.2	0.3	0.5
Forest and woodland ('000 ha.)	68330	3470	1896	5750	2126
Forest and woodland % of total	23	5.3	14.5	39	32.5
Percentage of deforestation (1980-1989)	2.3	0.4	0.9	4.0	3.5
Extent of agricultural land (million ha.)	169.5	20.8	9.2	2.6	2.0
% change between 1964-1980	4.4	8.3	2.2	44.4	11.1

Women's occupations in the subsistence sector in South Asia include farms, homesteads, forests, and communally shared areas. Neither women's rights over occupational space nor the matters related to their contributions are considered from the perspectives of social justice. Social norms and gender relations, inheritance, property ownership, institutional policies and procedures are not in favour of a transitional move. The question that needs investigation is how does feeling of ownership and responsibility leads to make a change in the management operation, and gives a sense of equity – socially, economically and environmentally.

The overall situation related to land use itself, as shown in Table 6, makes it clear that there had been only marginal changes with regard to the distribution of land area under agriculture. When women labour enrolment is compared with the land area under agriculture, it is quite evident that women continued to engage in farm-based production systems.

Table 6

Land Use by Crop Types in 1980 and 2000 (%)

Country	*Per capita cultivated land (ha.)*	*Agriculture*		*Permanent crops*		*Other crops*	
		1980	*2000*	*1980*	*2000*	*1980*	*2000*
Bangladesh	0.07	68.4	62.5	2.0	2.7	29.6	34.8
Bhutan	0.08	2.2	3.0	0.4	0.4	97.4	96.6
India	0.16	54.8	54.4	1.8	2.7	43.4	42.9
Maldives	0.01	3.3	3.3	6.7	6.7	90.0	90.0
Nepal	0.01	16.0	20.3	0.2	0.5	83.8	74.2
Pakistan	0.14	25.9	27.6	0.4	0.9	73.7	71.5
Sri Lanka	0.01	13.2	13.8	15.9	15.8	70.9	70.4

Source: ADB, 2003 – Key indicators.

The gender-specific implications of environmental stresses from the perspectives of human security, which are associated with livelihood security, reveal that majority of women in Asia are seriously affected due to their lack of rights to their workplace, resources and the environment. Therefore, the serious areas of our concern today include:

1. women's occupations and their access to and control over livelihood sources;

2. women's control over natural resources and means of assuring rights over water, forests, soil and biodiversity;
3. women's access to services for improving quality of life; and
4. women's environmental rights, primarily over occupational space.

Favourable policies, institutional structures, mechanisms and governance are the means for addressing these concerns. Many changes that have taken place in the local environments are beyond the control of women due to their lack of control. These have resulted in increasing women's insecurity and vulnerability. In South Asia, income, resources, solid capital and investable assets are disproportionately distributed between men and women. It is determined by patriarchally controlled social, economic and environmental systems on gender terms. Equal weight is needed to involve women, and protecting their rights over occupational space. In strengthening the three pillars of sustainable development, social, economic and environment deconstruction of gender is essential. Arguments raised in providing equal access to education, health and political freedom are to be extended to provide equal opportunities. On the one hand, the specially designed projects and programmes are expected to enhance women's participation and share in income. One the other hand, women are considered as implementation modalities. In the environmental domain the process has been rather slow and inconsistent. This may be due to the difficulty in making a transformation on women's equal citizenship in the environments. Therefore, the issue of women's capability and capacity to deal with local and global environmental change remains unaddressed. The efforts are needed to minimizing the effects of environmental degradation and global changes such as climate change on women.

Since 1975 the wave of interest and the pressure created primarily through international initiatives has been less effective in picking up environmental rights of women, by which progress has to be made more by their rights to resources at their disposal. A review of environmental justice and human rights issues (see Adeola, 2000) clearly stated the need for framing environmental rights as a component of human rights. In South Asia, the several decades of debate on women's human rights have been strongly focused on issues of violence. Yet, the violation of women's environmental rights has continued. Globalization, modernization, free trade, open economic policies and trade liberalization have contributed to this violation. Provisions opened up through Principle 1 of the Stockholm Declaration of 1972, and 20 years later through Principle 10 of the Rio Declaration on Environment and Development of 1992, have to be translated fully into strategies with action plans and programmes in South Asia taking into account constraints and needs. This shows that endorsements of women's issues into international agendas and agreements are the windows of opportunities and prospects for new directions to move on. While environmental legislation and strategies are focused and biased towards the issues of the environment for which community participation has been mentioning, the rights of the communities to their occupational space, resources and the broader environment have not been penetrated into national policy frameworks as needed.

Case studies conducted in several countries in Asia (e.g., Bangladesh, Nepal, Sri Lanka) in 1995 reveal that women's sources of livelihood are multiple, and the most crucial ones are the farms, and forests, most of which are used on customary grounds. The case study conducted in Khanmohona in Chittagong (Das, 1997) shows that system of inheritance allows to exclude women's rights to land. Irrespective of the work performed by women, no remuneration is available particularly for their home and homestead-based work including the agricultural crop production and processing. The case study conducted in Chalnakhel village in the central hills of Nepal (Bhadra, 1997) reveals that three spheres domains of women's occupations, viz., farms/fields, forests and the household, sustain family livelihood. Women's positions are justified on customary grounds and gender relations by which their labour is freely used, remuneration for work is excluded and workplace occupational security is ignored. The case study conducted in Labunoruwa village in the dry zone of Sri Lanka (Wickramasinghe, 1997) shows that women's occupational space is so diverse and includes paddy fields, slash and burn agriculture fields, home gardens, forests and common lands. Women's legal ownership over the private lands is limited to homestead of 10 per cent of the households or families. This indicates the inequity in the authority over decisions, handling remuneration and farm management. Implications of ownership being an area not researched into are a limitation of these case studies. The inferences make it clear that social justice for the drudgery of work performed by women to sustain the livelihood and family production systems has been taken into account beyond family well-being. Acquisition of control over solid assets, primarily the land, has not been considered as an equal opportunity or a personal choice, but a socially defined determinant on gender terms. Detailed analysis presented by Agarwal (1994), in her work on women's land rights, shows the variations in the systems of inheritance in South Asia. The rights to the physical environmental space open new windows looking into occupational safety and rights, security, as well as rights to deciding health of the village habitats, contamination-free resource base and risk reducing technologies for the local environments.

Biodiversity and the Environment

Biodiversity is a crucial aspect in the whole paradigm of women and environment. The linkages mediate through livelihood, culture and traditional practices. The social spectrum related to biodiversity is diverse and marked with distinct roles men and women play in regard to use and conservation. Social orientation makes it more realistic and acceptable to those who deal with these in their day-to-day lives. What biodiversity means to women living on land and its resources has been demonstrated over generations. For women, diversity of living species and their abundance, plants in particular, the richness in variety and its spread across land is central. Each of these aspects expresses the practical linkages with women's needs and their gender-specific concerns over sustainable management. Within this paradigm the socially accepted roles and responsibility over reproduction influence the resource management for subsistence. Biodiversity provides multiple options, security, reliance, richness and reduce vulnerability (see Table 7). It is a means of self-reliance over food security and livelihood, that enabling them to reduce the dependence on men's limited income for satisfying the needs of the families and communities. This implies that in the local environments women sustain the multiple connections (Wickramasinghe, 1992). Ways in which they make use of plants, parts of plants and the sub-systems are deeper. It includes a domain of traditional knowledge and practices as well. Enrichment through domestication and integration and also conservation, propagation and sharing of genetic materials of best qualities are integral elements. Studies focused on the sustainable management of home gardens – the mosaics of forest landscapes in Sri Lanka – are cases for demonstration (see Wickramasinghe, 1994). Situations pertaining to forest resource management also strengthen this point. Women continue in South Asia sustain the linkages between forest resources and non-forest living through their engagement in gathering, regeneration, and conserving the integrity (Sarin, 1995; Wickramasinghe, 1995).

Table 7

Key Areas of Women's Concerns and Associated Benefits of Biodiversity

Areas of concern	*Associated benefits*
Diversity of species	• Complementary benefits; • Reduced risks/vulnerability; • Multiple needs/priorities/output; • Richness and integrity; and • Multiple options.
Abundance	• Resistance to destruction; • Continuity/availability; • Security and reliance; and • Sustainability.
Variety	• Satisfying different preferences and needs; • Reduced vulnerability; • Multiple options; and • Diversity in output.
Spatial diversity	• Spatial connections and connectivity; • Resource conservation; • Aesthetic and amenity values; • Services and richness; • Harmony; • Multiple options; and • Reduced risks/hazards/vulnerability.

The features imbedded into the local culture including land husbandry, food and medicine provide tremendous amount of knowledge among rural women in South Asia in relation to their day-to- day living. The convention that each country has agreed upon need to be realized in relation to the domain of knowledge, practices and roles through which men and women of the communities make contributions. Debates on access to genetic resoúrces, traditional knowledge and benefit sharing under these circumstances are directly the matters of women's intellectual property rights in Asia.

Biodiversity being key area pertaining to the environment is an accepted ground reality. It is central to food security (Wickramasinghe, 1999 and 2001) where food and conservation culture as integral parts made a generation-long progress. The traditional knowledge, although has been subjected to fragmentation and commercial exploitation, goes from one generation to the next because the mechanisms of transmissions are oral and internal. Unless in-depth analysis of food habits and traditional medicinal practices, land husbandry, resource use and conservation practices, landscape diversity, environmental entrepreneurships, norms and attitudes over resource consumption is accomplished through research, the connection between women and the environment would not be fully covered.

The Windows of Opportunities

Recent initiatives on biodiversity conservation have made a substantial impact on women, particularly due to the formalization of this effort through state agency and many other institutions. Biodiversity conservation, for instance, is no longer a peripheral issue and the 1993 Convention on Biological Diversity (CBD) stimulated interest in recognizing and involving local communities including their traditional knowledge, innovations and practices. On the part of local communities, women's knowledge, experience and concerns over intangible services are the investable assets. In this regard, the most significant areas in translating CBD for providing local frameworks are directly linked with Articles 15 and 8.

The Article 15, by which the rights of the national governments to regulate access to genetic resources are recognized, has direct implications on rural women in South Asia. The whole dilemma is centred around the process and procedure followed by the national governments in regulating access and ways by which they recognized the rights of women who are the local custodians. How do individual nations handle this is a question in hand simply because in most circumstances the resource/source ownership is used rather than customary rights in regulatory mechanisms.

The next most crucial is the Article 8 by which the rights of indigenous and local communities on their traditional knowledge, innovation and practices are recognized. Institutionalization of women's traditional knowledge, innovations and practices is central to translating these (Wickramasinghe, 2003b). Why is it that women deserve special attention in the area of biodiversity and environment? The crucial areas of concern include:

- Roots of modern innovation on biodiversity conservation are stemming from the women's innovations of using local plants for the livelihood security. The formal commitment of state agency is therefore to integrating women and their sources. The inclusion of livelihood linkages that women maintain with resources/sources and contributed to conservation is a point for institutionalization.
- Humanitarian context of the traditional knowledge on plants and their uses for food security and medicinal purposes for both preventing and curing have been derived through trial and error. Such knowledge has provided incentives for in-situ conservation of biodiversity, for instances, in forest management as well as for ex-situ conservation of biodiversity. Women's resource rights are the condition by which knowledge and innovations could be easily endorsed without alienating in favour of commercialization.
- Many aspects of conservation and processing have been enriched with the local skills, knowledge and practices as well as by the ritualistic performances, which are locally significant, culturally sensitive and intangible. Therefore, the domain of knowledge cannot be extracted in isolation without

having an understanding of the art associated with rituals and holistic perception over natural life.

- The women's social relations and sharing practices have been the instruments for the extension of traditional knowledge and practical uses. The spatial areas under mosaics of natural diversity are extended over vast tracts or zones of natural habitats and ecosystems. Heterogeneous village ecosystems in Sri Lanka are its good examples. Zones are marked with specific composition functional linkages and contacts. The phenological cycles of the individual species, ecosystems and habitats, ecological conditions, processes, regional weather regimes favouring regeneration, complementary and nurturing effects of communities, methods of harvesting etc. are also integral elements. These are the properties inherited by women and the capital mostly carried forward by women.
- The heterogeneous village landscapes also reflect the socially defined roles inculcated into the village ecosystems for sustainability. The architect of every village has its own identity derived through linkages between human activity, needs and natural options. The greater diversity of both natural and domesticated plants that are found in space or landscapes is marked with strong life supporting potentials. The home garden landscapes demonstrate how does women's input make village ecosystems so diverse in composition, structure and sustain the linkages and perceptions.

Under these circumstances, issues of women's concerns are multiple. The foremost aspect is related to the biodiversity conservation and human sustainability. Maintaining richness and supportability are broader issues than matters pertaining to international regime on access and benefit sharing. The second aspect is associated with the international negotiations and the local frameworks for strengthening the linkages between intellectual property rights, traditional knowledge and genetic resources. The greater emphasis is to be placed on practices and technology. The third is the marked-based options for biodiversity conservation, which should provide multiple options for women's livelihood-based conservation initiatives. The greater tendency for excluding local food security, health and well-being of those who conserve resources for day-to-day consumption need to be avoided. It is important to note that traditional medicinal knowledge and the genetic material sources are tightened not only with ownership authorities but strongly with the local custodian. The fourth is that resource evaluations made in economic terms should be equipped to look into intangible, service and subsistence aspects. While state agency has become the access providers, the traditional knowledge, customary practices and regulations remain non-accommodated fragmented elements of the biodiversity. This implies that women-centred approach is essential for main-streaming biodiversity into land management in Asia.

Agro-diversity and Resource Management Regimes

Another characteristic issue in South Asia is the linkage between reduced agro-diversity and the increasing risk of food insecurity and vulnerability. The richness maintained by women in the manipulated production systems, farms and gardens has been a cultural phenomenon in South Asia. These have been integrated in favour of livelihood, which is a day-to-day reality of small-scale farm operators. The crucial problem is, as shown in the broad profile introduced in Human Development in South Asia 2002 (Mahbub ul Haq Human Development Centre, 2003), the deprivation of women. Accordingly, women are the invisible and unrecognized backbone of the South Asian agriculture. The significance of their role can be gauged not only by their high participation in farm and non-farm activities in rural areas, but also by their intimate connection to rural customs, traditions and values. Agro-diversity is the characteristic resulted from traditional practices that are closely associated with women's responsibility over human well-being. The integral elements of farm and land husbandry have provided diversity and variability in family diet, management of medicinal plants and plants for beverages, biomass for energy, fodder for livestock, mulch for soil enrichment. FAO (2000), based on various field data, revealed that the percentage of female engagement in agriculture is substantially higher than that of men in all the countries with a relatively low gap only in Sri Lanka. On the very outset, it is found that in their varied roles as agricultural labourers, de-jure landowners, de-facto household heads or the managers of homesteads, women are active participants in the agricultural sector (Mahbub ul Haq Human Development Centre, 2003). Women's linkage with the environment extends beyond division of labour and farm activities. The percentage of economically active women's labour in agriculture in these countries has increased outstandingly, except for India, between 1980 and 2000 (see Table 8). While changes in the enumeration attributed to this, there had been many factors enabling women to bear greater responsibility over farming.

Table 8

Percentage Increase in Economically Active Population in Agriculture (1980-2000)

Country	*Actual number 1980 ('000s)*		*% increase between 1980-2000*	
	Male	*Female*	*Male*	*Female*
India	125097	83668	33	17
Nepal	4152	2708	43	54
Pakistan	12888	5932	14	66
Sri Lanka	2067	790	23	71
Bangladesh	16298	13886	19	39

Source: Oxford University Press (2003).

The male migration for non-farm employment, increased land fragmentation resulted in smaller landholdings, and trends towards adopting high yielding crops requiring high labour inputs, are the causes for this trend. The women's authority over farm management decisions is not automatically linked with this increase in female labour force participation. Most of the opportunities are made available for women due to their preference to engage in village-based work even if the wage is relatively low and working conditions and hours are not favourable. This trend is not a reflection of transition of their inferior position in society.

Women labour in agriculture has increasingly becoming visible also due to demand for women's labour rather than integrating their knowledge, experience and practices for environmental enrichment. While resource management regimes adopted during the arena of technology transition have not been in favour of sustainable resource management, women in agriculture tend to lose their traditional knowledge due to lack of space to put them into practice. Reduced agro-diversity is a result of advancement of modern farm management regimes and displacement of women's traditional practices. Another attributory fact is the diminishing of reciprocal exchange of labour through which sharing, collective action, collaboration etc. have taken place during the past. Such social interactive engagement, over generations, has been a promising way to sharing knowledge, exchange genetic materials, food and planting materials through which agro-diversity has been enhanced. The self-confidence in using traditional management practices, as noted in Table 9, is also lost with the expansion of commercial crop production where family labour and reciprocally shared inputs have been replaced with purchased materials and labour.

Table 9

Traditional Management Practices Contributing to Increase Agro-diversity

Practice/regime	*Input*	*Advantage*
Minimum tillage	Labour	Little disturbance, controlled erosion
Organic fertilization	Compost waste, residues, dung, mulch	Soil rejuvenation, high soil moisture retainability
Mixed cropping	Variety and variability	Maximum output, high cropping index, multiple options, complementarity
Weed and pest control	Biological measures, complementary measures	Maintained useful wild species, reduced pollution risks
Tree integrated cultivation	Diversity	Complementary benefits, erosion control, reduce risks, soil and water conservation, stability
Rotations	Labour, reciprocal exchange	Maximum output, risk reduction, soil enrichment

While on the one hand paid work opportunities for women in agriculture contribute to their economic empowerment, on the other, the displacement of their traditional management practices that are of tremendous potentials to addressing deepening environmental problems, mainly land degradation, also takes place. The question here is who pays for managing agro-diversity, which is exclusively labour intensive and possible through a restorative process where such systems need new form of valuation either as cultural landscapes or hot-spots of biodiversity. Two requisites emerge here. The first is that the cultural forest gardens, paddy terraces in hilly areas, and the reserved riparian agro-forests that are found throughout South Asia need new form of recognition and evaluation. The second is that women are to recognized as environmental entrepreneurs in Asia with the potentials to make a paradigm shift adding new dimensions to modern conservation efforts. These are challenging issues because influx of artificial products and the expansion of crop monoculture have displaced the raw materials, technology and traditional skills. From the stage of restoring raw material base to the level of institutionalizing of technology, skills and knowledge, it is a national commitment to promote environmental enterprises, which are often labour intensive and locally possible. Alternative means to replace the disastrously expanding use of polythenes and plastic and rely heavily on restoration of the material base together with rights of women to supply sources and their capital investments.

From a perspective of ecosystems and landscapes the place, identity and recognition are always being important throughout humanity. Women in South Asia, irrespective of differences between countries, need recognition of space and identity under many circumstances. In this respect, the system of property ownership need changing. Equal opportunities to own land and manage resources should not be impeded by the ideology that women are more tightened up with the home and less capable of managing property. Similarly, the marriage system by which women lose their place of origin, recognition, and resource linkage with their entering into marriage and moving to the partner's home, should not be used as losing grounds. Instead, it should be considered as a capital movement and extension if favourable conditions are provided for women to replicate and transfer knowledge.

Women being influenced by the socially defined commitments and equipped with life experiences in providing basic needs, such as water, fuelwood, fodder and food for their families, are the experts in integrated resource management in their own habitats. Diversity is a practical means for catering these multiple demands. These resources are renewed with human inputs, which include nurturing, integration, enrichment, conservation, non-destructive use and exploitation (Wickramasinghe, 1994). The limits for extraction are guided by the preferences for maintaining the integrity of village ecosystem. The essence of WEHAB framework (UNDP, 2004), which deals with water, health, agriculture and biodiversity for energy and environmental sustainability, is also applicable for linking the ways of resource management that women have innovated for sustainable supply of basic needs for their families. Strong demonstrations for these integrated efforts are available, but scattered throughout in South Asia. The evolution of forest garden mosaics, consisting of individual home gardens in the lands devastated for Mahaweli settlements in the dry zone of Sri Lanka, is a good example. (Wickramasinghe, 2002). The women of the individual households have followed ecosystem restoration process through creating favourable conditions to house, and growing and nurture plants of multiple potentials for stability, sustainability and security. Food, medicinal output, fodder, mulch, shade and domestic biomass energy needs are the criteria used by women in selecting and designing the highlands allocated for putting up houses. The important lesson learned here is that, women, irrespective of education, income and other acquired assets, make a move if opportunities are opened up for them to undertake challenges to make a change. Requisites for them to make a wider transition are the windows of opportunities ensuring rights to their own environment as equal and capable citizens.

Conclusions

The negative social and economic impacts of environmental degradation on the one hand and the issues of inequity, marginalization, deprivation and demoralization on the other increasingly affect the South Asia region. In realizing the opportunities provided through many international conventions, two aspects are important. The first is the full understanding of the linkages between women and the environment. The second is the governance mechanisms by which women's environmental citizenship may be restorted. In Asia women and environment is an old paradigm marked with tangible, intangible and labour linkages. The linkages are affected on the one hand by the degradation of the environment itself, and on the other by the social, economic and policy trends that have not been able to facilitate a progressive move towards establishing equity in local contexts. Future prospects depend on the policy instruments and institutional mechanisms by which women's linkages with the environment need to be materialized enabling them to make decisions over their occupational space, livelihood sources, resource base and their management.

The women-environment dynamics is complex and diverse. Within the context of environmental space one area of crucial important is women's environmental citizenship. Evidences reveal that women's rights and access, which are traditionally gained through customary or on de-facto terms, differ from legally defined, formally recognized property ownership. Women's day-to-day association with land, water, soil, plants etc. is formally marginalized due to lack of spatial area and exclusion of traditional practices and knowledge from modern technology and management regimes. Women are considered as providers of implementation modalities. Mainstreaming under these circumstances for the sustainable management of renewable and non-renewable resources is a challenge. The social ideology presents women as a weaker section for whom resource management tasks are difficult. In addition, marriage through which spatial attachment gets fragmented, biological reproduction and home management commitments which hinder mobility, and poor negotiation and involvement in decision-making deny the women's environmental rights in South Asia.

The perspectives of environmental rights on which this chapter is structured deal with two crucial aspects. The first is the holistic nature of the women-environment dynamics by which elements are to be considered in integrity. The second is related to 'rights', where grounds for inclusion are entertained. These circumstances demand a paradigm shift in the arena of women and environment where equity needs to be guaranteed on citizenship grounds. This also requires a change in valuation that could accommodate value for women's input for the whole area of environmental sustainability while valuing subsistence and marketable goods, services and non-tangible – cultural and spiritual aspects. The legally defined men's property ownership incurs demoralizing and disempowering effects on women. These are detrimental to the integration of traditional knowledge, skills and experiences and as a result public participation in environmental management remains unaccomplished. Countries in South Asia should focus on promoting policies for assuring property and occupational rights of the carriers of knowledge and practices and also for the custodians of the local environments. Knowledge, irrespective of the differences in sources and the means of transmission, is a capital that women could offer in relation to their contacts, occupations and workplaces.

Environmental paradigm has to be intervened and engendered with gender mainstreaming instruments. It has wider potentials to address issues of empowering and capacity building that these countries have been involved for several decades. The consequences of inadequate attention given to the broad paradigm of environment is to be reversed through various paths:

1. The first is the empowerment and moralization of women. Women moving away from their own environments, occupations, land that they tilled and forests that they had close linkages with means continuing destruction to the environment. Whatever the measures that we intent to initiate should enable to empower women as custodians of their own environment.
2. The second is associated with the long-term health implications resulting from alienating women's access to traditional knowledge, healing practices and rituals. It is important to realize that the availability of local materials and plants

enables women to continue the remedial measures to treat ailments and reduced the gravity of their lack of access to modern health services and affordability. Women and poor families become more vulnerable to disease and ill-health.

3. The third is the issue of deepening crisis in food and energy security for which rural populations in Asia have relied largely on local produced food and biomass for energy.
4. The environmental degradation, which is heavily influenced by the crop monoculture and modern technology, has become a serious threat to land-based women's occupations and the linkages that they have maintained through tangible, intangible and labour inputs.
5. Mobilization and motivation of women as equal partners for promoting sustainability and healthy environment should be the national priorities. The water, soil, air, health, richness in agriculture, biodiversity etc. depend heavily on the social system where distinct needs, interests, capabilities and capacities of men and women are found.

Under these circumstances, there is a need to recognize women's environmental citizenship, and have citizens responsible for their own environments, occupational space, livelihood, health and resources. The women- environment dynamics need to be seen from four perspectives: the first is the sense of citizenship; second is the collective responsibility; the third is the rights of the future generations; and the fourth is related to decision-making, mutual respect and justice for all, free from discrimination. These areas are the challenges for every single state in South Asia.

REFERENCES

Adeola, F.O., 2000, "Cross-national Environmental Justice and Human Rights Issues: A Review of Evidence in the Developing World", *American Behavioral Scientist*, Vol. 43 (4), pp. 686-706.

Agarwal, B., 1994, *A Filed of One's Own: Gender and Land Rights in South Asia*, Cambridge University Press.

Agyeman, J., Bullard, R.D. and Evans, B. (eds.), 2003, *Just Sustainabilities: Development in an Unequal World*, Earthscan Publications Ltd., London.

Bhadra, C.K., 1997, "The Land, Forestry and Women's Work in Nepal", in Anoja Wickramasinghe (ed.), *Land and Forestry: Women's Local Resource-based Occupations for Sustainable Survival in South Asia*, CORRENSA, Peradeniya, Sri Lanka, pp. 74-87.

Cutter, S., 1995, *Race, Class and Environmental Justice, Progress in Geography*, Vol. 19 (1), pp. 111-22.

Das, S., 1997, "Women's Contribution to Homestead and Agricultural Production System in Bangladesh", in Anoja Wickramasinghe (ed.), *Land and Forestry: Women's Local Resource-based Occupations for Sustainable Survival in South Asia*, CORRENSA, Peradeniya, Sri Lanka, pp. 51-72.

Eady, V., 2003, "Environmental Justice in State Policy Decisions", in Agyeman, J., Bullard, R.D. and Evans, B. (eds.), *Just Sustainabilities: Development in an Unequal World*, Earthscan Publications Ltd., London, pp. 168-81.

Faber, D.R. and McCarthy, D., 2003, "Neo-liberalism, Globalization and the Struggle for Ecological Democracy: Linking Sustainability and Environmental Justice", in Agyeman, J., Bullard, R.D. and Evans, B. (eds.), *Just Sustainabilities: Development in an Unequal World*, Earthscan Publications Ltd., London, pp. 38-63.

FAO, 2000, *The State of Food and Agriculture*, Food and Agriculture Organization of the United Nations, Rome.

Mahbub ul Haq Human Development Centre, 2003, *Human Development in South Asia 2002: Agriculture and Rural Development*, Oxford University Press, Pakistan.

McLaren, D., 2003, "Environmental Space, Equity and the Ecological Debt", in Agyeman, J., Bullard, R.D. and Evans, B. (eds.), *Just Sustainabilities: Development in an Unequal World*, Earthscan Publications Ltd., London, pp. 19-37.

Middleton, N. and O'Keefee, P., 2001, *Redefining Sustainable Development*, Pluto Press, London.

Sarin, M., 1995, *Joint Forest Management in India: Achievements and Unaddressed Challenges*, Unasylva, Vol. 46, pp. 30-36.

Shiva, V., 1989, *Staying Alive: Women, Ecology and Development*, Zed Books, London.

—, 1991, *The Violence of the Green Revolution: Third World Agriculture, Ecology and Politics*, Third World Network, Penang, Malaysia.

Taylor, D.E., 2000, The Rise of the Environmental Justice Paradigm: Injustice framing and the Social Construction of Environmental Discourses, *American Behavioral Scientist*, Vol. 43 (4), pp. 508-80.

United Nations Economic Commission for Europe, 1999, Convention on Access to Information, Public Participation in Decision Making and Access to Justice in Environmental Matters, UNECE, Geneva.

UNDP, 1999, *Human Development Report*, United Nations Development Programme, Oxford University press, New York.

UNDP, 2004, *Energy for Sustainable Development in Asia and the Pacific Region: Challenges and Lessons from UNDP. Projects*, United Nations Development Programme, One United Nations Plaza, New York, U.S.A.

Wickramasinghe, Anoja, 1992, "Women Equity and Natural Resource Management", Occasional Working Paper in *Women's Studies and Gender Relations*, Vol. 1, 1992, The Centre for Research in Women's Studies and Gender Relations, The University of British Columbia, Canada.

—, 1993, "The Differential Impact of Deforestation and Environmental Degradation on Men and Women: Issues for Social Justice", *Journal of Human Justice*, Vol. 5 (1), pp. 46-57.

—, 1994, "Indigenous agroforestry system: An adoptable strategy for rehabilitation and sustainable management of degraded lands", in Panjab Sing, P.S. Pathak and M.M. Roy (eds.), *Agroforestry System for Sustainable Land Use*, Oxford and IBH Publishing Co. Pvt. Ltd., New Delhi, pp. 59-69.

—, 1995, "Gender patterns in the management of forest resources in Sri Lanka", in E.H. D'Silva and D. Kariyawasam (eds.), *Emerging Issues in Forest Management for Sustainable Development in South Asia*, pp. 81-84, ADB, Manila, 1995.

—, 1997, "Women Harmonizing Ecosystems for Integrity and Local Sustainability in Sri Lanka", in Wickramasinghe, Anoja (ed.), *Land and Forestry: Women's Local Resource-based Occupations for Sustainable Survival in South Asia*, CORRENSA, Peradeniya, Sri Lanka, pp. 89-141.

—, 1999, "The Local Context and Gendered Sights Related to Biodiversity Management and Food Security in Sri Lanka". Paper presented at the Technical Consultation on Gender Dimensions in Biodiversity Management and Food Security: Policy and Programme Strategies, M.S. Swaminathan Research Foundation, Chennai, India, 2-5 November 1999, sponsored by FAO/RAP, Bangkok.

—, 2001, Biodiversity Conservation from the Perspectives on Gender and Food Security. Research Report, National Science Foundation, 47/5, Maitland Place, Colombo 7, Sri Lanka.

—, 2002, "Farmers' initiatives in promoting agroforestry in Mahaweli settlements", *Sri Lankan Journal of Agricultural Sciences*, Vol. 39, National Agricultural Society of Sri Lanka, 2002, pp. 127-45.

—, 2003a, "Women and Environmental Justice in South Asia", in Agyeman, J., Bullard, R.D. and Evans, B. (eds.), *Just Sustainabilities: Development in an Unequal World*, Earthscan Publications Ltd., London, pp. 229-51.

—, 2003b, "Gender Mainstreaming: Strategy for Incorporating Traditional Knowledge into Mainstream Development, Sri Lanka National Strategy for Incorporating Traditional Knowledge into Development Practices", IUCN Sri Lanka Country Office, The National Science and Technology Commission (NASTEC), Sri Lanka, pp. 115-24.

3

Big Boys on the Block

The Intersections of Militarism and Patriarchy

Anuradha M. Chenoy

> "We are the big boys on the block in South Asia. And if there are going to be negotiations, it is better if they are through us than any foreign power, or even the United Nations" (Editorial on Sri Lanka, *The Hindustan Times*, May 12, 2000).

Militarization has been traditionally understood as the increasing emphasis on military power by states to further their national interests, with the option of using military threats and war as an extension of politics. When military methods are used to solve political issues, and the military starts dominating civilian institutions, with a simultaneous decline in individual freedoms and democratic institutions, states are said to be militarist. Militarization includes socially organized physical coercion, which describes the process of militarization underway on a global scale. Both state and non-state forces can be militarist in their method and ideology. Militarism implies emphasis on the military over the civilian in a state, and thus includes the wider structures that promote militarist methods.

Patriarchy is the social condition that privileges men over women and allows men to dominate over them. It is the value system that attributes qualities of superiority to men in the division of labour. The force and power in militarism are fixed in hierarchies that coincide with patriarchal practice. Both these categories have become entwined through historical time reflect in the ideological and institutional structures of states and society.

It is the ideology and practice of militarism and its linkages with patriarchy that provides a link with the violence in the state to the violence in society and within the home. Militarism is a component of states in either overt or latent forms. Thus, even democratic and liberal states that include notions of pacification in domestic politics may use it in their foreign policy gestures (e.g., NATO states). Militarism however is not confined to states. It replicates itself in anti-state and other political movements, that give up on political negotiation and resort to force and militarist values. This paper submits that both militarism and patriarchy are part of a hegemonic ideational structure that has over time subsumed social, political, psychological and economic relations and structures. This entwining that has occurred through history is expressed through power structures in state and society, and these concepts have become expressions of common sense and ideology. A feminist analysis of international security structures shows stark continuities in the period of globalization with the earlier periods of history. As barriers for the flow of information, capital and technology fall and nation-states change their role, as new nations emerge and one nation asserts a unilateralist dominance unparalleled in international history, the values of militarism and patriarchy underlie relations between genders. In this paper we attempt to unravel these two intersecting concepts of militarism and patriarchy, with reference to South Asia.

In History

History in ancient and medieval times was witness to the most stark forms of patriarchy and militarism. Both had their roots in the structure of the family and extended to the clan, the community and the state. The very division of labour from its simplest to its more complex forms implied that women's primary concern was reproduction, the home and the hearth, while that of men was production and protection. This protection was to come through force. The tasks of the clan, and then the state, were linked to the tasks of the patriarch. Protection, expansion and survival were negotiated largely through militarist means. Ancient myths, bardic traditions and historical analysis confirm this across geo-spatial spaces and cultures. All cultures had their 'men of steel' where men and steel (armour) were happily interchangeable. We are thus familiar, for example, with the Rajput warrior/male. The support he receives from the mother/sister for saving the 'honour' of both his land and his women. The fear to conform to these ideals was linked to becoming 'womanly' or 'wearing bangles'. The mother image came to be linked to territory (Dharti Ma). Both militarism and patriarchy developed simultaneously, were entwined while re-enforcing each other.

Early capitalism, colonialism and imperial expansion radically altered relations between men as more men participated in state structures and in anti-state movements. Relations of hierarchy and social mobility altered and new political spaces were created for them. Relations with women, however, remained largely unaltered. Women benefited only through the 'trickle-down' effect. Despite women's education (and but for some exceptions) the dominant social norms continued to confine them in their traditional roles. The onset of liberal democracy, liberty and freedom gave these rights first to men and only much later to women. The pacification that came with democracy in the western world was to a large extent confined to internal issues. Foreign policies involved expansion and colonialism based on militarist ideals and force in controlling empires and natives.

War and militarist methods defined for men, what 'maleness' meant. It was a confirmation of the masculine identity.[1] War and militarist values became a proof of manhood, and the fact that this manhood could be tested this way. This test also demonstrated male superiority. The test of superiority in the military field was extended to society through cultural and social practice. Literature, media, films and texts echoed these practices. The privilege and status given to men as warriors excluded others, especially women. At the same time, the military and the overall ideology of militarism also defines women as complementary or adjunct to men. Femininity is thus presented as a ('natural' and inferior) contrast to masculinity. Militarism re-enforced role models and behavioural patterns of men and women within the military and in society itself.

It is the ideology of militarism that presents violence as a 'normal male practice', one that should be linked with the male identity. That is why, we often hear acts of violence being condoned for young boys with the idiom "boys will be boys". Or, when most militant movements refer to their militias as "our boys". With this, aggression becomes an accepted code for men, whereas the pacific/victim is the natural code for women. Similarly, men seem to be designed to serve the state/polity whereas women are designed to serve men. The gender difference is a hierarchical difference, played out in positions of power and decision-making that ensures that the status of men remains superior in all structures and institutions. Moreover, the propaganda for patriotism and war promotes national unity and silences dissent, women are especially "shown their place" during this time. Subjugation of others is part of the militarist ideology that is also inculcated as a male practice. This 'other' can range from the other gender, to community, class, region, enemy nation, etc.

Society and state recognized (both legally and socially) the distinct but unequal roles, and favoured women's sacrifices for the state's wars. Women accepted male privilege and the male-militarist mystique. All of society and women within this internalized these values and even promoted them. States thus take care to honour the wives of soldiers killed in wars. The sacrifices made by mothers/wives are part of the traditions of all wars and of all countries. Here, it is important to note that just as war and militarism reinforced the traditional roles of women, it also had unintended consequences of changing some roles for women. Wars forced women to go to work in the absence of men or take up auxiliary tasks of war, and thus become part of public life. In many cases, when wars were over, men resumed their natural positions as leaders and often women went back to the home, as the state extolled the virtues of 'home-making'. Nonetheless, feminists themselves have conceded that wars did create new spaces and roles for women. At the same time, the public roles given to women during wars, reinforced militarist values and accepted women as part of an unequal hierarchy. Militarism and military values based on patriarchal tenets continued as basic norms.

Values and feelings of nationalism that characterized the 'modern period' further sustained the twin values of militarism and patriarchy. Many modern states, like the states in Europe, were linked with the rise of nationalism. The anti-colonial movements and the establishment of postcolonial states of Asia and Africa, came in the context of a constructed nationalism and the formation of identities linked to the nation-state. Nationalism was part of the ideology that built the modern state. Thus, nationalism has played a progressive role in history linked with the processes of modernization and secularization. Since patriarchy and militarism were endorsed by nationalism during these critical periods, they have been retained in the ideological and institutional structures of the state.

Nationalist movements encouraged the homogenization of identities against oppressive outsiders, colonial or feudal systems. At the same time, the nationalist movements built internal hierarchies and suppressed internal differences like class, gender, race, etc. These hierarchies and unequal power relations continued to exist and in some cases intensified in the newly formed nation-states, which were now run by the successful nationalist elite. These states in their new incarnation were based on the principle of maintaining the status quo in domestic politics and realism in international politics. It was only progressive movements and the push of democratization that forced state structures to concede rights and incremental social justice. Militarism and patriarchy have been constant aspects of these states.

In fact, a deconstruction of the new nation-states reveals that they attempted to maintain elite privilege that was patriarchal in nature. Nationalism was used to paper over the gender, class and other differences. Feminist scholars, systematically, showed how the nation was represented primarily by male voices in all decision-making bodies and how male agendas were continuously reinforced. Gender is central to the construction of the nation itself. Since nationalism draws heavily from cultural images from an imagined past, often going back to the idea of a culture that was destroyed because of foreign domination, nationalism reinforces traditional conceptions of women.[2] During the national movement in India, for instance, myths around the women as 'custodian of the past' or 'as heirs to wisdom and traditions' were propagated, while women were kept within boundaries set by the male nationalist elite.[3] Though women participated in the nationalist struggle, they continued to be kept within specific boundaries, and were not given the rights, promised them during the struggle.

In many nationalist discourses the nation is depicted as the 'motherland'. As Benedict Anderson has shown, the power of nationalism lies in its image of 'belonging' and of 'being home'. Women being associated with the home and the private domain reinforce the powerful imagery of merging the national community with the selfless and devoted mother. As this imagery appeals to male society, it simultaneously legitimizes male domination over women.[4] The language of nationalism is itself gendered and the image of the nation is often linked to the mother or mother goddess. As national identity is equated with gender, race and colour, women become identified with the nation and their bodies used to reproduce the boundaries of the nation and as transmitters of national culture.

Since women are identified as territory and linked with the 'honour' and control of this territory, rape has always been part of the act of war and conflict and women's bodies become, as Kandyoti has put it, "the privileged signifiers of national difference".[5] Here, the aggressor by violating the women attacks the honour of the enemy, and the act is symbolized as 'violating the national honour' of the 'other' – the enemy. This gendered nationalism is entwined with militarism that is inherent in both making and maintaining of the nation/state, and is part of the male and the state's discourse. Every war and occupation has used this symbolism and soldiers have raped women. Even, in the latest US attack on Iraq, Iraqi women have been raped in prisons and outside by American soldiers. Women's bodies are thus 'owned' by the community and are to be controlled by norms set by the male-dominated community.

At the same time, women also identify with the nation and are not excluded from it as other groups of different ethnicity, race or colour may be. Though nationalism attempts to fix hierarchies, yet it also plays potentially a progressive role. It was the force that enabled de-colonization and anti-imperialism and can resist the attack on the state from forces of globalization. Though nationalism is passe in the West, where state building is complete and states are secure from external or economic threats, nationalism can be a barrier used by Third World states against western economic hegemonies. As women identify with nationalism and become part of it, they also internalize and accept the gendered hierarchies that it enforces and the ideology of militarism that it promotes.

The danger of nationalism comes, when sectarian forces twist it for xenophobic purposes. The problem is that the slide from nationalism/patriotism to chauvinism/jingoism is easy and often goes undetected. That is why, many excuse national chauvinism as part of an exercise in nationalism. In instances of xenophobic nationalism, an attempt is made to construct an enemy 'other' as a threat. Since the 'other' groups are seen as disintegrative or secondary to internal unity and to territorial integrity or any other attribute of sovereignty. Moreover, everyone has a fixed place in a nationalist hierarchy (man, woman, native, foreigner, class, caste). This then legitimizes the state system in which violence is used as the ultimate arbiter of social conflicts. This process also attempts to curb the autonomy of women and also control their sexuality. Every attempt is made to reinforce powerful position of men in social, political and economic life. Women tend to be defined as 'dependents' and receive identification only in terms of their relationship to men as wives, mothers, daughters or sisters. Citizenship rights are limited/denied to them. And, 'national interests' defined in terms of male subjects.[6]

National chauvinism privileges or glorifies the positive characteristics of the dominant culture and poses it against the alleged inferior/inimical characteristics of the other nationalism. National chauvinists are thus prepared to use violence against the 'other' communities. Historically, the construction of nationalism has promoted the image of male domination and male leadership. The distinctions between nationalism and militarism are deliberately blurred. Literature and analysis of war associates men with combat, violence and activity, and women with peace, nurturing and passivity. These images are explained by biological, social and historical references. National chauvinism exaggerates the negative aspects of nationalism. Conflating manhood, combat and militarism, national chauvinism reproduces violence and glorifies it as a 'natural' expression of masculine and nation-state identity.[7] Thus, the image of the 'heroic' male warriors is extenuated to the behaviour of states. Success of a state, like the success of a man, is thus measured in terms of power, honour, valour, self-reliance, and other aspects linked primarily to 'male ego'. Clearly then, nationalism is often used as cover for militarism. National chauvinism has the closest links to militarization.

It is through the messages of nationalism that civil society can be militarized. Women are an important agency in militarizing civil society. Women carry this message through the message of a militant nationalism. The nation itself is symbolized as a woman, for example, Bharat Mata or Mother India. This symbolism helps evoke the most fundamental of all imageries. It is in this context that the forces that use militant nationalism like the Sangh Parivar (the right-wing groups led by the Bhartiya Janata Party) in India, have insisted on using the patriotic song "Vande Mataram" (Hail Mother). This song and the images it evokes of nation as mother, is used by the Sangh as a slogan, and even as a greeting in their morning assemblies. With this, women's bodies get replaced as national territory, to be protected and to be possessed. Just as the 'other' or enemy territory (symbolized also by the woman-mother image body) has to be violated and dispossessed.

Since civil society extends into the state and the state penetrates and influences civil society, the patriarchy and militarism of the state cannot remain an isolated phenomenon. It influences political culture, dominant beliefs and ideas as also state and social structures and institutions. Religious ideals, nationalism and popular culture absorb these values to present a complex and multiple system of ideologies, which include patriarchy and militarism. This ideational complex varies within societies and political cultures just as it varies between states.

In Theory

Militarism has been analyzed in many theories and discourses. Treatises on war like those by Clausewitz and Jomini and others have discussed the values and methods of militarism, and shown war as an extension of politics. Marxist theorists from Lenin to Rosa Luxemburg have shown militarism to be an intrinsic part of the expanding capitalist state. Gramsci, Hobsbawm, Bloch and others have stressed on militarism as an ideology. Many economists have shown militarism of states in terms of defence expenditure and the social and opportunity costs that are lost as a consequence. The relation of militarism and patriarchy, however, remained unexamined, until feminist writers questioned the power play in war and militaries. Simone de Beauvoir stated that it is not the sex that gives life that is accorded superiority but the one which kills – that is, the one that goes to war.[8]

Feminist scholars have critiqued theories of militarization as being inadequate in their explanation, since they did not take into account the gender aspect of militarization.[9] They argued that militarism as a social process depends on patriarchy and promotes and sustains military values. It is thus masculinity and not capitalism that links industry and military and patriarchal assumptions reinforce militarization and hegemony of the military industrial complex that maintain militarization.[10] The argument is that the inequality between women and men has been a fundamental cause of the social toleration of many forms of violence against women, and the perpetuation of war. Feminists show that militaries through time and world over have almost been a male preserve. Further, militaries are based on conscious political policies that construct state institutions for organized violence that is dependent on maleness.

Cynthia Enloe has pointed out that since militarization occurs during war and peace, and also in any part of society, that may or may not be controlled by the military, thus virtually anything can be militarized – toys, scientific research, motherhood, curriculum, etc. Enloe believes that the wide-ranging effects of militarism necessitates many explanations, and needs much more analysis from feminist writers.[11] It is thus the functioning of militarization in society that needs to be researched and the interconnectedness of patriarchal and militarist views that need to be analyzed to establish a gender perspective of militarization. Enloe argues that it is only when militarism is viewed as a process rather than as 'events' that the connections between war, militarism and other processes like oppression, colonization, division of labour, reproduction, and liberation, can be understood.[12]

Because the feminist understanding links masculinity with militarism, it is possible now to see how militarism functions in civil societies. Jill Steans argues that while there has been discussion on how ideas of masculinity fosters and support militarism, there is need for an analysis for the relation between masculinity and femininity in the context of militarism. Women contribute to the militarization of society in both material and ideological ways, from encouraging men to go to war, to playing a direct role in the war processes. But, the key issue is that in all these varied roles the incorporation of women has tended to reinforce the masculinity of war and justify militarism.[13] Feminists, thus, oppose the incorporation of women into the military, because that would increase the militarization of society as a whole and so undermine the work of peace and women's movements.

Feminists develop the link between militarism and other forms of domination and militarism and violence. Aggression and violence are related to the construction of masculinity and are also related to race and class. For example, the Sikhs are said to be a 'militant' race. This has in recent times been extended to religion, e.g., 'militancy and Islam'. Feminists emphasize the cultural underpinnings of militarism because of their fundamental assumption that the causes and consequences of militarization are not linked simply with war. Similarly, militarism is not the opposite of peace, but is part of the entire process that makes the methodology of war a part of daily life.

The linkages of masculinity and war have also been established through analysis of 'military thinking' and military values, both of which are masculinist in nature and essence. All armies are based on the concepts of training boys 'to be men', to 'bring out the man'. The basic attempt is to reinforce violent masculinity. This violent masculinity, however, is not restricted to the military as Connell has shown, it is extended to the state. Acts of violence are embedded in power inequalities and ideologies of male supremacy and that the connection of violence with ideology reveals the multiple character of social power.[14] One reason that makes it difficult to challenge both militarism and patriarchy is that the concept of power itself has both these qualities intertwined within it. State power in the period of globalization denotes both these qualities. US unilateralist policies set an example of this for other nations. The effect is a spiralling of militarist states, all seeking as India's former Deputy Prime Minister L.K. Advani stated, to be 'hard' states.

State violence is legitimized through the use of such key concepts as 'autonomy' and 'national interest', which are based on masculinized notions of social control and hegemony. Feminists have argued that both the ideology and the practices of the state are masculinized. The state thus arms men and disarms women. The major practices of the state like diplomacy, governance, etc., are formulated in a context of masculine ideology, designed to give the appearance of 'toughness' or even backed up by national interest and force.

At the same time, feminists have been divided on the 'essentialist' position that militarism is essentially masculinist and women are inherently peaceful. Feminist writers like Betty Reardon analyze the link between sexism and militarism, which is based on a view that men are by nature aggressive and that the social order must be maintained through force, and that sexism and militarism need each other. Jane Adams thus speaks of 'the eternal opposition' of feminism and militarism.[15] This construction defines the very nature of women as essentially a pacifist one. Since women were engaged with mothering and caring, there has been a gender stereotyping of women that helps re-enforce a structure of male power superior to that of women. In history, with the construction of gender stereotypes, males got identified as the idealized warrior and women as the pacifist with motherhood, 'household work', etc. This construction helps in re-enforcing patriarchal control.

The belief that women have a privileged or innate predisposition for peace and opposition to militarism is a constructed belief, which is disproved by history. An intermediate position, however, is taken by feminist writers like Jean Elshtain and others, who submit that women use their moral agency to preserve peace. Women thus have a historic link to the pacific 'other' but the challenge lies in transforming that identification into one that can speak to public power and challenge the warrior mentality, even though that warrior mentality is embraced by some women in the name of sexual equality.[16] Through history, women have always participated in the military system in various ways. Though they were never forced to join the armed forces, but the same social and economic forces shaped the ideas of men and women. Concepts of patriotism, imperial expansionism, colonialism and territoriality have been shared by both women and men. Women thus contributed to war efforts in their own way and national consensus on wars, fascism and anti-fascism has legitimized wars and militarization in all societies. And, in fact, women/wives have played critical roles in the military systems.

While feminism as theory and practice is set against militarism, however, women have remained engaged in the ideology and support of war as men. Feminists thus argue that the military plays a special role in the ideological structures of patriarchy since the very notion of combat plays a role in the construction of 'manhood' and justifies the superiority of men in the social order. Male superiority is established in the military through a variety of ways. This starts with recruitment, training, organization, ideology etc. At all these stages the emphasis is 'to make a man' and a distaste for anything 'womanly'. Thus, gender is central to the armed forces, and the state institutions work to construct particular forms of masculinity and regulate relations between them, as part of the vital conditions for the sustenance of these institutions.[17] Clearly, while it is possible to draw connections between militarism and masculinity, they are not identical, but have 'become entwined'.[18] Thus the masculinity of war is constructed to maintain gender difference and assign a lower role to women in the social and power hierarchy.

In South Asia

In South Asia, the entwining of militarism and patriarchy has its own variations and specifics. Within South Asian states these concepts vary in their intensity and practice. Thus, for instance, in Pakistan, the roots of militarism are more structural and overt since the traditions and institutions of democracy are historically shorter and interspersed with direct military rule. In Sri Lanka militarism developed in response to a secessionist movement with a deeply militarist character. In Nepal, the dominant ethnic group – the Gorkha – itself implied a militarist/protectionist force. The anti-state Maoist movement has all the characteristics of militarism that its ideologue Mao had advocated: "Power flows from the barrel of a gun." The Nepali state response to the Maoist insurgency is along typical militarist lines that have no regard for human right violations. This gives little space for alternate 'capture' of power theories. In India, the general belief was that given its long experience with democracy and non-alignment in foreign policy, it was basically pacific. However, when India has had to deal with any internal conflict of long standing, whether it is in the North East, Kashmir, Punjab or movements like the Naxalite movement and others, the state has happily resorted to largely militarist solutions.

In all the militarism of South Asia, the element of patriarchy remains a major component. As we showed in the earlier sections, militarism in all South Asia privileges the male, has sharpened the gender divide and has been always linked with 'manhood'. All the states and societies in South Asia discriminate against women in a variety of ways. Practices ranging from dowry deaths, female infanticide, violence against women and honour killings remain current and acceptable social practices. It is not necessary to list and give detailed reference since these practices are listed in our daily news reports. In instances of conflict and militarism, these discriminatory and patriarchal practices intersect. Two instances in May 2000 are enough to show how rampant they are. In Pakistan, the attempt by General Musharaf to pass a legislation against honour killings and blasphemy laws was withdrawn in the face of sustained hostility by the Mullahs and Islamic forces within the military. In India, while laws may guard against such practice, honour of women remains a major issue. For example, a panchayat in Punjab ruled that two feuding families would have to pay 'with the blood of a virgin girl' if they continued to feud (*Asian Age*, 22 May 2000).

In both instances (in Pakistan and India) conflict was linked to the honour of women. Women's bodies symbolized both protection and violation of honour. The autonomy of women was to be controlled by the patriarch whether in the state or the community. The women had no choice in the policy or decision. Honour was to be held and tested in the hands of the male/male-dominated community. The failure to protect honour was the fault solely of the woman, who had to pay for it either by her life or by forfeiting her virginity or honour.

The protection versus the violation of honour is similar to the protection/subjugation of territory. Women have had to pay a special price in these conflicts. In all conflicts, in South Asia, women's bodies are subject to the interplay of militarism and patriarchy through the concepts of honour and territory. Thus, whether it was the partition of India and Pakistan in 1947, the Bangladesh liberation war, the LTTE-Singhalese conflicts, the forceful removal of ethnic Nepalese from Bhutan in the 1990s, the Gujarat massacres in India 2002, or sectarian/communal conflicts throughout South Asia – all these have some common ingredients. All these conflicts involved ethnic or religious identity conflicts; women were a target of rape/mass rape and sexual crimes in all these conflicts, since rape was seen as violation of the honour or territory of the enemy. Thus, honour (*laj*) of nation/community/

woman becomes interchangeable in all these conflicts, revealing the deeply entwined nature and manifestation of the militarized and patriarchal discourse and its methodology.

The link between militarism and patriarchy is evident during every conflict, whether at local, national or inter-state level. For example, in Pakistan, in the locality it is honour killing. In India, poor and low caste village women are paraded naked when they go against caste/family tradition. At the national level, nuclear testing becomes a moment for 'testing the manhood' of both states. (Thus, statements like "we are not eunuchs".) Hijacking becomes a moment to identity politics. ("We Hindus are cowards", apropos "Muslims are bullies".) At the inter-state level, like during the Kargil conflict, gender divisions that emphasize male versus female roles get sharpened.

In South Asia, like in many other Third World societies, militarism is not restricted to states. Other movements for political mobilization and non-state or anti-state movements can be equally militarist. This is especially evident in movements that are based on fundamentalist agendas or religious chauvinism. For instance, in Pakistan, the two Islamist parties – the Jamat-e-Islami (JI) and the Jamiat-e-Ulema-e-Islam (JUI) – that were co-opted by the former military dictator Zia-ul-Haque and that propelled the implementation of the Islamic system in Pakistan's political structures. Both these parties educated students and youth and built a militant Islamic cadre. This cadre was eventually armed and became the base for the 'jihad' (privatized holy war) in Afghanistan in the 1980s. The JUI based itself on the Deoband school, and displaced the JI in its influence since its madrassas were responsible for producing the student militia – the Taliban.

These Islamic parties had the typical fundamentalist trajectory. They wanted a homogenized religion, of which they were the sole spokesmen. They advocated militant enforcement of religious laws as interpreted by them. Women were given a secondary role enforceable by these laws. Women's honour and family law was to be based solely on fundamentalist interpretations of Islamic tenets, etc. As a consequence, these parties that never had popular support in terms of electoral practice (with never more than 7-10 seats in parliament) dictated that shari'a law and parallel shariat courts be instituted in Pakistan. They have heralded the 'Islamic bomb' and presented pilgrims to Haj as 'messengers from a nuclear country'. Here then is a clear example of militarism, patriarchy, xenophobic nationalism that distorts religion to maintain these multiple oppressions.

In India, Hindu fundamentalist movements and parties like the Shiv Sena, VHP, RSS, combine the ideology of a militant nationalism that manifests itself in ways that reveal xenophobic nationalism and patriarchy. This is revealed in their multiple agenda that includes, for instance, building an image of India as one based on Hindutva, vandalizing or calling for the banning of films like 'Water' or 'Fire', that attempt to question the stereotypical role assigned to women, propagating the nuclear message into civil society through religious symbols like nuclear yatras (travels) or distribution of sand from Pokhran. The distribution of tridents, symbolizing a militant Hinduism and the creation of militias by groups like the Bajrang Dal are the more direct forms of militarizing civil society through religious symbolism that is being used by right-wing militant groups. The cultural nationalism of these parties targets the minorities on the one hand and attempts to control the autonomy of women on the other. The method of achieving and enforcing this agenda is a militant one, clearly showing the linkages of these phenomena.

It is not the state alone that has the potential for militarism or patriarchy. Many of the anti-state movements have absorbed and reflect this in their movements and in their method. The LTTE in Sri Lanka, Khalistan movement, the NSCN, the Kashmiri militants, the Maoists in Nepal, have all bypassed political negotiation and taken to the politics of militarism. Though they may have reason for alienation and anger, ultimately they have used militarist methods to fight the state and their own adversaries within the movements. They have sought to control the autonomy of women in different ways that include advocating dress codes, prohibiting abortion, imposing bans on some texts or local cultural forms, etc. At the same time, these movements have also attempted to use the agency of women in their movement within a patriarchal framework.

Similarly, other movements in South Asia like the LTTE in Sri Lanka, have responded to state oppressions by replicating their own repression by combining militarist methods, patriarchal discourse with their demands for secession or autonomy. In most instances, the response to state oppressions is countered through methods that replicate the state. Thus, even new states that are born out of a struggle against militarism and chauvinism of one kind or another, like Bangladesh, replicate the very oppressions that they had struggled against. It is therefore time to thus question both the states and the movements within them on the intersecting oppressions that phenomena like militarism and patriarchy generate.

Conclusion

Civil society is the site that legitimizes intersecting ideologies. The contest between ideologies promoted by the state and any other group that seeks to gain power and control takes place in the realm of civil society. The entwining of militarism and patriarchy with xenophobic religion or nationalism is located in civil society. Since the state is sustained by and extends into civil society, it often relies on structures such as these, to retain its power in civil society. Though the twenty-first century has established that democratization and women's liberation are irreversible phenomena, militarism and patriarchy combine with other ideologies to generate a system of oppressions that target and continue to control women. Women's movements and counter-ideologies have contested patriarchy and have been part of peace movements, yet their task to deconstruct and challenge militarism and patriarchy continues.

NOTES

1. Janna Thompson, "Women and War", *Women's Studies International Forum*, Vol. 14, Nos. (1–2), pp. 63-75, 1991. Thompson shows the male identification with war, we extend it to militarization.
2. Anderson, B., 1983, *Imagined Communities*, Verso Books, London; Yuval Davis, N. and Anthias, F., 1989, 'Introduction', Women, Nation State", Macmillan, Basington; Jayawardene, Kumari, 1986, *Feminism and Nationalism*, Zed Books, London.
3. Jayawardene, op. cit.
4. Steans, 1998, *Gender and International Relations*, Polity Press, Cambridge, pp. 115-116; Mosse, G., 1985, *Nationalism and Sexuality: Middle Class Morality and Sexual Norms in Modern Europe*, quoted in Steans, University of Wisconsin Press, Madison, p. 67.
5. Kandiyoti, D. Kandiyoti, "Identity and its Discontents", *Millennium: Journal of International Studies*, Vol. 20, No. 3, 1992, pp. 429-431.
6. Yuval Davis and Anthias, *Woman Nation, State*; Steans, p. 68.
7. Cynthia Enloe, 1990, *Bananas, Beaches and Bases: Making Feminist Sense of International Politics*, University of California Press, Berkeley; and Enloe, 1983, *Does Khaki Become You?* South End Press, Boston, MA; also, J. Ann Tickner, 1992, *Gender in International Relations*, Columbia University Press, New York.
8. Simone deBeauvoir, 1972, *The Second Sex*, Penguin, London, p. 95.
9. Enloe, Cynthia, 1987, "Feminist Thinking about War, Militarism and Peace", in Hess, B. and Ferree, M., *Analysing Gender: A Handbook of Social Science Research*, Beverly Hill, London, Sage; And, Enloe, C., 1988, *Does Khaki Become You? The Militarization of Women's Lives*, Pandora, London; Peterson, Spike, 1990, "Security and Sovereign States: What is at stake in taking Feminism Seriously?", in S. Peterson (ed.), *Gendered States, Boulder*, CO: Lynne Rienner, pp. 31-64; Anne Sission Runyan and V. Spike Peterson, "The Radical Future of Realism: Feminist Subversions of IR Theory", *Alternatives*, 16: 67-106.
10. Betty A. Reardon, 1993, *Women and Peace: Feminist Visions of Global Security*, State University of New York Press, Albany, p. 157.
11. Enloe, Cynthia, 1987, "Feminist Thinking about War, Militarism and Peace", in Hess, B. and Ferree, M., *Analysing Gender: A Handbook of Social Science Research*, Sage, Beverly Hill; And, Enloe, C., 1988,

Does Khaki Become You? The Militarization of Women's Lives, Pandora, London.

12. Enloe, *Feminist Thinking*, op. cit.
13. Steans, op. cit. pp. 115-116.
14. R. Connell, 1995, *Gender and Power*, Polity Press, Cambridge, p. 109.
15. Jane Adams, 1922, *The Long Road of Women's Memory*, The Macmillan Co., New York, p. 129.
16. Jean Bethke Elshtain, 1982, "Women as Mirror and Other: Towards a Theory of Women, War, and Feminism", *Humanities in Society*, Vol. 5, Nos. 1&2, Winter and Spring, pp. 29-44.
17. Connell, *The State, Gender and Sexual Politics*, op. cit.
18. Peterson, 1992, p. 48; Inger Skjelsbaek, 1997, Gendered Battlefields, A Gender Analysis of Peace and Conflict, Oslo, Prio Report 6/97, p. 48.

4

Agendas for Gender

Follow-up on the Beijing Platform for Action from a UNIFEM Perspective

Chandni Joshi

What made Beijing a unique landmark in the history of UN conferences was the strong message that ran through its build-up and the conference itself, viz., the accountability of all actors to the women of the world. For us in UNIFEM[1] it was the most important message. All of us – the member-states, the UN and other multilateral agencies, the NGOs, activists and others – made pledges to the millions of women of our planet through the dynamics of the Beijing conference and its build-up. Thus, not only was the Beijing conference important itself, it was equally important for what happened before and after it – nationally, regionally and at the international level. This continuum was one of the key factors of the conference. Women had worked extremely hard to create new political spaces where their voices were heard and consensus forged. Beijing was also significant for the strength and intensity of mobilization; the sheer sweep of issues covered; the large numbers who fought and kept vigil over every paragraph, every sentence and every word of the declaration and the PFA;[2] the debate which preceded the consensus: all of this and much more made the Beijing conference what it was.

PRE-BEIJING: A HISTORICAL PERSPECTIVE

Foundations for Beijing had already been laid by previous world conferences and summits. The first world conference on women in Mexico City in 1975 addressed the issue of gender equality. This was followed by a second world conference at Copenhagen in 1980 and a third in Nairobi in 1985. During the 1990s, at a series of UN world conferences held to set standards and directions that would take policy, planning and practice into the next century, women emerged as a global force for shaping international debates and providing a gender perspective on all development issues.

At the UN Conference on Environment and Development in Rio (1992), world leaders embraced the notion that the effective participation of women as environmental managers is vital to achieving sustainable human development. In Vienna, governments acknowledged that women's rights are human rights and that attention to gender-specific violations, such as violence against women, is necessary to fulfil the promise of human rights for all. In Cairo, gender equality and equity and women's empowerment, reproductive health and rights were recognized as cornerstones of effective development policies. In Copenhagen, the World Summit for Social Development recognized that the equality and the empowerment of women are not only essential to the survival of the human race but prerequisites for the achievement of the goals of productive employment, social integration and poverty eradication.

As progress towards women's equality was assessed during the years following the Nairobi conference, it became evident that a fourth UN conference on women was necessary to provide a clear blueprint for action. It was envisioned that this would aim at removing the remaining obstacles to women's full and equal participation in all spheres of life and mainstreaming women in all aspects of development.

> "Unfortunately, progress has not been felt by women at all levels of society, particularly at the grassroots....the purpose of the conference is not to emphasize the differences between countries of regions, but to use our diversity as a source of strength and

unity. We are going to share our different experiences in order to take action for a better world" (Gertrude Mongella, Secretary General of the Conference).

BUILD-UP TO THE BEIJING CONFERENCE IN SOUTH ASIA

In the South Asia region, a tremendous momentum of government and NGO partnership was created, building structures to facilitate the process to Beijing. India witnessed a most dramatic mobilization of women from all walks of life on the eve of the Beijing conference, something that owed its origins to the richness of the women's movement and to the abiding democratic spirit in which the Government of India and the movement continuously interacted with each other.[3] The need to establish a unit, which would facilitate a flow of information on and about the conference, to NGOs, particularly grassroots women NGOs, was felt. While doing tremendous work, it was sensed that they remained in the shadows only because they were away from metropolitan areas. Thus, the Coordination Unit was set up in December 1993, initiated by a group of donor agencies, who came together in the Inter-Agency Facilitating Committee for Beijing (IFCB), of which UNIFEM was a member.

SOME ISSUES FOR BEIJING

Besides national processes, there was a lot of international interaction taking place. Issues were discussed over a period of two years and spread across several sectors. For instance, in the sector on poverty, the issues of structural adjustments, economic liberalization and market orientation were debated. There was the question of equal pay for work of equal value. In health, it was the whole issue of not only reproductive health but all aspects of health. In environment, there was the entire question of biodiversity versus monoculture, women's traditional knowledge and the issue of intellectual property rights. And, in human rights, there were concerns, such as violence against women, uniform civil code on strengthening international monitoring and international machineries on handling issues of violence, and conflict, among others.

UNIFEM AND BEIJING

UNIFEM's role at Beijing was not limited to the official UN conference but extended also to the parallel NGO Forum on Women at Huairou. Its preparatory activities included a host of seminars and workshops, bringing together NGO and government representatives for the purpose of developing national strategies, giving participants training in leadership skills, negotiating techniques and fostering group cohesiveness. Much effort was taken to disseminate information about the Fourth World Conference on Women (FWCW), to open channels of communication among women's groups and create networks, to collect gender-related statistics and to orient government delegates, officials and journalists to women's issues. Thus, in the process to Beijing, at Beijing itself and in the period post-Beijing, UNIFEM played a crucial role, both in bringing partners together and in carrying the voices of grassroots women to Beijing. It mobilized other UN and donor agencies for collective support to the governments and NGOs. These were brought together to pool resources and provide coordinated support to the respective countries of the region. For example, in Pakistan, UNIFEM spearheaded the Process to Beijing and Beyond which involved the setting up of the MFU (Multi-donor Facilitation Unit) and raising funds, helping the government and NGO activities to run smoothly for two years. Similarly, in India, UNIFEM was a part of the IFCB (Inter-Facilitation Committee for Beijing Group, comprising donors), which was set up, along with the CU (Coordination Unit) to facilitate the process to Beijing. In India, four regional preparatory workshops were held simultaneously to assist people attending the FWCW and the parallel NGO Forum. They presented the NGOs who had been accredited to the NGO Forum or to the main conference, with the opportunity to be briefed on burning issues which had emerged from the Indian women's movement and the government and NGO endeavour over the past two years. This forum also assisted in then identifying and focusing on regional issue, developing a consensus, promoting networking, and honing advocacy and lobbying skills.

These were followed by the national preparatory workshop, where participants from the regional workshops shared their discussions and regional issues with participants from the other regions. Participants had the opportunity to meet representatives from the official delegation, including representatives from the Ministry of External Affairs (MEA), the Department of Women and Child Development (DWCD), the National Commission for Women (NCW) and pioneers of the women's movement, and to discuss with them issues that they felt should be highlighted as the Indian point of view at Beijing and plan for post-Beijing activities. It brought together women from the grassroots, representatives of the government, about 400 NGO delegates, prominent activists, and representatives of international agencies. A forum was thus provided where different voices, different concerns, different levels, all turned together towards the common goals of equality, peace and development. These workshops constituted a final and most important input, which played a key role in the effectiveness with which Indian women could make their voices heard at Beijing – as well as in guiding the way in strategizing and planning for post-Beijing activities.

Women's Expectations from Beijing

Some of the significant gains that the world's women looked for at the FWCW were:

- A new vision of development founded on women's realities and built on women's rights.
- Ensuring the provision of adequate resources, mechanisms and processes for accountability and implementation of this new vision.
- Consolidation and building of new bases of solidarity for the international women's movement as a global force that would move women into the 21st century.

- Strengthening of emerging new partnerships between civil society and government, which would work together in addressing common problems.

The FWCW took place in Beijing in September 1995. Over 40,000 women and men across the world met to assess how women's lives had changed over the past decade and took steps to keep issues of concern to women high on the international agenda. The conference in Beijing was unique in that, perhaps for the first time in history, very diverse partners created groundbreaking levels of commitment. What made that possible was the sheer force of the intellectual commitment derived from the vibrant women's movement. They had struggled hard to negotiate spaces and language through the many levels and layers of national, regional and global biases, prejudices and 'real politiks'. Delegates from UN member-countries looked at recent trends affecting the status of women with an eye to the future. They reviewed how women had fared in the areas of health, education, employment, family life, politics and human rights. Despite the progress made since 1975, it was found that disparities between north and south, rural and urban, and rich and poor, continued to concern women everywhere.

Beijing stood for participation in the broadest sense of the term. Women played a leading role in not only building a new vision of development, but also in articulating the implementation of systems and processes that would create a sustainable future for all. They asked for greater commitment, accountability and resources for the implementation of what had come out of the other various world summits and conferences. They sought to build on their collective gains and to respond to women's demands that substantial resources be invested to translate words into meaningful actions.

Women formed alliances across borders and across issues. They learned from each other, realizing that their concerns differed in degree and scope, but were similar in terms in causes and consequences. A major achievement of the conference was that gender, as a social construct of the relationships between women and men, was debated and appeared in the plan of action. There was a high degree of partnership between the various layers of structures of the conference – the UN and the NGO Forum – at national, regional and international levels. The visible result is agreement over the 12 critical areas of concern that shaped the organizing of the conference and the Platform for Action adopted by member-nations by consensus, and with reservations.

NGO Forum, Huairou

At the NGO Forum in Huairou, almost 4,000 workshops and panels were offered over a 10-day period. The international women's movement in Beijing was strong and diverse, committed to influencing the UN more than ever before. There was an evolution of the NGO Forum from being a rebel camp outside the UN grounds, to a legitimate partner, inside the UN halls. Political modalities had also changed – from confrontation to lobbying – to get points of view across. And, along with this, there was a structural change in the relationship of a social movement (the women's movement) to the inter-governmental process. Much of the success of the NGO Forum was due to the role of the facilitating committee, which worked with the NGO Forum Secretariat. Regional focal points, raised by representatives of the Conference of NGOs in Consultative Relationship with the United Nations and the NGO Committee on the Status of Women, worked with the New York secretariat. Largely responsible for the success of Beijing were the national and regional preparations. At these preparatory meetings, there was representation from all interested groups, especially the official delegates.

Beijing Platform for Action

The Beijing Platform for Action (BPFA) moved women a step forward from previous conferences. Through it (the BPFA is not a legally binding document, but a contract that governments made with each other and with the world's women), 189 governments committed themselves to achieving gender equality and the empowerment and advancement of women. It identified clear and practical sets of actions, assigning responsibility for implementation to various groups of actors to make sure that there was accountability to the women of the world and that it moved in the direction of equality for women. It enunciated strategic objectives and prescribed specific activities. It aimed at removing the remaining obstacles to women's full and equal participation in all spheres of life and at securing the mainstreaming of gender in all aspects of development. The PFA emphasized that women shared common concerns, and that the common goal of gender equality around the world could be achieved by working together and in partnership with men. It recognized that women cannot be treated as a homogeneous group. Some women face particular barriers to full equality and achievement because of their particular situation – race, age, language, ethnicity, culture, religion or disability.

The BPFA identified 12 critical areas of concern for women's advancement as under:

- Women and Poverty
- Education and Training for Women
- Women and Health
- Violence against Women
- Women in Armed Conflict
- Women in the Economy
- Women in Power and Decision-making
- Institutional Mechanisms for the Advancement of Women
- Human Rights of Women
- Women and the Media
- Women and the Environment
- The Girl Child

Implementing the BPFA is a multilayered, multifaceted task. It involves governments, NGOs and civil society. It also involves the UN system and its funds, programmes and specialized agencies. Taken together, all actors are accountable for achieving clear, measurable outcomes for women. Much of this work emphasizes linkages between the PFA and the results of other UN conferences. This approach underlines that women's issues are an integral part of any societal agenda, whether national or international, and that women's concerns are not their concerns alone but the responsibility of society as a whole.

Overview of the Situation of Women in South Asia

South Asia has the contrast of the presence of 'a few hundred women in the halls of power' and the situation of 'millions of women who do not have control over their own bodies much less their lives'. Though it has had women heads of government in Bangladesh, India, Pakistan and Sri Lanka, this has not translated into positive outcomes for the majority of South Asian women. The vast majority of women are illiterate, in poor health, invisible in national accounting systems, and suffer legal, political, economic and social discrimination in all walks of life. They also have the lowest rates of participation in their governance structure. For example, women hold only 7 per cent of parliamentary seats and 9 per cent of the seats in government cabinets. Only 6 per cent of the region's judges are women, and only 9 per cent of civil service posts are held by women, with less than 1 per cent of all female civil servants in decision-making positions in all countries of the region but Sri Lanka.[4] With the patriarchal system firmly entrenched in South Asia, structures continue to perpetuate gender-blind policies that take existing gender relations for granted, while women's particular concerns are relegated to "women's issues". So deep is the entrenchment, that gender biases are held not only by men, but women too. Women are the primary caregivers in all societies. They are responsible for ensuring survival for families ravaged by disease or conflict. Yet, when social development policies are drawn up, women are usually perceived merely as a vulnerable group in need of a special project.

Carrying the Beijing Torch in South Asia

UNIFEM's mission, policy framework and strategies were strongly endorsed by the Fourth World Conference on Women (FWCW). One of the commitments made at Beijing was that the implementation of the PFA would be followed through at the national, regional and global levels. Towards this end, UNIFEM South Asia works to preserve the continuum of Beijing at the national and regional levels, in different ways. For the Beijing +5 review process, it facilitated NGO processes through issue-based consultations, and supporting participation to regional and international forums. At the regional level, it hosts a biennial regional review to commemorate Beijing in partnership with governments of the region, to facilitate a collective stock-taking on the implementation of the BPFA and to promote sharing and learning. Participants include ministers responsible for women's development, secretaries and senior government officials of the Women's Ministries, members of the SAARC Secretariat, key NGOs, experts, activists and collaborating UN agencies. So far, five such reviews have been organized, debating on regional challenges and gaps, and formulating the future course of action with regard to following-up on the BPFA.

The First Regional Meeting Commemorating Beijing was held in partnership with the Department of Women and Child Development (DWCD)[5], Ministry of Human Resource Development, Government of India, in New Delhi, in 1996. The major objective of the meeting was to facilitate a collaborative regional policy dialogue on key issues concerning women's empowerment and to share experiences and perspectives. Focusing on the critical areas identified in the PFA, it provided an opportunity to take stock of achievements and challenges and to explore possibilities of ensuring continuity, mainstreaming and coordination. It was generally felt that there was an urgent need to identify areas of common concern and prioritize national and regional issues in the area of women's development, such as women in conflict situations/violence, trafficking, property and land rights and the adverse impact of economic policies. It was noted that that there was no system of ongoing sharing of information, including following-up on the BPFA, for which government-NGO collaboration was stressed.

Recommendations generated by the review included regional collaboration in several areas, such as research on women's contribution to the economy, social safety nets required in the context of structural adjustment policies and cooperation to eradicate trafficking in women and girls. It called for regional advocacy on home-based workers, in line with the ILO convention and consensus was also reached with respect to the need to form an

NGO – SAARC Women for Peace. It concluded with the unanimous agreement that such a regional stocktaking be made a biennial event.

The Second Regional Meeting Commemorating Beijing was held in 1998 in Kathmandu in partnership with the Ministry of Women and Social Welfare, His Majesty's Government of Nepal, which assessed progress made since the last review. Among other things, this meeting sought to formulate a regional strategy to expedite the implementation of the PFA. Regional partners and representatives shared modalities and experiences of gender mainstreaming carried out by different countries in their planning process. The joint declaration – the Kathmandu Forward Looking Strategies – noted that important strides had been made to fulfill commitments made at the Beijing conference, both in terms of national and regional initiatives. All South Asian countries had ratified Covention on the Elimination of All Forms of Discrimination Against Women (CEDAW) and almost every government in South Asia had taken steps towards the drawing up of plans of action, five-year plans and policies for the implementation of the BPFA. Recording the achievements made since the last review, it observed the progress made on increased commitment to combat trafficking and to making national statistical systems sex-disaggregated. It referred to the institutional mechanisms that had been built and the steps taken to incorporate gender sensitivity in policies, programmes, plans and in political, legal and economic institutions. Two issues that gained consensus for regional action as well as action within all the countries of the region were trafficking and violence against women.

BEIJING +5

Five years after 189 governments had adopted the PFA, they met again in a special session of the UN General Assembly in June 2000 to undertake a global review of the progress achieved and the challenges faced. Globalization and the economic empowerment of women, women, science and technology, women's leadership and human security and social protection were identified as cross-cutting themes. All of the South Asian nations participated in the Beijing +5 review. National governments prepared country reports, and alternative reports were developed by the women's movement and NGO sector in each country, though in some countries like Nepal, the government and NGOs formulated one analytical report. UNIFEM supported national and regional processes facilitating a broader participation of women's groups through task forces, which were set up for women for the review process. The South Asia Beyond Beijing Meet, which fed into the Asia-Pacific Regional NGO Symposium in Bangkok identified violence against women and girls, women and poverty, women's political participation and empowerment, as common priority concerns for the South Asia region. Trafficking of women and girls, special concerns for women like ageing and the girl child and women in situations of armed conflict were listed as areas of special concern. Information generated through the five-year review process provided the basis for identifying and articulating future priorities – globally, regionally and nationally. The focus was on best practices, obstacles encountered, vision for the future and identification of new and emerging trends.

Following five focus areas were identified at Beijing +5:

- Political will and commitment to create an enabling environment for the implementation of the PFA (including legal review and reform to ensure equal opportunities for women).
- Capacity building for the advancement of women and gender mainstreaming (including capacity building for women and girls and for actors responsible for achieving gender equality).
- Accountability for assessing the implementation of the strategies and actions in the PFA (including targets, benchmarks and a clear time frame for implementation).
- Cooperation and partnership for implementing the PFA within and between nations and regions (including cooperation between public and private sectors, within and among women's organizations).
- Assistance to women and girls currently subject to discrimination and disadvantages.

The review made apparent that progress to meet the goals and commitments of the PFA had been slow and uneven. In the outcome document, which was adopted by the plenary of the special session, governments agreed upon further actions to accelerate the implementation of the PFA at the national, regional and global levels, to actualize commitments to gender equality, development and peace. Governments and inter-governmental organizations recognized the contribution and complementary role of NGOs in ensuring the effective implementation of the PFA. Several areas were listed for action to be taken, and these included: the setting of goals and targets; increasing women's participation in politics and decision-making; reducing gender disparities in education; promoting women's human rights; reviewing and revising legislation; addressing trafficking; addressing emerging health challenges including HIV/AIDS; mainstreaming gender; and promoting sustainable development.

The Third Regional Meeting Commemorating Beijing was organized in collaboration with the Ministry of Women's Affairs and Social Security, Government of Maldives, at Bandos Island, in 2000. In addition to assessing progress made and learning and sharing, it provided a forum for both governments and NGOs to report back on the Beijing +5 process, unpack the outcome document in the regional context and formulate strategies to take it forward. Moreover, this review added new benchmarks to the roadmap which had already developed. Special sessions were organized on two of the major regional priorities that had been identified: CEDAW implementation and reporting and combating the alarming rise in the trafficking in women and girls. With CEDAW committee members and the UN Special Rapporteur on Violence against Women as resource persons, the review was considerably enhanced.

The consensus document – the Maldives Forward Moving Strategies – noted the progress made, particularly in the areas of drawing up of national plans of action and national policy instruments to implement the PFA. It recognized the move towards legal reforms and strengthening of laws, as well as expansion of institutional mechanisms for securing gender equality and equity. It recorded the increased commitment and development of plans of action to combat gender-based violence and trafficking of women and children and the intensification of efforts to make national statistical systems sex-disaggregated and reflective of women's contribution. As priority concerns for the future, it identified the areas of trafficking, information sharing, including best practices from the region, laws related to violence against women and poverty eradication strategies/programmes in different countries. As regional priorities, it flagged developing expertise in diverse areas, which included gender budget and gender audit, and creating monitoring mechanisms within countries to review the progress of implementation of CEDAW and the PFA. It recommended undertaking studies to assess the positive and negative impact of globalization on women as well as women's political participation, strengthening the national women's machinery and setting up institutional arrangement mechanisms.

The Fourth Regional Meeting Commemorating Beijing was held at Paro, Bhutan in May 2003, in collaboration with the Royal Government of Bhutan. Action taken on the last strategic document was examined and reviewed, continuing the process of collectively measuring progress and strategizing on areas of concern. While being a continuation of the process of regional sharing and learning, it provided an opportunity to focus on key regional priorities, identified at Maldives. These included: trafficking in women and girls, gender analysis of budgets, knowledge-based advocacy on CEDAW and engendering the census processes in South Asia.

The Bhutan Forward Moving Strategies notes progress, among other areas, in drawing up of national plans of action and national policy instruments to implement the PFA, of moving towards gender justice through legal reforms and proper application of laws and of increased efforts to combat gender-based violence, trafficking of women and children and in addressing risks and vulnerabilities of HIV/AIDS. This was the first time that HIV/AIDS was included in a declaration emerging from the regional reviews. It records progress made in sex-disaggregated data in national statistical systems and consensus in favour of increasing resource flows to women in national budgets. Some of the key recommendations that emerged included, promoting rights-based policies and programmes to eradicate feminization of poverty, and strengthening national processes and government-NGO collaboration to review the progress on full implementation of CEDAW, the BPFA and the Beijing +5 outcome document, linking it to reporting on Millennium Development Goals (MDGs).

It called for strengthened efforts to combat violence against women and increased national and regional collaboration to eliminate trafficking of women and girls. Support was advocated for processes to engender global trade agreements, for the promotion of enabling policies for women in the economic sphere and for continued strengthening of networks of women workers in the informal sector. It recommended taking forward the processes of developing and applying tools such as gender analysis of budgets, gender audit and engendered planning and monitoring at the national and local levels. It called for continued efforts to strengthen processes to increase women's participation in decision-making and intensified efforts to address the gender dimensions of HIV/AIDS. Increased sharing of information and knowledge, particularly in the areas of developing monitoring indicators, gender analysis of budgets, violence against women, women's political participation and gender dimensions of HIV/AIDS, was recommended. There was also consensus to continue the regional bi-annual process of reviewing progress in the implementation of CEDAW and the BPFA, facilitated by UNIFEM.

Progress on Key Issues Highlighted in the Commemorating Beijing Meetings

To follow up on key issues, which have been highlighted in the meetings commemorating Beijing, UNIFEM is working in partnership with governments, women's organizations, research institutions, NGOs, the UN system, bilateral agencies and other actors of civil society, to facilitate a more effective implementation of the BPFA.

CEDAW IMPLEMENTATION AND REPORTING

With its focus on substantive equality for women, which requires not only formal equality, but also equality of results in real terms, the CEDAW sets the pace for a dynamic, proactive approach to women's advancement. It is, in effect, the international bill of rights for women, and the most prominent international instrument for the advancement of women's rights. It is, today, one of the most widely endorsed human rights treaties in the history of the United Nations, currently ratified by 173 countries. The process has thus been catalyzed first and foremost by the will of nations, to give themselves a vision for putting people at the centre of development. Successive UN conferences and conventions have contributed to the setting up of a normative framework to convert this vision into reality. South Asia has been at the vanguard of this process and all countries in the region are signatories to CEDAW.

Efforts in the region are directed at deepening and expanding the process of implementation and reporting on CEDAW, in close partnership with governments, NGOs and CEDAW committee members. Through a process of knowledge-based advocacy with regard to reporting on CEDAW, the sharing of experiences is promoted through a transparent interactive mechanism. This enables governments, the women's movement, UN agencies and NGOs to jointly appraise progress on fulfilment of obligations under the Convention, with technical expertise provided by CEDAW committee members and International Women's Rights Action Watch (IWRAW) Asia-Pacific. Such exchanges promote mutual learning and assist the reporting process. In addition, the capacity of women's organizations to use CEDAW in their advocacy work is being enhanced and indicators developed to track progress on the implementation of CEDAW. Efforts are ongoing to link CEDAW reporting, with the BPFA and the MDGs.

Violence against women has become an important and critical area to be addressed for all stakeholders in the South Asia region. Many countries of the region have made progress in several ways, including by amending laws and establishing national women's commissions. Facilitating the implementation of human rights instruments to bring laws into conformity with human rights standards, efforts are continuing to make legal and judicial systems more responsive and gender equal to the concerns of women affected by violence. Diverse strategies are used, such as the creation of a regional lawyers' network, which has identified discriminatory laws with regard to violence against women in Bangladesh, India, Nepal, Pakistan and Sri Lanka, providing tools to advocate for appropriate reform.

Institutional mechanisms for gender justice are being strengthened through networks and innovative alliances. For example, the Gender and Judges initiative with SAKSHI (Delhi-based NGO) involves an innovative partnership with the judicial system. The judge-NGO partnership provides a unique model of institutional partnership, which has been decisive in transforming the stereotypical comprehension of equality and sharpening the focus from 'formal equality' to 'substantive equality', which has been propagated in the international conventions dealing with violence against women, like CEDAW. It has led to the creation of an Asia-Pacific Advisory Forum and Judicial Education on Equality Issues, with the judges in the forum becoming critical players in advancing the programme in their respective countries (Bangladesh, India, Nepal and Pakistan) and facilitating the process in the region at both the apex and lower court levels. While the project has been an NGO initiative, ownership of its design and delivery by judges makes this partnership quite unique, leading to increased gender-sensitive judgments in both India and Nepal on a number of issues.

Encouraging regional learning and sharing, interventions involve piloting community-based Zero Violence Zone initiatives, and strengthening the alliance between the law enforcement machinery and civil society organizations. By using a multidisciplinary response to curb violence, a dialogue has been initiated on the interplay of masculinity, gender and violence against women, empowering women with information on support services and their legal rights, and supporting efforts to increase the capacity of law enforcement agencies.

Campaigns have proved to be effective vehicles to highlight issues of violence against women. For example, the UNIFEM led

1998 Interagency Global Campaign, *"A life free of violence: It's our right!"* to celebrate the 50th anniversary of the UN Declaration on Human Rights, highlighted dowry, domestic violence, trafficking and women's legal rights in the South Asia region. Encouraging women to speak out and to challenge the culture of silence, which envelopes violence, it raised awareness of a diverse cross-section of society, fostering a range of partnerships. Giving visibility and an edge to an issue, hitherto considered private, the issues were taken to the UN General Assembly through the Global Video Conference, which marked the culmination of the campaign.

Combating Trafficking

Trafficking emerged as an area of critical concern, at the very first regional meeting commemorating Beijing, which was held to review the progress made in the implementation of the BPFA. It was noted here that though there were many groups, NGOs and coalitions doing good work on trafficking, they were often working in isolation and not in concert, leading to a lack of synergy. As well, there were differences on the definition of trafficking, and misconceptions regarding the issue. All subsequent meetings commemorating Beijing endorsed trafficking as an issue requiring urgent attention. This succeeded in creating a much needed strengthened response to the problem. At the meeting held in Bhutan in 2004 all regional governments, represented by ministers and senior officials, gave their commitment to taking forward the SAARC Convention on Trafficking, strengthening processes towards regional, bilateral and national dialogue involving NGOs, initiating legal reforms and promoting technical exchange. In addition, the strong commitment given by the SAARC secretariat at the 2004 meeting to address the issue at a regional level has provided the much-needed regional focus to address cross-border trafficking.

Regionally, efforts focus on prevention, rescue, rehabilitation and prosecution, involving strategic partnerships, with the police, doctors and lawyers, reaching out to a diverse group ranging from parliamentarians, to law enforcement officials, and the general public. New networks have been set up. These include the South Asia Professionals Against Trafficking (SAPAT), comprising police, and other professionals like lawyers, doctors and media persons, the Technical Advisory Group in South Asia (TAGSA), consisting of development experts, and a South Asia Forum Against Human Trafficking (SAFAHT), comprising NGOs and activists.

Supporting Research and Documentation

Due to the inherent nature of violence against women and the socialization processes, which encourage silence, there is a great dearth of hard data on the issue. To expand knowledge and understanding about the issue, two global assessments have been undertaken. Independent experts have looked at the violence women experience in conflict and post-conflict areas. As part of a global scan to review work taking place to counter violence against women, UNIFEM South Asia undertook a regional assessment in four countries of the region – Bangladesh, India, Nepal and Pakistan – in 2001-02. The assessment attempted to review current policies, achievements, challenges, key actors, and future potential of programmes to end violence against women. The overall sense that one gets from the scans is that of walking up an escalator that is going down.

Gender and Hiv/Aids

The rapid pace of the epidemic and its magnitude serve to make HIV/AIDS one of the most formidable health and development challenges of this century. The issue, however, is also one of gender, empowerment and human rights. This was endorsed at the Millennium Summit, where world leaders identified the eight most critical challenges for this century as the Millennium Development Goals (MDGs), with HIV/AIDS being one of them. The Bhutan Forward Moving Strategies (the consensus document of the Fourth Commemorating Beijing Meeting in Bhutan in 2003), eight governments, NGOs and representatives of women's groups called for an intensification of efforts to address the gender dimensions of

HIV/AIDS, using a multi-sectoral approach and building the capacity of individuals, institutions and networks in the South Asia region.

Initiatives on gender and HIV/AIDS seek to address vulnerabilities that put women at risk to HIV/AIDS, address gender inequalities in the context of care, treatment and support for women living with HIV/AIDS, build the capacities of organizations working on the issue, and forge linkages between positive women's networks, government and civil society. A unique pilot project on Equalizing Gender Relations in the context of HIV/AIDS in partnership with the Indian Railways in Vijayawada with the South Central Railways is ongoing.

Making Women Work Visible

The Third World Conference on Women in 1985, and a decade later the World Summit for Social Development in Copenhagen and the Beijing Conference, called for recognizing and measuring the remunerated and unremunerated economic contributions of women and for reflecting these in the national accounts, economic products and GNP. Governments affirmed the need to devise statistical means to recognize and make visible women's work (both paid and unpaid), develop methods to reflect the value of such work in national accounts, and examine the correlation between women's unremunerated work and poverty.

Since women are not perceived as economic entities, their work and contribution to the economy remain undervalued and underrecorded, leading to their invisibility to policy makers and development planners. To make women's work visible and to enable a more accurate reflection of women's contributions and productivity in national accounting systems, efforts are made to make census exercises more gender-responsive – a collective effort involving governments, UN agencies, statistical organizations, research institutions and NGOs. The results of the 2001 Census in India show a better recording of work participation, especially female work participation rate (FWPR), which increased from 22.3 per cent in 1991 to 25.7 per cent in 2001, which is approximately 36 million women. In Nepal, the definition of work participation rate has been modified to include livestock-related work done for subsistence and the recording of FWPR has increased by 10 per cent. Focusing on unpaid work, efforts are being made to increase awareness on the merits of the time use survey in estimating such work. In addition, regional cross- fertilization is promoted to make optimum use of knowledge and learning.

Gender Analysis of Budgets

Gender budgeting, as a tool for mainstreaming gender, is recognized worldwide. One of the reasons for this is perhaps the gap, which was evident at the Beijing +5 review, between expectations and achievements in the implementation of the BPFA. This was attributed to the shortfall in resources allocated to programmes for gender mainstreaming and the advancement of women. The Outcome Document noted that gender analysis of public budgets was emerging as an important tool to assist in the equitable use of existing resources. It called for the incorporation of "a gender perspective into the design, development, adoption and execution of all budgetary processes".

Gender budgeting initiatives in South Asia are a collective journey undertaken together by governments, in partnership with distinguished economists and feminists, research institutions, the UN system and key women's NGOs from the region. The diverse mechanisms used, include diagnosing the existing degree of gender inequality in budgets at different levels and in various sectors through studies; creating opportunities for a cross-fertilization of ideas and experiences through exchange visits; through national and regional meetings, taking recommendations to the implementation level; and by facilitating local and regional interaction with the knowledge and experience of regional and internationally renowned experts on gender budgets, to sharpen and refine the tool of gender budgeting, attuned to the local context.

Scorecard on Gender Equality

To track progress that the world is making towards gender equality, UNIFEM publishes a biennial report, "Progress of the

World's Women", with each edition having a thematic focus. The first report was prepared for the Beijing +5 review in 2000 and focused on the economic dimensions of women's lives. Progress 2002/Volume 1 focuses on women war and peace and Volume 2 on MDGs. In South Asia, the UNIFEM regional office prepares a "Progress of South Asian Women", biennially, as a background to the meetings commemorating Beijing. These present an analytical overview of the stocktaking exercises.

UNIFEM South Asia and the Processes Facilitated by it for Beijing +10

The processes outlined above served as useful mechanisms to keep the Beijing dialogue ongoing. They assisted in maintaining the continuum of the conference by tracking progress on commitments made, providing an opportunity to all stakeholders to reaffirm their pledges, re-energize their efforts and hone future strategies.

- A space was facilitated for women's groups through a South Asia Beijing +10 NGO Consultation, organized in Kathmandu, by South Asia Women's Watch and Beyond Beijing Committee (BBC), in June 2004. The priorities and concerns identified here were lobbied for at key NGO and governmental Asia-Pacific processes on Beijing +10 so as to impact them. These included the NGO Asia-Pacific Forum, the UN ESCAP inter-governmental meeting and the UN 49th special session at the CSW. The consultation culminated in the unanimous adoption of the "Himalayan Declaration", at Lalitpur, Nepal, on 20 June 2004 (for details, see Appendix III).
- Support was extended to representatives of select women's groups to participate at the Asia-Pacific NGO Forum held at Bangkok, from 30th June to 3rd July, 2004. Under the aegis of the Asia-Pacific Women's Watch, more than 700 participants from 35 countries of the Asia-Pacific region revisited the BPFA. It concluded with the adoption the Forum Declaration, wherein delegates re-affirmed their commitment to the BPFA and resolved to:

- carry on the spirit and realize the intent of Beijing,
- protect one another as defenders of women's human rights and peace, and
- assert themselves as equal partners in the creation of a just, democratic, humane and peaceful world.

Creation of Knowledge Products

A handbook, "Translating the Beijing Commitments into Action in South Asia", which focuses on the accountability mechanism of the biennial regional reviews and its features; and a visual narrative, "The Power of Doing", were screened, showcasing UNIFEM's work in the South Asia region. A comprehensive gender report, in the form of the publication, "Progress of South Asian Women 2005", was prepared. This provided the base document for the fifth ministerial meeting – Celebrating Beijing +10.

The Fifth South Asia Regional Ministerial Conference, held from 3rd to 5th May, 2005, in Islamabad, Pakistan focused on appraising the progress made by SAARC countries on the 12 areas of critical concern and the Forward Moving Strategies, which had emerged at the last biennial review. It dwelt on the gaps, challenges and opportunities, formulating an action plan for a more effective implementation of the BPFA. In addition, it paid special attention to the issues of: gender, livelihoods and resources; violence against women; women's representation, leadership and effectiveness; and engendering MDGs, PRSPs processes and linking BPFA, MDGs and CEDAW indicators, which had been identified as critical priorities for this conference. The conference deliberations culminated in the formulation of the 'Islamabad Declaration: Review and Future Action' (see Appendix I). Governments and civil society agreed to direct their efforts and actions on a two-year plan, focusing on the following areas, which were identified as priorities:

- Violence against women
- Economic empowerment of women
- Political empowerment of women
- Disaster preparedness and management
- Health and education

Delegates agreed upon specific actions to address the above and to develop and strengthen institutional mechanisms for gender equity and equality, which includes ensuring sufficient resource allocations and authority for national machineries for women; ensuring the integration of women's human rights and gender concerns by mainstream institutions into their policies and programmes; repealing/amending discriminatory laws against women and initiating integrated efforts to implement laws; ensuring gender analysis of budgets to support women's advancement; promoting men's and boys' participation in creating a gender just society; enhancing corporate social responsibility; strengthening partnerships with women's groups and civil society organizations; promoting a gender-sensitive media; acknowledging the positive contribution of the UNIFEM in carrying forward the Beijing process; and lobbying for sufficient resource allocations for the organization and appropriate status for it within the UN system.

The process of regional sharing and learning was continued and regional coordination and cooperation on issues of gender equality and women's empowerment promoted. Listing key concerns, regional priorities were identified, and an Action Plan adopted to address these.

For the first time, at such a meeting, elected women representatives from different tiers of governance, shared their stories of how they transformed power relations in order to create a new framework for political empowerment of women from the respective countries. Senior government officials and NGO experts from the region shared experiences on the MDGs, PRSPs and CEDAW processes along with information on Media and ICT as tools for women's advancement.

The delegates noted that to break the cycles of poverty, violence and gender discrimination, there was a need to accelerate progress and expand its reach. This meant determined implementation and greater accountability. The need for enhanced regional cooperation and the development of a comprehensive SAARC Gender Database was reiterated. Governments agreed to deepening and creating a new accountability instrument – the formation of a core group of Secretaries from the Women's Ministries to monitor the biennial regional action plans.

An action declaration, this focused on crucial gender issues for the next two years. These were identified as violence against women, the economic and political empowerment of women, disaster preparedness and management, and health and education. The need for developing and strengthening institutional mechanisms for gender equity and equality was also articulated. The issue of feminization of poverty, agriculture and migration as well as women's work in the informal sector continued to be a focus area for governments. Concerns were expressed with respect to the inadequate progress made in giving equal access to economic opportunities for women, including access to land and livelihoods that ensure dignity and personal security.[6] The governments of the region, while affirming their commitments to core women's rights issues, also recognized the need to work on disaster management as a priority and build intersectional linkages across all issues.

The Review is marked by a seriousness of purpose. For example, this meeting was organized around pivotal issues for women of South Asia, which had been identified by governments and civil society at the Fourth Biennial Regional Review at Paro in Bhutan in 2003. These included the issues of women's livelihoods, violence against women, with a special focus on trafficking in women and children and vulnerability to HIV/AIDS, women's political participation, as well as the need for monitoring mechanisms. In response UNIFEM had commissioned studies on these, prioritizing the need of the governments and harmonizing that with its MYFF goals.

There was consensus towards ensuring linkages between BPFA, CEDAW and MDGS as mutually complementary processes. Recommendations were made to integrate the Islamabad Declaration: Review and Future Action at appropriate multilateral fora, emphasizing the integration of gender perspectives in the high level plenary meeting to review the Millennium Declaration and

Goals. It was also recommended that CEDAW and BPFA be integrated into national indicators and other processes, including the medium term development framework (MTDF) to monitor achievement of the MDGs.

The Review also provided a strategic instrument for highlighting gender concerns at the Millennium Summit in September of that year, when nations came together for the five-year review of the MDGs. The findings and the recommendations that emerged from it, influenced and contributed to the ECOSOC consultation and to other processes leading towards the MDG review. As part of the preparatory process, UNIFEM was able to successfully carry the voices of South Asian women to the highest levels, by facilitating the presentation of the Islamabad Declaration to the public hearings organized in New York.

Another conference, which served to highlight issues of gender equality and their linkages to the achievement of the MDGs, was the "Regional Conference on Development Effectiveness through Gender Mainstreaming: Lessons Learnt from South Asia". Jointly organized by IFAD, UNIFEM and IDRC, this was an initiative of the IFAD-UNIFEM Gender Mainstreaming Programme in Asia, the recommendations of which were subsequently fed into the World Summit. They underscored the high costs incurred on account of gender inequality and the need for all stakeholders to work effectively on gender mainstreaming within a women's rights framework. Policy options, which governments could consider in mainstreaming gender in development programmes for the achievement of the MDGs, were also identified. Emphasis was laid on the fact that there was a need for going beyond the existing policy frameworks with regard to women in the formal and informal sectors, by providing conditions of 'decent work', reducing women's vulnerabilities especially structural violence against women, and enhancing women's individual and collective agencies, political voice and representation.

Thus, both the Review and the Conference provided a vehicle for focusing attention on the imperative of advancing gender equality and including the voices of women as overriding priorities in the MDGs reporting processes themselves. Enabling participation of delegates in processes at the national, regional and global levels, UNIFEM has consistently facilitated fora, such as these.

At the World Summit held at the United Nations in New York in September 2005, world leaders from more than 150 countries adopted a Summit Outcome that resolved, amongst other issues, to promote gender equality and end discrimination against women by 2015. They reaffirmed their commitment to a full and effective implementation of the goals and objectives of the Beijing Declaration and Platform for Action and the outcome of the twenty-third special session of the General Assembly, which they articulated as being an essential contribution to achieving the internationally agreed development goals, including those contained in the Millennium Declaration.

At the South Asia regional level, since the Islamabad Declaration in 2005, various levels of progress may be seen in some of the areas, which were identified for priority action. For example, the SAARC Gender Database, which has been continuously, advocated for in successive Beijing biennial review meetings. Both the Bhutan Forward Moving Strategies of 2003 and the Islamabad Declaration of 2005 echoed the need for having adequate mechanisms and tools to monitor progress of women, including the need for sex desegregated data according to region specific indicators. Its roots, however, can be traced to the Beijing Platform for Action, which among other issues, spelt out the need for sex desegregated data. Concerns regarding inadequate sex desegregated data and gender sensitive analysis had constantly been identified as important areas of concern, which required strengthening.

In response, the SAARC Secretariat and UNIFEM and its partners in South Asia, embarked on the process to develop a database prototype, which would act as the anchor for all data and information storage and retrieval. The establishment of a SAARC Gender Database is also a key component of the MoU between the SAARC Secretariat and UNIFEM, which has been endorsed by all seven member countries. It is envisioned as a G-Data Shop to facilitate engendered planning, advocacy and the identification of gaps and challenges. The countries will be collating and generating data on violence against women, especially trafficking, feminization of poverty and health including HIV/AIDs. Research on issues will be supported and quantitative and qualitative data developed according to the prototype agreed upon at the SAARC-UNIFEM Review Meeting held in August 2006, at Paro in Bhutan. Including both traditional and non-traditional indicators, the data will be consolidated into an institutional SAARC Gender Database at the SAARC Secretariat.

To keep the spirit and momentum of Beijing alive and to follow-up on the BPFA and the Islamabad Declaration, UNIFEM will be organizing the Sixth South Asia Ministerial Conference in 2007. This will be held in collaboration with the Ministry of Women and Child Development, Government of India, in New Delhi.

NOTES

1. The United Nations Development Fund for Women (UNIFEM) was created by the UN General Assembly resolution in 1976 as the Voluntary Fund for the UN Decade for Women. This was in response to the call from the women's movement for a fund within the United Nations system, to help improve the living standards of women in developing countries and to address their concerns. It was set up to be an aid to and advocate for women of the developing world, to give them voice and visibility.
2. Platform for Action.
3. Beijing – UN Fourth World Conference on Women – Anita Anand with Gouri Salvi.
4. Human Development in South Asia 2000.
5. Now a full-fledged ministry.
6. Islamabad Declaration 2005, inter-ministerial meeting supported by Goverment of Pakistan and UNIFEM.

Appendix I

ISLAMABAD DECLARATION: REVIEW AND FUTURE ACTION CELEBRATING BEIJING PLUS TEN, 2005

(Fifth South Asia Ministerial Conference, 3-5 May 2005)

1. WE, Ministers, Secretaries and Senior Officers of the Governments and SAARC Secretariat, women's groups, NGOs, and researchers from – Bangladesh, Bhutan, India, Maldives Nepal, Pakistan, Sri Lanka, and Afghanistan invited as an observer state, gathered at Islamabad on 3-5 May 2005 at the Fifth South Asia Ministerial Conference "Celebrating Beijing Plus Ten" jointly organized by the Government of Pakistan and UNIFEM South Asia Regional Office.
2. This conference acquires a special significance, since the year 2005, marks the tenth anniversary of the historic Fourth World Conference on Women held at Beijing in 1995 as well as the five-year review of the Millennium Declaration. We have all gathered in Pakistan after the 49th session of the Commission on the Status of Women to celebrate a ten year journey of regional cooperation and learning, reviewing our progress and identifying current challenges and road map for future action.
3. While recalling and reaffirming the commitments for the realization of women's human rights and gender equality made in the Beijing Platform for Action 1995, the outcome document of the Beijing + 5 and the resolutions of B+10 review at the 49th session of the Commission on the Status of Women and the substantive framework provided by the Universal Declaration of Human Rights, the Convention on the Elimination of All Forms of Discrimination Against Women (CEDAW) ratified by all countries of the region, Security Council resolution 1325 and all other relevant follow up documents adopted.
4. We acknowledge developments in the following areas:
   (a) The formulation of national policies and action plans to promote gender equality and the empowerment of women.
   (b) Increased access to education for women and girls.

(c) Establishment of national machineries on women and institutional mechanisms towards effective realization of women's human rights.
(d) Drafting new legislations and/or amending laws especially on violence against women, sexual exploitation and trafficking of women and children.
(e) Emerging jurisprudence on women's rights.
(f) Forging partnerships between governments, women's groups, civil society and interest groups, elected representatives, the media and the private sector.
(g) Increase in women's access to economic opportunity, credit, and employment.
(h) Enhanced affirmative actions towards increasing women's representation in political decision making at different levels.
(i) The adoption of policies on HIV/AIDS prevention, treatment and care.
(j) Adoption of regional instruments such as SAARC Social Charter and the SAARC Convention on Trafficking.

5. We recognize the gaps and challenges in implementation in the following areas:
(a) Inadequate implementation of plans, policies and programmes relating to women.
(b) Lack of expeditious enactment of legislation and non-repeal and amendment of discriminatory laws.
(c) Inadequate progress in meeting the commitments under Article 9 of CEDAW on gender equality in citizenship laws.
(d) The feminization of poverty and its further accentuation due to adverse effects of globalization.
(e) Inadequate progress in giving equal access to economic opportunity, land and livelihoods with dignity and personal security.
(f) Continued prevalence of all forms of violence against women, including in conflict situations.
(g) Inadequate commitment, awareness, measures and resources to combat violence against women.

(h) Inadequate attention to eliminating socio-cultural practices and mindsets that continue to discriminate and disadvantage women.
(i) The increasing prevalence of HIV/AIDS among women, particularly younger women.
(j) Lack of gender sensitive policies and interventions to combat communicable diseases, anaemia, TB, malaria etc.
(k) Inadequate progress in achieving women's equal representation in national legislatures.
(l) Inadequate, and lack of gender sensitive reproductive and sexual health information and services and care to women.
(m) Lack of sufficient male involvement and participation in promoting women's rights and substantive equality.
(n) Continued lack of gender perspectives in macroeconomic policies, trade negotiations, national budgets and investment decisions.
(o) Inadequate, reliable and relevant sex disaggregated data and gender analysis at all levels.
(p) Insufficient resource allocations, authority status for national machineries on the advancement of women, and their marginalization.
(q) The lack of regional cooperation and partnership initiatives to address problems of regional concerns such as trafficking in women and children, HIV/AIDS and promoting and protection of the rights of migrant workers.
(r) The increasing vulnerability of women in marginalized groups.
(s) The negative portrayal of women in the media.
(t) Inadequate initiatives to address the needs and concerns of women in remote areas and in disadvantaged communities.
(u) Inadequate progress in meeting and monitoring time bound commitments.

6. In light of the above, we agree to prioritize our efforts and actions on a two-year plan on the following areas:

(a) Violence against women
(b) Economic empowerment of women
(c) Political empowerment of women
(d) Disaster preparedness and management
(e) Health and Education

7. In pursuit of the above priorities we will:
   (a) Develop and strengthen institutional mechanisms for gender equity and equality
      (i) Ensure sufficient resource allocations, authority and status for national machineries for women including women's ministries and national commissions.
      (ii) Ensure that mainstream institutions integrate women's human rights and gender concerns into their policies and programmes, and establish appropriate gender management systems.
      (iii) Repeal/amend discriminatory laws against women and initiate integrated efforts to implement laws.
      (iv) Ensure gender analysis of budgets and identification of allocations and expenditures at all levels needed to support women's advancement.
      (v) Promote men's' and boys' participation in creating a gender just society.
      (vi) Enhance and encourage corporate social responsibility.
      (vii) Further strengthen partnerships with women's groups and civil society organizations,
      (viii) Promote and strengthen gender sensitive media,
      (ix) Acknowledge and appreciate the positive contribution of the UNIFEM in sustaining and carrying forward the Beijing process and advocating women's rights in the region and lobby for sufficient resource allocations for the organization and appropriate status for it within the UN system.
   (b) Ensure linkages between Beijing Platform for Action, CEDAW and MDGS as mutually complementary processes
      (i) Recommend to integrate the "Islamabad Declaration: Review and Future Action" at appropriate

multilateral forums and through these emphasize integration of gender perspectives in the high level plenary meeting to review the Millennium Declaration and Goals.

(ii) Recommend that CEDAW and Beijing Platform for Action are integrated into national indicators and all other processes, and the medium term development framework (MTDF) to monitor achievement of the Millennium Development Goals.

8. Eliminate violence against women (VAW) and girls

(a) Ensure that international commitments under CEDAW and Beijing Platform for Action and the outcome document of the Beijing + 5 meeting are fulfilled in regard to elimination of violence against women.

(b) Prioritize the following:

(i) Law and administrative reforms and actions to address violence against women, through health and other relevant initiatives.

(ii) Ratification of the SAARC Convention on Trafficking by all member countries.

(iii) Use existing research in law reforms, policy formulation and programmes and encourage further research.

(iv) Reform of the criminal justice system to make it more responsive to violence against women and sensitization of the judiciary, the administrative and law enforcement machinery particularly the police and health professionals to violence against women.

(v) Consider ratification of the Optional Protocol to CEDAW.

(c) Promote concrete actions – safety net, support systems and leadership development to address the reality of violence in women's lives which exposes which inter alia women to HIV/AIDS.

(d) Promote and strengthen gender sensitive community based interventions to address VAW.

(e) Check negative forces and strengthen civil society to promote zero tolerance against VAW.

9. Economic Empowerment of Women
    (a) Provide adequate infrastructure to support women's economic opportunity, independence and livelihood that ensures dignity and personal security.
    (b) Provide and strengthen adequate social security systems.
    (c) Ensure that women's contribution is visible in the national accounting system.
    (d) Protect the rights of women workers in both the formal and informal sectors and home-based work.
    (e) Support women's right to own property and land, to inheritance, to equal access to credit, to be fully employed and to receive equal remuneration for work.
    (f) Ensure the participation and voice of women in the formulation of macro-and micro-economic policies.
    (g) Address the need to promote shared responsibility in care-giving roles in the family and prevent women from being overburdened by multiple tasks and responsibilities.
    (h) Support and facilitate processes to engender global and regional trade agreements and treaties.
10. Political empowerment of women
    (a) Secure political will of the States, political parties and other actors along with mechanisms for implementation of gender sensitive electoral codes and legislation for affirmative actions for women in the legislatures and to prevent any reversal or dilution of affirmative actions already taken.
    (b) Work towards ensuring that women are directly rather than indirectly elected.
    (c) Create an enabling environment to allow women legislators to participate in and contribute to the deliberations and decisions of the elected bodies of which they are members.
    (d) Ensure greater representation of women as office bearers and candidates.
    (e) Ensure gender analysis of budgets and identification of allocations and expenditures at all levels needed to support women's advancement in the political arena.
11. Emergency situations and disaster preparedness

(a) Ensure women are at the centre of the rescue, relief and recovery efforts, and at all levels of decision making and planning in all types of natural disasters and conflict situations.

(b) Support and promote regional women's networks and ensure that the needs of women and realities of women's lives are reflected in national policies and actions through the phases of relief and recovery and post conflict reconstruction.

(c) Work towards capacity building of women and to ensure appropriate allocation of resources to deal with emergency situations.

12. Concrete Immediate Actions

(a) Propose that in the next two years the SAARC gender database housed at the SAARC Secretariat is organized, resourced and equipped to address the full range of challenges on sex disaggregated data and is able to share best practices from the region on gender equality.

(b) Incorporate SAARC and country level indicators for the MDGs that reflect commitments made under Beijing Platform for Action and CEDAW.

(c) Agree to meet, discuss and review progress on the Islamabad Declaration: Review and Future Action at the annual session of the UN Commission on the Status of Women with the assistance of UNIFEM.

(d) Agree to hold six monthly meetings of secretaries of national machineries of the member states and to address the issues of trafficking of women and children and review of the "Islamabad Declaration: Review and Future Action" to be sponsored by the UNIFEM.

(e) Agree that civil society groups of the region will participate in the public hearings being organized by the UNSG on MDGs to give their inputs in the formulation and expansion of indicators relating to MDGs.

(f) Each government will develop a plan based on this document with time bound goals and targets within the two year frame and shared it within the region

(g) A website to be created to share information.

Appendix II
NOTES ON CSW

At the 49th Session of the CSW

Delegates representing governments and civil society organizations from the region to attend the Review were supported. The session was marked by debates on various resolutions on emerging issues for women around the world filed by various governments. The resolutions focused on *economic empowerment, gender mainstreaming, trafficking in women and children, Tsunami disaster response and armed conflict.*

Critical issues that were highlighted at the CSW included: (a) Linkages between the MDGS and the BPFA (b) Response to the Tsunami (c) Women's leadership in disaster response and management (d) Women's rights to inheritance and property (e) Trafficking in women and children (f) NGO briefings, which provided an information hub and a forum to network with NGOs from around the globe

Launch of Publications

A global monitoring report "Beijing Betrayed" and subtitled "Women World Wide Report that Governments have failed to turn the Platform into Action" by Women's Development Organization (WEDO) in collaboration with women's groups worldwide was launched on 3rd March 2005. UNIFEM's publication "Pathways to Gender Equality: CEDAW, Beijing and the MDGs" was also released at the CSW. The publication identifies specific ways in which the three frameworks correspond to and support each other and suggests resources and entry points for engaging in the process.

Adoption of Resolutions: Ten resolutions were adopted at the CSW covering the following areas of concern: *Gender Mainstreaming, HIV/AIDS, Women in Afghanistan, Women in Palestine, Indigenous Women, Women and Natural Disasters, INSTRAW, Economic Advancement of Women, Trafficking, and a proposal to consider appointing a Special Rapporteur on Laws that*

Discriminate against Women in 2006. The resolutions on Indigenous Women and on Women and Natural Disasters represent new areas of concern and important gains.

Side Event at CSW: Through a Community of Practice Session on 'Enabling Accountability Mechanism: Voices from South Asia', organized on 1st March 2005, UNIFEM South Asia, shared the tools that it has developed in the region to foster accountability enabling mechanisms. Through a Panel Discussion, insights were provided into the diverse dimensions of the unique process, which has been facilitated by UNIFEM and effectively used by governments and the women's movement, to follow-up on commitments made in the BPFA and CEDAW; accelerate progress in their implementation; and link the obligations and commitments embodied in the BPFA and CEDAW to the achievement of the MDGs. This also served to spotlight the key role that UNIFEM plays in South Asia, in bringing different partners together and in carrying voices from the ground to the highest levels of policy and decision-making.

Some key issues that emerged at this session were:

- Women's ownership and rights as a key strategy for gender equality
- The need to protect and sustain women's livelihoods and entrepreneurship with the opening up of the economy
- The need to adopt this mechanism of South Asia as a best practice and extend it to other regions
- To explore how ICT opportunities can be used more aggressively for women's development and gender equality by UNIFEM.

Side Event at CSW: UNIFEM Asia Pacific and Arab States Regional Programme on Migration, organized a Migration Panel on "Claiming and Celebrating Women Migrant Workers' Rights: Paradigm Shifts and Innovative Practices" on 28th February. Nepal being one of the pilot countries and a country of origin was represented by a high level government delegate from the Ministry of Labour and Transport Management, who spoke as a panelist. Other panelists included a government representative from a country of employment (Jordan), a migrant worker and a NGO working on migration. The session sought to share new perspectives and innovative practices by different stakeholders in addressing women migrant workers' concerns in countries of origin and employment. It also sought to ensure that issues of concern and recommendations for change inform the deliberations and outcome document of the CSW Beijing +10 Process.

Appendix III
HIMALAYAN DECLARATION ON BEIJING +10
Lalitpur, Nepal

Alarmed that rampant globalization, neo-liberalism and unregulated privatization have contributed towards the intensification of poverty, social injustice, illiteracy, structural violence, resulting in extreme forms of discrimination and exploitation of women in the region;

Concerned that the adverse policies of the international financial institutions and the developed countries have devastating impact for the exercise of human rights of women and have jeopardized the quality of life and equitable employment opportunity for women,

Recalling the provisions enshrined in the Universal Declaration of Human Rights; the Convention on the Elimination of All Forms of Discrimination Against Women, the Beijing Platform for Action, the Outcome Document; the Convention on the Rights of the Child; the SAARC Convention on Trafficking and other regional and international instruments relating to women's rights;

Reiterating the fact that militarization of the region has escalated violence against women and children with grave risk of displacement, unsafe migration and exploitation thereby increasing extreme vulnerability of women;

Understanding that the women in the region have largely been disenfranchised from the mainstream political processes and marginalized from the power structures;

Realizing that sustainable human development incorporates substantive equality between women and men, respect for human, economic, social, cultural, civil and political rights, the elimination of poverty and the preservation of the environment is possible only through an equitable distribution of the world's resources between south and north, poor and rich, women and men.

We the 160+ delegates from South Asian countries assembled in the South Asia Beijing+10 NGO Consultation held in Kathmandu, Nepal on June 19-20, 2004, from Bangladesh, India, Nepal, Pakistan and Sri Lanka, representing various women's organizations, NGOs *and civil society organized by South Asia*

Women's Watch and hosted by Beyond Beijing Committee have unanimously adopted the following "Himalayan Declaration."

Our Mission Statement

1. We, the representatives from South Asia are all bound together by a common identity which expresses itself both in our linkages and the struggles for the empowerment of women in our respective countries.
2. These links have strengthened us individually and have led to a growing regional solidarity. Today, in the context of the contemporary socio-political environment, we feel it is imperative to develop and further strengthen a South Asian perspective for women's empowerment in the region.
3. As women our lives are subject to control through predominantly patriarchal structures and discriminatory laws and institutions, often justified on the basis of religion, customs and cultures which has led to increasing restrictions on our space and access to resources.
4. Increasing incidence of rape, dowry deaths, honour killings, acid attacks, women's humiliation in public, and the violence perpetrated by castism and religious fundamentalism leave us vulnerable both in the private and public sphere.

   We urge the countries of South Asia to

- Take comprehensive measures to address root causes of conflict situations, initiate and strengthen processes towards negotiated political settlements to internal and cross-border conflicts and ensure the participation of women at all levels in these efforts; reduce military budgets and channel those resources towards the expenditures related to the social sector.
- The states must take effective measures to arrest the adverse impacts of globalization specially on women; the state must ensure the protection of workers, food security, and the protection of environment and livelihood of people; keep off privatization of the sectors that meet the basic needs of people like water, health care, education stop the corporatization of agriculture.

- The state must not abdicate its social responsibility towards its people.
- Create a code of conduct for corporate reasonability to comply with international human rights standards relating to women.
- Take immediate measures to stop systematic and gross gender-based violence and violation of women's human rights; repeal/amend all discriminatory laws and adopt gender just laws meeting the standard of international human rights laws and treaty obligation;
- Adopt all national, bilateral and regional laws and treaties with the goal of combating the heinous crimes of trafficking, sexual exploitation and slavery of women.
- The states should come up with a fix time frame and ensure minimum of 33 per cent of reservation for women at all level in political and all levels of decision making.
- Adopt special affirmative measures, as a principle of positive discrimination, for dalit, marginalized, single, aging, minority, indigenous, refugee and disabled women.
- Withdraw all declarations and reservations from CEDAW and CRC and ratify the Optional Protocol of CEDAW, the Refugees Convention, the Statute of the International Criminal Court, the Second Optional Protocol to the Geneva Convention, and the UN Convention on the Protection of Rights of Migrant Workers and their family and implement the provisions of above conventions and protocols.
- All states must strengthen national machineries and increase substantially the budgetary allocations for the empowerments of women in order to fulfill commitments made under PFA.
- Consultative process with women's organizations, NGOs and civil society needs to be strengthened by the governments of the regions.

We, the women of South Asia who comprise more than 50 per cent of the regional population are strengthened by our firm commitment to continue our struggle to establish substantive equality in all spheres of life. We call upon all the governments of the region to fulfill the commitments made in Beijing, other international fora that fully implement BPFA, CEDAW and other international instruments, national action plans on women of the respective countries within the given time frame.

We urge upon the development partners and relevant UN agencies to prioritize South Asian Women's concerns in their agenda and extend all necessary financial and technical assistance.

Since achievement of the goal of Equality, Development, and Peace is the international commitment of all the governments of the region, we call for full implementation of the goal by the year 2015.

Adopted on June 20, 2004, Lalitpur, Kathmandu, Nepal.

Appendix IV
BANGKOK COMMUNIQUÉ

The high-level intergovernmental meeting to review Regional Implementation of the Beijing Platform for Action and Its Regional and Global Outcomes was held in Bangkok from 7 to 10 September 2004, and was attended by 44 members and associate members of ESCAP, United Nations bodies, programmes and specialized agencies, representatives of intergovernmental agencies and observers from non-governmental organizations.

WE REAFFIRM OUR COMMITMENT to the consensus Beijing Declaration and Platform for Action and the outcome of the twenty-third special session of the General Assembly.

WE ACKNOWLEDGE the gains made including:

- The formulation of national policies and action plans to promote gender equality and the empowerment of women.
- The establishment and the strengthening of national machineries or institutional mechanisms for the advancement of women.
- Improved women's health, including maternal and reproductive and sexual health, nutritional status and longer life expectancy.
- The formulation and revision of domestic laws and regulations to eliminate discrimination against women.
- Affirmative actions to increase women's participation in politics and decision-making.
- Increased access by women to education and a significant decrease in women's illiteracy rate.
- Improved economic empowerment of women.
- Active and enhanced participation of women's non-governmental organizations and civil society.

WE ACKNOWLEDGE THAT THERE ARE GAPS in the full implementation of the Beijing Platform for Action, including:

- The insufficient catalytic role of national machineries for the advancement of women in the national planning and policy-making process.
- The lack of policies, legislations and programmes to protect women migrant workers' human rights.

- The lack of reproductive health information and services or care to women, particularly young women and adolescents.
- The lack of regional cooperation and partnership initiatives for combating trafficking in persons, HIV/AIDS and promoting the protection of women migrant workers and global market mechanisms.
- The limitation of financial and human resources for promoting gender equality.
- Women's disproportionate representation among the poor (feminization of poverty).
- The high prevalence rate of HIV/AIDS in the region particularly among women.
- The low level of women's participation in decision-making at various levels.
- The persisting violence against women including trafficking of women and children and girl child marriage.
- The lack of reliable and relevant sex and age disaggregated data and gender statistics.
- The persisting portrayal of women and girls as sexual objects and commodities in media and information and communication technology.

WE RECOGNIZE THE NEED TO ADDRESS THE FOLLOWING CHALLENGES:

- Combating continuing violation of human rights and all forms of discrimination against women and girls.
- Strengthening of women's national machineries and institutional mechanisms.
- Improving allocation of financial and human resources and increasing allocation of financial resources.
- Developing gender-sensitive indicators and sex disaggregated statistics for measuring progress.
- Forging close cooperation and partnership with stakeholders.
- Creating an enabling environment to support policies and affirmative action programmes to ensure women's access to economic resources and opportunities, education and health, and including reproductive health.

- Increasing the accessibility, availability, affordability and quality of reproductive health services, especially for poor, young and marginalized women.
- Reducing the vulnerability of women and girls to HIV/AIDS.
- Promoting gender mainstreaming as a systematic approach to ensure gender-responsive implementation of policies and plans to be institutionalized.
- Addressing the negative impacts of globalization and trade liberalization such as job insecurity and violations of labour rights.
- Providing adequate social and legislative protection to vulnerable women.
- Reducing and alleviating poverty.
- Supporting and recognizing community and independent media to counter the negative and stereotypical portrayal of women and girls.
- Protecting women and children in situations arising from militarism, war and armed conflict, and in particular, from the use of rape and sexual violence and hostage-taking as a strategy of war.
- Mainstreaming of women in environmental decision-making at all levels in the context of environmental degradation and pollution, climate change, and their impact on gender.

FURTHERMORE, WE RECOGNIZE the importance of ensuring linkages and cross-fertilization with commitments to the Convention on the Elimination of All Forms of Discrimination against Women, Security Council resolution 1325 (2000) on women, peace and security, International Conference on Population and Development Programme of Action, the Millennium Declaration, the internationally agreed development goals, including those contained in the Millennium Declaration, which are recognized as effective in realizing women's human rights and gender equality.

We encourage the strengthening of cooperation and partnerships, and the commitment to allocating increased resources by governments, non-governmental organizations, development partners, and regional, international and intergovernmental agencies.

We therefore renew our commitment to the full and effective implementation of the Beijing platform for action.

We offer this communiqué as the Asian and pacific contribution to the meeting on the global review and appraisal of the implementation of the Beijing platform for action to be carried out by the United Nations Commission on the status of women at its forty-ninth session to be held in New York in March 2005.

Source: E/ESCAP/BPA/Rep.
28 October 2004

5

Legal Pluralism, Minority Identity and the Uniform Civil Code Debate

Flavia Agnes

In the Indian context, the issue of family law reform is entangled within the polemics of identity politics and minority rights. The debate revolves around the enactment of a Uniform Civil Code (UCC) with sharp polarization between those who support the demand and those who oppose it. While the anti-UCC segment is symbolized by Muslim fundamentalists, the pro-UCC lobby has two components driven by two different ideologies – the Hindu right wing and secular and women's rights groups. This polarization leaves very little space for voicing misgivings about the feasibility of an all-encompassing code, within a culturally diverse pluralistic society.

The secular groups supporting the demand from the perspective of women's rights view gender as a neutral terrain, distanced from the contemporary political events. But, within a complex social, political and economic structure, the demand of gender equality cannot be confined within a linear mould of granting uniform rights to women of all communities. In order to be relevant to women's lives, there is an urgent need to contextualize the demand within a comprehensive framework, inclusive of political and economic diversities.[1]

While this demand was initially articulated by the women's movement, after it was communalized within an anti-Muslim political agenda, some women's groups reframed it as 'reform within personal laws'. But, the media has continued to highlight the UCC controversy, with its inherent anti-Muslim bias. The bias is also reflected in the manner in which the historical Shahbano judgment of 1985 and the subsequent Muslim Women's Act of 1986 are commented upon in the media, obviating the more recent court rulings which have granted significant rights to Muslim women. This essay brings to the fore these latent biases and as well as the recent developments within the Muslim Personal Law brought about through judicial proclamations which have gone unnoticed because the media has failed to highlight them.

The Supreme Court, the Media and the UCC Debate

Periodical pronouncements by the Supreme Court, urging the state to enact a Uniform Civil Code (UCC), have received wide media publicity. The myriad opinions expressed in support of the UCC are governed by three distinct undertones, i.e., gender equality, national integration and concepts of modernity imbedded within notions of middle class morality.

The gender concerns project the demand for an all-encompassing and uniform code as a magic wand which will ameliorate the woes and sufferings of Indian women in general and Muslim women in particular. This concern places gender as a neutral terrain, distanced from contemporary political processes. From this point of view, the agency for change within communities becomes highly suspect. Minority women are projected as lacking a voice and an agency either in their own communities or through the process of litigation to claim their rights within existing structures. It projects the state intervention in the form of an enactment of a uniform code as the only option to bestow gender justice upon minority women.

At another level, for the liberal, modern, English educated, middle classes, the demand is laden with a moral undertone of abolishing polygamy and other 'barbaric' customs of the minorities and extending to them the egalitarian code of the 'enlightened majority'. This position relies upon the western model of nation-state and liberal democracy and scorns simultaneous sexual relationships in the nature of polygamous marriages in the name of modernity, but at the same time, endorses sequential plurality of sexual relationships (through frequent divorces), and also the more recent trends of informal cohabitations, which are gradually gaining legitimacy and social sanction.

Within a communally vitiated political climate, the demand also voices concerns of 'national integration' and 'communal harmony' and projects Muslims as the 'other' both of Hindus and the nation. At times the distinction between these two terms collapses and they become interchangeable.

It is indeed a matter of grave concern that this position, advocated by the Hindu right wing, received a boost through judgments pronounced by the apex court of a secular and pluralistic state, and more often than not by the presiding Chief Justices. It is interesting to note that no matter what the core issue litigated before the Supreme Court, the comments regarding the enactment of a UCC are always made in reference to 'national integration' and either a veiled or direct insinuation against Muslim law, thus creating a fiction that Hindus are governed by secular, egalitarian and gender just family code. The latent message is that it is high time that this code was extended to Muslims to usher in modernity and gender equality among them.

This communal posture of the apex court becomes evident when we examine the constitutional challenges to archaic and sexist provisions of Hindu law. For instance, when in 1984, the Delhi High Court upheld the archaic provision of restitution of conjugal rights under the Hindu Marriage Act which was challenged on the basis that it violates freedom and equality, not only was there no mention of a UCC and 'national integration' but the court went further and ruled: "Introduction of constitutional law in the home is most inappropriate. It is like pushing a bull into a china shop. It will prove to be a ruthless destroyer of the marriage institution and all that it stands for. In the privacy of the home and married life, neither Article 21[2] nor Article 14[3] have any place."[4] Later in the same year, the Supreme Court affirmed this decision in Saroj Rani[5] and overruled the Andhra Pradesh ruling which had struck down this provision as unconstitutional.[6]

While the blame for igniting the UCC controversy must lie primarily with the Supreme Court, the blame for repeatedly fanning it and keeping it alive in popular parlance lies with the media. While the Shahbano judgment[7] provided the first impetus for highlighting the polarized opinions into mutually exclusive segments – the progressive-modernist in support of a UCC and fundamentalist-obscurantist in opposition, it has continued to frame the issue within these binaries even when the lines between these two sections have become blurred. In the two decades since the Shahbano ruling the ground realities have changed substantially. The demolition of the Babri Masjid,[8] the rise of the Hindu right wing, the burning of Christian churches in South Gujarat, the communal carnage[9] which engulfed the state of Gujarat in February-March 2002, accompanied by gruesome sexual violence upon Muslim women – have all been factors that have necessitated a re-examination of the earlier call for a UCC, ostensibly to secure the rights of minority women. In the context of the anti-minority political events, many secular and women's rights groups have been compelled to withdraw their support to a UCC propagated by the Hindu right wing.

What is even more relevant is that the Bharatiya Janata Party (BJP),[10] the dominant segment of the National Democratic Alliance (NDA)[11] coalition, itself has abandoned this agenda once it came to power in 1999 though this was an important plank in its election manifesto (along with the assurance of building a Ram Mandir at Ayodhya at the site of the demolished mosque and abolition of Article 370[12] – a cultural trishul[13] – a three-pronged attack against Muslims). Rather strangely, in its election manifesto for the parliamentary elections which were held in 2004, the demand for a UCC was dropped in order to retain its non-fundamentalist partners of the NDA who were opposed to this agenda. [In a dramatic turn of events, the ruling NDA coalition government lost the elections and a Congress-led secular coalition – United Peoples Alliance (UPA) –

was voted to power, and since then the hype regarding the enactment of a UCC has receded.]

Despite this, the polarization in the media continues and the same old controversy gets whipped up time and again and is savoured with relish by the English speaking urban, liberal, middle class. And this class, which is otherwise indifferent to political processes, becomes the ardent defender of the demand for the UCC. Every time the Supreme Court makes a comment, what one sees in the media are images of *purdah*-clad Muslim women and opinions of Muslim religious leaders opposing the demand. Many times, the core issues litigated before the Supreme Court are blotted out and the call for a UCC is projected as a pronouncement against the Muslim minority.

For instance, the judgment pronounced by the then Chief Justice, Justice V. N. Khare in John Vallamattom case in August 2003 concerned a Christian priest's personal freedom to make a bequest of religious-charitable nature.[14] But a stray and uncalled for comment[15] regarding the UCC helped the media to convert a judgment in defense of personal freedoms and cultural plurality into one in defense of UCC and hence, anti-minority. Ironically, the next day and through the weeks that followed, the newspapers were flooded with reports and editorials on UCC with quotes from Muslim religious leadership and Muslim intelligentsia at one end and women's rights activists at the other, while the judgment itself was relevant neither to the Muslim identity nor to women's rights.

Similarly, in the Sarla Mudgal[16] case of 1995, the core issue before the court was conversion and bigamy by Hindu men. Here again, neither Muslim law nor rights of Muslim women were issues before the court. The court was examining the rights of two Hindu wives and the validity of two marriages by a bigamous Hindu husband – the prior one under the Hindu law and the subsequent one contracted after a fraudulent conversion to Islam. Despite this, the parties to the litigation were all Hindus and continued to be so. But, unfortunately, the judgment and the media publicity that followed focused primarily on UCC in the context of nation, national integration and minority identity. Of the three judgments, the Shahbano alone had an aggrieved Muslim woman at its core.

And this controversy warrants a re-evaluation in the light of subsequent developments.

Revisiting Shahbano and the Controversial Muslim Women's Act

The facts of the Shahbano judgment, which first raised the controversy around UCC, are now history. It would suffice to mention that the Supreme Court elected to comment upon Islam and the Muslim Personal Law while deciding the right of maintenance under a secular and uniform statute. But this was not the first instance of the apex court upholding the right of the divorce Muslim woman for maintenance. Two significant decisions of the Supreme Court delivered by Justice Krishna Iyer in 1979 and 1980 in Bai Tahira[17] and Fuzlununbi[18] had placed the divorced Muslim woman's right of maintenance under this provision upon a secure footing, without arousing a political controversy.

The unwarranted comments evoked a communal backlash. Relenting to the pressure exerted by the Muslim orthodoxy, the government introduced the Muslim Women's Bill which sought to exclude divorced Muslim women from the purview of Section 125 of the Code of Criminal Procedure (CrPC).[19] This move by the ruling Congress, led by Rajiv Gandhi, came to be projected as the most glaring instance of the defeat of the principle of gender justice for the Indian women as well as the defeat of secular principles within the Indian polity.

This move met with severe opposition from secular and women's rights groups. As the debate progressed, the media projected two insular and mutually exclusive positions, i.e., those who opposed the Bill and supported the demand for a UCC as modern, secular and rational, and those opposing the UCC as fundamentalist, orthodox, male chauvinist, communal and obscurantist. To be progressive, modern and secular was also to be nationalist and conversely the opposing faction could be labelled as anti-national. As the controversy escalated, the Muslim was defined as the other, both of the nation and of the Hindus. Muslims, in turn, could be mobilized to view this as yet another threat to their tenuous security. The rigid approach of the Muslim leadership provided further fuel to the Hindu right-wing forces in their anti-Muslim propaganda.

Ironically, the fury which was whipped up, seemed to be divorced from the core component of the controversy, a paltry sum of Rs. 179 per month, far too inadequate to save the 73-year old ex-wife of a successful Kanpur-based lawyer, from vagrancy and penury. The raging controversy and the communal turn of events finally led Shahbano herself to make a public declaration renouncing her claim, strengthening the popular misconception that Islam subverts economic rights of women. If this entitlement was against her religion, she declared, she would rather be a devout Muslim than claim her right of maintenance. A sad comment indeed, warranting reflection from campaigners on both sides of the divide. The statute, passed under a party whip, led to a further strengthening of the Muslim appeasement theory in judicial discourse and in popular media.

The hurriedly drafted and hastily enacted statute was full of loopholes. But, despite its limitations, the Act was of immense historical significance, as the first attempt of independent India, to codify the Muslim Personal Law. But, the positions across the divide were so rigid by then, that they left no space to contemplate upon this milestone. It is only when the dust raised by the controversy settled down that one could examine the relevance of this statute titled, Muslim Women (Protection of Rights on Divorce) Act, 1986 (MWA). But, since it was enacted amidst protests from women's rights groups and progressive social organizations, it was viewed with suspicion and foreboding by these sections. Hence, the first response of the protesting groups was to challenge its constitutionality, rather than examine its viability.

While the writ petitions filed by various organizations were pending in the Supreme Court, the Act gradually unfolded itself in the lower courts. Appeals from the decisions of various High Courts gradually started accumulating, along with the original writ petitions. What was intriguing was that while the writ petitions were filed by groups agitating for women's rights, the appeals were from husbands aggrieved by the verdicts of various High Courts. If indeed the Act was depriving women of their rights and was enabling husbands to wriggle out of their economic liability, why were the husbands finding themselves aggrieved by the orders passed under a blatantly anti-women statute? Lurking beneath was a faint suspicion that perhaps the manner in which the Act was unfolding itself in the lower courts, was indicative of a different reality, defying the premonitions. This fascinating phenomenon provided the first indication that perhaps the ill-famed Act could be invoked to secure the rights of divorced Muslim women.

A seemingly innocuous clause, which had missed the attention of protesters and defenders alike, had been invoked by a section of the lower judiciary, to pronounce judgments, which provided greater scope for protection against destitution. Section 3 (1) (a) of the Act stipulated that a divorced Muslim woman is entitled to a reasonable and fair provision and maintenance to be made and paid to her within the 'iddat' period by her former husband. This clause had been invoked by the judiciary in defense of Muslim women's rights.

Though initially just a trickle, the judgments were a pointer towards a possibility. They affirmed that the new Act was to protect the rights of divorced Muslim women and not deprive them of their rights. They further stressed that any ambiguity within the Act must be interpreted in such a manner as to reconcile with the proclamation contained in the title of the Act. Banishing divorced women to a life of destitution would not amount to protecting their rights as stipulated by the statute, they declared.

Suddenly, the lump sum provisions for future security, which the courts were awarding within the framework of Islamic principles, seemed to be a better safeguard against destitution, than the meagre doles which they were entitled to under Section 125 of the CrPC. A reading of the judgments indicates that the Act had rid itself of the agenda of alleviating vagrancy and destitution among divorced women and had extended itself to the claims of women from a higher social strata. The statute enacted in haste, at the insistence of the conservative leadership, seemed to have boomeranged. A concerned and sensitive judiciary, carved out a space for the protection of women's rights from what appeared to be an erroneously conceived, badly formulated and blatantly discriminatory statute, without invoking a political backlash. Drawing on the Islamic concept of 'mataaoon bil ma'aroofe' (fair and reasonable provision), the courts opened a new portal for the protection of divorced Muslim women.

The ruling of the five-judge Constitutional Bench headed by Justice G.B. Pattanaik in Daniel Latifi,[20] pronounced on 28 September 2001, finally put its seal of approval on these positive interpretations. The Supreme Court held that the Act is constitutionally valid and upheld the positive interpretations given by various trial courts in respect of fair and reasonable settlement for a life time! So, after this ruling, there is no ambiguity whether a divorced Muslim woman is entitled to maintenance for three months or a reasonable provision for a lifetime. Despite this, the media failed to take note of it and the landmark ruling received hardly any media publicity.

Muslim Women, Dominant Ideologies and the Media

Law is not merely a statute; its essence lies in the manner in which it is unfolded in law courts. The empty words of a statute come to life in trial courts where they are contested, interpreted and validated. Right from 1988, the courts have engineered divorced Muslim women's rights through innovative interpretations of the Muslim Women's Act (MWA), ushering in a new set of rights within the established principles of Muslim law. Several judges declared that 'provision' contemplates 'future needs' and that the parliament has replaced one set of obligations of a Muslim husband with another. The claim under the Muslim Women's Act does not operate through a rider of sexual purity. The judicial pronouncements delivered divorced Muslim women from the cumbersome burden of recurring monthly dues, which hinged upon post-divorce chastity.

But rather unfortunately, within the communally vitiated atmosphere, the advances made by divorced Muslim women under MWA have been invisibilized and glossed over by the media. During the Shahbano controversy, the denial of rights of a meagre maintenance dole was lamented by all and sundry, notwithstanding the fact that the maintenance awarded to the wife of an advocate with a flourishing practice was just Rs. 25 in the first instance and Rs. 179 in appeal. So long as the debate could be used as a stick to beat the community with, these minor details did not seem to matter. What did matter is the fact that a communal campaign could be mounted upon a patriarchal paradigm and thereby legitimized.

The demand for a UCC was couched as a 'liberal and modernizing mission'. The irony lay in the fact that the groundwork for mounting this campaign was laid by the women's movement, with genuine gender concerns, but firmly located within the cultural ethos of the mainstream. Within this framework, a similar appeasement of Hindus, by strengthening coparcenaries by various legislative measures, could be deliberately ignored. The 'modernizing mission' is an important tool for establishing racial and communal superiority and is used constantly by dominant classes and hegemonic cultures. During the colonial rule, the introduction of the Anglo-Saxon legal structure was seen by the British administrators as an important forte of its civilizing mission and that the Hindu society could rid itself of its barbarism and enter an era of 'civilization' through it. An image of the cruel and superstitious native who needed Christian salvation was deliberately constructed by the Evangelists. In post-independent India, a similar framework is being used to justify the barbarties against the minority communities through the dominant ideology.

One needs to examine the invisibilizing of the Muslim women's struggle within the cultural construct of these hegemonic claims. The communal fervour could be sustained only by denying the fact that the Act provided for an alternate remedy, far superior to the one that had been denied to Muslim women under Section125 of the CrPC; by negating the fact that since 1988, the Act was being positively interpreted by various High Courts in the country by awarding substantial amounts as 'settlements'; by glossing over an important development in the realm of family law, that of determination of economic entitlements upon divorce, rather than the prevailing right of recurring maintenance. So, even while homes of poor Muslim women were looted, gutted and razed to the ground in various communal riots, while teenage sons of Muslim women were killed at point blank ranges in police firings, while Muslim women were raped under flood lights in post-Babri Masjid riots, the mainstream continued to lament over Muslim appeasement and denial of maintenance to 'poor Muslim women/the Shahbanos'.

One could overlook even this. Perhaps, there was a justification. Denial of maintenance by husbands was perhaps as loathsome as rape of women in communal riots. In the ultimate analysis, it was the 'poor Muslim woman' who suffered. So far so good. But, how can one logically explain the recurring motif of 'Muslim appeasement' even after the Supreme Court decision in the Daniel Latifi case, when the controversy was finally laid to rest by upholding the constitutional validity of the Act and simultaneously securing the maintenance rights of Muslim women? In actual term the rights secured by the Supreme Court are superior to the rights of maintenance which a Hindu woman is entitled to.

And yet, the rhetoric continues. And is used yet again, in defence of the Gujarat carnage. "They had it coming ... they have been 'appeased' beyond tolerance. Why should they demand a separate law in a secular country? Why should they be allowed to marry four times? Why are Hindus alone bound by an obligation of maintenance?" What is startling is that the grievances are mouthed not only by Hindu extremists but also by centrists, the liberals, the people who inhabit my social space, the urban, cosmopolitan, middle class. Within the cultural ethos of the mainstream, an injustice to a Muslim wife gets magically transformed into a Hindu injury which could be invoked to justify communal carnage. Without this tacit approval by the middle class, the recent Gujarat carnage could never have spread so wide nor so deep.

The rhetoric conveniently overlooks the fact that abandonment and destitution of wives is as rampant among Hindus; that the matrimonial faults of adultery and bigamy are evenly distributed across communities; and that Hindus, Christians and Parsees, with equal zeal, guard the patriarchal prerogatives within their respective personal laws. Further, that around 80 per cent of all women burnt in their matrimonial homes are urban middle class Hindus! That patriarchal prerogatives cannot be abandoned even when a law is being codified is something we have learnt in the process of Hindu law reforms. Even when codification is sought in the name of either 'uniformity', 'national integration' or as a 'civilizing mission' these prerogatives will be retained. The saving of Hindu undivided family (HUF) property under the Hindu Succession Act is a glaring example of this. The Hindu urban and rural propertied class and family business establishments have gained the maximum concessions of tax benefits due to this. Any move to abolish this even under the guise of a UCC will be opposed vehemently by this class, as it will upset their apple cart. For them, the UCC debate is confined to abolishing the 'barbaric' Muslim culture of polygamy and to liberate the Shahbanos, while simultaneously turning a blind eye to the sexual promiscuity and multiple sexual relations among them. The women bound in these relations can easily be discarded as 'concubines', 'mistresses' or partners of contractual agreements, *maitreyee karars*[21] (this is the modern term for these alliances) lacking legal validity and devoid of any rights, as one experiences during contested claims of maintenance by these women.

Viewed within this background, the struggles of individual divorced Muslim women who defied their culture and tradition and dictates of patriarchy have to be acknowledged as acts of assertion. Divorced Muslim women had to fight every inch of the way for their rights right from the trial courts in small district towns right up to the Supreme Court. Their crucial right of survival hinged upon interpretations and explanations of simple words like 'within/for' 'and/or' 'maintenance/provision', disjunctures and conjuctures of words and phrases.

In the final battle in the Supreme Court, both sides – the women's rights groups who had challenged the constitutionality of the Act as well as the Muslim religious leadership who had pressed for their claim that the Muslim woman's entitlement ought to be limited to three months of 'Iddat' period-lost out. Who emerged victorious was the divorced Muslim woman who had waged a relentless battle to defend her rights. It is time the media should take note of this silent revolution waged by individual Muslim women and acknowledge the fact of their agency in bringing about changes within their personal laws.

Monogamy, Morality and Maintenance

Since the entire issue of maintenance to Muslim women is in the centre, it would be interesting to contextualize sexual morality and its co-relationship to claims of maintenance. I have mentioned earlier that the claim under the Muslim Women's Act does not operate through a rider of sexual purity. It would indeed be interesting to explore how this co-relationship between sexual purity and maintenance claim is played out in court rooms. Within the Indian family law, women's economic claims arising out of a marriage contract are confined to recurring monthly maintenance. It is only under the Muslim Women's Act, the principle of determining economic rights upon divorce has been introduced in the Indian matrimonial jurisprudence.

A large number of deserted Hindu women, particularly from the lower strata, find it more convenient to claim this right under Section 125 of the CrPC, rather than under the provisions of their personal law, i.e., the Hindu Marriage Act, as the proceedings under Section 125 of the CrPC are summary and are situated in the proximate magistrate's court than the distant district court (except where family courts have been set up). This otherwise innocuous section came into public focus during the Shahbano controversy in 1985 and is retained in public memory due to the furor it caused at the time. But, the notions of sexual morality with which this section is governed as not received due attention in contemporary feminist legal discourse.

The stipulation under clauses 4 and 5 of this section that a woman who is living in adultery is not entitled to maintenance, provides the armour for husbands to entangle women in vicious and dilatory litigation over a pittance of maintenance. A careful scrutiny of reported cases in any law journal would reveal the extent to allegations of sexual promiscuity are made to subvert women's claims. To give an example, a journal widely used by lawyers practising matrimonial law *Divorce and Matrimonial Cases* (DMC) for 2001 reports around 45 cases under the title "Maintenance". In almost half of these, sexuality and morality were the core issues which were contested. An important point to note is that from litigation in the magistrate's court, the cases went through cumbersome processes to the higher courts for them to merit a reporting in the law journal. Hence, they reflect only a tip of the iceberg. In each of these cases the women were assaulted and driven out. Most of these cases also contained allegations of dowry harassment. But, none of these women had filed a criminal complaint under Section 498A of the IPC. All they did was to file an application for maintenance and it is then that the husbands lashed out with allegations of sexual promiscuity.

The layered and multiple contexts through which sexual morality surfaces, as per the norms of patriarchy, serve only one end – to challenge the legitimacy of women's claims. It is a clear case of "heads I win and tails you lose". The allegations ranged from adultery on the part of the wife and disputing paternity of the child to allegations of a subsisting previous marriage of the wife, husband's subsisting first marriage, allegations of concubinage and husband's subsequent marriage. But, the issues of sexuality, morality and polygamy, whichever way they emerge, can always be turned against the woman's claims of maintenance. For instance, it really does not matter whether the woman's previous marriage or the husband's previous marriage is in dispute. So long as sexuality is pitted against maintenance claims, it is the woman who has to pay the price.

Scanning through the judgments one can see a positive trend emerging, where the courts have upheld the women's claims and disallowed the husbands' contentions. But, despite this, the prevalence of Section 125 (4) and (5) provides the scope for the husbands to entangle the deserted women from the lower strata, in prolonged, cumbersome and costly litigations. And, negative rulings, though less frequent, still prevail. I have quoted from a judgment of the Allahabad High Court to convey the extent of humiliation a woman goes through during these litigations: "If the man and woman choose to live together and indulge into sex no such marriage status can be conferred automatically by their so living upon such a woman. She is not entitled to the legal status of a wife in the eyes of law and society. Law and society treat such women either as concubine or a mistress ... The two may agree to live together to satisfy their animal needs. But such a union is never called a marriage. A woman leading such a life cannot be bestowed with the sacrosanct honour of wife. No marital obligations accrue to such a woman against her husband. Such a wife must be termed as an adulterous."[22]

One measure, which is being suggested to resolve the ambiguity of a Hindu marriage, is compulsory registration of marriages. This rigid stance of morality would lead to placing all Hindu marriages in a straight jacket and invalidating all unregistered marriages. This will only serve to make the situation worse for women of this category. This would indeed be regressive and deprive them of the presumption of marriage due to prolonged cohabitation, and the presumption of legitimacy of children which is presently available under the India Evidence Act.[23]

Conclusion

In this concluding section, I would like to highlight some of the latest developments on this issue. The positive trend found in some recent suggestion for reforms is to validate the rights of second wives/cohabitants. For instance, the Malimath Commission report[24] has suggested that the term 'wife' under Section 125 of the CrPC should include "a woman who was living with the man like his wife for reasonable long period". Though the report has several anti-women recommendations, this particular positive one needs to be highlighted.

The recently enacted Domestic Violence Act takes the issue even beyond and seeks to grant rights of residence to cohabitants and women in informal relationships and protect such women from domestic violence. This provision was endorsed by the Parliamentary Standing Committee on Human Resource Development, in its 124th report, in the following words: "The Committee is aware of the fact that in our society there are numerous cases where a man and a woman, though not legally married, live together as husband and wife ... The Committee, therefore, suggests that the Bill should be suitably amended to include those women also who have been living in relationship akin to marriages and in marriages considered invalid by law."

The Act, which was passed in August 2005, provides the scope for protective injunctions against violence, dispossession from the matrimonial home and alternate residence. It also provides the scope for claiming economic protection, including maintenance. The wide definition of domestic violence – physical, mental, economical and sexual – brings under its purview the invisible violence suffered by a large section of women and entitles them to claim protection from the courts. The scope of protection against violence extends beyond 'wives' in legal marriages to not only daughters and sisters but even women in informal relationships. Entire gamut of women, whose marriages are suspect due to some 'legal defect' on the ground that essential ceremonies were not performed or that the man or the woman has an earlier subsisting marriage can no longer be used to deny women the crucial rights of residence and maintenance.

While these are welcome trends, how do we connect them to the debate on UCC which is mounted on the plank of monogamy? It is not my intention here to hold a brief for sexual promiscuity of either men or women – be they Hindu, Muslim or even Christian or Parsee. All I wish to do is to raise an uncomfortable question: when de-linked from rights of maintenance and residence, would the claim for monogamy still survive as a plank for the UCC discourse. Or, even further, whether concepts of gender equality, national integration and sexual morality are artificially superimposed upon the UCC discourse by vested communal interests and whether, in the context of recent developments, the binaries in which the debate is located has become redundant. And even more daunting is the question: what innovative measures are needed to protect the crucial economic rights of women within the family and in informal sexual relationships, even beyond their right of residence and maintenance and the confines of personal laws.

For instance, in February 2005, a Bench presided over by Chief Justice R.C. Lahoti pronounced a landmark ruling in a case titled B.P. Achala Anand vs. S. Appi Reddy[25] which affirmed the rulings of the various High Courts since the eighties and breathed new life into the right of women to the matrimonial home. It also incorporated into the Indian law, the legal dictum of the English law, "deserted wife's right in equity". Where a husband who was statutory tenant of the matrimonial home, deserted his wife and left the house, the apex court held that the landlord could not turn her out so long as she paid the rent and performed the conditions of the tenancy.

At the other level, there have also been welcome developments within the Muslim Personal Law itself, advancing the premise of 'reform from within'. One such important development is the 'model *nikahnama*' which was endorsed by the Muslim Personal Law Board in June 2005. Muslim marriages are contracts and hence Muslim law recognizes the right of the wife to stipulate conditions at the time of marriage. Over the years, operating from a patriarchal social structure, the provision of stipulating conditions within the marriage contract had been rusted through disuse. But, in order to overcome several discriminatory provisions like the husband's right to pronounce arbitrary and capricious oral divorce (triple *talaq*) and the husbands right to contract bigamous marriages, women's groups had worked on various models of '*nikahnama*', through which the husband binds himself at the time of marriage. In addition, the 'model *nikahnama*' also prescribes that *mehr* amount could be stipulated in cash, valuables, shares, securities or immovable property like dwelling house or agricultural land.

While it is true that Muslim law provides the scope for these conditions to be included in the *nikahnama*, and the women's groups had worked out various models of such marriage contracts, unless it received the approval of the All India Muslim Personal Law Board, it would have remained in the periphery to be used by the conscious and alert few. The adaptation of a model *nikahnama*, which included clauses of arbitration prior to divorce, substantial amount of *mehr*, will go a long way in the struggle for reforms of personal laws from within. Hopefully, the message will reach out far and wide among the illiterate Muslim masses in rural India, who are in desperate need of such protective clauses. The only way to reach out to them was through the well oiled mechanism of the Muslim Personal Law Board.

In conclusion, I would like to emphasize that during the Constitutional Assembly debates, due to the communal conflict and political upheaval of the times, the provision for the enactment of a Uniform Civil Code (Article 44) was placed in Part IV of the Constitution, as a directive principle of state policy and not in Part III, i.e., as a fundamental and legally enforceable right. For nearly four decades after independence secular and women's rights groups viewed the enactment of a UCC as central to weed out gender-based discriminations in personal laws. But, since the issue of UCC has always been linked to political constraints of the time, the recent incidents like the rising wave of Hindu fundamentalism, the anti-Muslim political agenda and the gruesome communal violence unleashed upon the Muslim community have led to the creation of an insecure Muslim minority which regards the personal laws as an integral part of its threatened political identity.

It is this realization that has led many women's groups to reframe the demand for gender justice into a new language of 'reform from within', i.e., involving the community in bringing in reforms, as well as challenging specific instances of gender discrimination in courts. This may be a slow and painful process, but in the present political scenario, the only one that has yielded results. Within this framework, it is important for the media to keep a tab on the subtle changes that have taken place within the personal laws of various religious communities, in both predictable and unforeseen directions. One important development is the manner in which the norm of Hindu monogamy itself has weakened through legislative and judicial interventions, providing protection to a large number of women who are trapped in informal or bigamous marriage relationships, weakening the ideological premise of UCC which was aimed at introducing the concept of monogamy within Muslim marriages.

NOTES

1. For a more detailed discussion on the evolution of personal laws in India, see Agnes, F., *Law and Gender Inequality*, New Delhi: Oxford University Press (1999).
2. Right to life.
3. Right to equality.
4. *Harvinder Kaur v. Harminder Singh*, AIR 1984 Del 66.
5. *Saroj Rani v. Sudarshan*, AIR 1984 SC 1562.
6. *T. Sareetha v. T. Venkatasubbiah*, AIR 1983 AP 356.
7. The Supreme Court judgment, *Mohammad Ahmad Khan vs Shah Bano Begum*, AIR 1985 SC 945.
8. The 450 years old mosque was demolished by Hindu fundamentalists on 6th December, 1992 who claimed that the mosque was built on the site of an earlier Hindu temple and that it was the birth place of the Hindu God Ram. The demolition was followed by countrywide riots. In Bombay alone around 1,000 people were killed during these riots.
9. On 27th February, 2004 a train carriage was set on fire allegedly by Muslims. Following this, the Hindu fundamentalists aided by the state apparatus inflamed riots in several cities of Gujarat. The number of people killed in these riots were estimated to be around 3,000. Many scholars and legal activists state that 'riots' is not the appropriate term to be used as the killings were aided by the fundamentalist political party which was in power in Gujarat at this time. Rather ironically, the party came back to power with a thumping majority in elections held later in the same year.
10. The Hindu right-wing political party with an explicit anti-Muslim ideology.
11. The BJP was the dominant party of this alliance which came into power in 1999.
12. This Article gives special status to the state of Jammu and Kashmir. It provides several concessions to the local people. There had been protests to such a status from the rightist parties.
13. The three-pronged weapon (trident) of Lord Shiva. This weapon has been used by the Hindu group known as *Shiv Sena* as a Hindu symbol.
14. *John Vallamathom v. Union of India*, AIR 2003 SC 2902.

15. "It is a matter of regret that Article 44 of the Constitution has not been given effect to. ... A common civil code will help the cause of national integration by removing the contradictions based on ideologies...."
16. *Sarla Mudgal v. Union of India* (1995), 3 SCC 635.
17. *Bai Tahira v. Ali Hussain Fideali Chotthea*, AIR 1979 SC 362.
18. *Fuzlunbi v. K. Khadil Vali*, AIR 1980 SC 1730.
19. This is a general legal provision and is meant to safeguard women from destitution and moral depravity. Though the remedy is of a civil nature, it is situated within the Criminal Procedure Code. Till 2001, there was a ceiling of Rs. 500 and the courts could not award an amount beyond this. The courts usually would award a meagre some of Rs. 100-Rs. 200 as one Supreme Court judge expressed "to keep a woman's body and soul together". The ceiling has been removed in 2001 through an amendment.
20. *Danial Latifi v. Union of India*, 2001 (7) SCC 740.
21. This term is used for marriage agreements between two people who lack the legal capacity to enter into a valid marriage. For instance, if the man has not obtained a divorce from his wife, he enters into the marriage agreement with the subsequent woman, and conveys to her that there is a valid contract between the two. But courts have ruled that such marriage contracts are not valid. So, in case there is a dispute, the woman is left high and dry, devoid of all her rights, as the contract is not a legally valid contract.
22. *Malti v. State of Uttar Pradesh* I (2001) DMC 204 (Allahabad).
23. Under Section 50 of the Act, if there is a cohabitation for a reasonable length of time, even if the wife does not have a valid marriage certificate or any other proof; the presumption will be in her favour that she is living in a legally valid marriage. It is for the opposing party to disprove the presumption. This presumption is applied to civil matters but not for prosecution for bigamy under the criminal law.
24. I am referring to the "Committee on Reforms of Criminal Justice System" constituted by the Ministry of Home Affairs, Government of India, which was headed by Dr. Justice V.S. Malimath. The committee brought out its report in March 2003.
25. AIR 2005 SC 986.

6

Globalization, Resistance and Change

Reflections on South Asian Women's Experience

Indu Agnihotri

Women in South Asia have acquired increased visibility in the public sphere in recent decades. However, this does not necessarily signify an improved status. In fact, in all countries in this region, the mass of women today face impoverishment, loss of livelihood and assets, and are victims of violence that is unprecedented both in nature and scale. Their vulnerability and marginalization find reflection in their being a significant component of struggles and social movements launched in recent years. This assertion of agency is not a matter of choice. Rather, it is a struggle for survival at both, an individual and, a collective level – a struggle in which they have shown remarkable resilience and will to overcome adversity.

The South Asian Region

South Asia bears the stamp of a shared history, even as the lives of the people change as a consequence of its integration into the larger global economy. Given its varied topography and a long history of evolution of communities with varied livelihood patterns, social life has been marked by diversity of cultural practices and political formations. While re-invented Orientalism, espoused by proponents of imperialism assigns to some countries and civilizations an inherent characteristic of backwardness, the fact remains that patterns of change are determined by deeper historical processes; the 'backwardness' of this region is also a result of imperialist policies which led to uneven development and obstructed structural transformation. These impediments make it difficult to achieve sustained economic growth in South Asia today while integration into a capitalist market on unequal terms serves to perpetuate imperialist hegemony.[1] Meanwhile, the last quarter of the 20th century has seen an unbridled expansion of capitalism across the world made possible by the 'collapse' of the socialist bloc and the creation of a unipolar world. The unilateral declaration of war against countries such as Iraq represents overt forms of imperialist aggression while globalization aims at re-ordering the world economy to suit the needs of corporate capital which functions at a transnational level and owes accountability to none.[2] This is facilitated by restructuring the state and through international treaties which ensure unequal access to world resources and markets in direct and indirect ways.[3] Globalization represents the ideological offensive of neo-liberalism to push market-oriented reforms and facilitate capital flows to maintain capitalist profits; at the country level it is marked by a package of liberalization and privatization of assets and resources. It is accompanied by the ideological offensive of free-market ideology, which asserts that globalization is "shaping a new era of interaction among nations, economies and people" and, accompanied by the new infotech revolution, "it is increasing the contacts between people across national boundaries – in economy, in technology in culture and in governance".[4] Votaries of liberalization draw a contrast between the 'freedom' of open economies as against the 'controls' of planned or semi-planned economies to argue that economic reforms usher in an age of greater freedom and choice. This has proved to be a potent symbol for acceptance of the globalization model by the middle class: regardless of the ideological hegemony of imperialism over people and nations, as well as the structures in which markets and new technologies are embedded, the impression conveyed is that 'newness' and 'interaction' usher in an age of equal opportunities.

Analysis of women's status in South Asia today can be undertaken only in the context of these macro-level developments. The states in this region have a chequered political history, presenting a range of political formations from monarchy, constitutional monarchy, democracy and military regimes, or even a combination of these with a propensity for frequent change. Tensions emanating from the differential basis of integration into developmental and democratic processes have often surfaced violently in the social polity of the region and as issues of 'identity politics', resulting in a fluid and volatile situation which reflects shifting socio-political alliances at the local level and in the changing international context. Social movements in the region have chosen to focus on issues of substantive democracy and not to foster complacency about formal adherence to democracy. Globalization and fundamentalism have emerged as the major challenges with women as specific targets. Though some women from the upper sections have made gains, their power and status are in stark contrast with the experience of the vast mass which is part of the poor and marginalized. Militarization and nuclearization of the region have further escalated the scale of conflicts in the region. Continued tension between countries is used to justify high budgetary allocations for defense and 'security', seen only in military terms. There is escalation of armed conflict, perpetuated by both governments as well as their opponents looking for military solutions to political problems. Violent conflict affects women at different levels but certainly increases their vulnerability: caught up as they are in a number of roles, both as combatants and as targets of attack.[5]

Women's increased participation in struggles in South Asia today reflects the unequal burden on them. While this is often brushed aside as resulting from age-old patriarchal traditions, there is a need to examine whether globalization processes mitigate inequalities or reinforce them? Does globalization bring increased freedom, choice and new opportunities to all and equally so? Can women fare better when social inequalities are exacerbated? Do these represent the persistence of older forms of discrimination or does integration into a free market global world provide vested interests with fresh opportunities to unequally pass the burden on to women, thereby giving rise to new or more intense forms of patriarchy? What is the differential impact of these processes on women across different sections of society? There is a need to evolve an engendered critique of development processes to intervene for pro-women changes.[6]

This paper argues that women's lives are marked by stress due to the enhanced burden of work and poverty and they are directly embroiled in the dynamics of social change in the region. Many articulate the will to impact institution-building processes for democratic governance. As they simultaneously straddle different worlds in their everyday life, prevailing social perceptions singularly ignore their multiple roles and focus only on women's nurturing role in the family, projected as an autonomous and unchanging unit. But, the family is embedded within the broader social frame, within relations of production and it may be worthwhile to explore how the family bears the brunt of these changes to emerge as a site of conflict as the social crisis deepens. Ironically, the fresh wave of orthodoxy sweeping South Asia in the new global era, attempts to push women back into an imaginary past invoked in the name of 'tradition' and 'identity' even as they negotiate fresh openings alongside the ravages of the modern world. Politics in the region reflects the dangers of regressive ideologies. Women confront re-configured patriarchies and free market ideology, while state and fundamentalism vie with each other to further restrict their choices. Meanwhile, beneath the jingoistic slogans fanning fundamentalist mobilizations and hostilities built up around caste, culture, region, religion, language and nation, there runs a bond of commonality of both – women's oppression, as well as their struggle for survival and the search for alternate paths to peace, progress and development.

Impact of Globalization on South Asia

Evidence from countries across the world suggests that some groups are receiving fewer benefits from improvements in national income, health and education. Successive Human Development Reports record the problem of increasing disparities on the basis of region, countries and within regions. Income disparities are increasing, indicating wider gaps between people at the top and those at the bottom: the gaps show skewed development and concentration of rural, female-headed, indigenous and ethnically marginalized groups in the lower income group. They draw attention to the 'egregious failure' of the developed world and their leaders, to "help the poor and the unemployed in the developing world". The US, committed to transferring 0.7 per cent of its combined GDP to developing countries as aid, has given no more than 0.1 per cent of its GDP; that too to nations in which Washington is known to have strategic and political interests. The rich nations have failed to open their markets to the goods and commodities produced by the poor of the developing world, especially when opening up would have come at the expense of their own producers.[7] While there is a need to examine specific aspects of development and change at the country level, it may help to note the trends at the world level: in 1999 the assets of just three billionaires counted for more than the combined GNP of all the least developed countries and their 600 million people. By the late 1990s, the one-fifth living in the highest income countries had 86 per cent of world GDP, 82 per cent of world export market, 66 per cent of FDIs, and 74 per cent of world's telephone lines. The corresponding figures for the bottom one-fifth were 1 per cent, 1 per cent, 1 per cent and 1.5 per cent respectively.[8]

Despite vast differences in the economies, certain common features and problems emerge in South Asia: all are caught in the Debt and Dependence Syndrome and have acquiesced to IMF loan conditionalities by formally adopting the Structural Adjustment Programme. Sri Lanka, the first in the region to adopt the aid package of the IMF-World Bank, was followed by Pakistan, Bangladesh, India and Nepal. This involved financial and organizational reforms for compliance with WTO norms and trade agreements which effectively ensure that transnational corporations control the world market in a wide range of commodities and facilitate free flow for capital in countries and sectors where such access was earlier restricted through policies devised at the national level.

It is now conceded that there is no 'new vision' or 'one-size-fits all' solution to problems of the developing world nor can structural constraints be overcome by global strategies. Stiglitz, a former chief economist at the World Bank, has questioned the "appropriateness of particular policies for particular countries" as well as pointed to the need for developing countries to take charge of their own futures.[9] Further, "long-term initiatives to halve hunger and poverty will fail without fundamental restructuring of the global trade system – particularly in agriculture – that includes rich countries dismantling subsidies, lowering tariffs and leveling the playing field," so that the poorest countries escape poverty traps.[10] The terms and rules are, thus far, loaded against developing countries and uneven burdens are borne by the poor both within and among nations.[11] Reports point to the "growing exclusion and deprivation in certain regions of the world," which has dislocated traditional livelihoods and local communities, and threatens environmental sustainability and cultural diversity. "As the current process of cross-border interaction and interconnectivity gathers speed, there is increasing debate not only about inequalities between countries but also about inequalities within countries, and its effects on people, families and communities. ...The debate on globalization is fast becoming a debate on democracy and social justice in a global economy." There is growing concern about globalization, since "...its advantages are too distant for too many, while its risks are too real".[12] Premised on the new paradigm is a definition of 'good governance' as per IMF-WB norms which makes aid conditional upon adherence to norms. This is tantamount to denial of the democratic right to determine policy making at the national level: the state in South Asia is under pressure to 'withdraw.' Effectively, the idea of the 'roll back' is that the Third World countries give up on its 'welfare' commitments while it must continue to intervene on behalf of capital to maintain and provide an environment suitable for investment and production.[13] Since the face of poverty in this region is increasingly a 'feminine' face, this has direct bearing on women's status.

While the experiences of South Asian women are marked by diversity of both cultural practices and political formations, certain trends are visible at the regional level with globalization offering, at best, a very narrow range of choices. As the poorest and 'most deprived' region in the world, South Asia is also the least gender-sensitive; it has the fewest literates and the largest number of the most malnourished. The region has the lowest per capita GNP and is home to nearly 40 per cent of the world's poor; over 500 million live below the poverty line, with basic human needs remaining unmet; 395 million are illiterate, of which 60 per cent are women. Achievement of 48 per cent adult literacy, despite substantial increase since the 1970s, records the lowest in the world with more children in South Asia being out of school than in the rest of the world and two-thirds of those out of school are female. The largest number of malnourished are in South Asia, leaving sub-Saharan Africa far behind despite the much higher GNP growth rate and an increase in food production in South Asia. About 260 million lack access to even rudimentary health facilities and 337 million to safe drinking water; 830 million have no access to basic sanitation facilities while over 400 million go hungry every day. The discrimination women are subjected to is evident from the fact there are only 94 women for every 100 men – translated as 74 million 'missing' women. South Asia has emerged as a region with the highest human deprivation: measured in human capabilities and access to opportunities; this far exceeds income deprivation and contrasts sharply with the presence of large armies and modern weapons. Military spending has gone up since 1987 in proportion to GNP and approximately US$ 14 billion are spent annually on two of the largest armies in a region where till some years ago the ratio of soldiers to doctors at the end of the 90s stood at 6:1.[14]

It is now accepted that the basic assumptions of economic reform policies were wrong on three counts with regard to South

Asia: firstly, conditions were not right for introducing reforms; secondly, the link between public and private investment was ignored when South Asian governments cut back on public expenditure; and thirdly, the use of capital-intensive technologies affected small producers the worst. Negative indicators are the only aspect in which the region still stands united. With SAARC failing to take off, intra-regional trade among the nations is as low as 3.9 per cent of the region's GDP even as illicit trade networks thrive. Resources, such as land, remain concentrated and the benefits of growth are recycled among small elites. Women bear the greatest burden of human deprivation in South Asia. The region's Gender Equality Measure (GEM), which reflects economic and political opportunities open to women as compared to men, shows the lowest value (0.23), among all regions in the world. Though Sri Lanka stands out with relatively high human development indicators, women in South Asia largely "suffer greater poverty of educational, health, economic, political and legal opportunities, relative both to their male counterparts and to women around the world.... are several factors that transcend class, religion, culture and locality and affect the lives of all South Asian women".[15] The depth of poverty, particularly for the bottom 20 per cent income group, cannot be imagined. Nor can it be covered up by the glitz of modern markets.

Response from Women's Studies

Growth of inequalities, some argue, does not necessarily reflect that gender inequalities are inherent to globalization processes; these may depend on the specific location of women as well as the general political situation. The question that needs to be answered is whether in societies grounded in patriarchal cultures can gender-based gaps be narrowed when social inequity is on the rise? There is evidence to show that while macro-trends affect all marginalized groups, they are not gender neutral.[16] The international debates, of the 70s and 80s, generated an ideological critique of economic development and social policy. The new international packages are based on models indifferent to gender divisions in household and national economies.[17] While patriarchy emerges as a necessary concept to critique development, in view of multiplicity and overlapping forms of oppression, the mediations between patriarchy and other forms of classification such as caste, class and religion or ethnicity need to be more specifically examined. The focus on South Asian women, as a descriptive though non-homogeneous category, serves a useful purpose to lay out the contextual terrain within which women's issues and experiences need to be examined.

Research in the area of women's studies focuses on globalization, work and women's lives from a range of perspectives. With overwhelming evidence of the impact of globalization policies on women in South Asia showing a decline, a few champion neo-liberal strategies while others attribute this to flaws in implementation: while some economists taking a broad universalist approach are positive about the impact of trade liberalization on gender, the feminist view focuses on micro-level complexity, employs multi-dimensional concepts of gender and is less positive about the impact of trade liberalization on gender: the two perspectives occupy different domains and are not easily integrated.[18] Some refer to an 'unevenness' and, 'mixed' impact; others draw attention to the phenomenon of 'feminization,' and 'flexibilization' to argue that since there is increased mobility, there is a window of opportunity. On the contrary, several case studies show that the restructuring of labour contracts in the name of flexibility "is much more likely to take place in a gender differentiated way than to be a force for overcoming the sexual division of labour".[19] An overwhelming range of scholars have, however, observed that "capitalist market forces and employment based on imperialist exploitation cannot liberate women from patriarchal exploitation that is the very condition for their entry into wage labour in multinational factories producing for the world market. In the long run, capitalism and imperialism only perpetuate and may even reinforce patriarchal relations of production, which in turn reinforce capitalist and imperialist relations of production".[20]

Does increased labour mobility lead to breakdown of the entrenched patterns of work distribution and allocation along lines of the sexual division of labour? Can the weakening of state structures reduce its intervention to enhance women's, and men's, ability to access basic needs and services and does the efficiency of the market integrate them into the developmental processes despite their location in groups/communities denied access to the means of production? While answers to specific questions would vary, depending on the region, country or social group being studied, the overall thrust of the neo-liberal offensive towards increasing social inequalities is now well-documented. Very early on when these policies were adopted doubts were expressed as to "whether the new economic policy directions are sufficiently informed and alive to all the major stresses and constraints faced by the Indian economy and consequently, whether the initiatives/ remedies are not concentrated on a narrower range of ailments which can create their own distortions on a wider socio-political-economic front. The experience of other countries, with policies aimed at achieving stabilization (correction of macro-economic imbalance in the short run), and structural adjustment (modifying structural parameters of the economy so as to control imbalances as well as to stimulate growth in the middle term) do suggest that there are some groups which take the brunt of these policies more than others: one such group being poor women".[21]

Significantly, a basic constraint has been the non-availability of data on a disaggregated basis. This makes comparisons, both country-based as well as between male-female ratios, difficult since comparable data sets are difficult to obtain. Nevertheless, some headway has been made in recent years with the official agencies, specifically since the Human Development Reports initiative came to be adopted at the regional and national levels. State agency initiatives have been complemented by debates on methodological issues as well as specific interventions pertaining to definitions and categories used in both qualitative and quantitative analysis and systems of national accounting (SNA), which largely make women's work and contribution invisible and obliterate by ignoring or under-estimating household based services. Studies have pointed to the need to draw on time-use statistics though it is widely felt that much more needs to be done in this direction.

Impact on Women in South Asia

The Asia-Pacific region witnessed both changes and catastrophes accompanying globalization processes. The instabilities which showed up in the mid-90s drove home the point that with the market, power and wealth get concentrated in the hands of a select band of people, nations and corporations.[22] Women experienced the depth of suffering, brutality and indignities over the past decade, which was marked by an overall increase in concentration of incomes, resources and wealth among a few – be they individuals, corporations or countries. It was found that "the benefits of competitive markets and other mainstays of globalization such as information technology have been skewed towards the elite minority of South Asian women. The new markets, tools, and rules of this global era have failed to alleviate the poverty of most of South Asia's women".[23] On the whole, planned policies have made no positive intervention for women's entry in the labour market and whether micro-initiatives can counter macro-trends and deal with constraints in the face of reduced intervention by the state remains an issue.[24]

Promoting gender equality is a key objective of the Millennium Declaration adopted by the UN in 2000 to eradicate poverty, promote human dignity and equality and achieve peace, democracy and environmental stability. While space does not allow for detailed discussion with regard to each country, certain trends are delineated. Maldives and Bhutan, also part of SAARC, are not discussed since not much information is available.

Sri Lanka, dependent on a single commodity for export – tea – was adversely affected by falling international prices. As job opportunities and incomes declined, the country became torn with ethnic strife and armed insurgency good enough to push it many decades backwards. The country, first to adopt SAP, has seen a collapse of the modern welfare state and the throttling of both democratic debate and institutions even as women have experienced the ravages of militarization in their daily lives.[25]

The divergence between economic growth and human development is greater in Pakistan. Since the early 1990s, the problem of poverty has been intensified because of the slowing down of economic activity; SAP imposed heavy burdens on the poor; while the burden of indirect taxation has fallen disproportionately on the lower income groups. As rural poverty increased so did male out-migration in the 1990s, making reliance on women's earnings vital for the economic survival of poor households. Dependence on agricultural wage work, as the main source of employment, is still higher for rural men than rural women though there is evidence of their increasing involvement; the large majority of rural women still work as unpaid family labour; 1991 data indicates that female labour force participation rates in rural Pakistan range between 43 and 57 per cent. Women continue to be seen as a group marginal with their needs not being addressed in macro-economic policies.[26]

Bangladesh had an early success in reducing poverty but subsequently since 1985 poverty rates have risen faster than any historically observed so far. Increasingly, with loss of land and livelihood, it also became clear that families could not survive on incomes of 'male breadwinners' alone, forcing and felicitating women's entry into factory employment. Women garment workers in Bangladesh are in the centre of debates on labour market patterns, feminization, labour standards and the MFA clauses, specifically in the context of quotas. The country's economic security is in jeopardy with private patents having grave implications for community rights. Cuts in subsidies make competition for local producers more difficult to withstand. In the sphere of banking and finance, the gates have been opened to foreign giants without development of an internal institutional base. This shall result in casting many to 'death'.[27]

Nepal, one of the least developed countries in the world, is integrated into the global market at a highly disadvantageous level. The political elite, represented by the three dominant caste groups, controls most of the land and resources and the 1990s have seen mobilization around these issues. Approximately, 40 per cent of the population lives in absolute poverty in abject conditions. Women, who contribute more than men in terms of agricultural work as well as within the household economy, find that the number of hours they work have increased in the last decade with a shift to cash cropping. There is also an increase in non-agricultural activities. Studies talk of 'asymmetry' and a downward trend in women's control over decision-making with the increase in cash transactions and in terms of women's asset holding and credit facilities. Migration amongst women in the age group of 12-25 is high, exposing them to trafficking and renders them vulnerable to crime and violence; "income inequalities have increased, tearing the existing social fabric which may lead to an explosive political situation".[28]

India shares with its neighbours some of the root causes for its social backwardness and also a visible increase in social as well as gender-based disparities. It records poor human development indices. There is concentration of land in most states, except in Kerala and West Bengal and a high degree of differentiation; the landless rural masses lack employment and the purchasing power to acquire minimum food requirements and the cities are teeming with migrants in search of employment. There have been rapid changes with globalization: in patterns of work, in nature of consumption and access to goods and services. This has led to increasing insecurities and a volatility of incomes along with a collapse of stable livelihoods. Development policies have failed to generate a more socially equitable system and there are glaring inequalities based on caste, class and gender with women being the most discriminated against in all these sub-categories. This is reflected in the intensification of various social struggles, including struggles by women.[29]

Targetting the Peasant Base of South Asian Economies

While globalization primarily conjures images of urban industrial growth, entry into the agricultural sector has been a primary focus of MNCs and a visible expansion of agro-business operations into remote corners of South Asia is being achieved through cuts in agricultural subsidies, waiving of exemptions through WTO, the Uruguay Rounds and the invoking of TRIMS. In a classic replay of the colonial economy syndrome economic expansion aims at developing the metropolis with no backward or forward linkages with the local economy developing. The results in India have become obvious in recent years with the combined phenomenon of farmers' suicides and starvation deaths. Further, reduction of public investment in infrastructure reinforces existing regional inequality in availability of required facilities. While more is known about the Indian situation, there are similar developments elsewhere in the region.

In India, rural employment during the period 1993-94 to 1999-2000 grew at the very low annual rate of less than 0.6 per cent per annum, lower than any previous period in post-independence history, and well below the rate of growth of rural population. The WTO agreement on agriculture, signed in 1995, affected developing countries adversely since the highly subsidized products of the developed world were dumped on the international market with a clear advantage while the Third World producers could not compete. Agriculture, which still accounts for nearly two-thirds of the working population in the rural areas and 70 per cent of rural women's employment, has had to bear the main brunt of these imbalances; changes affect women the most and the burden too falls disproportionately on women from small or marginal farmer families and rural labour households. Over the 1990s, the rate of growth of foodgrain production dropped; rates of growth of farm business incomes declined and there was a significant shift in income distribution in the economy away from agriculture. Farmers are being squeezed by rising costs of inputs, reduction of subsidies, and reduced public investment in the rural areas; even as their products compete with imports from developed countries which are based on high and rising real levels of actual subsidy. This has a negative impact on the demand for agricultural labour. The livelihood crisis of the farming community has disproportionate adverse effects on women and girl children given the existing gender inequalities. Market-induced diversification of agricultural production marks a shift away from food to cash crops, placing the lower ranks of the peasantry at greater disadvantage vis-à-vis the international market for basic food requirements. Free trade regimes ensure participation of the poor on unequal terms in market transactions in the agrarian sector. In the face of a prolonged fall in global primary product prices, unable to obtain private or bank loans, poor and small peasants have been the first to lose what little land and other assets they had. Suicides, owing to indebtedness, started as far back as 1998. Data shows a rise in landlessness and generalized distress with even former rich peasants being reduced to penury and low purchasing power. Members of cultivating households, who had never worked earlier for wages, are now forced to hire themselves out for labour. The massive rise in farm debt and loss of rural purchasing power is reflected in an unprecedented decline of foodgrain absorption per capita in India. This has come down to 155 kg per annum as compared to around 175 kg only six years ago implying an even larger decline in rural India. "India's farmers and labourers are taking the biggest beating ever since colonial times and the great depression." The impact on women is both direct and indirect: faced with shortages women and girl children are disproportionately disadvantaged in the household.[30] These shortfalls are accompanied by cuts in food subsidies and curtailment of the Public Distribution Scheme.[31] Clear links can be established between the cuts in spending on poverty alleviation schemes which checked rural debt and the declining health of the people. One estimate puts the figure for poverty levels in India as high as approximately 75 per cent of rural households. This is concentrated in households comprised of rural labour, *Dalits* and those which are women-headed: categories which repeatedly emerge as overlapping in aspects of human development and poverty indices. In fact, total annual subsidy on food in India is actually only about 0.6 per cent of national income, which is much lower than what farmers in the 'North', who also dominate the global wheat market, continue to get.[32] A correlation may be drawn between the increasing destitution of women and the policy of reduced availability of public work concomitant with cuts in government spending. With reduced opportunities for off-farm work, women from the landless groups have become more vulnerable. In agriculture women are involved in cultivation operations, livestock husbandry and off-farm activities. While much of this work is in the subsistence sector, wage work component remains high. There is large-scale displacement of women from traditional work, forcing many to migrate. Increasing social violence against women has also to be understood against this backdrop. Meanwhile, in the South Indian states, which deviated from the SAP requirements, during this period poverty declined.[33]

The opening up of the agricultural sector has brought back contract farming whereby farmers sell their produce to the multinational corporations (MNCs) at a price determined exclusively by the latter for agro-processing or seeds. Fewer than 10 transnational companies today virtually control the worldwide food chain; less than five companies control 98 per cent of the world's export market in the following products: wheat, corn, coffee, tea, pineapple, cotton, tobacco, jute, and forest products. Global monopolies promote corporate control of food supply, extending their domination to nations' economic and natural resources while omitting and erasing community rights.[34] Further, the rich biodiversity and indigenous knowledge conserved through traditional community-based systems, in which women traditionally played a significant role, today stand threatened. New agreements such as TRIPS encourage private ownership and piracy of indigenous knowledge: MNCs such as W.R. Grace, RiceTec Inc., Sabinsa Corp., Monsanito and Pioneer Hi-bred/Du Pont, all from the USA, sought to register patents on neem, basmati, black pepper and sarson.[35] Further, nearly 3,000 varieties of genetically engineered crops, developed, field tested and grown in the US are up for sale by companies such as Monsanto, Ciba-Geigy, Du Pont and Upjohn along with the largest commercial seed companies which have invested in genetic engineering to expand their control over the increasingly monopolized food industry through new seeds and patent laws. Several lakh women in India and other parts of South Asia have been protesting against these through nation-wide campaigns.

Similar disturbing developments can be seen with regard to aquaculture. FAO and the World Bank openly support environmentally harmful technology models which contribute depletion of marine resources through trawl fisheries. Several hundred miles of shoreline in India and Bangladesh are adversely affected. Apart from economic vicissitude, changes in coastal farming patterns have made the coastline more vulnerable to natural calamities. The introduction of sluice gates and fish ponds etc. interferes with both fishing activities and the spread of flood water.[36] Marine authorities actively collude with MNCs and large private companies to give them access to natural resources. Commercial aquaculture of the 1980s and 1990s which promotes mono-culture marks a significant change in the cultural as well as working lives of the coastal people. In India marine produce rose from 92,691 tonnes in 1983-84 to 2,44,000 tonnes in 1993-94, with large tracts of cultivable land in Orissa, Andhra Pradesh and Tamil Nadu becoming prawn farms resulting in decline of wage work available, increase in distance covered in search of work as well as dependence on a contractors or middleman, drastic decline in animal husbandry work, and village commons becoming unavailable. The work available to women under prawn cultivation is strenuous, marginal and low paid: clearing of moss from tanks, catching prawn seed from the sea, de-shelling snails and peeling prawns and piece-rate and contract work are common; although cash wages have gone up slightly the number of days of work have gone down. There is a shortage of drinking water and wood fuel; even open fields for toilet purposes are no longer available. Further, subsistence requirement for food also have to be met from market purchases.

The traditionally high involvement of women in agriculture in the region is borne out by the fact that in Nepal it is estimated to be as high as 93.7 per cent, anything between 78 per cent and 86 per cent for India, 66.4 per cent for Pakistan and 41.5 per cent for Sri Lanka.

In Bangladesh, 70 per cent of the people have become functionally landless and a huge segment lives below the poverty line. The early 1990s witnessed a drastic slowdown in growth of rice production in Bangladesh; a high incidence of male desertion and burgeoning of female-headed households with no resources or assets. Of the over 21 million women in the labour force, a significant section is in agriculture and the female component in the rural labour force has increased. Privatization of state-owned enterprises and withdrawal of subsidies, particularly from agricultural inputs and consumer subsidies, as well as imposition of user fees in health services have had an adverse impact.[37]

In Sri Lanka, SAP had an early and "overall impact as well as adverse consequences for women in their multiple roles. While growth rates increased, exports grew and entrepreneurs, exporters and business flourished, terms of trade deteriorated..." A spiralling cost of living affected low income families, unemployment rates of women doubled that of men from the eighties; the benefits of economic growth did not 'trickle down' and female-headed households were most adversely affected. The major casualty was the reduction in the food subsidies and the 'conversion' of the food ration to food stamps of fixed value decreased the calorie consumption of the poor. The proportion of the female labour force aged between 10 and 14 years doubled by the mid-80s. Women's rights were eroded through land settlement policies, including in the Mahaweli Development Programme even as workloads increased. Whereas earlier state policy was supportive of small-holding agriculture, this changed under the IMF-WB conditionalities. In 1996 a World Bank study estimated that in the years to come, 1.8 million small-farm farmers would have to give up their agricultural activities. While the plantation sector still engages 68 per cent of the agricultural women, in paddy farming they carry out only 30 per cent of the tasks. Trading in formal and informal sectors is a male-dominated activity. Employment of women in agriculture declined from 61.3 per cent in 1969-70 to 49.1 per cent in 1980-81 resulting in a high level of out-migration of rural women to urban areas or overseas, concomitant with the breakdown of agriculture and cottage industries. With the opening up of the economy GDP went down, and agricultural production declined and from being a country which had achieved successes in human development and low income disparities alongside relatively high food securities, after two decades of SAP Sri Lanka was reduced to being a country of extreme forms of poverty, hunger, child, malnourishment, and a low birth rate, alongside other compendiums, such as high level of inequalities, socio-political unrest, war and repression. Several hundred thousand women ended up moving to Free Trade Zones set up in the country since 1978; others went to the Middle East as maids. Today, infrastructural support is being provided to woo multinationals while the agricultural communities are forced to give up livelihood patterns evolved over thousands of years. While many blame this on the civil disturbances, the contribution of SAP to this situation needs to be explored. Since women's activity is primarily concentrated in the informal sector, growth strategies which adversely affect the informal sector are likely to further undermine women's role and status.[38]

The SAP experience in Sri Lanka and elsewhere has been described as a 'one-way process' in which developing societies have had to adjust to the needs, demands and conditions of developed countries. Clearly, the international division of labour "not only extracts the surplus from the labour of workers but in its convergence with the gender division of labour and patriarchal social relations, reinforces the subordination of women workers". Market liberalization has not generated employment growth commensurate with economic growth even as marked structural shifts have taken place in the economy from agriculture to manufacturing and services. Several local industries such as handloom 'collapsed' through inability to compete in the market economy, and the lack of diversification in the rural economy. The policy bias against the small producer has not been conducive to development in the small scale and informal sector in which the majority of women workers are located.[39]

In Pakistan, "the vast majority of women in the less industrialized South still live in rural agrarian economic structures and their issues are inextricably linked to macro-level issues of the economy, poverty, environment and rural agro-industrial development." The thrust towards large-scale farming and capital formation is detrimental to the social sectors and less-advantaged citizenry. Rural poverty has increased considerably in the 1990s and so has reliance on women's earnings, making it vital for the economic survival of poor households. Dependence on agricultural wage work as the main source of employment is higher for rural women although most still work as unpaid family labour. The

1991 data for Pakistan indicated that female labour force participation rates in rural areas ranged between 43 per cent and 57 per cent, with evidence of increasing involvement with increase in male out-migration.[40]

In Nepal, there is continuous reference to degradation of the resource base, mainly land and forest. In a remote district, Humla, 350 people died in 1998 due to hunger, when the subsistence crop failed and government could not make food available due to lack of funds to transport food. A large number of families moved across the Indian border walking 7-8 days, while others just died. It was earlier estimated that 33 of Nepal's 75 districts would be food-deficient by 2000 while only seven would be food-surplus. The hill districts have emerged as areas of chronic food shortages. Nearly 47 per cent of the hill population experience food deficits, while productivity of land has stagnated in the Terai region as well, despite increasing use of fertilizers.[41] The proportion of people below the poverty line increased from 40 per cent in 1975-76 to 49 per cent in 1991-92. Nepal has reported a decline in food securities from the mid-1980s onwards and this period has seen its conversion from rice-exporting status to being a rice-importer as well as dependence on imports to meet atleast 30 per cent of its foodgrains requirements. While commons and grazing lands are being converted into private property by influential people, skewed land ownership patterns deny the majority of households any access to land. Since non-farm employment being unavailable, rural households have faced greater hardships in earning their livelihood in recent years and the majority need to do multiple types of work to survive. There is an evident decline in per capita food production, resulting in 65 per cent of children in Nepal between the age of six months to six years being malnourished, female children and women being particularly affected. Meanwhile, the government responsibility for food distribution has been curtailed resulting in 'unequal spatial distribution of food'. Seven government companies, which provided the institutional framework for support of prices of agricultural products and maintained buffer stocks for emergencies, were dissolved. Unequal access to food often overlaps with the traditional caste divisions, with 65-67 per cent of households of occupational castes featuring in the BPL category. Connectivity with markets, in the absence of increasing labour opportunities, has exposed the population to newer risks, including the outflow of local population and, more specifically, trafficking in women. The prevailing deficit in food consumption is not the result of a particular disaster, but is persisting from year to year. Clearly, the continuing unequal terms of trade have adversely affected food security in the rural areas.

The subject of women's rights to land and forests, along with that of access to resources and food security, has emerged as a central concern in social movements in the region.[42] Recent developments have destroyed the agrarian economy of the South Asian region and made the landless poor more vulnerable. Today, there is a real possibility of the 'family farm' disappearing as has happened in countries such as Thailand, and to some extent Sri Lanka, countries which adopted the liberalization model much ahead of the others. What are the social implications of this since the family farm has existed in South Asian history as a primary unit of community life, social organization and is also a primary decision-making unit? What implications do these trends have for women, more so when change comes alongside fundamentalist ideologies which harp upon women's 'traditional' roles? In contradiction with the politico-ideological climate, many regions which were previously home to these agricultural communities are today promoted as eco-tourism spots or as farm land for urban elites while women, denied work opportunities closer to home end up getting caught in sex-trafficking rackets in order to provide for their families. Nepal, Bangladesh and India are important junctions in this nexus while Pakistan too has emerged as important, especially for trafficking in children. The links between policies, the emerging social reality and the nature of political conflict emerging in South Asia need to be explored further.

Women and Work in the Urban Economy

In South Asia, only a very small section of women are in formal sector employment, except in Sri Lanka where women comprise nearly 45 per cent of the workers in this sector. Although it is seen to be increasing in India, it is still only 18 per cent while the corresponding figure for Nepal is 15.6 per cent; in Bangladesh women are 13 per cent in the public (formal) and 22 per cent in the private (formal) sector. Women's role in the informal sector has clearly grown even as the informal sector itself has grown throughout South Asia. It is estimated that in Bangladesh, women labour force in this sector grew from 44 per cent in 1983-84 to 75 per cent in 1995-96. Data for Nepal suggests that 83.7 per cent women were self-employed with no separate data being available for the informal sector.[43] In India, there was a corresponding growth from 93.97 per cent to 95.79, between 1981 and 1991. Globalization processes have been marked by industrial slowdown and de-industrialization in countries such as India. NSS data showed a very significant deceleration for both rural and urban areas, with the annual rate of growth of rural employment falling to as low as two-thirds of a per cent over the period 1993-94 to 1999-2000. This was "the lowest rate of growth of rural employment in post-independence history".[44]

Attention has repeatedly been drawn to continuing poverty and its relation with inadequate employment generation. This becomes crucial with attempts to rationalize and restructure the economy and the state moving from a model of significant control over modern industry to lesser involvement, as is happening in India. It was thus far recognized that planned strategies were required to ensure social goals and therefore large-scale investments were made in core areas. There is a change even in these areas despite evidence that the dynamic sectors in industry were precisely those in which the state had invested. Multi-national companies (MNCs) and transnational corporations (TNCs) enjoy uncurbed rights to exploit the vast markets and cheap labour of these countries. Outsourcing of jobs has taken various forms over the years: within a country from organized to unorganized sector and movement of manufacturing jobs from high wage countries to low wage countries. The movement of IT sector jobs from countries in the North to countries like India, China and Brazil is one of the newer forms of outsourcing, specifically in the IT-enabled industries. A fifth of the 'Fortune 1000' firms already have a back office address in India with a likelihood of increase.

In Bangladesh, while the new export sector of readymade garments has provided employment to women, total employment in aggregate manufacturing has declined in both relative and absolute terms. Garment factories had gone up from just four in 1978 to 2,400 in 1995, employing 1.2 million workers, 90 per cent of whom were women under the age of 25, comprising 70 per cent of women in wage employment in the country. Nevertheless a "significant deindustrialization, particularly in the traditional sectors which have suffered from import penetration"[45] was observed. Open unemployment has risen from 1.8 per cent of the labour force to 4.9 per cent while underemployment in 2000 was estimated to be as high as 31 per cent. Some argue that poverty and continuing economic crisis opened a 'window' of opportunities for widening of women's role in the economy. Women's cheap labour led to their share of the labour market in garments, textiles, pharmaceuticals, electronics and food processing, particularly shrimp exports. In two export promotion zones 67.5 per cent of the workers were women in the early 1990s. Wage differentials, to the tune of almost 50 per cent, made female labour an attractive, proposition, particularly in the garments industry. Though women occupy critical space in export-oriented industries, the chances of 'fair practices' being carried out remain limited as the implementation of social clauses threatens competing demands of the market for profits. Questioning the benefits of integration of women into the global market, scholars have pointed to the "insecurity of employment, enforced overtime, absence of benefits such as maternity leave". Studies of urban employment point to the extreme volatility across organized and unorganized sectors, particularly in manufacturing. These contribute to an extreme and continuous pressure on the wages and incomes of the majority of women workers to levels far below subsistence levels.

The euphoria over globalization was justified by many on the grounds of 'feminization' of the labour force. Sri Lanka entered the network of Third World Free Trade Zones in 1978, by establishing the Investment Promotion Zone at Katunayuake. The work remains concentrated in ill-paid categories and insecure conditions with low bargaining potential, in the lower ranks of the industrial pyramid, subject to authority and repressive controls exercised by managerial staff as well as state apparatus. Studies show that women found work conditions so appalling that four strikes took place between 1980 and 1984 in a unit which had a 95 per cent female workforce; work stoppages also took place in other units to protect denial of minimum wage and long hours of work, for improvement of toilet facilities and payment of wages before the Christmas festivities.[46] The real face of 'work opportunity' in urban industries in the global era can be seen from the fact that on occasions women garment workers in Sri Lanka, as also leather workers in NOIDA, India, protested restrictions on the use of the toilet in number of times and duration of visits, including on pregnant women; as well as on breaks to drink water. Struggles met with a combined and ferocious onslaught from the employers and governmental machinery with attacks on union members being a common feature, along with aggressive sexual behaviour by male supervisory staff. While their transformation into urban workers partially liberates young women from rural paternalistic control structures, they also become subject to new forms of subordination.[47] Subsequently, women's employment in the urban sector did not increase in any consistent or substantial manner; pointing to the fact that 'feminization' emerges as a temporary strategy to take advantage of lower wage rates prevailing for women workers and peters off as equalization occurs.[48] In Pakistan, the women's workforce remains a fraction of a fairly small industrial workforce. The contract system makes women's visibility even poorer, although electronics and other TNC-controlled industries do employ women, mostly in the Punjab province. Women are also found in food, textiles, footwear, printing and publishing and drugs and pharmaceuticals, mainly in the small-scale sector but employment in the formal sector is below 5 per cent. From 1989 onwards, a more liberal policy was adopted by the Pakistan government in the face of increasingly larger number of women being drawn into the job market since urban households could no longer subsist on single incomes.[49]

Certain common features are visible in South Asia: it appears that "employment generation in South Asian countries has so far not benefited much from WTO".[50] Changes visible in the labour market are in the direction of flexibility, casualization and informalization of employment, and proliferation of what are variably called atypical, precarious, or contingent jobs – some of the phrases commonly used to describe salient aspects of these changes. While some still argue that it is "difficult to generalize about the gender impact of globalization," nevertheless it is clear that new employment creation has been in the nature of "irregular, often precarious forms of work" with proliferation of "informal activities, subcontracting, part-time work, self-employment and home-based work". Demand for women's unpaid labour increases with economic distress but is "injurious to women because it tends to strengthen the 'homemaker' stereotype. An unequal burden of domestic work at home and a marginal position in the labour market might tend to reinforce each other, making it harder for women to break out of the role of dependent and secondary bread-winner within the family".[51] There are several studies of the urban informal sector and women's labour in Asian countries and the broader implications of these trends. Home-based work – a survival strategy for millions of families – for capital helps to further cut costs. For the worker, even the status of a 'worker' is in limbo and attempts to cover these millions of women through some kind of legislation have failed.[52] In developing economies slow growth accompanied by growing competition and costs involved led to decreasing formal sector employment and a tendency for women's employment in the formal sector to diminish in relation to that of men as visible in the 90s.[53] Evidence suggests that recessions, economic stagnation and slow growth have more negative effects on women's employment than that of men. Studies point to the apparent commonality of economic experience across the very disparate countries of the region, which differ in size, resource endowment, particular social and political configurations and patterns of constraints with regard to increasing inequalities of income, deceleration in employment generation, stagnation or increase in levels of poverty, relative decline of manufacturing, and deterioration in the quality of employment. There is evidence of market failure, at both macro-economic and micro-economic levels, as well as strong evidence of close positive link between public and private investment, leading to a demand constraint in view of unequal asset and income distribution and a limited home market.[54]

There are long-term implications of these changes: women have emerged on a regular basis as workers; while this places some women at an advantage in terms of status within the household and has implications for intra-household dynamics as well as for their self-image and self-esteem, given the fact that the large majority enter a stagnant and depressed job market this cannot be seen only as a positive development.[55] Characteristically, state and social response to these developments remains by and large unchanged and they continue to be viewed as supplementary or subsidiary workers. While the transition to urban areas as workers partially liberates young women from rural paternalistic control structures, they also become subject to new forms of subordination. Concentrated in the lower ranks of the industrial pyramid, they are subjected to authority and repressive controls exercised by managerial staff as well as state apparatus.[56]

A pertinent question asked is: does 'work' always empower women? The presumption that paid employment ends discrimination and improves women's status has been critically examined by several scholars. A distinction is drawn with regard to the oppression faced by women in terms of transition from private patriarchy to a form of public patriarchy. The former is based on the "relative exclusion of women from arenas of social life other than the household and the appropriation of their services by individual patriarchs within the confines of the home. Public patriarchy is based on employment and the state; women are no longer excluded from the public arena, but subordinated within it".[57]

Paradox of Increasing Oppression and Growing Aspirations

In South Asia, today, there is a visible paradox between women's changing aspirations and the growing violence against them.

Retrogressive political ideologies, fundamentalism and state power present a combination, which makes this violence socially acceptable even though the link between economic policies, violence and fundamentalism is rife with tension. Insensitivity to the growing violence against women has increased and women's lives are circumscribed in numerous ways. Fundamentalism cements the link between patriarchy and right-wing forces at the ideological plane to make possible a neo-liberal 'grandslam'. Not surprisingly women have been outspoken critics of both the economic and the political fall-out of globalization. The women's movement consistently counters projection of a homogenized construction of the woman and attempts to speak on behalf of the wide mass of women in the region. Predicated on the non-homogeneity of the category of 'woman' and the diversity of experience, it challenges stereotypes of women's roles within patriarchal constructs at several levels. Much has been written in recent years on how communal violence and ideology 'reconfigure' women's experiences and facilitate the formation of particular identities which then determine women's position vis-à-vis communities and the state.[58] Dichotomies of 'good' and 'bad' women are invoked and the notion of honour of a community gets tied up with perpetration of violence against women of the 'other'.

Significantly, perceptions of women's roles are also caught in the cleft between glamorous images of the 'new' woman of the global era and the sanctions imposed by fundamentalists. While the competitive spirit of globalization projects both achievement and oppression as phenomenon born out of individual experiences, fundamentalist assertions deny the commonality of gender-based violence by asserting divisive community-based identities. Women come under pressure from the contentious claims of rival fundamentalisms; militant activists in different regions who also impose their respective 'codes' on women. These pose an immense challenge for the contemporary women's movement since it has to position itself in favour of women's right amidst the maze of identity politics, even as women become targets of violence inflicted upon them by militants who have themselves shown scant respect for human/democratic rights it has to stand up against majority fundamentalism to assert diversity and pluralism as basic tenets; at the same time, it needs to articulate its opposition to violations of human rights by the state in the name of national security. The fact remains that the success of women's organizations in countering violence is contingent upon the strength of democratic polity in the region. This, in turn, is today dependent upon social movements countering imperialist globalization.

In this context it is important to interrogate the link drawn between free market ideology and its projection as being synonymous with modernity when the driving force is imperialist globalization which embraces modernization even as it connives with fundamentalism and a regressive social order. There is an evident complicity of so-called modern phenomenon with ideologies which uphold patriarchal discrimination. The intensification and spread of dowry and dowry-related violence in India offers a clear example of how consumerism perpetrates crime which is sought to be passed off as 'tradition'.[59] Similarly, there are the so-called 'honour' killings, "indicative of a reformulation of the traditional discourse of honour as a means to justify the murder of women for social and economic reasons".[60] Every second a Pakistani woman is now believed to be a direct or indirect victim of violence. Practices that were earlier "confined to rural pockets in feudal and tribal belts have now spread to urban centres" and are indicative of "retrogressive social attitudes not only among the law enforcement agencies and the judiciary but also among the highest political decision-makers". In the Pakistan Senate, a resolution condemning 'honour' killings was not only thrown out but abusive language was used against women. 'Honour' killings are today also regularly reported from Haryana and Uttar Pradesh in North India. The disjunction between the image and the social reality adds to the intensity of social conflict, resulting in violent eruptions.[61]

The reality defies a homogenized construction of the woman is evident from the fact that alongside the victim of 'honour' killings stands the 'new woman' – professional, entrepreneur, manageress, executive, officer – who features prominently in public space in many parts of Asia. She definitely stands to gain from the process of reforms, through the expansion of horizons both in the personal and public domains; she imbibes the slogan of equality and opportunity to be more articulate and assertive; she is the independent young woman projected by the media who is constantly being asked to make choices, no matter that the choices offered to her are within the parameters of free market ideology. She straddles the metropolitan space in Third World countries, presented through a world of fashion and glamour, flashing new energy, supreme confidence taking in the infectious freedom in the air; yet she carries within herself the perplexities born of a social dilemma.[62] This is personified by the commodified woman, brand ambassador for consumer products, projected as the new role model who appears to symbolize achievement and independence in the most individuated form co-existing with the secluded woman. This phenomenon throws up new icons represented in India by Sushmita Sen and Aishwarya Rai alongside militant fundamentalist women leaders. While opposition to these new icons comes from the women's movement, right-wing ideologues also decry 'western' culture in opposition to indigenous values. Thus, there is a continuous need for the movement to interrogate crass commercialism and exploitation of women's bodies from a progressive standpoint and to challenge retrogressive perspectives of opposition to the changing reality based on perspectives which further restrict women's spaces.[63]

The response of the state, how it views women in its official policies and the abdication of its role assumes significance in this context. There is a continued need to pressurize the state which interacts with individuals, social groups as well as institutions with purposeful bias and without neutrality. The state operates within unequal structures as well as through structures which maintain and perpetuate inequality. Homogenized conceptions of womanhood and fundamentalist prescripts serve as instruments of moral policing even as policies ignore the needs of the vast mass of women who constitute the labouring poor and workers. Even as the corporate world uses the brand icons to promote consumerism, the state denies to the masses basic facilities which adds to women's physical burdens while it also rules out the scope for developing a social dynamics which may facilitate social change.

The combined effect of corporate globalization and retrogressive ideology is most visible in the response of South Asian states to the issue of son preference and the 'missing' girl child. The new ideological onslaught bolsters discriminatory attitudes towards women and uses the iconic woman to boost consumerist sales. However, it does feel the need to question prevalent ideological perceptions which allow new technologies and scientific achievements to perpetuate son preference and pre-birth sex selection. Though the adverse sex ratio is a feature common to the region, issues of reproductive rights and women's health continue to be seen primarily in the context of their reproductive role and states are eager to achieve 'targets' of control of women's fertility rather than address the problem of the missing girl child. Inclusion of the health agenda in every multilateral aid agreement and MNCs gives a push to hazardous contraceptives which continue to be tried, tested and continue to be imposed on Third World women.[64]

The assertion of agency by women in South Asia in the face of such odds signifies the tremendous fortitude and courage with which women in this region have stood up to the challenges thrown. Recent decades have seen women actively in the forefront of movements for democratic change. Further, in movements which may not strictly fall within the ambit of what is stereotypically seen as women's issues, they have emerged as active participants, organizers and even leaders. Despite social opposition and repression, they have joined the ranks of those working for literacy, against displacement, for environmental protection and against alcoholism. They have braved the wrath of the state in the fight against state-supported fundamentalism and the onslaught on human rights; worked for peace in riot-torn situations and fought to build unity in the midst of ethno-religious divides and voiced their opposition to criminalization of politics and militarization. At the end of an eventful century and the most remarkable millennium in the history of humankind, one can surely join the great social historian of our times, E.J. Hobsbawm in emphasizing that women's assertion of active agency is one of the most significant expressions of the democratic upsurge in this period.[65] This has been most visible on the political front at the level of women's participation in institutions of decision-making, particularly in local self-government. However, since "political marginality cannot be countered only by a numerically expanded presence", local democracy, decentralization and political representation, including reservation, have emerged as significant issues to achieve the goal of social transformation not merely to confront patriarchy but also as an attempt to widen the democratic base of political institutions.[66]

This is important at a time when the democratic process itself is being undermined through political structures at the macro level, particularly through the intervention of the Bretton Woods institutions. Can women's role in decision-making be enhanced while democratic processes are subverted? The political processes that globalization generates aim at undoing the ideological gains of the twentieth century. The new structures and protagonists of world power are relatively anonymous and lack accountability. The power of the macro-structures and mega corporations is too enormous to be wished away or presumed to be likely to wither away. While nation-states buckle under these immense pressures, social movements which uphold transformative social agendas need to intervene. The women's movement has emerged as one of the most powerful and sustained blocs struggling against imperialist globalization to strengthen forces of peace, progress and development, so that in the new millennium the world can become a better place to live in. As the South Asian experience shows, these are complex issues to which responses have to be negotiated through concrete interventions as well as ideological debate and the women's movement has to continuously prepare itself to withstand the challenges that lie ahead.

NOTES

1. S.J. Huntington, 1997, *The Clash of Civilisations and the Re-Making of the World Order*, Touchstone, New York. Also see Bipan Chandra, 1979, *Nationalism and Colonialism in Modern India*, Orient Longman, Delhi.
2. V. Prashad, 2000, *War Against the Planet*, Leftword, New Delhi. Also see Noam Chomsky, 2001, *Propaganda and the Public Mind,* Madhyam, Delhi.
3. P. Patnaik, 1995, *Whatever Happened to Imperialism and other essays,* Tulika, New Delhi. Also see R. Axtmann, 1996, *Liberal Democracy into the Twenty-First Century: Globalisation, Integration and the Nation State,* Manchester University Press, Manchester.
4. For more on globalization and related processes, see World Commission on the Social Dimension of Globalization, *A Fair Globalisation: Creating Opportunities For All,* ILO, Geneva, 2004. also cf. *Human Development Report* (henceforth HDR), UNDP, OUP, New Delhi, 1999, p.25.
5. Gender Equality, Executive Summary, *Striving for Justice in an Unequal World*, UNRISD, Geneva, 2005.
6. See *Womenspeak, United Voices Against Globalisation, Poverty and Violence*, Six Women's Organisations, Delhi, 2000.
7. UNDP, *HDR, 2003*, Oxford, Delhi, 2003, p.48; also *HDSA, 2003*: *The Employment Challenge,* Mahbub ul Haq HDC, Oxford, Karachi, see Overview.
8. *HDR, 1999,* see Chap. 2.
9. J.E. Stiglitz, *Globalization and its Discontents,* Allen Lane, 2002,
10. *HDR, 2003,* p. vi.
11. *HDSA, 2001, Globalisation and Human Development*, Karachi, p. 15.
12. ILO, *A Fair Globalisation,* p. 3
13. cf. P. Patnaik, 2003, *The Retreat to Unfreedom: Essays on the Emerging World Order,* Tulika, New Delhi.
14. *HDSA, 1997*, Oxford, Karachi; also see *HDSA, 1999*, the Crisis of Governance, Oxford, Karachi.
15. *HDSA, 2000, The Gender Question,* Oxford, Karachi, p. 33.
16. Sparr, P. (ed.), 1994, *Mortgaging Women's Lives: Feminist Critiques of Structural Adjustment*, Zed, London. Also see I. Tinker (ed.), 1990, *Persistent Inequalities,* OUP, New York; Heyzer, N. and G. Sen

(eds.), 1994, *Gender, Economic Growth and Poverty: Market Growth and State Planning in Asia and the Pacific,* Kali, New Delhi.

17. Ruth Pearson, 2000, "Moving the Goalposts: Gender and Globalisation in the 21st Century", in S. Caroline (ed.), *Gender in the 21st Century,* Oxfam; also see D. Elson, 1995, *Male Bias in the Development Process*, Manchester University Press.
18. Veena Jha (ed.), 2004, *Trade, Globalisation and Gender-Evidence from South Asia.* Also see Madhu Kishwar, "A Half-Step Forward: The Thwarting of Economic Reforms in India", *Manushi,* Nos. 92-93, pp. 51-80.
19. D. Elson, 1996, "Appraising Recent Developments in the World Market for Nimble Fingers", in A. Chhachhi et al. (eds.), *Confronting State, Capital and Patriarchy: Women Organising in the Process of Institutionalisation,* ISS, Netherlands.
20. Linda Y.C. Lim, 1997, "Capitalism, Imperialism and Patriarchy: The Dilemma of Third World Workers in Multinational Factories", in Visvanathan (ed.), *The Women, Gender and Development Reader,* Zed; Moser, C., 1993, *Gender Planning and Development Theory, Practice and Training,* Routledge, London; Mukhopadhyay, S. 1992, *Impact of Structural Adjustment Polices on Women: Some General Observations* (unpublished). Also see *Shifting Sands, Women's Lives and Globalisation,* CWDS, Stree, 2000.
21. *The New Economic Policy and Women, a Collection of Background Papers* to 6th National Conference, IAWS, Mysore, 1993.
22. C.P. Chandrashekhar and Jayati Ghosh, 2002, *The Market that Failed: A Decade of Neo-liberal Economic Reforms in India,* Leftword, New Delhi, p. 146. Also see J. Ghosh, 2002, *Export-Oriented Employment for Women and Social Policy,* UNRISD.
23. *HDSA*, 2000, p. 67.
24. Ghosh, J., *Trends in Economic Participation Among Women in Asia-Pacific Region*, http//www.macroscan.com
25. S. Jayaweera, 2000, "Socio-Economic Development in Sri Lanka: Trends Since the Social Summit", in *South Asian Women, Global Perspectives and National Trends,* CENWOR, Colombo.
26. *Economic Survey, 1998-99,* Government of Pakistan, Finance Division, Islamabad, 1999, p. xi; *Pakistan NGO Review, Beijing Plus 5,* op cit. p. 61; *National Plan of Action for Women,* Ministry of Women's Development, Islamabad, 1998.

27. *HDSA, 1999*, p. 13; Naila Kabeer, 2001, *Bangladeshi Women Workers and Labour Market Decisions: The Power to Choose*, Vistaar, New Delhi; also see Siddiqui, H.G.A., *Globalization and Economic Security*, and Barar, M. K., 1999, *Globalisation and Employment Scenario in Bangladesh*, papers presented at Dhaka, Conference on Security.
28. Acharya, M., 1998, "Globalisation Process and the Nepalese Economy: Its Impact on Employment and Income in Nepal", in M.K. Dahal (ed.), *Impact of Globalisation in Nepal*, NEFAS.
29. www//macroscan.com and Proceedings of the Seminar on Globalisation and the Women's Movement, CWDS, New Delhi, 2005.
30. See U. Patnaik, 2004, "The New Colonialism: Impact of Economic Reforms on Employment and Food Security in India" in M. Bhattacharya (ed.), *Globalisation: Perspectives in Women's Studies,* Tulika, New Delhi. Also see, The Costs of Free Trade, http//www/macroscan.com
31. M. Swaminathan, 2000, *Weakening Welfare: The Public Distribution of Food in India*, Leftword, New Delhi.
32. U. Patnaik, 2004, "Principal Tasks on the Agrarian Front", *Social Scientist*, Vol. 33, Nos. 7-8, July-August.
33. See Papers, 2004, National Seminar on Globalisation and Women's Work, VVGNLI, NOIDA, March 25-26, unpublished.
34. Dawkins, K., 1996, *U.S. Agricultural Policy and the Uruguay Round: Implications for Food Security and Global Democracy,* presented in International Conference on Globalisation, Food Security, and Sustainable Agriculture, New Delhi (henceforth Food Security, New Delhi, 1996).
35. Quoted from letter to Mike Moore, Director General, WTO, on behalf of the Citizens and Gram Sabhas of India, in September 1999, unpublished.
36. Custers, P., 1997, *Capital Accumulation and Women's Labour in Asian Economies*, Vistaar, New Delhi, Chapter 8.
37. Crow, B., Why is Agricultural Growth Uneven? Class and the Agrarian Surplus in Bangladesh, in Rogaly et al; also see Siddiqui, T., "Bangladeshi Women in Transition: New Frontiers of Marginalization", paper presented at Regional Consultation on Women's Rights: Impact of Armed Conflict, Sectarian Violence and Religious Fundamentalism in South Asia Forum for Human Rights, Lahore, November 1998.

38. See papers presented at Conference on Food Security, New Delhi, 1996; Anoja, W., Global Trading Practices and Poverty Alleviation in Sri Lanka: A Gender Perspective in Seminar on Gender Impact of Trade Liberalisation, UNIFEM, New Delhi, 1995. Also see Beneria, L. and Sen, G., "Class and Gender: Inequalities and Women's Role in Economic Development: Theoretical and Practical Implications", *Feminist Studies,* 8(I), 1982, pp. 157-176.
39. S. Jayaweera, 1989, *Women and Development: A Reappraisal of the Sri Lanka Experience,* CENWOR, Colombo; also S. Jayaweera, "Socio-Economic Development in Sri Lanka and Trends Since the Social Summit", in *South Asian Women: Global Perspectives and National Trends in the 1990s,* CENWOR, Colombo, 2000.
40. Pakistan NGO Review, Beijing+5, NGO Coordinating Committee for Beijing+5, Lahore, 2000 also, National Plan of Action for Women, Ministry of Women's Development, Islamabad, 1998.
41. For this section, refer to Adhikari, J. and Bohle, H.G., 1999, *Food Crisis in Nepal, How Mountain Farmers Cope*, Adroit, Delhi, pp. 4, 25, 145ff.
42. Agarwal, Bina, 1994, *A Field of One's Own: Gender and Land Rights in South Asia,* CUP, Cambridge. This was also reflected in a theme Plenary in the World Social Forum, Mumbai, 2004; V. Shiva, and Menon, H., *Trade Liberalisation and the Corporatisation of Agriculture Food Security, 1996,* in Food Security, 1996; also see Commission Paper, "Agrarian Crisis, Migration and Impact on Women", 7th National Conference, AIDWA, Bhubaneshwar, 2004.
43. *HDSA*, 2000, pp. 60-61.
44. *HDSA*, 2003, p.34.
45. See *HDRSA*, 2000 and Options for Women in the Textile and Handloom Sector in Bangladesh, in V. Jha, 2004; *HDSA*, 2003, p.42; also Kabeer, op. cit.
46. Hossain, H., "Global Economic Integration and Open Borders: Impact on Women" and A. Rehman, "Trade Liberalisation and its Impact on Women: The Case of Bangladesh", in South Asian Seminar on Gender Impact of Trade Liberalisation, UNIFEM, New Delhi, 1995; I. Mazumdar, "Impact of Globalisation on Women Workers in Garment Exports: The Indian Experience", in V. Jha 2004. Also see Mazumdar, "Emergent Contradictions: Globalisation and Women Workers in India", CWDS, 2004, unpublished; Jayakody, S. and Goonatilake, H., "Industrial Action by Women Workers in Sri Lanka: The Polytex Garment Workers", in Heyzer, N. (ed.), *Daughters in*

Industry: Work, Skills and Consciousness of Women Workers, in Asia, APDC, Kaula Lumpur, 1988.

47. Goonatilake, H. and Goonasekere, S., "Industrialization by Women Workers in Sri Lanka: Working Conditions Inside and Outside the Investment Promotion Zone" in Heyzer (ed.), op. cit. and I. Mazumdar, "The Effects of an Urban Environment Upon the Lives of Women: A Case Study of Women Industrial Workers in Noida", CWDS, New Delhi, 1999, unpublished.
48. J. Ghosh, Trends in Economic Participation and Poverty among Women in the Asia Pacific Region, op.cit. http//www.macroscan.com
49. Said Khan N., *Industrialization, Culture and Women Workers in Pakistan*, in Heyzer (ed.), op. cit.
50. *HDRSA*, 2003, p. 78
51. 1999 World Survey on the *Role of Women in Development: Globalization, Gender and Work,* United Nations, New York, 1999, p. viii.
52. Mies, M., *The Lacemakers of Narsapur: Indian Housewives Produce for the World Market*, Zed, London, 1992. Also Chhachhi, A. and Pittin, R. (eds.), *Confronting State Capital and Process of Industrialisation,* MacMillan, 1996; Mukhopadhyaya, S., *Labour Market Analysis and Employment Planning*, ILO, Working Paper 32, 1989.
53. Standing G., "Vulnerable Groups in Urban Labour Process: Labour Market Analysis and Employment Planning", ILO Working Paper 13, 1987. Also Standing, G. and Tokman, V. (eds.), *Towards Social Adjustments: Labour Market Issues in Structural Adjustment,* ILO, Geneva, 1991; Standing, G., *Unemployment and Female Labour,* MacMillan, London, 1992.
54. *HDRSA, 2003*, pp. 2, 28.
55. Rao, Rurup and Sudarshan (eds.), *Sites of Change: The Structural Context for Empowering Women in India,* FES-UNDP, New Delhi, 1996. See discussion, pp. 118-132. Baker, I., "Women's Employment in Comparative Perspective", in *Feminisation of the Labour Force: Paradoxes and Promises* in Jenseon, Hagen and Reddy (eds.), Oxford, Polity Press, 1988; and Beneria, L., and Feldoman (eds.), *Unequal Burdens, Economic Crises, Persistent Poverty and Women's Work,* Boulder, Westview, 1992.
56. Goonatilake, H. and Goonasekere, S., "Industrialization by Women Workers in Sri Lanka: Working Conditions Inside and Outside the Investment Promotion Zone" in Heyzer (ed.), op. cit.

57. Sangari, K. and Chakravarty U., 1999, *From Myths to Markets*, Manohar, New Delhi; "Deniz Kandiyoti, Identity and its Discontents: Women and the Nation" in Williams and Chrisman (eds.), *Colonial Discourse and Postcolonial Theory: A Reader*, Columbia University, New York, 1994.
58. Sarkar, T. and Butalia, U., *Women and Hindu Right: A Collection of Essays*, Kali, New Delhi, 1995; also Sarkar, T., "Pragmatics of the Hindu Right: Politics of Women's Organisations", *EPW*, 34(31), July 31 August 6, 1999, pp. 2159-2176; RSS, "The Ideological Onslaught Women", AIDWA Publication Series, New Delhi, 1999. Also Jayawardena K. and de Alwis, M., *Embodied Violence, Communalising Women's Sexuality in South Asia,* Kali, New Delhi, 1996; Rouse, *Shifting Body Politics: Gender, Nation, State in Pakistan*, Kali, New Delhi, 2004.
59. I. Agnihotri, "The Expanding Dimensions of Dowry", *Indian Journal of Gender Studies*, May-August, 2003, Vol. 10, No. 2, pp. 307-319.
60. *State of Human Rights in 2000*, HRCP, Lahore, 2001.
61. Chowdhury, P., "Enforcing Cultural Codes: Gender and Violence in Northern India", *EPW*, 32 (19), 10-16 May, 1997, pp. 1019-1028; "Women's Equality", January-March, 2004, AIDWA, New Delhi, and AIDWA Report, Bangalore Conference, 1998.
62. Sen, K., "Indonesian Women at Work, Reframing the Subject" in Sen, K. and Stivens (eds.), *Gender and Power in Affluent Asia,* Routledge, London, 1998.
63. John, M.E., "Globalisation, Sexuality and the Visual Field and non-issues for Cultural Critique", in John, M.E and Nair, J. (eds.), *A Question of Silence, the Sexual Economies of Modern India,* Kali, New Delhi, 1998.
64. For more on sex ratio, see S.B. Agnihotri, *Sex Ratio Patterns in the Indian Population: A Fresh Exploration,* Sage, New Delhi, 2000; *Seminar* Unhealthy Trends, 489, May 2000; J.A. Gupta, *New Reproductive Technologies, Women's Health and Autonomy, New Freedoms New Dependencies?,* Sage, New Delhi, 2000; also see Mohan Rao, *From Population Control to Reproductive Health: Malthusian Arithmetic,* Sage, New Delhi, 2004.
65. E.J. Hobsbawm, *The Age of Extremes: the short twenth century 1914-1941,* Viking, New Delhi 1994, Chapters 10-11.
66. *Seminar,* May 1997.

7

Challenges for Women's Empowerment and Education in South Asia

The Goal is Empowerment of Human Values

Kamla Bhasin

We in the women's movement in South Asia are concerned mainly with the empowerment of those women who are disadvantaged and dispossessed; the women who have been disempowered. These women, who constitute a substantial portion of our societies, are like the roots of trees, which are not visible, which are not recognized and admired for their contribution but which carry the entire weight of the tree. These women are strong, resilient, wise and hardworking. They are survivors. If they had not been so tough, the strong winds of injustice and inequality would have blown them out of existence by now. They are the last bastions of sanity, sustainability and hope.

I wish to pay my tributes to millions of such women in Asia and elsewhere by singing one of my songs – a song of hope, a song about women's determination to be the masters of their own destiny.

We have decided to dispel darkness
We have decided not to remain uneducated.

With all our might we will learn to read
We will learn to read and understand the world
We will open our minds and broaden our horizons.

With all our might we will learn to write
We will learn to write our own destinies
No more will we sit and curse our fate.

We will master skills and master knowledge
We will dream of a brand new world
And walk with pride we have decided.

Our life partner will be a knowledge
Which teaches us our rights and responsibilities
Which empowers us to fight injustice
We have decided, yes we have decided.

In this paper I will provide the context of South Asia and raise some key issues related to women's empowerment and education.

The Affluence and Poverty of South Asia

South Asia consists of seven countries, namely, Bangladesh, Bhutan, India, Maldives, Nepal, Pakistan and Sri Lanka. Till 1947, three of the larger nations (Bangladesh, India and Pakistan) were one country. While India is almost like a continent and has more than a billion people, Maldives and Bhutan are small with only about 200,000 and 1.7 million inhabitants respectively.

The most ancient and advanced civilizations flourished in South Asia. This region gave birth to Hinduism, Buddhism, Jainism and Sikhism, four main religions of the world, and it has been home to Judaism, Christianity, Zoroastrianism and Islam. Not just religion and philosophy, but medicine, astronomy, astrology, architecture flourished here. Along with highly evolved forms of dance and music, the most sophisticated of crafts, this region developed very advanced agricultural practices, water management and harvesting systems. The most powerful and unique endowment of South Asia has been its ethos of normative human living in harmony with the laws of nature. This has become manifest time and again in the life examples of millions of its people; in the revelations and teachings of countless prophets and has been encoded in the institutions of religion and in the folk traditions.

It was the affluence of this region, which attracted a host of invaders and colonizers. Like the story of the Americas, Australia and Africa, the story of South Asia during the last 500 years has been that of systematic plunder, impoverishment and disempowerment by colonial powers and their local counterparts. South Asia became the shining jewel in the crown of British Empire. No wonder, while Britain flourished, South Asia lost its shine and glory.

Today, when the only measure of affluence is economic, South Asia is called the home of the poor. Over 50 per cent of the world's poor live here. India alone has more people living in absolute poverty than the entire population of Africa.

In 1992, this is what the ministers of the seven South Asian countries said about the state of their children:

> "A quarter of the world's children live in South Asia. Every day, many of the children of our region are exposed to the scourge of poverty and economic deprivation. Every day, many of them still needlessly die or suffer from diseases caused by lack of clean drinking water or inadequate sanitation. Of the 35 million children born each year, over 5 million die before the age of five. The majority of the survivors, particularly girls, do not develop to a fraction of their potential. About a quarter of maternal deaths in the world occur in South Asia" (The Colombo Resolution on Children, 1992).

THE MAN-MADE POVERTY OF SOUTH ASIA IS IMMORAL

Poverty is only one side of the story. There are other sides too. Actually, South Asia today is a bundle of contradictions, for example, along with over 500 million people living in poverty, some of the most affluent people with the most expensive lifestyles also live here. South Asia has got its share of local industrial magnets and local multinational corporations. While almost 30 per cent inhabitants of Mumbai live in the most inhuman of slums, this city is the most expensive in terms of renting office space. More expensive than Hong Kong and Tokyo.

Along with having the lowest levels of literacy (in some pockets female literacy is as low as 5 per cent), South Asia has areas where literacy levels are as high as 90 per cent (Maldives, Kerala in India). This 'poor' region has produced some of the most brilliant economists, scientists, computer wizards and continues to supply millions of doctors, engineers, nurses, scientists, plumbers, electricians to the 'rich' world. South Asian brain worth billions of dollars is sucked away every year.

Millions die in South Asia of totally preventable diseases like Malaria, diarrhoea, but it has some of the most sophisticated medical centres.

While millions of South Asians lack access to safe drinking water, two South Asian states (India and Pakistan) have developed nuclear capabilities and they spend very large amounts of scarce resources on armed forces and armaments.

When it comes to women, South Asia has the most patriarchal of communities where the birth of girls is considered the worst misfortune and it has matrilineal and matrilocal communities where girls and women are held in very high esteem. It has areas where the sex ratio is as low as 750 women to 1,000 men (Haryana and Punjab in India) and areas where there are more women than men (Kerala in India). While millions of South Asian girls never see the inside of a school, thousands of our women have achieved the highest in education and learning possible anywhere.

South Asia has had six women heads of state – Srimao Bandarnaike (Sri Lanka), Indira Gandhi (India), Khalida Zia, Sheikh Hasina (Bangladesh), Benazir Bhutto (Pakistan) and Chandrika Kumaratunga (Sri Lanka). But, the overall participation of women in legislative bodies and in political parties has been and continues to be abysmally low.

Thus, there are clearly two South Asias – the South Asia of the affluent and the South Asia of the impoverished. The two are interconnected. The affluence of one causes the impoverishment of the other; the power of one causes the disempowerment of the other. Because the poverty of South Asia is man-made, it is 'immoral'.

The Process of Impoverishment Continues; Now in the Name of Development

South Asia has enough natural, human intellectual and spiritual resources to eradicate poverty. Yet, the process of impoverishment continues. In 1985, in a South Asian workshop organized by the Freedom from Hunger Campaign/Action for Development of FAO, men and women representatives of NGOs and people's organizations stated:

> "It is generally agreed now that the development strategies and programmes implemented during the last three decades have failed to effectively tackle the causes of rural poverty. The benefits of whatever development and growth has taken place have not trickled down. Landlessness has increased and so has poverty, unemployment and inequality. Peasants, landless people, the small fisherfolk, plantation workers and women have been marginalized. In addition to this, through environmental destruction, the very resource base of the people is being rapidly destroyed."

Since this declaration, the pace of economic reforms in South Asia has accelerated manifold. Unbridled consumption is being promoted with no concern at all for ethics and morality. The magic of market and free trade is being propagated. Those few who can intervene in the markets and benefit are indeed happy, but the poor of South Asia already know that the market is neither free nor fair. They are experiencing the pains of double-digit inflation, concentrated mostly in the prices of food and necessities; they are experiencing the dehumanization caused by rising unemployment.

Millions of South Asians have become development refugees, sometimes as a result of large dams; sometimes because their lands were bought over by large agri-business companies; sometimes because large multinational companies were given fishing rights, and rights to do large-scale shrimp cultivation; sometimes because rich outsiders were given contracts to cut their forests, and so on.

Unable to face these adversities, many Sri Lankan and Indian farmers commit suicide every year; as a result of pauperization thousands of crafts people in India are finding it difficult to survive; thousands of Nepali parents are selling their daughters to Indian flesh traders; thousands of women from Kerala and Sri Lanka are leaving their homes and families to work as maids in the Middle East, and so forth.

The high rates of unemployment and underemployment, worsening living conditions, social disintegration and alienation have been creating and/or fuelling ethnic and communal conflicts and violence in South Asia. Virtual civil wars are going on in several parts of Bangladesh, India, Pakistan and Sri Lanka.

The present paradigm of development is creating a mad craze for materialism, consumerism and unsustainable lifestyles. Selfishness, competition, corruption, intolerance, violence of all kinds and disregard for life itself are becoming more intense and widespread. There is a loss of values, norms, ethics and morality and this is what threatens our common future and existence.

Women in South Asia are at the Bottom of All Hierarchies

It is indeed difficult to make general statements about women in South Asia because of the vast differences between them. They belong to different classes, castes, religions and communities. They have very different roles, status, position and condition. But, on the whole, one could still say that almost all women in South Asia suffer from patriarchal structures and ideologies; they experience gender inequalities and subordination. Women lag behind their men in all indicators of social and human development. South Asia has the most adverse sex ratios for women in the world, in spite of regions like Kerala and Sri Lanka where these ratios are not adverse to women. Life expectancy for women is lower than that of men, women's health, nutritional and educational levels are significantly lower than that of men. Women are concentrated in low skilled and low paid jobs, they get lower wages and income than men and they hardly own and/or control property and means of production. The number of female-headed households has been increasing and they are amongst and poorest in our countries. The participation of women in political and social decision-making is abysmally low. They are excluded from jural authority. They have no say in the formulation of social, economic, legal and political rules, which govern their lives and keep them subjugated.

Not in all, but in large parts of South Asia, girls live with disadvantages, burdens and fears. They carry the burden of neglect, of discrimination, of household work, of looking after siblings, of work outside the home, etc. Girls live with fears – fear of being aborted, fear of being poisoned, fear of being neglected and allowed to die, and fear of not getting adequate affection, care, nourishment, medical attention and education. Our daughters also live with the fear of sexual abuse ranging from playful manhandling to rape. After marriage they face the fear of loneliness, maladjustment, and mental and physical torture.

Then, there is the fear of being sold – sometimes in the name of marriage, sometimes for child labour or prostitution. They are commodities, objects of pleasure, objects to be used and discarded. They are rape victims, victims of harassment in buses, gardens, factories, offices, even in temples. No place is safe for them!

A daughter (i.e., woman) is forever homeless. Father's home is not her's – nor is the husband's home her's. She is a home-maker but not an owner of homes. She is a farmer, but does not own any land, she grows food but has no control over it.

The situation of women and girls has been so alarming in South Asia that our seven governments have had a joint campaign on the girl child.

Development Programmes and Policies Have Further Victimized Women

As a result of the women's movement in South Asia and globally, there have indeed been some positive changes for women; for example, there is growing gender awareness as a result of which women's subordination is recognized and the need to challenge it is accepted by all; violence against women is recognized and condemned; and women's participation in all decision-making bodies is seen as important. There have been improvements in some legal provisions, in educational and job opportunities for women, and policy statements have become more gender-sensitive. There is some increase in the number of women participating in government and non-government development agencies and programmes. South Asian governments have set up women's bureaus, commissions and departments and/or ministries to look into gender issues.

But, alongside these positive changes, the process of disempowerment of women, particularly of poor women, continues. Unfortunately, most of the official development programmes and policies followed in South Asia have belied the hopes of disadvantaged women. The research done by feminist scholars and activists during the last two decades has shown anti-women biases and effects of the programmes and policies which have almost exclusively been formulated by (elite) men. To give a few examples: in Nepal women used to be the main farmers. But development programmes designed by foreign and national experts ignored them completely. They planned everything for men. This has meant that women farmers have been losing control over resources and decision-making power. The story is the same in the other countries of South Asia

In Bangladesh and India hundreds of thousands of women used to make a living by pounding rice. When the rice mill was introduced, men were given or they took the ownership and jobs, and women became unemployed.

Large-scale destruction of forests in South Asia has affected the entire cycle of nature. It has led to floods and famines. What does this mean for women? It means that they now have to walk for several more hours to fetch water, to collect fuelwood and fodder. It means their men migrate to cities in search of work leaving them to cope with daily life alone. Their burden of work has increased further, their struggle to survive has become more tedious, and their existence has become more precarious.

In industry the situation is similar. In India, in the textile industry, many women were employed. When the textile factories were modernized, women were thrown out. As we know so well, women are always the last to be hired and the first to be fired. They continue to be in the least skilled and lowest paid jobs. Newer forms of exploitation are to be seen in the electronic and garment industries in Bangladesh, Pakistan, India and Sri Lanka.

Then, there is modern media reducing our women to commodities and objects of sex, unleashing all kinds of violence against them, and depicting them as the playthings of men. Pornography, prostitution, sex tourism etc. have been increasing, often all in the name of and connected to 'growth' and 'development'.

Case studies have shown that trade liberalization has negative impacts on women as producers and consumers, specially in sectors related to essential needs like food and clothing. In Maldives, when exports in fisheries increased, women's participation in the fisheries declined from 62 per cent in 1977 to only 20 per cent in 1990.

In a newspaper article, Vandana Shiva refers to an ICSSR study in India which has shown that growth in agro-processing linked to foreign investment and exports was creating joblessness. Overall, in the agro-processing sector, employment was going down. Exports of agricultural commodities have led to increased food prices and decline in food entitlements.

Women have been acutely aware of and alarmed by these trends. In 1989, women activists and scholars from five South Asian countries said the following in a South Asian Feminist Declaration:

> "As women our lives are subject to control through predominantly patriarchal structures and family laws and institutions, often justified on the basis of religion. The onslaught of capitalism and imperialism in the post-independence period has led to increasing restrictions on our space and access to resources and a destruction of our traditional skills and knowledge systems....

...Along with other marginalized communities we have been subject to increasing levels of state, community and family violence. Our voices are not heard as we are excluded from the political process which projects class privileged dynastic rule, whether by men or women leaders. The disintegration of civil society: the increasing centralization of authority in the hands of the state, often backed with fundamentalist sanction, leaves us vulnerable to constant attack inside and outside our homes. Growing statistics on rape, dowry deaths, incidents of acid throwing, the stripping of women as acts of revenge, the concerted attack by religious fundamentalists to keep us propertyless and resourceless, the continued denial of our contribution to subsistence and reproduction, are shared experiences....

...These processes are occurring in the context of increasing militarization. A declining proportion of yearly budgets are being allocated to health and education while there are massive increases in defence spending. Since the 1980s defence expenditure has escalated phenomenally in all the countries in the region. The diversion of resources for military spending results in unproductive consumption of energy and non-energy materials and the diversion of labour and industrial production from socially useful production....

...Women, adivasis, dalits and small peasants have been the most debilitated in this process. Women now work longer hours than before seeking fodder and fuel to maintain increasingly impoverished families. The acceleration of the twin processes of privatization and commercialization has had very specific effects on women, particularly poor rural women. The provisioning of families has shifted even more onto the bodies of women as the number of female headed households increase in the countryside. More women are being drawn into wage work but in invisible, irregular and low paid sectors of the economy. New avenues of employment in the world market factories have instituted another form of exploitation as women are barricaded into restricted industrial zones subject to patriarchal control within and outside the factory. IMF conditionality and structural adjustment, programmes will intensify these processes,

> particularly with the withdrawal of already scanty social and welfare services."

The following quote from the Draft Platform for Action for Beijing shows that what South Asian women are facing is actually a global and ongoing phenomenon:

> "Macro-level economic policies have adversely impacted women and families, specially those in poverty. The restructuring of the economy is driving women into insecure employment, unemployment, unprotected home-based production and dangerous working conditions. Diminishing social security systems and services are becoming the reality of women's daily lives. Inequities in the quality of life, nutrition, health, education and opportunities for a full and productive life increased from region to region within nations. Poverty increased both in absolute and in relative terms and the number of women living in poverty increased in all regions."

The above statement sums up the impact of macro policies on women in South Asia and in other countries. It shows clearly that the process of women's disempowerment is going on unabated. While the talk of women's empowerment becomes louder, the reality of women's lives becomes worse.

Let People Not be Enslaved by Free Markets

It is in this context of privatization, globalization and trade liberalization that we are talking today about women's empowerment. These two words – women's empowerment – mean very different things to different people. Some people would like women to be empowered so that they can serve the interests of economic growth and free markets better. For them the goal is a certain kind of economy and women's empowerment is a means to achieve that. The goal is freedom of the markets, not freedom of women. They believe, or atleast they want everyone else to believe, that structural adjustments will ultimately help everyone; the magic of the market will bring well-being to everyone.

However, as I have said earlier, a large number of women and their organizations as well as people's organizations and NGOs in

South Asia and elsewhere are convinced that the present paradigm of development can only further marginalize and disempower the disadvantaged women and their families and therefore it needs to be challenged. According to them, women need to be empowered not to serve the present system but to challenge and change it. If we agree with this, then, it is not enough to speak only about women's equality and empowerment. Along with these we must talk about the changes which are necessary in the economic, political and information systems, both at the micro and macro levels. Equality for women within the existing system will not be the complete answer. If women walk into and strengthen the present paradigms and cosmologies, the world will not change.

The 21st century needs a new paradigm of development, a paradigm which respects nature, and works in harmony with nature; a paradigm which is people-centred and people-oriented; and a paradigm in which women and women's perspective are centrally located. This new paradigm will not be obsessed with money or profits, or power, but it will be guided by certain values and principles like equality, justice, well-being for all, cooperation, peace and non-violence, democracy and participation, decentralization of control over power and resources, etc. While it is important to deal with the present situation, to use the spaces available within the present system for improving women's lot, it is imperative to have a vision of the society we wish to create. Our short-term strategies should be guided by a vision, by certain values and principles, so that instead of strengthening the present unsustainable paradigm of development, our work slowly but certainly challenges it. Our work will be transformative only if we have a clear vision. Reformism and radicalism, realism and idealism are not contradictory but complementary. The main challenge before us is to define our vision and the values and principles which will guide this vision. We must remember that positive visions are powerful instruments of change.

We need to say clearly and loudly that it is not the poor who are inferior or underdeveloped but those who exploit and oppress them are inferior, those who dominate and kill are inferior, those who hog all the resources are inferior, those who live in palaces in the middle of slums are inferior, and those who pollute with their big cars are inferior. The so-called developed people and countries are not developed, they are anti-development, anti-life. They are not rich. They are poor – poor in compassion, poor in sensibilities, poor in fair play. They are not super human as they are often projected on our TV screens, but they are inhuman, they are dehumanized. Only dehumanized people can sell Coco Cola in villages which have no safe drinking water, only dehumanized people can produce and sell weapons, pornography, violent films, and the like.

My question to all of us is: can women initiate a movement to devalue power, domination, consumerism so that the rich feel ashamed not the poor, the rapists feel ashamed not the raped, and those who always want to control feel ashamed not those who are controlled? Can women initiate and lead the process towards equity, justice, and sustainable livelihood?

My answer to this question is: If anyone, it is empowered women who can heal the world.

Women need to be empowered so that they can put a halt to destructive processes and also put things right before it is too late. I say this, because I feel a large number of women still retain seeds of regeneration. In the present scenario women's so-called backwardness can be a boon, a blessing. They can offer solutions because they are backward, they are not integrated, not educated, and because they have not progressed too much on the wrong paths.

That what has been derisively called feminine contains the key to our survival. What is feminine? Nurturing, caring, selflessness, being emotional, being like nature, creative, non-violent, non-linear, non-specialized, circular, etc., have all been labelled feminine and therefore looked-down upon, marginalized or crushed. Killing of the feminine is what has made our world today so inhuman. We need to reaffirm these feminine values.

I am not talking of women. I am talking of feminine principles and, values. I am calling them feminine only because patriarchy has called them that, male philosophers, scientists have called them that. I am happy to call them human values, which they are. But, today, these human values are to be found more easily in women than in men – not because the female body has some special limbs or glands producing them, but because of historical reasons.

The main question which we face today as feminists, adult educators, literacy activists is – through all our projects and programmes to empower women, what is it that we want women to be, to become? What kind of power do we want women to have? What is our definition of women's empowerment? Do we want them to be like men, or compete with men in order to have better positions within the present system? Women to head weapon's industry? Women to control Coco Cola corporation, Barbie Doll incorporate, pornography industry, or women to head corrupt political systems? In other words, does it change anything if instead of having male cancer cells we have female cancer cells? The question is, how do we fight the cancers which are plaguing our societies and not how to change the sex of cancer cells. Are women more competent to deal with these cancers?

Well at least women are less responsible for creating these cancers and that is a good enough qualification to begin with. But I go a little further. I believe women are more equipped to save the world and I say this for the following reasons.

My first reason is – because they are at the bottom of all hierarchies women know what harm inequality can do, how it can maim, kill, destroy. Because they are at the bottom, if their energies are released, they can shoot up. Like an ordinary loaf of bread, they are capable of rising. They have led the feminist movement, which talks of inequality in every home. Women are the ones who have exposed all 'isms', which have left half of humanity out of their purview. They are pleading against dualities like inside-outside, private-public, body-mind, nature-culture, subjective-objective, emotional-rational, etc. They are asking, for ecological and integrated ways of thinking and being. Women are the ones who have given us the potent slogan, "Personal is the political". They are the ones who are pleading to internalize struggles against all hierarchies. Women have been saying let us all begin with ourselves; let us all start fighting the patriarch, dictator, exploiter sitting in each one of us and we will see rays of light entering, forcing their way from all sides.

Women are more equipped because they create, feed and nurture with their own bodies; because they give birth from their own blood and flesh; and because they speak and act passionately against violence, against war. No wonder, they have led the peace movement everywhere.

Women are more equipped because they have been and continue to be involved both with production and reproduction; they have thus taken care of both economics and of human beings. As a fellow feminist Gita Sen says, "women are the workers in both spheres [reproduction and production], those most responsible and therefore with most at stake, those who suffer the most when the two work at cross purposes, and those most sensitive to the need for better integration between the two".

Women are more equipped to lead us out of the present ecological crisis, because through their personal experience and their history they are closer to nature and therefore they are more likely to protect nature. The very survival of billions of peasant families is intertwined with the survival of nature. No wonder, women have also been in the forefront of the environment movements the world over and in South Asia. Amongst the women it is the working class women, the indigenous women (and men) who are more capable of showing us the way. We educated, middle class women have lost the passion and lost our connections with nature. Many of us have become honorary men.

Women are more equipped because purity, goodness, nurturing, caring for others have been thrust upon them. At least for the last 2,000 years they have more experience of practising these values. They have picked up the pieces after all wars, have healed after and during all killings, and have forever cleaned the mess created by men.

Men have more physical strength, but women have much more resilience and resistance. Many people have said if men had to bear children, there will be no more births. When it comes to it, women are militant and immovable. They stand like rocks in the face of adversity. This is what we have seen in many people's struggles in South Asia.

The biggest threat to the 21st century is violence, violence of all kinds, and if women get organized they can show the way out of this violence. Mahatma Gandhi and Vinoba Bhave said decades ago that the future, the new age, must be based on non-violence and love and therefore it must be led by women.

That 50 per cent of humanity which was not consulted, and which did not participate in creating the present world, needs now to take the lead to create a humane world. Today, women face the challenge to find their own 'dharma', their own essential nature, to refine it, strengthen it, and radiate in it. They have to believe that they can help in the creation of a new culture, a new civilization which is bio-philic or which loves life, which is based on love and compassion not on competition, a civilization which is not dying to be victorious but which is keen to live. They have to take men along, make them practice 'feminine' qualities and become partners in creating a new world. There has been feminization of poverty. Let us now feminize their politics and polity.

Empowerment is a Dynamic and Political Process

Now, a few words on women's empowerment. About ten years ago, my friend Abha and I were doing a workshop with rural women in Bihar. Most of them were extremely poor (materially). They possessed almost nothing. We asked them what their dreams were – what would they ask for if some God(dess) offered to make all their desires come true. Their answers baffled us, their wisdom challenged our narrow notions of development. Their list of desires contained the following:

- my own identity
- leisure and time to dream
- recognition and respect
- love
- affirmation
- freedom

Satisfaction of basic needs like food, shelter came somewhere towards the end of the long list.

Since women's empowerment is connected to development, let me tell you how an old man from Tehri Garhwal in North India defined development. He said, development is greening of the heart. What an insight!! Genuinely green or happy hearts, cannot be ruthless, exploitative, domineering, greedy.

According to me, empowerment of women will make a difference only if our notion of power is different from the present notion of power.

Empowerment for us cannot mean power over others, or power to control more than our share; it should mean power to be, power to control one's own greed, avarice, violence; power to nurture, heal, care for others; power to fight for justice, ethics, morality; and power to achieve inner growth leading to wisdom and compassion.

Women's empowerment is a process, which is both ongoing and dynamic and which enhances women's ability to change those structures and ideologies that keep them subordinate. This process enables them to gain more access to resources and decision-making, gain more control over their own lives, and gain more autonomy. It is a process, which enables women to have self-respect and dignity, and also improves their self-image and social image.

The process of empowerment is a political process, because it aims at changing existing power relationships.

The goal of women's empowerment is not just to change hierarchical gender relations but to change all hierarchical relations in society, i.e., class, caste, race, ethnic, North-South, etc. Because gender relations do not operate in a vacuum, and because they are related to and influenced by all other economic, social and political systems, one cannot change gender hierarchies without changing other systems and hierarchies.

Women's empowerment is not and cannot be separated from the empowerment of nature, empowerment of all the marginalized people and countries. Women's struggles and movements, therefore, need to be closely linked to peace movements, ecology movements, workers and peasants movements, human rights movements and movements for democratization and decentralization of society. These different movements are different aspects of the same struggle, different segments of the same dreams, therefore, there is need for strong connections and alliances between them.

I believe that while talking of empowerment of women, we must also talk about empowerment of feminist thinking and ideology, empowerment of principles like equality, justice, democracy and sustainability. This means, we do not support all women, irrespective of what they stand for. We do not empower women dictators, women patriarchs, just because they are women. We recognize that women can also be patriarchal and dominating and that some men can be and are our partners in fighting patriarchy and other hierarchical systems. Our struggle is for certain principles and for a society where men and women have equal opportunities to live, grow and participate.

In other words, not just women, but women's perspectives need to be empowered because women are not just a separate sector. Women's concerns, perspectives and visions are necessary on every issue – be it militarization, human rights or sustainable development. Every issue is a woman's issue.

Empowerment of women has to be done at all levels, and in all sections if it is to become strong and widespread and make a difference. Effective networking is required between grassroots level women activists, intermediary level activists, women in the government, media women, women politicians, women academics, women artists, women entrepreneurs etc. We also need networking between those working at the micro level, and those working at the macro level. We also need support from sympathetic men at all levels.

Empowerment of women is not a one-way process, in which some activists can go and empower others. It is a two-way process in which we empower and get empowered. This is an ongoing journey for all of us. No one can become empowered for good and then become an expert in empowering others.

Women's empowerment has to be multidimensional and integrative. This process may include some or all of the following:

- Making women's contribution to society visible, i.e., showing that women in addition to being deliverers of children and homemakers are farmers, labourers, artisans, professionals, they have always been involved in production, and their contribution to GDP has always been major. They are producers of life itself and managers of natural resources.
- Making women and society recognize the knowledge, capabilities and skills that women have had and still have, particularly in areas of agriculture, health, handicrafts etc.
- Creating a social environment, which gives women self-esteem and self-confidence.
- Providing opportunities for girls and women to realize their full potential and to have choices and not to be pushed into only a few traditional roles and occupations. Giving them an education which empowers rather than domesticates.
- Enabling women to take decisions about their own lives: whether, when and whom to marry, whether and when to have children, whether and what to study, etc. also, to take decisions about family matters, community and national affairs. Enhancing women's political participation at all levels.
- Facilitating an awareness amongst women and men about girls and women's genuine needs, their status within and outside the family, their rights and responsibilities.
- Providing facilities and resources available to women to meet their basic needs of food, clothing, shelter and their special needs in health and security.
- Providing women access to and control over means of production, property and other resources and control over income.

Issues Which Need More Attention

Different approaches and strategies have been tried out in South Asia for setting into motion the process of women's empowerment. I wish to point out some areas which are crucial for women's empowerment, but which have not been given adequate attention in the past. These areas need to be looked at very carefully and effective strategies have to be developed to deal with them.

Women's lack of control over property and other productive resources is an important reason for women's inferior status. It is this which makes women feel insecure all the time. In her recent book *A Field of One's Own: Gender and Land Rights in South Asia*, Bina Agarwal has very convincingly argued that gender gap in the ownership and control over property is the single most important factor affecting women's economic well-being, social status and empowerment. This issue needs to be addressed urgently at all levels.

Lack of access to gainful employment is another important issue. While much stress is laid on who brings in the cash, women are denied opportunities of learning and developing skills to bring in cash, and to be gainfully employed. Women's household work is not valued and if they do not bring in cash, they are devalued, considered a burden, a liability. Research done by Amartya Sen and Jean Dreze has come to the conclusion that greater involvement with outside work and paid employment does tend to go with less anti-female bias in intra-family distribution. Therefore, they suggest that female participation in 'gainful' economic activity is a material factor in combating the special deprivation of women in many parts of the world. In South Asia we have talked a lot about income-generation activities for women, but most of these have failed to help women. They have increased women's workload without enhancing their income much. This issue needs careful consideration.

Sharing of household and child rearing work is another area which needs to be looked into because that is where maximum subordination of women is located. Women slog all the time, have no leisure, no opportunity to study, to grow. This is a big hurdle in the path of women's equality and empowerment. Women's drudgery can only be reduced if others in the family share her work. Boys and men should share mothering, caring and nurturing activities to provide time to women, to rest to have time for themselves, and to develop other interests.

It is in these areas that women are exploited, where they suffer materially and men benefit materially from patriarchal structures. These are the areas which are the most difficult to challenge and change. Without understanding and dealing with these issues it will be difficult to change the situation of girls and women in South Asia.

Control over women's sexuality is another area which needs to be studied, understood and addressed. Early marriage, *purdah*, restrictions on women's mobility, which are all ways of controlling women's sexuality, have drastic implications for girls and women.

The other important area to be addressed is that of ideology which justifies and perpetuates patriarchal structures, practices and behaviour patterns. Media are a powerful creator of ideology and we all know how sexist and anti-women most media have been and are. Considerable amount of work has been done to change media images of women but unfortunately things have only become worse.

Religion is also a creator of patriarchal ideology. Religious texts and mythologies, religious and cultural customs which preach and justify male superiority also need to be challenged much more than we have done in the past. This is indeed an area which we should tread cautiously but tread it we must. It is an area which will not change overnight but if we keep silent about it, it will never change. Religions, which justify caste, class, gender hierarchies, cannot be accepted uncritically in the present day and time. Religious laws, which go against our constitutions, which deny women their fundamental rights, need to be questioned. What and how we do this very sensitive task needs to be discussed and planned carefully to avoid hurting sentiments and backlash.

Formal Education and Knowledge Have Subordinated and Disempowered Women

On the issue of education for women's empowerment, let us take a quick historical look at what education and knowledge have done to women in the past.

In the beginning of human kind both men and women created knowledge. Feminist and other anthropologists tell us that women discovered agriculture, initiated certain crafts; they were the first healers; they developed medicine.

However, during the last few centuries, when creation of knowledge became a separate and formalized activity, men of the leisured classes took almost total control over it. Learning, education and creation of knowledge became the exclusive preserve of upper class (and upper caste) men. There has also been a domination of western science and knowledge over the science and knowledge systems of other cultures.

So-called learned men created formal, organized, modern religions which abandoned the feminine principle of power, dethroned goddesses and established male gods and male religious hierarchies. In the new scheme of things women had no role in defining religion. This is why, all modern religions are patriarchal. They have defined male as superior, as the master, the husband. They have debarred women from religious authority.

Male religious heads defined ethics, morality and law. They defined the status, roles and responsibilities of men and women; they defined masculinity and femininity. To date, most personal laws are based on religious laws and are therefore full of double standards, and injustice against women.

Since education was closely linked to religions, women were systematically debarred from education also. Some Hindu religious texts said that molten wax should be poured into the ears of those women and lower-caste men who dare even to listen to the Vedas or religious treatises. No wonder, even today, 75 per cent of all illiterate people in the world are women. In South Asia, girls and women lag behind boys and men in literacy and in all educational achievements.

Because men from the leisured classes (and castes) have had exclusive control over the creation of knowledge, they have had the power to define, to name. Male doctors have defined female body and illness. Male psychologists have been telling us what is female psychology. Male historians wrote history and ignored her completely with the result that women have neither had a history nor a sense of their own contributions to society. Male economists have defined what is work and what is of value and of course according to them women's work is neither work, nor valuable. Even our languages are patriarchal.

Different analyzes of present-day textbooks and primers for women's literacy programmes have concluded that even they are sexist, biased, they perpetuate patriarchal beliefs, and therefore end up in domesticating women instead of empowering them.

This kind of male knowledge discounts experience-based knowledge. Only book knowledge and degrees are considered valuable, respectable and relevant. This is why, mothers who educate the whole world are not considered educators; women who nurse and treat are not considered healers; women who do 60 per cent of agricultural work are not considered farmers, they are just wives of farmers.

This kind of patriarchal knowledge has done injustice to women, by discounting women's knowledge, by marginalizing women's contribution, by first defining and later turning women into subordinates. Such education and knowledge systems are responsible for creating a strong patriarchal ideology. They have and can only domesticate women and not empower them. But worse than this is the fact that knowledge based on the experiences of half of humanity has itself been half-true, half-valid, defective. Obviously, this is not the kind of education which can help empower women.

In the recent past the most exciting and revolutionary change which has taken place is that a large enough number of women have started creating knowledge. During the last 150 years women got educated, started researching and challenging patriarchal knowledge. Women historians are now challenging male history, women theologians are challenging male religions and theologies. The same is being done by women sociologists, anthropologists, doctors, lawyers, educationists, adult educationists, etc.

Women are looking at textbooks, literacy primers and other pedagogic to weed out sexism; they are scrutinizing colleges and university systems to see sexist biases; they are looking at NGOs and finding that most NGOs are male dominated; they are experiencing and analyzing that comrades in left parties and in trade unions can also be patriarchs.

This kind of work by our sisters and foremothers has not only empowered us, but also enabled us to break our ignorance and silence and to stand tall. This work needs to be expanded. Education of women is indeed the most important component, the most important intervention for women's empowerment provided both the contents and methodology of this education are pro-women.

The Kind of Education Women Need

We have to strengthen and multiply not only those ongoing efforts to educate women but also acquire information and knowledge which helps them challenge patriarchal knowledge, norms, values and behaviour patterns. Women need education not only to read and understand the word but to read, understand and control their own world; and help them not only master the three 'R's but to be masters of their own lives and makers of their destinies. They need education to acquire the necessary analytical skills to understand the fast changing realities of life, and also give them the confidence and strength to refuse to submit to conditions of indignity and inhumanity. If we are involved with women's literacy, then literacy classes for women should become nuclei for consciousness raising. They should help women form strong groups so that they can gain more and more control over their lives, help them break their silence, and make them visible. These classes should create an atmosphere which allows women more freedom, and gives them more opportunities to realize their full human potential. Education for women's empowerment will have to be an ongoing process of collective action and reflection. Our educational efforts should be built on women's existing knowledge and skills; they should affirm women, bring out the best in each one of them.

The methodology of women's education has to be participatory and non-hierarchical. Women must be involved in setting their own agenda and priorities, their own pace of learning. The educational process should make them feel good about themselves, build their confidence and self-respect, unleash their creativity, make them feel energetic and joyous; in one word – EMPOWER them.

The educational atmosphere should be such that it helps the participants discover knowledge for themselves in a dialogical group situation, where everyone (both trainers and trainees) participates with a questioning and open mind.

Besides everything else, our educational efforts must provide to the participants some clarity on our vision of sustainable livelihoods, vision of the society we want to create, some understanding of our common goals.

We need education which will not only help the participants in the search and acquisition of new skills and knowledge but also acquire and strengthen values like justice, equality, honesty, truthfulness and solidarity amongst oppressed groups. It should also create or release energies in women to act with conviction and courage in their various struggles at different levels. At the same time, it will not lead to more competition and ambition but create trust and solidarity amongst women. It should help them form associations and networks at different levels.

Education should also help women develop an analytical and questioning mind and a scientific approach to understand the realities around them. It should help them see the connections between micro and macro realities, between micro realities and macro policies, and between the local and the global.

Education should be such that it liberate the participants from the burden of readymade answers, which are given by the dominant cultural and political structures. It should encourage women to investigate the nature of reality from their own angle, encourage them to see for themselves whether what they are being told by others is consistent with the reality.

Education should also start a process of questioning and challenging authority and domination. This can be done by creating an atmosphere for everyone to open up, to ask questions, to criticize, and to feel the need for constant vigilance.

Besides everything else, education should be fun and joy. We must do away with the oft seen and heard dichotomy between joy and work, entertainment and serious job. Surely, work can be fun, serious job can be entertaining.

Many organizations in South Asia are making genuine attempts for women's empowerment. They are experimenting with different approaches, focussing on different areas of women's lives, i.e., health, education, wages, employment etc. In Bangladesh, there are Nijera Kori, BRAC, Gonoshasthyo Kendra, Saptagram Nari Swanirvar Songstha and hundreds others. WAF, Sindhyani Tehreeq, Aurat Foundation and many others are working in Pakistan.

In India, there is SEWA, ASTHA, Working Women's Forum, the Chipko Movement and hundreds others.

There are also some government efforts which have been genuine and successful; e.g., the PCRW in Nepal and Women's Development Programme and Mahila Samakhya Programme in India. All these experiments need to be reviewed from time to time, readjusted, expanded and multiplied.

But empowerment of women is not just done or possible at the grassroots level. There are many other inputs which are necessary (and are being provided). We need good training groups, feminist researchers, publishers, feminist film-makers, poets, singers, doctors, lawyers, etc. It is the joint efforts of all these and many more people – both women and men, which is leading to and will lead to women's empowerment.

Finally, I want to say that whether it is our work for women's empowerment, for sustainable development or for human rights, we have to bring into it feelings, emotions, passion and values.

There must also be a lot of joy and creativity. These struggles are going to be long. We cannot have long, serious, unhappy faces for too long. So, let us sing and dance our way to a better future, a just future. Asia has been known as the "Land of the Rising Sun". Let it also be known as the "Land of Rising Daughters".

8

Gender Imagery in American and Indian Advertising

Some Comparative Notes

Lucinda Joy Peach

The view that gender is socially constructed, and that the differences between males and females are produced by the social experiences people have, rather than biology alone, is held by many of us who teach from a feminist perspective. As a result, we understand that the images displayed in various forms of media socialize us and shape our understandings of both femininity and masculinity (Wysocki, 2002). Among various forms of media, advertisements in particular both reflect social ideas about gender as well as shape these ideas. Advertising constructs a quasi-fictional world of gender imagery which provides models by which we gauge our personal identities (Griffin, 1994: 492).

Given the prevalence of gender imagery in advertising (Griffin, et al., 1994: 491), along with the significance of advertising in shaping the dominant gender images in modern society, this essay will consider some of the normative dimensions of gender advertising. Since media depictions of gender have been considered by most scholars to be more pervasive and influential in shaping women's identity than men's, I will focus on images of women in advertising. Nevertheless, since the social construction of gender is a process in which men and women are mutually constituted in binary opposition to one another, consideration of advertising's influence on women's identity will necessarily include some consideration of men's identity as well.

Much of the research on gender in advertising has been conducted in the United States and Europe, and may not fully describe the ways that gender is portrayed in advertisements across cultures. Indeed, there has been little attention paid to how Western women are portrayed in advertising in other cultures and its impact on non-Western women in those cultures (Frith, 2004: 1). Yet, the impact of Western advertising on the global media is significant. It plays an important role as an agent of socialization, perpetuating culturally specific or localized beauty standards such as thinness as universals. With the rise of international media corporations and the spread of international editions of women's magazines, these conventions are being spread quite rapidly around the globe (Shaw, 1999).

In addition, the almost exclusive focus on Western media is unfortunate because the depiction of gender, and women's bodies in particular, may have radically different consequences in Western and non-Western cultural contexts. For example, scholarship conducted on depictions of gender in Western contexts are rooted in an ethos that women have acquired certain rights in relation to their bodies, including the right to display them in public without fear of retribution or punishment and the right to take pleasure in them. These are rights which are not universal for women in many countries, especially non-Western ones.

In South Asia, for instance, cultural traditions historically have dictated women dress modestly, and such traditions remain widespread today (Frith, 2004: 1). As the authors of a study of Indian magazine advertisements point out, "while the 'new' Indian woman may be similar to the Western woman in so far as education and workplace aspirations are concerned, her cultural experiences may be different" (Singh and Schoenbachler, 2002: 7).

Magazines remain a popular medium for dissemination of cultural norms and values in both American and Indian societies. Women's magazines are among the most desirable of vehicles for advertisers, since they are aimed at the sector of the population increasingly more responsible for purchases. As an editorial on the Strategic Management Website proclaims: "The strength of these magazines rests principally on the crucial role of women in the consumption process. The front cover of a magazine is the vehicle by which the consumer distinguishes one magazine from another and serves to label not only the maga zine but also the consumer who possesses it" (Strategic Management Editorial, 2004).

Since the representation of gender has become such a dominant feature of modern-day advertising in India, it is often called the social resource 'used most' by advertisers. Yet, there has been very little published research on Indian magazine advertising at all, never mind gender advertising, despite recent feminist scholarship on the role of gender on other forms of media, including film, television soap operas, romance novels and stories in women's magazines, and so on. For all of these reasons, this essay will focus on gender advertising in Indian magazines and how well the analysis of American and other western advertisements seems to apply in this different cultural context.

Issues with Gender in Advertising

Jean Kilbourne, an expert on the impact of advertising, especially on girls and women, begins her newest book *Can't Buy My Love* (Touchstone, 1999) with the following observations:

> If you're like most people, you think that advertising has no influence on you. This is what advertisers want you to believe. But, if that were true, why would companies spend over $200 billion a year on advertising? Why would they be willing to spend over $250,000 to produce an average television commercial and another $250,000 to air it?

While we might think that advertising does not affect the way we see the world, Kilbourne argues that "we internalize these advertisements, and they unconsciously alter the way we perceive normalcy" (Bryant, 2004). In particular, advertising has a significant influence on our understanding and social experience of gender altogether.

Scholars and other observers of gender images in the mass media have noted a number of problematic aspects of the gender imagery in American advertising. These include the objectification of women and valorization of "the male gaze," the promotion of negative gender stereotypes, especially of women, the creation of harmful ideals, such as the "beauty myth" with its unattainable standards of physical perfection, again, especially of women, the "eternal youth" myth that valorizes only youth; and the effect of encouraging unsafe and/or unhealthy activities, such as extreme dieting and eating disorders, cosmetic surgeries such as breast enhancement and weight reduction, smoking, drinking, alcoholism, and so on. After discussing each of these, I will make some preliminary assessment of the extent to which these problems are also apparent in Indian magazine advertisements.

Objectification

Objectification refers to the process whereby persons are effectively turned into objects by the way they are portrayed. Rather than being valued as subjects, they are depicted and/or treated as objects. Women's bodies are more likely to be shown to advertise products than men's. More often than not, "advertising portrayals depict women in a narrow range of primarily traditional roles, encouraging the view of women as sexual or decorative objects and creating unrealistic and undesirable ideals for women to uphold" (Williams, 1995; Horner, 1998). Advertising often objectifies women by reducing them to their bodies, and often to certain parts of the body, such as breasts, torsos, legs, or buttocks, rather than the whole body. Many advertisements reinforce women's insecurity about the adequacy of their bodies by asking women to view themselves as a collection of discrete parts, each one in need of major renovation (Jacobsen and Mazur, 2004). Such portrayals emphasize the view of woman as an object to be disciplined, manipulated, and viewed by others, especially men (Rohlinger, 2002).

In recent years, men are also being objectified in advertising, although the message is different. Media portrays the ideal man as physically big and strong, and the ideal woman as small and taking up little space. The tough and powerful man considers compassion and sensitivity signs of weakness and displays what Kilbourne calls "contempt for the feminine qualities" (Bryant, 2004).

An important aspect of objectification in media generally is "the male gaze". This refers to the way the camera focuses on the body of a woman as reflecting a hypothetical or actual male viewer. Indeed, Indian feminist scholar Mary John contends that "the difference between the sexes has been associated with visual processes – to be sexualized as a 'woman' is to be objectified as an image to be looked at, while the power of 'man' is in his gaze, the pleasure and anxiety generated by the desire of looking" (John, 2000: 372). Sociologist Erving Goffman's now famous analysis of advertisements supports this assertion. Goffman's research showed that males are much more often depicted as looking directly at women than vice versa, and that this contributes to the objectification of women in real life (Goffman, 1979).

Goffman also attributed different types of gaze with male and female models in advertisements. Male models typically gaze directly at the audience. Conversely, female models often engage in the mental drift, in which the female model does not make eye contact with the audience but instead allows her gaze to focus in the distance, on a small object, or on the protective male character. This withdrawal entrusts the woman's physical and mental safety to the dominant, superior man, who may or may not be physically present within the advertisement (Rohlinger, 2002). Goffman's work also suggests that women engage in passive touch behaviour that positions them as ornamental objects in advertisements. He argued that this type of visual cue strips women of their instrumentality and reinforces their subordinate position in the social hierarchy.

While Goffman and other researchers have focused on Western advertising, communication researchers studying images of women in Indian advertising have noted that the gaze differs across culture and gender (Frith, 2004: 2; Griffin et al., 1994). Nonetheless, the way that the male gaze objectifies women seems to operate similarly in American and Indian magazine advertisements. A study of gender in magazine advertising in the US and India by Griffin, Viswanath and Schwartz found that perhaps the most common way that the subordination or portrayal of women as accouterment to men was ritualized was through presenting women as the accessories of men. The frequency with which such poses by women as subordinate or accessories of men were used was very similar in Indian and US advertisements, occurring in 30 per cent of their study sample (Griffin et al., 1994: 495, 499).

Similarly, studies on the projection of women in Indian advertisements in the past have shown that women were mostly projected as glamorous or enticing, whether they were used to sell cosmetics, fabrics, jewellery, domestic appliances, suitcases, scooters or stationery. Men's clothing advertisements invariably used admiring women by the side of the male models, creating the impression that "all a woman desired was a man dressed in sophisticated garments" (Strategic Marketing Editorial, 2004). Such advertisements, which have been described as portraying "fashion model poses," share the characteristics of depicting women as "sights" to be looked at, as passive and inviting, and as welcoming the gaze of the anonymous (male) viewer (Griffin, et al., 1994: 497). In fact, the study by Griffin and others found that the greatest similarities between US and Indian magazine advertisements involved the "conventions of Western fashion pose," including the portrayal of women next to men as subordinate and/or decorative objects, lying provocatively on beds, sofas, or the ground, revealing a feminine touch or engaging gaze (Griffin, et al., 1994: 501).

In addition to their general objectification, images of women are often sexualized, which sends the message that men may "possess" women's bodies (see Frederickson and Roberts, 1997). Evidence that women are more sexually objectified than men has been found in many media realms, including fashion and fitness magazines (Rudman and Verdi, 1993), MTV (music television) commercials (Signorielli, McLeod, and Healy, 1994), and prime-time television commercials (Lin, 1998; Murnen et al., 2003). Although sexual images have been used to sell products since the very beginning of the industry, in recent decades, the prevalence of sexual imagery has become more common, explicit, exploitative and violent. Researchers concluded that female nudity and erotic content had become quite commonplace in contemporary US advertising by the mid-1980s (Frith, 2004: 2).

One significant difference between Indian and American advertising is that the display of female anatomy is much more explicit and frequent in American advertisements than in Indian ones (ibid.). Similarly, while depictions of "sexual pursuit" in both Indian and American advertisements almost always portray men as the pursuers and women as the pursued, such depictions occur three times more often in American advertisements than in Indian ones (Griffin, et al., 1994: 496). Indian advertisements are more likely to portray women in "neutral/other" ways than to portray them as sex objects. Nonetheless, although, some stereotypical portrayals of women in Indian advertisements decreased in the nineties (e.g., "housewives, concerned with looks"), they were more likely to be portrayed as sex objects in the nineties (Das, 2000).

The findings that Indian women are less sexually objectified in advertisements than Western women are consistent with other studies of the use of Western and Asian models in Asian advertising. For example, one study found that Asian magazines used Western female models more frequently in clothing advertisements whereas Asian female models were used more in advertisements for beauty products. In addition, Asian magazine advertising reflects that a higher proportion of Western models are of sensual or sexy beauty types (i.e., the model is posed in a sexual way, usually wearing sexy attire or tight-fitting, revealing clothes) whereas a higher proportion of Asian models is either of the "classical" or the "cute" or "girl next door" beauty type. These differences may indicate that the objectification of women's bodies is racially or culturally based, as Western models are more often featured in advertisements for body-related products – even in Asian magazines, whereas Asian models are used more often in advertisements for facial beauty (Frith, 2004: 7).

A number of scholars have made connections between the objectification and sexualization of women in media imagery and tacit cultural understandings that women are appropriate objects of physical and sexual violence and abuse. For example, Kilbourne opines that "men would not oppress what they see as equal," but advertisements that objectify women encourage men to think of women as unequal and inferior. She explains how advertisements that eroticize rape and sexualize women contribute to creating a society that has less trouble digesting violence against women.

Kilbourne gives an example of such objectification, describing how some advertisements show young women with their mouths covered. This depiction might seem harmless, such as a turtleneck sweater pulled up over the young woman's mouth or an advertisement for nail polish with her hand across her mouth. Or, it might be much more sinister, such as an advertisement for a CD featuring a young woman with her lips sewn shut. Kilbourne explains that on the surface these advertisements sell sweaters and nail polish and CDs, but they are also selling the idea that women should be silent. This may not be intentional on the part of the advertisers, but we get the message whether it is intended or not (Bryant, 2004).

This technique of objectifying women as sex objects is evident in an Indian advertisement for Motorola phones with digital photo capability. The photography conveys the same message that women are objects who should be silent by cutting off the heads and necks of the two presumably young women who are dressed in school uniforms and standing on bleachers, leaving their objectified lower limbs to be ogled by a male who is peeking up at their legs from below where they are standing on the bleachers. Thus, the objectification and sexualization of women's bodies is by no means only an American phenomenon, but has infiltrated the magazine advertisements of other countries, including India, despite significantly different cultural contexts with different standards of modesty for explicit portrayals of sex.

Promotion of Negative Stereotypes

A second problem area related to gender images in advertising is that they promote negative stereotypes. Past research indicates that both men and women are portrayed in stereotypical ways in magazine advertisements in most parts of the world. However, most scholars agree that these stereotypes are more negative, and thus more damaging, for women than for men. Although it is important to be sensitive to cultural differences, which certainly do exist, especially between the US and India, for example, studies have shown that "sex-role stereotyping tends to be surprisingly consistent across different countries" (Furnham and Mak, 1999: 431).

Scholars have pointed to four primary stereotypes of women that are prevalent in advertising:

(1) sexual objects,
(2) homemakers,
(3) dependent on men, and
(4) ornamental or decorative objects seldom shown as making important decisions or doing important things (Das, 2000).

These four types of stereotypes are remarkably similar across US and Indian cultures, due in large part to a significant extent, perhaps, to the effects of globalization, and the adoption of Western advertising conventions by Indian advertisers. A study of TV commercials, for example, found that commonalities included the greater use of men as authoritative central figures, with women more often depicted as users of products; frequent portrayals of men as interviewers or professionals while women are given dependent or secondary roles; men more often portrayed during leisure/outdoor or business occupations while women are more frequently shown at home, confined to a domestic setting; males more often older than the females; and males depicted in association with pleasurable rewards, whereas females more often used to advertise products oriented to social or self enhancement (Furnham and Mak, 1999: 432-33).

Until very recently, Indian magazine advertisements portrayed women primarily in their stereotypical roles. Women were shown either in the kitchen cooking food, washing a bucketful of clothes, bandaging wounds or feeding their husbands and children. In addition, women are more often depicted in domestic settings in Indian magazine advertisements than in American ones. Authors of the study making this finding in fact observe that "Indian ads showing mothers in the kitchen or serving meals to the family appear more similar to American ads from the 1950s or 1960s than they do to American ads in our 1985-87 sample" (Griffin et al., 1994: 496).

However, during and since the 1990s, the image of the "new Indian woman" is explicitly cultivated in Indian advertising. Women are shown less frequently as dependent upon men while men are less likely to be depicted in themes of sex appeal, dominance over women and as authority figures (Strategic Marketing Editorial, 2004). Advertisements have also started portraying women more frequently as career-oriented and in non-traditional activities and are constructing the persona of the "new Indian woman". Nonetheless, while it is harder to find images in recent magazine advertisements that depict women as only homemakers, depictions of women in professional roles continue to be limited. A study of television commercials conducted as recently as 1999 confirmed that available evidence shows that women are usually depicted at home, and they most commonly appeared in commercials for domestic products (Frith, 2004: 3; Furnham and Mak, 1999: 432-33).

In both US and Indian advertisements, women are used to sell different types of products than men. Following traditional stereotypes, advertisements selling home and body products are female dominated, whereas advertisements for automobiles and sports products are male dominated (Singh and Schoenbachler, 2002: 23; Furnham and Mak, 2003: 433). While the percentage of neutral or non-traditional product advertisements in Indian magazines with a female in them increased from 38.7 per cent in 1987 to 62.6 per cent in 1994, the opposite was true in the case of men, who were less likely to appear in advertisements for non-traditional products (i.e., female-oriented and neutral products) in 1994 than in 1990 or in 1987 (Das, 2000).

However, women were also portrayed in traditional ways in advertisements for neutral products. Some of the common stereotypical portrayals of women seem less prevalent in Indian advertisements, however. For example, Indian advertisements are more likely to portray women in "neutral/other" ways and less likely to portray them as sex objects. This is consistent with research on advertisements in other parts of Asia, which show statistically significant differences in Western models more frequently being posed in sexy dress than are Asian models (Frith, 2004: 5). However, the softening of stereotyped female role portrayals in more recent Indian advertisements seems to be primarily due to increases in neutral portrayals rather than increases in portrayals of women engaged in non-traditional activities.

Further, there are still a number of Indian advertisements which convey the message, more and less subtly, that women are dependent on men. An advertisement, for example, conveys this message through showing the man using his visa card to pay the bill following dinner with his female companion at a fancy restaurant. Standing alone, this is not worthy of comment, but when it is not accompanied by similar depictions of the female in a couple paying, it sends the message that men continue to be the primary breadwinners, on whom women are financially dependent. Similarly, advertisements illustrating the point that women are shown engaging in activities that are not important continue to be fairly common. An example is an Indian advertisement for Nitco Tile, portraying a young Indian women in blue jeans and sleeveless sweater lying happily on a bare floor (presumably newly tiled). The advertisement suggests that women lives of leisure with nothing better to do but lie around and admire their floors!

One other way that gender stereotypes operate in advertising is in relation to the informational content about the products being sold. The findings of a study of Indian advertising suggest that while most advertisements in general contain information, that more advertisements targeted at women contained no information at all. This indicates that Indian advertising targeting women tends to contain less and different types of information than does advertising directed at men (Singh and Schoenbachler, 2002: 23). In addition, this study found that advertising directed at women included significantly more hedonistic themes and less themes such as achievement and success. Interestingly, although sex is used far less often to sell projects in India than in the US, this study found that sex was more likely to be used in advertisements targeting women. Whether this stereotyping is due to the influence of Western advertising strategies or indigenous ones, it seems to have a negative impact on India women.

Promotion of Impossible (and Harmful) Ideals

A third problem with the way gender is depicted in advertising is the creation of impossible ideals for appearance. These ideals include what have been or can be called "the beauty myth," the "eternal youth myth," and the "ability to buy perfection myth," all of which may result in unhealthy behaviours, even addictions. Far greater pressure placed on women to conform to these ideals than is imposed on men.

The Beauty Myth

The term "beauty myth" was coined by Naomi Wolf as the title of her book *The Beauty Myth: How Images of Beauty Are Used Against Women* (1992) to describe how the images of women in advertisements create impossible standards of beauty and thinness for "real" women to live up to. One study of American advertising found that one of every 11 commercials has a direct message about beauty (this isn't counting the indirect ones) (Dittrich, 2004). In America, at least, the image of the ideal beauty typically is a model less than 25 years old, over five feet nine inches tall, weighing less than one hundred twenty pounds, and without wrinkles, blemishes, or pores. In American, the ideal beauty has typically been blonde, and certainly white skinned.

That Caucasian ideal seems to be prevalent in India today as well, as suggested by the actresses, models and music stars who typically adorn the front pages and style sections of the national newspapers and many advertisements that appear in Indian magazines. For example, a L'Oreal advertisement on the inside-front cover of the Indian edition of *Cosmopolitan* shows a very young looking, light skinned, blue eyed woman with flawless skin and wide lips. Women of colour, when they do appear in magazine advertisements, are usually exoticized and marked by their "Otherness", as an Indian magazine's advertisement for Louis Vitton handbags featuring an African woman dressed in gold lame shorts and top and high heels in the middle of the desert clearly illustrates.

Advertising also promotes unrealistical ideals for women's weight and body size. A study conducted in 1984 found that the average size of idealized woman (as portrayed by models) has become progressively thinner over the years, and has stabilized at 13-19 per cent below physically average weight. It is then not surprising to learn that women generally are less satisfied with their bodies than men (Horner, 1998; American Association of University Women, 1990; Dittrich, 2004).

Wolf criticizes the media for disseminating such narrowly defined and unrealistic illusions of unobtainable perfection because of how they negatively affect women. Researchers have found that repeated exposure to the thin beauty myth ideal via the various media renders these images seemingly achievable and real. By inviting women to compare their unimproved reality with the air-brushed, 'beauty myth' models, such advertising images work to erode women's self-esteem and satisfaction with their bodies. The term "beauty" is reduced to a mere decorative quality, which makes women appear ornamental and valued only for their appearance.

The "Eternally Young" Myth

A second harmful consequence of female-gendered images in advertising is the promotion of an obsession with youth. "If little girls are presented as sex objects, grown women are depicted as children" (Jacobsen and Mazur, 1995: 80). Images of women used in advertisements in women's magazines have become progressively younger in the past thirty years. Cultural and aesthetic trends apparent in examining advertisements over time, as well, indicate a trend towards using models who look girlish and waiflike, with feline or childlike features, as opposed to top models of the 1980s, who had square jaws and broad shoulders, which emphasized a powerful, mature look.

The media also uses female teen celebrities to sell products, ideas, and values. Models in their 20s are used to market anti-ageing products. When models or actresses known to be in their late 30s and early 40s are hired for anti-wrinkle product campaigns, their faces are airbrushed to appear a decade younger. The beauty myth is especially harmful to young women who, from their early teenage years, are bombarded by images on how to look, how to dress, and how to attain an ideal body. Through "ideal body" advertising and programming, these images play an indirect role in the promotion of body image distortions. This role starts with the mass media's influence on young women's development of the internalized ideal body. Unfortunately, adolescent girls not only turn to advertising for image guidance, but often maintain this ideal image no matter the consequences.

Studies reveal how advertising and other media encourage young girls to compare their own bodies to what they see in the media and, inevitably find their own bodies lacking. It is the norm for young girls in the United States to feel dissatisfied with their bodies and how they are willing to go to any length to turn their bodies into ones similar to those they see in the media. The pressure to look like a model makes it difficult for children and youth to accept and love their bodies as they are, which can lead to a negative body image, less confidence and decreased self-esteem (Snow, 2000). These problems are also evident in Indian magazine advertising. For example, an advertisement for "Ever Youth" clear skin complexion mask depicts a young woman's face with a caption telling her how she can attain and preserve a clear and youthful complexion.

The "Ability to Buy Love" (or Perfection) Myth

Advertisements promise us instant happiness through buying products. The "Ever Youth" advertisement just mentioned is one example of how products are packaged to promote this idea that beauty (and thus happiness) are just a bottle away. By promising the fast solution of every problem, instant gratification as something you can buy, something you can take that will make you feel better instantly, something that will end boredom, advertising also feeds addiction.

Kilbourne explains that advertising creates dissatisfaction with our unembellished selves. "And at some level, Kilbourne says, when the accumulated stuff doesn't do the trick [to make us happy], we feel there's something wrong with us. We don't think that the ideal image of beauty that is put in front of us is impossible; we think we just haven't learned how to put the eyeliner on right, or we didn't buy the right kind. It works for Cindy Crawford, so why doesn't it work for me?" (Bryant, 1998). One disturbing consequence of girls' and women's exposure to advertisements is the lengths to which they are willing go to achieve the beauty myth ideal, including unhealthy weight loss regimens using harmful weight loss medications, liposuction, breast augmentation and other forms of cosmetic surgery, taking up or not quitting cigarette smoking, spending inordinate amounts of money on clothing and cosmetics, and so on.

One study concludes that "women who internalize the thinness-as-beauty ideal may engage in extreme and often pathological behaviors in order to achieve and maintain a slim figure" (Horner, 1998). In addition to concern about thinness, the beauty myth has propelled some women and even girls into considering or actually undergoing cosmetic surgery, especially breast implants that have been promoted by the media and plastic surgeons as a way to increase the psychological and social well-being of females (Jacobson, 2000). While such advertising promoting diet and weight loss, health and fitness, and cosmetic surgeries, is not yet pervasive in Indian advertising, there are signs that the trend is in that directions. For example, an advertisement appearing in *India Today* promises "permanent fat reduction" illustrated only by the thin, muscularly sculpted torso of a woman.

According to Kilbourne, one reason that magazine advertisements that objectify women and use sexual images are so successful is because they attract attention. "Just saying the word 'sex' or showing a woman's breast is an effective way to get people's attention. These sexual images yoke the product with our basic desires, as if by buying the product, we were going to get, not just sex, but love. We know that isn't really true but it's hard not to believe it on some level. By now we have all seen so many of these images all through our lives that there is an immediate connection and reaction. Buying the product=sex=love" (Bryant, 2004).

This sales strategy has become increasingly prevalent in Indian magazine advertisements as well. As women have made significant progress in education and employment over the past 40 years, and have become more self-reliant and independent, advertisers have targeted women as the primary market for products and services in India. Indeed, extensive market research has resulted in a trend to address many advertisements for goods and services to a growing class of urban middle class woman who have independent salaries or an increasing control in purchase decisions.

Although some advertisers have been careful to avoid a "Westernized" image of the "new" Indian woman, but have instead attempted to construct a cognate, pan-Indian gender identity, thereby maintaining India's distinctive cultural markers despite increased economic globalization and further development of an open market system (Strategic Marketing Editorial, 2004), other advertisers have clearly adopted Western models, techniques and stylistic conventions. While the advertising techniques may be similar, the consequences are undoubtedly not the same, given the different cultural contexts into which these advertisements are being disseminated.

This contributes to the promotion of Western images as the ideal standard by which beauty as well as all other markers of value and worth are measured, a message that is especially problematic when articulated in advertising in non-Western societies. In the Indian context, the proliferation of images of Westernized women can be viewed as part of a larger trend towards cultural "homogenization" which many fear is the inevitable outcome of globalization. Through the various media, the West is having an increasing influence upon the more affluent sector of the Indian economy, a trend that is especially prominent in Indian women's fashion magazines.

Even though Indian advertisements use Indian models with traditional dresses, they are being increasingly replaced with Western models, models in Western outfits or models with other Western attributes. According to one commentator, "this osmosis of traditional culture with Western culture not only reflects the metamorphosis of women in society but also reveals the new Indian market – a revolutionised consumer marketplace" (Strategic Marketing Editorial, 2004). In addition, a comparative study of images of women in weekly US news magazines (*Time* and *Life*) and weekly Indian magazines (*India Today* and *Illustrated Weekly of India*) found that many of the Western advertising conventions and poses for women were being transferred across cultures and that female models in India were adopting poses and displays that conformed closely to gender portrayals in the advertising of the industrialized Western nations (Griffin et al., 1994). The authors of this study note that the proliferation of branded advertising in the increasingly open markets of nations such as India and China has provided standardized images of gender (and what it means to appear "attractive") (ibid.). The effect of this new trend on gender ideals in India has yet to be fully revealed, but initial indications are not promising.

Summary and Conclusions

There are numerous similarities between gender advertisements in American and Indian magazines. Nonetheless, significant differences remain. One comparative study of Western and Indian magazine advertisements observed that there are several factors that should have led to even more liberal portrayals of women in Indian magazine advertisements, such as the increasing number of middle class consumers and their higher levels of education and decision-making. Yet it found that women for the most part are still portrayed in very traditional ways in Indian magazine advertisements. Although Indian society is changing, it is still a patriarchal society. Consequently, portraying Indian women in non-traditional ways may not be accepted as easily in Indian society as in Western ones.

One area which needs further research is the impact of Western female models and beauty myth ideals on Indian women. As John argues:

> We clearly and urgently need to have a better appreciation of how women are addressed by the beauty business: in what ways

they consent to the new and impossible standards of sexual attractiveness beamed at them, what levels of consumption are now considered normal if not necessary, or what aspirations lead so many to hone their skills and their bodies in the hope of a modeling career" (2000: 374).

To what extent are these Western images replacing indigenous aesthetics of female beauty? To what extent are such images viewed as foreign and thus not representative of normative standards for Indian women? What is the impact of the proliferation of these Western images on the Indian advertising industry as well as on Indian women's own understandings of their beauty and attractiveness?

Overall, similar kinds of depictions of men and women in Indian and Western advertisements suggests that the problems with gender advertising in the United States are also prevalent in India. The ways that gender advertising objectifies women, depicts them as sex objects, promotes the beauty myth, and encourages unhealthy behaviours suggests the gender advertising in India, as the US and elsewhere in the world, has negative consequences for the status of women in both cultures. In addition, the predominance of magazine advertisements featuring Western or Westernized women is also potentially harmful to the self-esteem and self-acceptance of Indian women whose appearance is markedly different. Since economic liberalization and globalization make it more difficult to eliminate or even reduce the powerful effects of these advertisements, the impact of Western ideals and norms on Indian cultural understandings of gender and how they are manifested in advertising must also be seriously assessed.

REFERENCES

Bryant, Erica, "Can't Buy My Love: Jean Kilbourne Takes on the World of Advertising," Blue Jean Online, http://www.bluejeanonline.com/features/features_archives/features0301b.html

Curties, Mandi and Corina MacKay, "Interview with Naomi Wolf," on line at Greeenleft Website, http://www.greenleft.org.au/back/1991/33/33-24.htm (1991).

Das, Mallika, "Men and Women in Indian Magazine Advertisements: A Preliminary Report," *Sex Roles: A Journal of Research*, 43: 9-10 (November 2000), pp. 699-717 on line at http://www.findarticles.com

Dittrich, Liz, "About-Face facts on BODY IMAGE," on line at About-Face Website, http://www.about-face.org/r/refs/media.shtml

—, "About-Face facts on the MEDIA," on line at About-Face Website, http://www.about-face.org/r/refs/media.shtml

Faludi, Susan, *Backlash: The Undeclared War Against American Women* (New York: Crown, 1991).

Frith, Katherine Toland, Hong Cheng and Ping Shaw, "Race and beauty: a Comparison of Asian and Western models in women's magazine advertisements," *Sex Roles: A Journal of Research*, 50: 1-2 (2004), pp. 53-61.

Furnham, Adrian, and Twiggy Mak, "Sex-role stereotyping in television commercials: A review and comparison of fourteen studies done on five continents over 25 years," *Sex Roles: A Journal of Research*, 41: 5-6 (1999), pp. 413-37.

Gallagher, Margaret, *Gender Settings: New Agendas for Media Monitoring and Advocacy* (London: Zed Books, 2001).

Griffin, Michael, K. Viswanath and Dona Schwartz, "Gender Advertising in the US and India: Exporting Cultural Stereotypes," *Media, Culture, and Society*, 16 (1994), pp. 487-507.

Hornor, Marianne, "The 'who', 'what', 'when', 'where' and 'why' of 'How' Advertising Works," http://www.ciadvertising.org/studies/student/98_fall/theory/hornor/who.htm (1998).

Jacobsen, Michael and Laurie Mazur, "Sexism and Sexuality in Advertising," in M. F. Jacobson and L. A. Mazur (eds.), Marketing Madness: A Survival Guide For A Consumer Society (Boulder, CO: Westview Press 1995), pp. 74-87, on line at Media, Power, and Culture, School of Journalism and Mass Communications, Kent-State University Website, http://www.personal.kent.edu/~glhanson/readings/advertising/wom eninads.htm (accessed May 3, 2004).

John, Mary, "Globalisation, Sexuality and the Visual Field: Issues and non-issues for cultural critique," in Mary John and Janaki Nair (eds.), *A Question of Silence? The Sexual Economies of Modern India* (New Delhi: Kali for Women, 2000), pp. 368-96.

Kilbourne, Jean, *Deadly Persuasion: Why Women and Girls Must Fight the Addictive Power of Advertising* (New York: Free Press, 1999).

—, Can't Buy My Love (New York: Simon and Schuster, 1999), excerpted on her websites: http://www.jeankilbourne.com and http://www.cant-buymylove.com

—, Killing Us Softly: Advertising's Image of Women (Northampton, MA: Media Education Foundation, 2000) (video documentary).

—, Slim Hopes: Advertising and the Obsession with Thinness (Northampton, MA: Media Education Foundation, 1995)(video-recording).

—, Still Killing Us Softly: Advertising's Image of Women (Cambridge, MA: Cambridge Documentary Films, 1987)(videorecording).

Murnen, Sarah, Linda Smolak, J. Andrew Mills, Lindsey Good, "Thin, Sexy Women And Strong, Muscular Men: Grade-School Children's Responses to Objectified Images of Women and Men," *Sex Roles: A Journal of Research*, 49: 9-10 (November 2003), pp. 427-37, on line at http://www.findarticles.com/p/articles/mi_m2294/is_9-10_49/ai_1108 13265

Reading. Anna, "Women, Men and the Mass Media," World YWCA Website, http://www.worldywca.org/common_concern/sept1997/ wm_media.html (1997).

Rohlinger, D. Andrea, "Eroticizing Men: Cultural Influences on Advertising and Male Objectification," *Sex Roles: A Journal of Research*, 46: 3-4 (2002), pp. 61-74, on line at http://www.findarticles.com

Singh, Tanuja, and Denise Schoenbachler, "Women's Advertising in Developing Nations: An Analysis of the Thematic and Information Content of Indian Magazine Advertisements," *Journal of Asia-Pacific Business*, 4(2) (2002), pp. 3-28.

Strategic Marketing Website Editorial, "Perspectives: Female role portrayals in Women's magazines," Strategic Marketing Website, http://www.etstrategicmarketing.com/smNov-Dec1/persp_women.ht m (2004).

Verma, Manish, Gender Roles in Advertising (PhD dissertation research, unpublished, on file with the author at Himachal Pradesh University, Shimla, H.P., India).

Wolf, Naomi, *The Beauty Myth: How Images of Beauty Are Used Against Women* (New York: Anchor Books, 1992).

Wysocki, Diane Kholos, "Using film to teach Women's Studies courses: a teaching aid recommendation," *Journal of International Women's Studies*, 3(2) (2002), pp. 70-74.

9

Violence
A Norm against Women in South Asia

Manjeet Bhatia

It is violence when the female foetus is aborted; when there is no celebration with the birth of a girl child; when children (usually girl child) are denied schooling in order to get help in domestic chores or to look after the younger siblings; when young boys are trained to be offensive; when the adolescent boy considers growing as a sanction to harass girls.

It is violence when spaces get gendered, and girls develop psychological fear of darkness and for boys/men it becomes an opportunity to exercise power; when child marriage takes place and one partner pays a greater price due to lack of opportunities to her; when family does not invest in women and women lack property rights.

It is violence when married women are not allowed to visit their native family or are not allowed to work outside home.

It is violence when women are objectified – in social norms and traditions, in media, in family when she is forced to use her body for living and she is sexually assaulted specially in disturbed and wartime situations; when she is sexually violated to settle political scores.

> It is violence when she is the 'honour' of the family and thus is an object that can be traded or killed to protect that honour.
>
> It is violence when men are made beasts by a system of thought which accepts that they can kill their own sisters and wives in the name of culture, tradition and family honour.
>
> It is violence when new economic opportunities make working women robots in gendered spaces;
>
> It is violence when political opportunities for women come without the social support.

The above rhetorical introduction identifies the many violence against women. Violence as is understood today goes far beyond the physical and encompasses many abuses that deny the woman her rights.

It will be quite illuminating to understand what according to some South Asian activists are the causes of violence against women:[1]

> *Masculinity defined at women's expense*
> We consider women as valuable property – to be protected from damage and presented to the husband in a prime condition. This morbid obsession with preservation of virginity is at the very root of the behaviour patterns of men in our society. When a man wants real revenge from his enemy, he will invariably try to degrade his opponents' women. He is inflicting irrecoverable damage to the property of his opponent. – Pakistani man, volunteer NGO worker and researcher
>
> *Drunkenness*
> Sometimes sexual violence is due to inebriation. Even, say, wanting to protect yourself with a condom – the women are scared to ask the man when he is drunk. The women think that he will get aggressive and shout and beat her up. – Sri Lankan woman, NGO executive director
>
> *No property rights for women*
> The root cause of violence against women and girls is their lack of property rights. A woman is born as another's property, not her own. Legally, she has no rights, up to age 35. – Nepali woman, lawyer

> *Inequality is taught*
> The kind of education that is imparted tends to veer towards discrimination against women. You know the role models that are portrayed, the kinds of stories that are taught to students – where the man is the bread-earner and the woman is the housewife. – Nepali woman, journalist

> *Misuse of religion*
> Generally, religion is used as a tool to oppress women. – Pakistani man, political activist

> *Economic exploitation*
> Also, upper-caste dominance and capitalism ... both are leading to more and more violence against women... Basically, dowry harassment by in-laws takes place because they want to extract money assets.... It's very funny; people would rather not invest in their daughter's education and personality development but keep accumulating money for her dowry! – Indian woman, who works with prostitutes

> *Others*
> Causes of violence against women are: one, the fact that she is a woman; two, society looks at the woman as inferior; three, men's violent nature and culture of male dominance; four, lack of education; five, the recent phenomenon of women being attracted to vagabonds. – Indian man, lawyer (who did not explain his fifth point)

The above activists give cultural reasons that can provide some insight into the understanding of the basis that perpetuates violence against women and girls in the changing and newly emerging socio-political environment of South Asia.

The continuum on which we can locate violence against women and girls range from sex slavery and objectification on the one hand to sexual harassment at work place on the other. Whether it is girl child being forcibly married off and considered property by the families or the *adivasi* women being sexually exploited the women is socially constructed to be economically dependent and put in vicious circles of low worth. If she tries to transcend this circle, her traditional sexual identity becomes an impediment and she is denied a dignified environment to do remunerative work. *In short, it is denial of agency*. Women's life can be seen as a continuum with one end being the right to survive and the right to dignity on the other.

If we see the activists' opinion on the causes of violence against women/girls against this background of the region, it is easy to see that violence could be a way of life here, where the woman's low worth traps her in an inescapable vicious cycle of violence and subjugation.

Activists have often related violence to cultural norms and practice. This is the usual perception, till we recognize the materiality link with violence. It does not mean that ideology or norms do not play a role in perpetuating violence against women and girls. The materiality relation to violence further defines and brings into focus the causes of violence. This link gets further defined in the present era of globalization, where new relations of production are emerging and they are forming new set of relations with the existing relations, norms and practices.

These new set of structures and relations have exploded certain myths. For instance, well-entranched cultural ideas like sons are preferred over daughters as they are required for performing last rites; it is with sons that a lineage survives, and sons are the old age investment, or that daughters have to be given away in marriage and investing in them is like watering a plant in other's courtyard or that huge amount of money is required for dowry to be given at the time of marriage, can be seriously questioned.

In today's times of globalization last rites is hardly the overwhelming consideration for son preference. It is material consideration of prosperity and economic control that reinforces the cultural norms and that is the reason as to why, sex-selective abortions to kill the female foetuses are the choice of the affluent and urbanized in India.

South Asia is a region spotted with internal turmoil. Violence in the region is mainly political in nature and is very volatile. Nepal, Sri Lanka, Pakistan and India are all embroiled in political strife of different natures. People of Nepal after sustained people's movement have recently further democratized their country by curbing the powers of the monarchy. The ethnic struggle for identity in Sri Lanka continues to claim human life and keeps the island burning. Conflicts based on regional aspirations plague both India and Pakistan. The gender impact of these political violences needs to be carefully looked at.

Historically, turmoil and conflict expresses itself through the violation of women's bodies. In this region, in particular, whether it is during war, communal violence or settling political scores, these are women who are always at the receiving end though it may not be always apparent. Chenoy refers to such violence against Sri Lankan women in this volume.

The birth of Bangladesh also gave birth to children of rapes, (over 200,000 Bengali women were raped during the war of independence). Communal violence in the recent riots in state of Gujarat, India, expressed itself through rape in a way where it seems rape is the norm rather than an exception. Violence against women is a norm which gets worse during conflicts/riots and war.

An activist revealed that in his interaction with men of a resettled colony in Delhi, he discovered that "men think that a woman has to be regularly abused or scolded to keep her under control. She is slapped even if she does not put the right amount of salt in the husband's food". Such kind of violence may even surface in the so-called educated community. Use of abusive language (usually a derogatory reference to female genitals or the suggestion of sexual violation of a female relative) is a way of humiliating the woman. For men, in some regions, using gender-biased abuse as a part of daily vocabulary is so normal that mostly they are not even aware of the implications of the abuse. In the first instance of the woman being slapped violence becomes a way of life, whereas when abusive language is being used it is the violence of marginalization and silencing.

There have been several cases of rape in moving cars in the capital city of India. Women in big cities live in the paradox of expanding opportunities and shrinking safe spaces. Recently, a woman working in Bangalore (the city with lot of IT multinational companies in Karnataka, a southern state of India) call centre was raped and killed by the driver of the car that company provided. Though such incidents generate a lot of media attention as well as an intense debate on the safety of women, yet a life of dignity and independence, even for the well-educated woman, appears to be a distant dream.

Cultural construction of womanhood, it appears, is static, and is unable to accept woman as an independent human being. The woman, who has freedom of thought, space and a mind of her own, is now made the target of violence.

In this region, democracy though valued is not practised in its true spirit. Democracy makes space for change of values and for voices from the margins. Traditionally, women are less valued in this region, though the paradox is, they are often worshipped as deities.[2] To challenge such identities democracy does offer public space that would be difficult to find in the traditional order. But it does not come without its own struggles, mainly for two relational reasons. Firstly, democracies in this region are at the best semi-democracies, because they reflect and respond to the traditional seats of power and control. A closer look at the process of elections and the elected representatives shows that publicly power is vested in traditional caste and class structures. It is these structures that perpetuate violence against girls/women. They continue to have control and define social identities.

Secondly, since democracy offers space to build new centres of power or/and challenge the traditional ones, new forms of violence against women/girls also emerge in this system. For example, the following incident in Bangladesh is testimony of how political election processes can be an instigation for violence:

> Mahima, a young woman, was raped by three youth activists of the BNP (Bangladesh National Party) and one youth activist of Jamaat-e-Islam, part of the ruling coalition, in what was suspected to be a politically motivated action against her father, an Awami League worker in a village in Rajshahi Division. The rapists took photographs of the rape scene and told the family

they would be distributed if a complaint was made. Following Mahima's suicide on 19 February, police brought charges against the four culprits. A court sentenced them to death in October. Their appeal against the death sentence was pending.[3]

In India, women getting elected to panchayat[4] have been exposed to a confrontation with traditional seats of power without any social change in their support. As a result, many of the elected women members have faced violence.

Here is a typical case as reported by Shail Mayaram:[5]

"Shanti Devi, a Dalit[6] Sarpanch in Tonk district's gram panchayat Polyara was continually harassed for the entire term of four and a half years that she held office. Her clothes were ripped off by the former Rajput[7] sarpanch of her panchayat and later an attempt was made on her life when his son pursued her in the fields on a tractor. Her initial attempts to file a criminal case failed in the face of police intransigence.

It is to be noted that the assailants were protected by a political party. Shanti Devi could register a case under the Scheduled Castes and Scheduled Tribes Atrocities Act, but justice in such cases is nowhere to be reached. In her report, Mayaram further states that "the witnesses, however, terrorized by the ex-sarpanch, who was a Rajput, turned hostile and refused to testify in her favour". The policeman only proved to be the agent of patriarchy. Shail points out that "the investigating policeman told her that he would give a favorable report only if she spent a night with him". The 'untouchable' woman sarpanch from Raigarh was thus silenced by the policeman with a threat of a physical violation of her body.

Interestingly, the powerlessness of women in the social structures gets utterly exposed as usually women do not even get support from her own community. Shanti Devi got no support from her family and caste community. They were more worried about the future of young girls of their community in finding marriage partners than standing with her in fighting for justice. Mayaram writes, "it took a very intense group session and a good deal of probing at a workshop in Tonk before Shanti Devi was even able to tell her story"[8] that too on the prompting of a colleague Muslim sarpanch who was witness to her trauma.

The so-called 'love marriages' challenge the traditional structures of power too. Especially, in an agricultural community, which traditionally has immovable assets. Patrilocal marriage being the norm, such marriages based on individual choice can upset ownership of land if girls marry outside community and demands property rights.

The stranglehold of traditional structures and the extent these structures perpetuate itself is clear from the following analysis of 'honour killings' in a district of Haryana,[9] India.

Jatmati, an activist associated with the All India Democratic Women's Association (AIDWA) for past fifteen years in the state of Haryana shared her and her team's experience and understanding of 'honour killings' in this region in a recent seminar[10] and pointed out that in Haryana, traditionally, inter-caste marriages are not allowed. Prospective brides and grooms are sought within the same caste, taking care not to select individuals from the first three gotras[11] and neighbouring villages.

She very rightly notes that in marriages done on individual choice are seeds of egalitarian society and this threatens the status quo in the community. Those in power in this system have vested interest and thus feel threatened by young people wanting to marry outside their caste.

For instance, the marriage of an upper caste girl with a dalit boy has the potential of caste power slipping into the hands of erstwhile-dominated groups and thus, blurring the identities and the power equation of both the communities. It can lead to major upsetting of social structures. Such concerns have been expressed when the activist and her team confronted panchayat members on specific cases.[12] Thus, it is best to contain such potentially radical revolts by killing in the name of honour and tradition. Interestingly, almost all social and administrative structures including the police participate in maintaining the status quo by not only not treating the killing as a crime but by falling in line with the power structures.

Jatmati and her team's survey about the socio-economic status of the young couples daring to challenge the social norms, reveals that the girls who get killed generally belong to poor or lower-middle class families and have had some educational exposure. Comparatively better students who show above average intelligence, generally choose trustworthy and responsible partners. The boys' economic status is often not a paramount consideration. It is not that all young people have the choice to get married to their chosen partner. Very often, the boy buckles under family pressure and the girl is betrayed. Those who choose to honour their relationship and decide to get married are well aware of the possible violent out come.

In an interaction with a couple who had eloped and hid themselves and had to go without food and job for days lest the girl's family discovers them it was revealed that the girl had to forfeit her property rights and all relations with her family.

The research notes that it is usually the families of the victims, relatives and people from their *gotra* (community) who kill. But, the whole process is led by members of the caste panchayat and the khap panchayat.[13] Usually, a small group of men, well aware of the implications of these marriages, lead in these killings. They are not simpleton villagers. On the contrary, they are educated. They use modern techniques for farming and daily living. They take the benefits of the caste and patriarchal systems to arrogate social and economic power for themselves. Others get sucked into these violent designs as they get carried away in the name of brotherhood and honour of the community. Actually, majority of the people have nothing to do with the violence. They get involved, I think, because this is the only way to claim and assert an identity in a situation where no other identity is possible. The threat of being outcast at the village level is a real one that can have far-fetching consequences for the individual family. Dalits and women are never allowed in these panchayats. Both groups remain powerless in the community. Village community has close networks and powerful identities that is dynamic and impacts everyday life. Any intervention in this matter on the basis of individual rights is bound to create conflict in this social context.

The state administration lacks will to intervene in these matters as individuals holding key administrative/political positions belong to these powerful sections of the community. Chief Minister and other ministers visit these panchayats and are honoured by them. In the given situation, in which political, administrative and social factors have become a nexus to protect traditional structures of power, any intervention seeking redressal or change is deliberately marginalized. Though it seems that these structures are extremely rigid and impossible to break through, recent initiates show that spaces for a more democratic approach may be formed if acceptable alternatives are provided.

Uninvited, AIDWA activists sat through one such khap panchayat and in spite of initial resentment by the panchayat members, the activists presented their point of view. The following is a jist of what happened:

> Once the discussion of the khap panchayat got over, the activists requested that they be allowed to speak. Initially, this request was rejected. Later, after some convincing, the activists were allowed to speak. They pointed out to the assembled panchayat that major social issues like dowry, infanticide and unemployment are not subjects of discussion whereas an issue like a marriage of choice becomes the subject of paramount concern.
>
> The activists mentioned that women are being bought[14] at a price everyday from different areas irrespective of caste or class. How is it that caste does not become a matter of concern then? The panchayat ultimately protects rapists and kill lovers. Is this justice? Where will such things take the community? When the activists spoke, everyone listened attentively. It was obvious that the members of the panchayat were not interested in developmental issues that would actually change the qualitative life of the community but wished to focus only on those issues that would help in reinforcing power structures and caste

> hegemonies. The facts were put truthfully and in a straightforward manner before them and it was apparent to all that the activists had no personal agenda or vested interests. Actually, a large section of the society's interests are not served in the process of working of these panchayats, and in the kind of issues that are taken up for discussion.
>
> So, ultimately, the working of these panchayats goes against the interests of the majority of people. But, nobody speaks on behalf of the majority. So, in reports that suggest that the entire village community decided on an issue, it is more likely that the decisions of a few selfish people and their vested interests are being thrust upon the majority. It is a superficially constructed will. Women, dalits and poor do not participate in this decision-making process. The voice of the people is not heard not because they have no voice but because they are not allowed to participate.

It will not be surprising if almost similar report comes from other parts of South Asia. Though most of the nations of South Asia practise democracy as the basis of their governance, yet the real power lies with the traditional socio-political, religious structures rather than with the people. The representatives of the people and the government more or less continue to accept these structures because they perpetuate the class and caste hegemonies. The issue of gender is always lost in the process. But, it must be stressed that perhaps democracy and democratic processes are the only alternatives available in which these power structures can be confronted by strategic interventions and the initiating of meaningful dialogue.

Women/girls trying to traverse new spaces for work also face new forms of violence that surface as the pervading assumptions of low worth and identities get subsumed to these spaces. It is in the confrontation between pre-conceived gender-biased assumptions and the efforts to release one from these identities that women face newer forms of violence. Here, I would like to cite study, done by Padmini Swaminathan in South India[15] of women factory workers, to illustrate the dynamics of this confrontation.

The study showed that most of the respondents felt overburdened with double duties of housework and remunerative work. World over studies have pointed out development invariably has meant more work for women. The following narration by an unmarried respondent, aged 25, and working in a garment unit in MEPZ, is quite illuminating:

> We wake up every morning at 5.30 a.m. My sister cooks and leaves for work. I help a bit with the cooking. Then I clean the courtyard, draw kolam, wash dishes, sweep and swab the house and such other activities in a hurry and leave without even being able to eat. I have to run because at 8.55 a.m., the company rings a bell. We have to be inside before that. At 9 a.m., they ring another bell. By then we should have started our work. If we are even 2 minutes late, the gate is locked and we have to return home. There is no other way. The company timings are from 9 a.m. till 6 p.m. Compulsory overtime of one hour has to be done in the evening everyday. If necessary, one hour in the morning and two hours in the evening have to be done. "Those not doing this can stay home" – that is how strictly they talk without even a little bit of conscience. The company provides no bus facility. For those who come from a distance an amount of Rs. 100 per month is given. I walk daily for 15 minutes to reach the company. It takes the same amount of time in the evening. When there is urgent work, like in the past three years, in the morning from 7.30-9 a.m. and in the evening from 6-8 p.m. overtime had to be done. Those who disagree to do overtime are given one week's or one month's leave and asked to discontinue after that. So, the company gets to pay one less salary for a month. Not only that, they dump the extra work on someone else. But if the workers do not get salary for a month and have to stay home, what will happen to the family?

The wage employment enhances the individual worth, yet it creates newer conflicts. It is recorded that wage income has enabled families to improve the quality of food, yet the women are unable to eat before going to work due to lack of time and lack of appetite due to the stress.[16] A divorced woman, aged 28, staying with her parents and working in MEPZ, told us:

> Daily after completing all the work at home, when I go to work, I feel fed up. In all the hurry, I do not feel like eating in the morning.

Overburden of work has been reported by all married and a few unmarried respondents. Poor infrastructure in terms of fuel and sanitation and unhelpful attitude of men, add to the burdensome nature of the work. Men wage earners too have similar harsh working conditions but in their case the woman provides a supporting role whereas when a woman goes to work, she is not provided any support from her husband or any other male relative and has to manage both home and the place of work.

It is important for women to become wage earners. Their wages have the potential to open up closed spaces where women traditionally inhabit. It offers possibilities of negotiating identities. But, the confidence that women get as a provider comes at a heavy cost because she continues to play all the traditional roles in addition to the wage earning. The wage also usually goes in repaying loans either to fund the education of their brothers, supporting business of male members or marriage of younger siblings. Padmini Swaminathan notes that a corresponding support from a male relation is hardly available. For example, not many men would borrow money to support the education of a woman relative.[17]

So, the woman stretches herself to be part of the new spaces yet allocation of the material benefits in her favour does not happen.

In another study, conducted at the industrial town of Chengalput, close to the metropolitan city of Chennai in southern India, where most of the units are pharmaceutical units, the focus was on the transformation of the occupational profile of labour force and the social implications of this change. The members of the lower strata of society, or the dalits who had been previously engaged as agricultural labourers, have now shifted to doing work in these industrial units. The study was to evaluate if the dalit peasants had benefited in terms of social upward mobility with the agrarian economics changing to industry-based economy. It is interesting to note the effects of such shift on women. The study reports that, as far as women are concerned, there is no substantial change. In fact, they face greater harshness at MEPZ due to "...compulsory overtime, immediate retrenchment, if worker refuses overtime, impossible targets, restricted use of toilets, preference for unmarried girls and pervasive practice of sexual harassment..."[18]

Bottle washing is usually women's job. Usually, a woman worker is expected to wash 1,000 bottles a day. Most manage to wash only 700 to 750. Similarly, the garment units also set unachievable targets for individual worker. The quantum of work is laid out and it is expected that in an hour 100 and in 8 hours 800 pieces have to be finished. Those who are not able to meet the target have to compulsorily do overtime. If worker still fails, her identity card is taken away which implies her attendance cannot be marked both at the time of exit or entry, as a result salary gets cut. A young woman in a garment factory said:

> We cannot complete 800 pieces in one day. Only if we work extremely hard can we finish that. From morning till noon we work very fast. But, in the afternoon, it is not possible to maintain that speed. We do not have the strength... The back hurts a lot. Hands and legs feel weak. Legs swell up. Even if we lift our heads while stitching we are shouted at. After all this if we have to go home and do the housework, pay attention to our family, we will just die.

The above experiences show how the woman's private identity moves into the arena of the public and spaces for reinforced violence are created.

Factory workers have also reported sexual harassment at their work sites. A married garment worker, aged 38, and working in MEPZ, said:

> The men who work with us and the supervisor speak with double meanings. They harass us regardless of age. They look at newly married women and say, "this sister worked very hard last night and is sleeping here". If the bra is visible, "wow, the banian looks new" and they laugh. If the saree has moved, they say, "good morning". On Sundays and on leave days, when we have

> overtime, they drink a lot on the premises. The manager also ogles at the women when he gets an opportunity and flirts... They behave as if they are threatening a dog to get the work done. ... Generally, women are not respected in the company... They do not make eye contact while talking. They look at the breasts instead and their eyes seek our consent. If we question this or go against any of this, we get a memo...

The newer spaces created by the changing economy in most South Asian countries are as much gender biased as the traditional spaces that the woman occupied. It means that the prejudices that were voiced and perpetuated against the woman in the familiar spaces of her home and immediate environment, are now being perpetuated openly and blatantly in an unfamiliar and new space of remunerative work. Further, the woman is now confronting a collective group of men on regular basis who violate and humiliate her. This is not the same as the humiliation and subjugation that a woman may feel within the confines of her home or as an agricultural labour.

The woman's entry into non-traditional spaces cannot alone be the reason to explain the increase in violence against her. The new spaces create their own relation of production. Women working in agricultural economy could not have faced the harshness the woman has to face at the hands of factory managers. Gender blindness in these industrial/office spaces, which are not gender sensitized or deliberately ignore the women worker's plight, adds to the violence that the woman already faces in patriarchal household structures and familial relations, which continues to exercise its hold on her.

Limitations of Law

Women's movements in this region have succeeded to different degrees in making legal interventions to address the issue of violence against women and girls. Table 1 gives an overall view of the various laws passed by the governments to check violence against women and girls in South Asia.

Table 1
Laws Computing Violence Against Women in South Asia

Country	*Domestic violence*	*Rape and sexual assault*	*Sexual harassment*	*Marital rape*
Bangladesh	2	1	1	0
Bhutan	0	1	0	2
India	1	2	2	0
Maldives	4	0	0	0
Nepal	4	2	0	2
Pakistan	2	4	0	0
Sri Lanka	4	2	2	2

Updated version of table referred in Progress of South Asian Women 2005: A Series for the Fifth South Asia Regional Ministerial Conference Celebrating Beijing Plus Ten, United Nations Development Fund for Women, UNIFEM

Key: 0 = no provisions or unknown; 1= specific legislation; 2=non-specific legislation; 3=non-specific legislation, being planned, drafted or reviewed; 4= specific legislation, being planned, drafted or reviewed.

Source: Appendix 1, Legislation on violence against women by country, "Not a minute more: Ending Violence against Women", UNIFEM, New York, 2003, p. 90.

I understand that it requires certain kind of activism to make legal theory intrinsic to the feminist's practice of social theory. Operation of law goes hand in hand with making of law. Operation of law "holds the possibility of a tool for political transformation in the position of women, a possibility yet unrealized."[19]

Presently, law is discriminatory and perpetuates patriarchal norms; community-based laws surely do so. For example, let us see the manner in which the judicial process was appropriated in a case in which a woman was punished for a crime she had not even committed. Vasudha Dhagamwar refers to this story about a Marathi nomadic tribe by Laxman Gaikwad.

The story tells us traditionally those who delivered 'justice' in Gaikwad's tribe were called *talangay* and no woman was part of the panchayats that deliberated on specific cases. Hearing was done in full view of large crowd of male witnesses. The involved parties had to pay for such sittings and the travel fare of the members of the *talangay* for each hearing. A panchayat could sit for two to three days. Once the decision is arrived at and fine determined, there would also be feast provided by the parties. The feast would include meat, chicken and liquor which are all ingredients of male entertainment.

In this specific case, an impromptu panchayat at a wedding, where groom's family raised objection to the fact that the bride's mother's mother 'kept' a man of another caste. The bride's mother, though, was married within caste. Her daughter could not get married without washing away the sins that her granny had committed.

The panchas, who sat to deliberate on the matter, had no doubt that the mother of the bride has to be punished before the marriage can take place. Vasudhaji writes, "some wanted her to eat excrement; some wanted her to be fined a sum of Rs. 2,000; some suggested the tip of the nose to be cut. And finally, a man more moderate than others suggested that her head should be shaved... The poor woman was summoned and fell at everyone's feet, by way of self-abnegation and apology."[20] She had to apologize and punished for a crime she had not committed.

"The women's head was speedily shaved without using soap to soften the hair and her shaven head was smeared with bright orange mercury paste, normally used to anoint stone idols. It would make her stand out and would probably have made the sore head burn. After the terrible experience the mother of the bride hid herself in tirrible humiliation. The day ended with a feast of a whole pig and plenty of liquor provided by the bridal couple to the *talanga*."[21]

Such deliverance of justice through an unwritten legal system that the community has traditionally acknowledged is very much an accepted practice in many parts of South Asia today. The above story is an illustration of such practices in a community at a point of time in history; today, the practice continues but is varied and perhaps operates in a much more subtle way than it did in the Marathi tribe of the story. The central issue of course being that in such practices the woman is totally made invisible and her voice is completely silenced. Such traditional systems of justice deliverance not only outcast the woman from the process but also from defining the crime as well.

In another context, similar marginalization of the woman may be discerned. The Indian Muslim community debated the Muslim women's case of discrimination in the rules of *nikahanama* and women activists expected self-correction. In spite of what was considered a reformist move, the outcome was disappointing. Muslim women's rights organizations were unhappy over the modified *nikahnama* as it was finally proposed. "As per the draft, the wife continues to have no right to divorce the husband without his consent. However, the man is allowed to do so despite her unwillingness."[22] The activists feel that the proposed *nikahnama* only perpetuated the existing discrimination. They also demanded a parallel system of justice and women be allowed to take domestic disputes to court of law.[23] This shows how a traditional system of understanding of justice still permeates into modern-day initiatives and remain as gender insensitive as before.

Women's movement in South Asia has succeeded in bulldozing the state to make certain progressive laws without much corresponding ethical or value change in the system. Perhaps, there is no other way. The vicious circle has to be broken either by the change in values of the society in favour of women or the progressive values have to be commanded through law. Since gender justice is not the priority issue with the successive governments of South Asian countries, the only alternative left is to consciously change the legal system into it being more gender sensitive and at the same time strives towards a corresponding change in value system.

As far as deliverance of law within a community space is concerned, it is effectively the patriarchal local rural community all over South Asia that defines the concept of justice in which the woman is excluded thereby perpetuating further violence against women and girls. Such systems of justice may even perpetuate violence against women for the 'crime' committed by a family member. A Pakistani woman was raped because her brother was having an affair with a girl of another community. Women's abysmal status in this region is very clearly reflected in the manner these systems of justice operate. At the local level she is an outcast and the formal legal system of the constitution is too distant.

Violence against women in South Asia is a norm. Culturally, she is disadvantaged and it cripples her *being* for rest of her life. When a woman struggles to traverse newer pastures in order to redefine herself and to remove sticky patriarchal identities, she faces new forms of violence as if in vengeance. This happens in all the spaces that she dares to inhabit – in factories, in political arenas and in personal relationships. As she straddles in the new spaces formed by changing economic conditions, the myth of the woman being chivalrously protected by the patriarchal society is conspicuously shattered.

NOTES

1. As reported by Ruth Finney Hayward, in *Breaking the Earthenware Jar: Lessons from South Asia to End Violence Against Women and Girls*, UNICEF, 2000, p.16.
2. In this region goddesses are worshipped which is the ideal image of a woman. In practice, it mostly amounts to ordinary women expected to emulate them which results in lot of stereotyping of women.
3. Amnesty International, report, 2003.
4. The lowest rung in governance.
5. Shail Mayaram, 'New Modes of Violence: The Backlash Against Women in the Panchayat system' in Karin Kapadia (ed.), *The Violence of Development,* Zed Books, London, 2002, pp. 406-7.
6. Low caste.
7. Higher caste.
8. Mayaram, op. cit.
9. Haryana is a northwest state of India. It is one of the rich states where child sex ratio is falling alarmingly.
10. CWDS seminar in March 2006.
11. It is sub-division of caste.
12. Sonia and Rampal; Darshana and Ashish cases.
13. Khap panchayat is made of caste panchayats of a few neighbouring villages.

14. Due to declining sex ratio number of women in marriageable age is reducing and in some cases women from outside the state are brought and also bought. In an interview conducted by the author in Kurukshetra district of Haryana, a case of marriage with woman from Himachal Pradesh was reported by the Sarpanch.
15. Studies based on the lives and experiences of garment workers of Madras Export Processing Zone (MEPZ) and "The Costs of Work" as cited in "The Trauma of 'Wage Employment' and 'Burden of Work' for Women in India" by Padmini, Swaminathan in *The Violence of Normal Times*; Kalpana Kannabiran (ed.), Women Unlimited, New Delhi, 2005.
16. Research shows that allocation in households is determined by female contribution and not by prosperity alone. (see: Satish Agnihotri, *Sex Ration Patterns in the Indian Population*, New Delhi, 2000, p. 272).
17. Ibid., p. 103.
18. Ibid., p. 100.
19. Kannabiran, Kalpana, (ed.), *The Violence of Normal Times*, Women Unlimited, Delhi, 2005, p.4.
20. Ibid.
21. Ibid.
22. *Lawyers Collective*, December, 2005.
23. Indian justice system allows communities to retain their personal laws.

10

THE SOUTH ASIAN GIRL CHILD

HER RIGHT TO EDUCATION

Manzoor Ahmed

The topic of right to education of the girl child combines two elements – the right to education and knowledge of the girl child and the instrumental nature of this right in fulfilling other rights of the girl child as a person and as she grows up to be an adult and a citizen. This is in accord with the generally accepted interpretation of the right to education – a right in itself and as a means for fulfilling other human rights. In addressing the subject, in this paper, following four points will be covered:

(a) The context for survival and development of the girl child in South Asia.

(b) Education as a right and as an instrument for fulfilling all human rights.

(c) Where does South Asia stand in fulfilling the right to education of the girl child.

(d) What can be done to promote and protect the right to education of the girl child in South Asia and her development as a person and a citizen.

A premise that underlies this discussion is that, even as the girl child and women in our societies are subjected to grave discrimination and deprivation, these cannot be overcome by focusing exclusively on the plight of the girl child. The total structure of injustice and exploitation in society that creates and perpetuates the underclass, the excluded and the marginalized also nurtures and sustains discrimination and injustice against girls and women. Misogynist values and practices are the products of a long history and an entrenched culture of a social structure and polity that thrive on social division and exploitation in different forms. The solutions lie in a structural approach, not in attempts to alleviate isolated symptoms of discrimination, which in any case cannot be very effective or self-sustaining.

The struggle against gender inequality is not about sharing equally the deprivation and injustice suffered by all children. It has to be a struggle for claiming the rights of all children and overcoming at the same time the special disadvantages and extra burdens of the girl child. This position is not in conflict with:

- Recognizing and taking action against the "multiple jeopardy" of the girl child – her being a member of social groups which are disadvantaged in various ways and her being a girl and, therefore, subjected to additional discrimination in her own groups and in the larger society.
- Affirmative action and positive discrimination in favour of girls to compensate for historical and current disadvantage.
- Gender-disaggregated and gender-specific data, analyses and research and gender audit of programmes.

In fact, these measures are necessary to identify and analyze the problems and guide effective actions against disadvantage and discrimination of all forms in which gender-based discrimination is often deeply ingrained.

A second related premise is that, to paraphrase Amartya Sen, gender disparity in education is not one problem, but a collection of many problems. Sen wrote about seven types of gender inequality in South Asia – ranging from higher mortality rates for girls and women to inequality in access to basic services and discrimination in the household. All of these affect the fulfilment of human rights including the right to education and development of the girl child. The multiple origins and causes of the phenomenon of gender inequality demand a multifaceted and comprehensive response.

Close to half of the population in the nations of South Asia are children under 18, who will be adult citizens in the next decade and the next generation. As workers, they will turn the wheels of the economy. As citizens, they will have their say in large and small decisions of the nation. And, as members of the community and the family, they will be the actors in civil society and will decisively influence the future of the following generation – their own children. Two-thirds of the citizens in the year 2020 in South Asia have already been born and the leaders of our nations in the second half of the 21st century are now in their early formative years. Will the new generation carry on the legacy of gender inequality, causing deprivation and disempowerment to half of the population and the heavy social and personal costs that this situation entails for the whole society? If the answer is no, then, action has to be taken now to set a new course in policies, priorities, values and practices.

The Context of Survival and Development for the Girl Child

As the late Mahbub ul Haq famously wrote about South Asia: "... it has emerged as the poorest, the most illiterate, the most malnourished, and the least gender-sensitive region in the world". He did add a note of optimism when he said that South Asia also "has the potential to become the most dynamic region in the 21st century if there is massive investment in human development" (HDSA, 1998: 2). He would have agreed that a large part of this massive investment, not only in resources, but also in a change of values and creation of a new vision for the future, must be directed at improving the life prospects of the girl child in South Asia.

Despite progress made in the last two decades on various indicators of children's survival, health and development in South Asia, the region has not met most of the goals set for children for the year 2000 at the World Summit for Children in 1990. The region is in competition for the dubious distinction of being the most laggard on many of the indicators among all developing regions. Some basic statistics for around 2000 will bring the point home (Table 1).

Table 1

Some Indicators of the State of Children in South Asia, 2000

Indicators	*South Asia*	*Developing countries*	*World/Least developed countries*
Under-five mortality rate, 2000	100	91	83
% under-five underweight, 1995-2000	46	28	-
% children enrolled in primary school	71	80	82
% households using iodised salt, 1997-2000	55	70	69
% children receiving Vit. A supplement, 1999	35	50	80 (LDC)
% children with low birth weight, 2000	25	15	14
% children immunized, 2000	58	-	70+

Source: UNICEF, Progress since the World Summit for Children, A Statistical Review, 2001.

The state of girls and women in South Asia is most poignantly illustrated by the story of "100 million missing women" made well-known by Amartya Sen (1990) and addressed by others (Mazumdar, 2001; Agnihotri, 2002). In describing the context for development of the girl child and fulfilling her right to education, specific mention can be made of the health and nutrition situation and the situation of children in need of basic protection from threats to their human existence.

HEALTH AND NUTRITION OF CHILDREN AND WOMEN

As noted, the child mortality rate in South Asia is higher than the average of 91 for all developing countries and higher than for each developing region except Sub-Saharan Africa. The major killers of children – diarrhoea, acute respiratory infections, measles and malaria – still remain a serious threat. On top of these, the new hazard of the HIV-AIDS pandemic looms large. The worldwide campaign to eradicate polio has recorded impressive progress. Yet, South Asia, along with conflict-torn African countries, remains the last hurdle to reaching the final goal of global eradication. The maternal mortality rate in South Asian countries is among the highest in the world with an average of 430 deaths per 100,000 live births.

Half of the children under five in South Asia are underweight for their age. An equal proportion suffers from stunted growth. Almost a quarter of these children is categorized as severely underweight and stunted – below two standard deviations from median reference point. A quarter of the children is born with low birth weight – a significant predictor of child survival and adult health status. Half of the children and two-thirds of women suffer from iron deficiency (anaemia). The poor nutritional status of children and women in South Asia is the worst among all developing regions.

Special health needs of adolescents and women are beginning to receive some attention but effective programmes serving substantial numbers are yet to be commenced. A major health challenge in South Asia is to ensure that the special needs of pregnant women, reproductive healthcare of women, and the special health needs of adolescent girls and boys, so far given sparse attention, are met effectively.

Protection of Children in Special Need

The progress being made in protecting the rights and meeting the needs of children in the mainstream of society brings out in sharper relief the plight of large numbers of children who are marginalized and excluded in one or another way from the care and services which are their right. The total numbers in these excluded groups in South Asia add up to a very substantial proportion of the total child population.

Because of uncertain definitions of situations which call for special protection measures for children, overlapping categories, and just the lack of adequate data, precise numbers are difficult to establish. But, the numbers easily add up to at least a quarter of all children. As in most situations of deprivation and disadvantage, girls are the victims more often than their proportion in the population would suggest. The overlapping categories of especially difficult situations for children include:

- The worst form of child labour in which perhaps 100 million children in South Asia find themselves.
- Trafficking of children cross-border and within countries for sexual and economic exploitation.
- Absence of care and protection from families due to abandonment by or death of parents.
- Displacement of children due to civil conflicts and violence.
- Use of children in war in combatant and non-combatant roles.
- Physical and mental disabilities that impede normal growth and development of children or their participation in educational and other services. If the standard ratio of "1 in 10 with a degree of disability" is applied, this category will add up to over 50 million children, at least a quarter of whom will require specialized services beyond what can be offered by regular social services.

These situations of extreme deprivation and hardship are present in all the countries of South Asia and in which millions of children are trapped. Juan Somavia, Director General of ILO, calls them the "lost children". As he put it, "The lost children are the most exploited, the poorest of the poor: child soldiers, girls in brothels, young bonded workers in the factories, sweatshops, fields and homes of our seemingly prosperous globe. They are robbed of their health, their growth, their education – and often even their lives" (Somavia, 2000: 27).

Education as a Right and a Vehicle for Achieving Other Rights

Before discussing the education right of the girl child, it would be useful to establish a common reference point about the concept of the right to education.

The concept of the *right to education* is well established now. International treaties such as the Convention on the Rights of the

Child (CRC), the Convention on Eliminating All Forms of Discrimination against Women (CEDAW) as well as the twin United Nations conventions on civil and political rights and cultural, social and economic rights have all proclaimed the right to education for all. These agreements among nations have drawn international attention to the issue and have underscored the obligation of the international community to assist national authorities to fulfil this right. However, national constitutions and laws in general, including those in South Asia, also have recognized in a largely similar language the right to education for all children. The issue, therefore, is not as much the legal formulation of the right to education as the will to implement the existing law. Specific laws and regulations are necessary and useful in implementing the rights. However, if the will is lacking, laws themselves cannot be a substitute, as the controversy over the 83rd constitutional amendment in India on compulsory education suggests.

The intent of both international treaties and national laws are to proclaim the entitlement of all children to a level of basic education as defined in each national context. The right of universal entitlement does not extend beyond basic education, but it includes the right to equitable and non-discriminatory access to other levels of public education.

Education is also a vehicle for promoting other rights. In the human rights literature, the argument is made about the indivisibility of rights and the mutual complementarity of different domains of rights. However, the right to education and its fulfilment as a public and social service play a unique instrumental role in promoting and protecting human rights in general. Education can serve this unique role by:

(a) raising the level of awareness and knowledge about human rights;
(b) empowering and enabling people to exercise their choices; and
(c) developing attitudes, values and behaviour that create a social and moral environment for fulfilling human rights.

The concept of education as an inherent right and as an instrument for fulfilling other rights is the basis for the *rights-based approach to educational development*. The protagonists of this approach have found it useful in various ways, including the following:

- arguments for advocacy in education,
- criteria for analysis of the educational situation,
- formulation of policies and objectives,
- designing teaching content and classroom practices,
- planning "inclusive" education,
- establishing obligations of various parties including the state, society, parents, the international community and other actors in education, and
- allocation of resources.

The rights-based approach offers a new perspective and new tools for promoting implementation of the education rights. Its value lies more in strengthening the implementation effort rather than brandishing the rights as a "stick" over the head of errant governments.

The Educational Challenge: Where does South Asia Stand

Very substantial progress can be reported in basic education in South Asia since the 1970s. Adult literacy rate has reached from 38 per cent in 1980 to 47 per cent in 2000 (UNICEF, SOWCR 2004). Primary education enrolment has almost doubled since the 1970s to the gross rate of 90 per cent and the net rate of 74 per cent. In absolute numbers, these gains are huge, and in terms of percentages also the progress is impressive.

However, the facts remain that at the beginning of the new century:

- Almost half of the adults in South Asia or some 400 million are still illiterate. Nearly two-thirds of them are women.
- On a net basis, taking count of those attending and not attending school in the prescribed primary school age-group, nearly one quarter or 60 million children are not in school. Again, two-thirds not in school are girls.
- One-third of those who enter primary school drop out before reaching grade five – thus failing to acquire a functional and sustainable level of literacy and numeracy.

The problems in respect of access, participation and achievement manifest themselves in multiple disparities for the groups deprived of education. Despite progress in the past decade, especially in Bangladesh, in narrowing the gender gap in primary school enrolment, South Asia retains the dubious distinction of having the largest gap among all regions in primary school net enrolment rates between boys and girls. This gap varies in percentage points from 11 in Bhutan and 14 in India to 35 in Pakistan. Only Bangladesh, Sri Lanka and Maldives have achieved gender parity in primary school enrolment (these data are based on SOWC 2004; see Statistical Annex).

Gender inequality, expectedly enough, is bound up with overlapping layers of disadvantages related to being poor, linguistic and ethnic minorities, nomads, refugees, rural residents, slum dwellers, and working children.

Table 2

Multiple Layers of Disadvantage: Illiteracy Gap in India (% literate)

Rich urban male	90%
Poor urban male	59%
Poor rural male	47%
Poor rural female	24%
Poor rural scheduled caste female	17%

Source: HDSA, 1998, p. 4.

Poverty and other disadvantages arising from social exclusion that impede children's participation in education are inextricably linked with the phenomenon of working children. It is a catch-all category that includes a large proportion of South Asian children. The children may be engaged in relatively benign work, which may even facilitate school attendance by helping in defraying direct and indirect costs of schooling. The category also includes children engaged in work in extremely harmful, hazardous and slavery-like situations, which are threats to children's life and limbs, not to speak of being impediments to their education.

Because of the wide array of situations that constitute child labour, quantification of the problem has been difficult. Surveys that include recognized categories of paid labour of children underestimate children's work including some extremely harmful and hazardous forms of work in the informal economy such as children employed as domestic help and children subjected to commercial sexual exploitation. Estimate of child labourers in India cited often is around 44 million in the mid-1990s, in the age range of 5 to 15 years. The number in Pakistan is about 19 million and a survey in Bangladesh provides a figure of 6.3 million (HDSA, 1998: 7). In Nepal, 57 per cent of the population in the 10-14 year age-group is considered to be economically active (HDSA, 1998).

The 60 million children, about two-thirds girls, who have not enrolled in or dropped out from primary school, largely overlap the category described as child workers. Sufficient disaggregated data and analysis do not exist to show clearly the situation of girls among the overlapping categories of working and non-enrolled children.

There is no dearth of policy statements, strategies and programmes to achieve the goal of education for all and fulfilling the right to education for all children including the girl child. Vimala Ramachandran wrote six years ago about the gap between intention and action in respect of girls' and women's education in South Asia. She cited the 1986 National Policy on Education of India as a glowing example of a statement of intention. In its chapter titled "Education for Women's Equality" it was said,

> ...education will be used as an agent of basic change in the status of women. In order to neutralise the accumulated distortions of the past, there will be a well-conceived edge in favour of women. The national education system will play a positive, interventionist role in the empowerment of women. It will foster the development of new values through redesigned curricula, textbooks, the training and orientation of teachers, decision-makers and administrators, and the active involvement of educational institutions. This will be an act of faith and social engineering... (Ramachandran, 1998).

After a change of government, the 1986 national policy in India was reviewed in 1992 but was accepted with small modifications. The section on women's inequality was brought forward from chapter 4 to chapter 1 in the new Programme of Action to indicate a higher priority to the issue (GOI, Programme of Action, National Policy on Education, 1992).

A surge of new initiatives and creative ideas was seen in India in basic education following the 1986 Education Policy in the form of programmes in different states such as Andhra, Rajasthan, Karnataka, Uttar Pradesh, Bihar and Gujarat supported by different external donors. Since the mid-1990s, the District Primary Education Project (DPEP) became the overarching nationwide effort that attempted to co-opt and absorb the strategies and lessons from the previous decade. It spread to 272 districts, more than half of the total in the country, in 18 states. Reducing disparities in participation, especially in gender, and improving quality are its main aims.

The common features of the district-based plans in DPEP have a strong gender focus. An extensive repertoire of measures drawn from experience has been applied in DPEP:

- Formation of mothers' committees or PTAs to promote a dialogue between parents and the school.
- Free reading and writing materials for children of the poor.
- Free uniforms for girls in some districts.
- Mid-day meals for children, preferably cooked so as to ensure that the girl child gets her share.
- Tie-up with the health department for health check of students.
- Construction of toilets – preferably separate for girls and boys.
- Ensuring women representation in village education committees.
- Appointment of additional women teachers and ensuring the presence of at least one woman teacher in each school.
- Establishing early childhood care and education centres in or close to the primary school.
- Co-curricular or after-school activities for girls.
- Expanding the Mahila Samakhya Programme (women's empowerment) especially, where poor and lower caste families live.

- Village surveys to identify girls and boys not in school.
- Provisions for non-formal education for those not able to participate in formal schools.
- Monitoring girls' enrolment and dropout.
- Periodic achievement tests for all students.
- Eliminating gender bias and stereotyping in textbooks.
- Selecting school sites in consultation with the community and applying criteria including girls' easy accessibility.
- Training and orientation on gender issues for existing and new staff.
- Equitable representation of women at all levels of staffing.
- Sensitizing Village Education Committees regarding accommodation for staff, especially women.

This inventory of measures represents the full gamut of policy and action recommendations that one can imagine, although all measures are not being applied in every district. Progress is being made. Yet, according to the global EFA monitoring report of 2003, India is "at risk of not achieving" the gender parity goals in either primary or secondary education by 2015, if the present trends continue. Adequate data for Pakistan and Nepal were not available for EFA monitors to make a projection, but it cannot be any more promising. Bangladesh has achieved gender parity in primary education, but is at risk of not achieving the goal in secondary education by 2015 (UNESCO, 2003).

Two questions stand out. First, in spite of policies which are hard to fault and strategies and programmes which are based on lessons from experience and backed up by resources, why are the goals so elusive? Secondly, even if numerical parity is achieved, as in the case of Bangladesh primary education, how significant is that accomplishment?

The two questions are clearly interrelated, as the Bangladesh case will illustrate. Bangladesh takes pride in achieving gender parity in enrolment at the primary and the lower secondary levels. A thorough analysis of how this happened has not been undertaken. Government actions that appear to have made a major contribution include raising public awareness about girls' education since the adoption of the compulsory primary education law in 1990, increasing recruitment of women teachers, grain distribution, and lately cash grants, to students from poor families, and stipends and exemption from tuition for girls in rural schools at the secondary level. The work of the vibrant NGO sector in Bangladesh in organizing women's groups, expanding the scope of economic activities for women through mico-credit, and non-formal education activities have brought about a change in awareness and aspirations in rural communities. BRAC, the largest national NGO in the world, has pioneered a "second chance" non-formal primary education programme in which 70 per cent of the participants are girls, who have been left out for different reasons from the formal system. The teachers of the 34,000 BRAC one-room primary schools are all women.

This accomplishment in Bangladesh should not be underestimated, However, parity in enrolment so far has meant equal participation in a system with a high rate of dropout and non-completion and extremely poor learning achievement. In fact, the performance of girls is even lower than the average low level (Education Watch, 2000). There is still much to be done to build a culture of gender equality in education and claim the right to education and development for girls (Groundwork, 2002).

It would be possible to construct a list for each of the countries in the region of actions taken in recent years to achieve universal primary education. Why does the target date for fulfilling the promise of primary education with acceptable learning achievement for all keep receding?

While many appropriate individual steps are being taken, there are systemic weaknesses, which hobble the steps taken and reduce their effectiveness. There is also the absence of a strength of resolve that is necessary to imbue sufficient energy into the actions to ensure successful outcomes and close the gap between rhetoric and reality. Vimala Ramachandran calls it, more generously, the gap between intention and action.

The systemic weakness, evident in all of the countries lagging in basic education, is epitomized by an excessively centralized structure of management and a bureaucratic tradition to go with it. It keeps all large and many small decisions regarding the primary school in the remotest village in the hands of a few officials in the capital city. In India and Pakistan this concentration of authority in some instances may be at the state or provincial capital level rather than in the national capital, but that hardly makes a difference for the village school.

The highly centralized structure denies the stakeholders in the educational system – parents, communities, non-governmental organizations and the civil society at large – an active role. It also stands as an obstacle to greater transparency in decision-making, accountability of various actors in the education system, and the fight against endemic corruption.

Insufficient commitment, despite the rhetoric including constitutional provisions and compulsory education laws in some countries, is reflected in inadequate allocation of public resources for education. Public spending in education in South Asia, although increasing slowly in the 1990s, still remains low compared to other developing regions, both as a percentage of GNP and as a ratio of total government expenditure. Recent statistics for public expenditure for education as share of GDP ranged from 1.8 per cent in Pakistan to 5.2 per cent in Bhutan. Others fell in the middle with India at 4.1 per cent, Maldives at 3.9 per cent, Nepal at 3.7 per cent, Sri Lanka at 3.1 per cent and Bangladesh at 2.5 per cent (HDR 2003, Table 9, data for the latest year between 1998 and 2000).

Allocation of public expenditure however says nothing about what is actually spent or how effectively. A recent survey of the Ministry of Human Resource Development in India revealed that on an average less than half of the central government allocations to the states for Sarva Shiksha Abhiyan (SSA – the Hindi acronym for EFA) was actually spent in seven states in financial year 2002-3. SSA is the national umbrella programme for basic education which includes DPEP. The concerned states are Andhra Pradesh, Bihar, Haryana, Kerala, Orissa, Maharashtra and West Bengal, most of which still have millions of children out of school (*Indian Express*, 2 October, 2003). In Bangladesh, due to rampant corruption and mismanagement, the government decided recently to discontinue the nationwide literacy programme called the Total Literacy Movement and close down the Directorate of Non-formal Education of the Ministry of Primary and Mass Education.

The lack of resolve is also manifested in the pervasive phenomenon of decision-making – be it appointment of teachers, location of schools, or selecting vendors for construction or supplies – influenced by partisan political interest and influence-peddling rather than by educational and good management criteria. In Bangladesh, there is much talk about criminalization of the political system, which in turn corrupts and undermines the governance process. Perhaps, the situation is not very different in the other countries of the region. It all adds up to a massive failure of governance of public services and institutions.

What can be done?

The continuing discourse on rights of the disadvantaged and the excluded, among whom girls and women are the large majority, points to the direction that has to be followed in addressing the problem of the failure of governance. Four points can be underscored before attempting to draw conclusions about what can be done in South Asia to fulfil the right to education of the girl child.

Addressing the Burden of the Excluded

Religious, ethnic and cultural minorities bear disproportionately the burden of deprivation from social services (HDSA, 1998). There is an overlay of gender in all of these incidences of deprivation. To cite a few instances at random:

- Official statistics about literacy rates are generally problematic because of varying definitions and imprecise measurement methods. United Nations estimates, published in the Human Development Report, show that the gender gap in adult literacy around 2001 was 19 percentage points in Bangladesh, 23 points in India and 29 points in Pakistan (UNDP, 2003).
- At least a quarter of the population of India falls under the categories of scheduled castes, adivasis, dalits, and backwards classes – subject to and vulnerable to a wide array of

discrimination and exclusion in relation to mainstream national development, participation in social services and voice in the governance structure (Nambissan and Sedwal, 2002; Sujatha, 2002).

- After six years of signing an agreement in 1997 between the tribal communities of the Chittagong Hill Tracts in Bangladesh and the government that ended an insurgency movement of the tribal inhabitants, the government appears to be dragging its feet in implementing the agreement to recognize tribal autonomy and remedy past injustice, while the tribal leaders are accusing the government of bad faith. *Education Watch* reports a pattern of unequal participation and achievement in education among the ethnic and cultural minorities, although there is a higher rate of literacy in the Hindu community (Education Watch, 2001).
- Sri Lanka has paid with 60,000 lives in its 17 years of ethnic war arising from the grievances about discrimination and insufficient recognition of the identity of the Tamil minorities. In spite of overall progress in education, 100,000 children in the conflict-torn north and east of the country remain out of school.

The larger question of how the minorities of various kinds are given full participation in social services and governance structures in the multi-ethnic and multi-cultural societies of South Asia has remained largely unaddressed. Respect for diversity is an essential aspect of human rights. Similarly, respect for ethnic, linguistic, cultural, national, gender and hybrid identities is a prerequisite for a democratic society. Despite being a region with great diversity, a majoritarian political culture holds sway, contradicting the fundamental principles of inclusive democracy.

According to Radhika Coomaraswamy, "No South Asian nation has successfully developed a strategy that preserves and promotes diversity to foster peace and prosperity. The turn of the century sees existing structures that support diversity facing ever more strenuous tests, and the region seems more fragmented and factional – and tragically more violent – with each passing year" (International Center for Ethnic Studies, 2000).

PARTICIPATION AND PARTNERSHIP: THE ROLE OF THE CIVIL SOCIETY

Highly centralized state institutions, aided and abetted by a control-oriented bureaucratic culture, and weak political institutions in South Asia have, not encouraged a participation of the civil society and partnership between the government and non-governmental entities in governance. A "statist" approach originating in colonial and feudal history relies upon the state authorities dominated by an elite to take the responsibility for "organizing", "controlling" and "guiding" society.

South Asia has a lively and strong sector of non-governmental organizations (NGOs), social movements, community-based organizations (CBOs), consumer groups, cultural groups, professional bodies, and religion-based service and development organizations. Social groups, such as the poor, minorities of various categories, and women, excluded from governance and public services, sometimes have sought to assert their identity and their claims through their own organizations.

The relationship between the state and the civil society organizations, especially the development NGOs in South Asia, has moved, on the whole, from an adversarial position to mutual tolerance and ambivalence. The "statist" mindset, the power of bureaucracy, and the centralized administrative structure have impeded the development of a relationship of partnership, cooperation, complementarity and mutual trust.

THE VEHICLE OF LAW AND THE SYSTEM OF JUSTICE

The basic elements of the modern system of civil and criminal justice have been in existence in most of South Asia for over a century. In Nepal it has been in operation in the present form since the promulgation of the 1951 Interim Constitution. However, a basic deficiency of the judicial system in the region is the lack of effective access to justice for the majority of the people due to high cost compared to people's income. This is aggravated by corruption and inefficiency of the agencies associated with the administration of justice such as police and the prosecutors.

The higher courts – the Supreme Court and the High Courts in each country – enjoy greater public confidence than the lower courts. The higher courts have occasionally taken a pro-active role in their rulings on human rights and public interest litigation.

Judicial activism has been described by Indian jurists as "social action litigation," which is broader than the concept of "public interest litigation" – a practice familiar in North America. The former is a strategy not merely to advance group rights and interests but also a strategy for civil society monitoring and involvement in the realization of social and economic rights.

The "activism" of the Indian judiciary has been justified in the courts as an effort to make them "the last resort for the oppressed and the bewildered" (Goonesekere, 1998: 234). The Indian Supreme Court's admission of social action suits makes it worthwhile for non-governmental social action groups to take the legal route to promote rights – to undertake research into a problem, work together with media and other partners and bring a well-documented brief before the court. This approach can be effective in a judicial environment, as in India, where the superior courts have wide power of judicial review under the national constitution. Similar authority to the High Courts is given by the constitution in Bangladesh, Nepal and Pakistan.

Synergy of Efforts is Critical

Education is the means by which people become more autonomous, more capable of assessing circumstances and making informed choices, and more adept at taking advantage of available opportunities. The network of educational programmes and institutions is spread widely and potentially capable of reaching the whole population. Education, therefore, can become an important vehicle for promoting a synergistic approach to serving the multi-dimensional needs of growth, development, and personal fulfilment of the girl child, youth and women. Educational programmes and institutions can be the anchor to which various activities can be tied and implemented in an integrated way, responding to specific conditions and needs of the beneficiaries.

For example, the multiple and complex circumstances that place children in various categories of protection needs invariably call for sensitive and responsive provisions for education, counselling, social and financial support and sometimes specialized services in a coordinated way – impossible to be provided by conventional sectorally divided social services.

All these point to the need for moving towards a synergistic approach that makes social services responsive, flexible and accountable to the intended beneficiaries. The essential features of a synergistic approach would include:

- decentralization to bring decision-making close to the loci of action;
- meaningful, as opposed to token, participation of the major stakeholders, especially the intended beneficiaries; participatory planning and management including a strong role for community organizations; partnerships, whenever appropriate, between public, private, NGOs, and community actors;
- accountability at the community level, especially to the principal stakeholders;
- transparency and openness in the decision-making process; and
- encouragement from the central authorities to greater synergy and appropriate changes in the legal, administrative and procedural provisions.

A move towards a synergistic approach from the conventional approach is certain to evoke strong resistance from various vested interests who benefit from the present pattern or are just insecure about change. These may include politicians who do not want to give up their control of patronage, unions of civil servants, and business and commercial groups who find it convenient to deal with a central organization. Sustained and determined efforts will be needed by civil society "activists" and committed professionals to overcome the resistance.

A Framework for Action

What can be done? Three strands of action are proposed – not something totally new, but doing more systematically and with more energy what may be already there to a degree. The three strands are: (1) seeking a higher political profile for effective policy dialogue and advocacy, (2) promoting more effective action to claim and establish the right to education and development of the girl child as well as the boy child, and (3) making the education system an instrument for fighting misogynstic values and behaviour in our societies:

1. *Make the state of children and women count politically*: A strategy for taking a politically "activist" stance needs to be developed. The elements of such a strategy would include:
   - Wide dissemination of the issues, conclusions and action points raised in this presentation and in similar discourse in national and regional languages.
   - Bringing together activists, organizations providing services, researchers and academics concerned with children and women in each country.
   - Cooperation with and formation of a broader alliance with others such as groups working on human rights, children's and women's issues, environment, and minorities.
   - Working with parliamentary groups, political parties, media, and professional bodies in social sectors.
   - Promoting national, regional and local "child watch" and "gender watch" reports.
   - Supporting policy research and policy dialogue leading to more open, participatory and informed process of education policy making.
2. Support effective implementation of education reform policies and programmes – bridging the gap between rhetoric and reality, intention and action:
   - Promoting a stronger commitment to education reform and change through a comprehensive and systemic approach in sector/sub-sector reform, decentralization with accountability, professionalization of management, and renunciation of partisan politicization of education.
   - Building partnerships for efficient, effective and synergistic delivery of social and development services – bringing together the stakeholders including the government, community organizations, NGOs, the private sector and the civil society in general at local, district, state/province and national levels.

- Finding enough resources – it is a matter of political choice – and ways of holding governments and politicians accountable and answerable for the use of the resources.
- Promoting the use of the legal system to claim the rights of the disadvantaged and the excluded – using the instrument of social and public interest litigation.
- Developing a regional perspective to share, to learn, to challenge, to inspire each other and to address issues that require regional cooperation; working with SAARC on a regional focus and regional norms and standards, and build alliances and networks of the advocates for human rights, children's rights and human development in the region.

3. Encourage a pro-active gender agenda in education through:
   - Gender audits of content, pedagogy and management.
   - Making human rights and gender sensitivity an explicit part of content in appropriate ways at all levels of education.
   - Making educational institutions and NFE and literacy programmes a bastion for combating misogynistic signals from the larger society.

Statistical Annex

A. Adult Literacy Rate(%)

Country	*1990*		*2000*		*2004*	
	Male	*Female*	*Male*	*Female*	*Male*	*Female*
Bangladesh	44	24	49	30	50	31
Bhutan	51	23	61	34	–	–
India	62	36	68	45	73	48
Maldives	95	95	97	97	96	96
Nepal	47	14	59	24	63	35
Pakistan	49	20	57	28	62	35
Sri Lanka	93	85	94	89	92	89
South Asia	59	34	66	42	70	45
Developing Countries	76	59	81	67	83	70
World	81	69	84	74	84	72

Source: UNICEF, State of the World's Children 2004 & 2006, Table 5

B1. Primary and Secondary School Enrolment

Country	*Pri. School Gross*		*Pri. School Net*		*Sec. School Gross*	
	Male	*Female*	*Male*	*Female*	*Male*	*Female*
Bangladesh	100	101	88	90	45	47*
Bhutan	82	62	58	47	7	2
India	111	92	78	64	57	40
Maldives	131	131	99	99	53	57
Nepal	128	108	77	67	58	43
Pakistan	93	54	83	48	29	19
Sri Lanka	107	104	97	97	70	75
South Asia	107	87	80	65	53	39
Dev. Countries	105	96	84	77	59	52
World	104	96	85	79	65	59

Gross enrollment refers to number of children enrolled in a level (primary or secondary), regardless of age, divided by the population of the age group that officially corresponds to the same level. Net enrolment refers to the number of children of the age group that officially corresponds to a level of schooling and enrolled at that level, divided by the total population of the same age group.

* Lower secondary level up to grade ten only.

Source: UNICEF, State of the World's Children 2004, Table 5.

B2. Primary and Secondary School Enrolment

Country	*Pri. School Gross*		*Pri. School Net*		*Sec. School Gross*	
	Male	*Female*	*Male*	*Female*	*Male*	*Female*
Bangladesh	94	98	84	86	45	50
Bhutan	–	–	–	–	–	–
India	111	104	90	85	58	47
Maldives	119	117	92	93	62	71
Nepal	126	112	75	66	50	39
Pakistan	80	57	68	50	26	19
Sri Lanka	101	110	–	–	84	89
South Asia	106	97	86	80	52	44
Dev. Countries	108	101	88	83	61	57
World	108	101	88	85	66	63

Source: UNICEF, State of the World's Children 2006, Table 5.

REFERENCES

Agnihotri, Satish, 2002, "Survival of the Girl Child: Tunneling out of the Chakravyuha," Second Annual Lecture on the Girl Child of South Asia, India Alliance for Child Rights, New Delhi, 8 December 2002.

Campaign for Popular Education (CAMPE), 2001. Education Watch 2000, A Question of Quality: The State of Primary Education in Bangladesh, Dhaka, University Press Ltd.

Goonesekere, Savitri, 1998, *Children, Law and Justice: A South Asian Perspective*, New Delhi: Sage Publications.

Government of India, 1992, Programme of Action, National Policy on Education, Delhi: Ministry of Human Resource Development.

Groundwork, Inc., 2002, "Overview of the Status of Gender Equality", Dhaka, USAID, Basic Education Policy Support Activity, May 2002.

Human Development Centre, 1998, South Asia Human Development Report 1998, Islamabad.

Indian Express, 2 October, 2003.

International Center for Ethnic Studies, 2000, "Conference on South Asian Diversity and Pluralism," Colombo, November 16-18, 2000.

Mazumdar, Vina, 2001, "An Issue of Survival? Whose? Or of What?" Second Annual Lecture on the Girl Child of South Asia, India Alliance for Child Rights, New Delhi.

Nambissan, Geetha B. and Mona Sedwal, 2002, "Education for All: Situation of Dalit Children in India." in R. Govinda (ed.), *India Education Report: A Profile of Basic Education*, New Delhi: Oxford University Press.

Ramachandran, Vimala, 1998, "The Indian experience" in Bridging the Gap between Intention and Action: Girls' and Women's Education in South Asia, Bangkok and New Delhi, UNESCO-PROAP and ASPBAE.

Sen, Amartya, 1990, "More Than 100 Million Women Are Missing," *New York Review of Books*, 20 December, 1990.

— 2001, "Many faces of gender inequality", *Frontline*, 9 November, pp. 5-14.

Somavia, Juan, 2000, "The Lost Children" in United Nations Children's Fund, Progress of Nations, New York: UNICEF.

Sujatha, K., 2002, "Education among scheduled tribes" in R. Govinda (ed.), *India Education Report: A Profile of Basic Education*, New Delhi: Oxford University Press.

UNESCO, 2003. Gender and Education for All: The Leap to Equality, EFA Global Monitoring Report, 2003/4, Paris.

United Nations Children's Fund 2000, Progress of Nations, New York.

— 2001, Progress since the World Summit for Children: A Statistical Review, New York.

— 2000, State of the World's Children 2001, New York: Oxford University Press.

— 2003, State of the World's Children 2004, New York: Oxford University Press.

United Nations Development Programme 2003, Human Development Report 2003, New York: Oxford University Press.

11

TRAFFICKING IN WOMEN AND CHILDREN

THE SOUTH ASIAN REALITY

Nandita Baruah

For years the South Asia region has been a hot bed of paradoxes – from hosting the largest democracy in the world, to hosting the most volatile regional civic unrest, the sub-continent has fuelled constant need to monitor and safeguard civil society of its varied problems.

Illiteracy, poverty, class clashes, natural calamities, political and ethnic unrest have all constantly increased vulnerabilities of marginalized groups, and made them susceptible to gross violation of human rights.

Political and civil vested interests groups have taken advantage of factors emanating out of the region's many paradoxes, to find newer ways to exploit the marginalized classes. In addition, migration across national borders in the region has increased the social exploitation of marginalized persons – trafficking being paramount on that list.

The push for the donor community to meet its commitment to the UN Millennium Development Goals of poverty eradication has in turn contributed to the development of a broader perception and understanding of the issue of trafficking in the region, and guiding the work done to address it. In this context, the work of different international and global organizations and institutions addressing trafficking has played an important rôle in bringing about a change in perception and response at the national as well as the regional levels. The role of non-governmental organizations (NGOs) has also been very critical in this area.

In the last decade, the varied initiatives taken by governments, NGOs, civil society and the donor community have thrown up important lessons and also created a platform for a meaningful dialogue to address the issue.

Till very recently, the term "trafficking" was not precisely defined in international law despite its inclusion in a number of international legal agreements. The recent attempt by the international community to develop a consensus definition revealed major differences of opinion concerning the ultimate end result of trafficking, its constitutive acts and their relative significance. Definitions of trafficking have tended to reflect the priorities and perspectives of promoters. For example, an organization concerned with orderly migration has naturally emphasized the migration aspects of trafficking. One concerned with the human rights of women has tended to place women at the centre of the definition and identify human rights violations as the critical defining factor. Those seeking to advance the cause of women working in prostitution have preferred a different definition of trafficking to those who consider all forms of prostitution intolerable.

In 1994, the General Assembly of the United Nations referred to trafficking as "the illicit and clandestine movement of persons across national and international borders... with the end goal forcing women and girl-children into sexually or economically oppressive and exploitative situations for the profit of recruiters, traffickers, crime syndicates as well as other illegal activities related to trafficking such as forced domestic labor, false marriage, clandestine employment and forced adoption". Five years later, the UN Crime Commissions took up the spirit of this definition by proposing a distinction be made between trafficking on the one hand, and migrant smuggling on the other. Smuggling of migrants has now been defined as "...the procurement, in order to obtain, directly or indirectly, a financial or other material benefit, of the illegal entry of a person into a State Party of which the person is not a national or permanent resident". Trafficking in persons is defined as "...the recruitment, transportation, transfer, harboring or receipt of persons, by means of threat or use of force or other forms of coercion, of abduction, of fraud, of deception, of the abuse of power or of a position of vulnerability or of the giving or receiving of payments or benefits to achieve the consent of a person having control over another person for the purposes of exploitation. Exploitation shall include, at a minimum, the exploitation of the prostitution of others or other forms of sexual exploitation, forced labor or services, slavery or practices similar to slavery, servitude, or the removal of organs".

Through the work of the Crime Commission, the international community has now decided that trafficking means much more than the organized movement of persons for profit. The critical, additional factor separating trafficking from migrant smuggling is the presence of force or coercion throughout or at some stage in the process – that force or coercion being for the purpose of exploitation. It appears, therefore, that an individual who pays a group or organization to facilitate her or his illegal entry into a state will be considered, prima facie, a smuggled migrant. This will be the case even if that person was misled about the dangers of the journey irrespective of the treatment she or he receives at the hands of smugglers provided there is consent to the original transport and provided an exploitative relationship does not develop between the two parties. Similarly, the organized and illegal cross-border movement of an individual for purposes of prostitution will not be considered trafficking in the absence of coercion – that coercion being specifically directed at securing the exploitation of the individual. The only situation in which non-coercion movement will be considered trafficking is when the individual involved is a child.

Trafficking versus Sex Work: The Definitional Impasse

Despite the definitional framework provided by the recent UN protocol and other international treaties and conventions, one critical element which remains contentious within the anti-trafficking framework is the legal or social status of women in sex work.

Several policy approaches to the legal regulation of sex work have emerged over the years, and it is necessary to examine the underlying basis as well as the policy implications of each before arriving at any individual decisions or opinions.

1. *The Criminalization Construct*
   (a) The approach is largely moralistic in its construct. It takes two different forms: abolition or toleration. Both approaches view sex work as a social evil, and promote the idea that such immoral conduct should be criminalized.
   (b) The toleration approach is based on the assumption that sex work is an inevitable social evil. Legislation based on this approach is generally silent about whether the activity itself is legal or illegal. It criminalizes the outward manifestations of sex work such as soliciting, brothel keeping and trafficking. In India, the Immoral Trafficking Prevention Act, 1986 adopts this approach.
2. *The Decriminalization Construct*
   (a) The decriminalization approach is the outcome of new world feminist construct of female sexuality. It makes a distinction between sex work and trafficking. It is based on the assumption that sex work can be voluntary and is a personal choice and thus a personal matter between consenting adults. It advocates for complete decriminalization of voluntary sex work and all related activities and the abolition of laws that criminalize such activities. Voluntary relationship between sex workers, pimps, brothel owners and landlords as well as the practice of sex work must be removed from the scope of criminal law, and all specific criminal laws that apply to sex work be repealed. It seeks to make sex work a subject of the general laws.
   (b) The decriminalization approach addresses forced sex work as a separate issue, with the recommendation that

the existing legislation relating to trafficking, especially in minors, fraud, coercion and forced labour be strengthened. This approach was debated among sex workers rights groups at the First and Second Sex Workers Conferences in 1997 and 1998 at Calcutta.

3. *The Legalization Construct*

The legalization approach is similar to decriminalization insofar as it involves taking the subject of sex work outside of the realm of criminal law. But it does not make a clear distinction between consensual sex workers and trafficked sex workers. In contrast to decriminalization, the strategy involves legalizing and heavily regulating sex work through a whole host of zoning and licensing laws. The legalization approach is based on the assumption that a balance must be drawn between 'public' health and 'public' need. Its objective is to curb the worst side-effects of sex work, such as the spread of sexually transmitted disease, including the HIV virus. The primary features of this approach are:

(a) *Zoning*: Zoning keeps the women in a working women's ghetto. It segregates them into a separate part of the town or locality. It restricts their private spaces because they are considered to be public women. If they venture out of the zone, their civil liberties are restricted.

(b) *Licensing*: Licensing involves the issuing of licenses, registration and disbursement of health cards to the women by state authorities.

(c) *Mandatory check-ups*: This practice has received the greater emphasis in the light of the HIV pandemic and the myth that women in sex work are responsible for transmission of the virus. The woman is compelled to submit herself to checks-ups or else face imprisonment.

(d) Legalization implies the recognition of sex work as a lawful activity by the state. However, the experience of those jurisdictions, which have introduced zoning and licensing laws, indicates that this approach results in excessive state control, ghettoization of sex work, and forced/discriminatory medical and health surveillance, which is usually mandatory rather than voluntary. This approach is not new and was operational in several countries at the beginning of this century, including in India.

While the debate on the best approach continues to remain unresolved, the different agencies/organizations working to combat trafficking in South Asia have tried to arrive at an acceptable programmatic construct, which would best promote and protect the interest of the trafficked victim and survivor.

Country-Level Efforts in South Asia to Combat Trafficking

Till very recently, in South Asia, the issue of cross-border trafficking was not a priority at all. While countries like Nepal and Bangladesh, which were main sending countries, were very keen to have the receiving countries acknowledge their role in the process of trafficking, the receiving countries like India and Pakistan did not want to acknowledge the cross-border dimension as being a major contributor to the problem. This polarized divide made it extremely difficult to address the issue of cross-border trafficking in any effective manner as countries played the "blame game" without wanting to take responsibility to arrest the problem. The consensus to view the issue as a cross-border problem with regional dimensions was lacking.

However, in the last couple of years, there has been a marked change in the attitude of most of the South Asian governments. One of the key shifts has been the growing consensus among countries in the region to view trafficking as a cross-border issue with clear regional dimensions, which has to be addressed jointly. The signing of the SAARC Convention on Trafficking is the strongest indicator of such a shift. Certain other key events have also impacted upon the larger environment within which anti-trafficking work is taking place. This change has been visible in the variety of actions that have come to the fore in the last year. Countries in South Asia have tried to bring about specific legislation addressing the issue in a broader perspective and not limiting it to prostitution as was the case so far. The Government of India has redrafted the Immoral Trafficking Prevention Act,

1956, so that it moves away from victimizing the victim and addresses more effectively the issue of punishing the traffickers. The Government of Nepal had as early as 1986 enacted a special law to deal with human trafficking. In recent years, due to extensive lobbying and advocacy by NGO/women's activist groups, the inadequacies in this law are being examined and a new Human Trafficking Control Bill has been proposed. In Sri Lanka, the heavy sentencing to those convicted for paedophilia has sent out signals about the seriousness of the government to deal with the problem. The establishment of a nodal agency like the National Child Protection Agency in Sri Lanka has also been instrumental in dealing with sexual exploitation of children. The Government of Bangladesh has also shown interest in defining strategies to arrest the increasing incidence of trafficking in women and children. Bangladesh has set up an inter-ministerial task force to effectively address the issue of trafficking. The Bangladeshi cabinet has approved the death penalty for crimes against women, including trafficking, rape and murder.

Bangladesh

Trafficking in women and girl children has been a major concern in Bangladesh, as the number of women and children being trafficked is increasing each year.

Political Commitment: The Government of Bangladesh has been taking a keen interest in this issue. It was the Prime Minister of Bangladesh, whose proactive role made possible the Male declaration of 1997, which has laid the stage and commitment to have a SAARC Convention on Trafficking. A National Plan of Action on Trafficking and Sexual Exploitation of Children is being drafted. NGO representatives have been involved in the drafting process.

- Police estimate more than 15,000 women and children are smuggled out of Bangladesh every year and as on February 1998, there were 200 Bangladeshi children and women awaiting repatriation in different Indian shelters ("Boys, rescued in India while being smuggled to become jockeys in camel races", www.elsiglo.com).

- 27,000 Bangladeshi women and children have been forced into prostitution in Indian brothels (Centre for Women and Children Studies Reports, "Women Forced into Indian Brothels," June 1998).
- More than 15,000 women and children are trafficked out of Bangladesh every year (Police estimate www.webpage.com/hindu/daily/980220/03/03200004.htm 19).

Strengthening Legislative Instruments/Acts: The Suppression of Immoral Trafficking Act, 1993 provides punishment for forcing a girl into prostitution. Abatement by having custody or charge of the girls is also a crime. Section 11 of the Act prohibits the detention of any female child under the age of 18 against her will in any house, room or place in which prostitution is carried out. 1998 onwards through a series of amendments the penalties prescribed for trafficking and other VAW-related offences have been made very stringent. Even to the extent of death penalties in some cases. Nevertheless, there has also been some criticism from NGOs and activists that such stringent punishments tend to bring down conviction rates. But, the strong penalties are symbolic of the government's seriousness to address the issue. The legal Act 'Nari O Shishu Nirjaton Domon Ain", 2000 (Suppression of Violence Against Women and Children Act, 2000) has provisions for tough punishments for committing the above mentioned crimes.

Bangladesh had signed the Optional Protocol to the Convention on the Rights of the Child, on the Sale of Children, Child Prostitution, and Child Pornography in 2001. The Government of Bangladesh has, in its CEDAW report, stated the gravity of the problem and has also talked about strengthening of border posts. However, in the same report, they have also expressed the difficulty in controlling border crossing due to the sheer length of Bangladesh's border with India and Burma, which makes it impossible to prevent people crossing the borders.[1]

In the last couple of years the government has tried to address the gaps through certain specific targeted interventions. The

Ministry of Women and Children Welfare is implementing a project to combat child trafficking. The project has been working to strengthen the control mechanisms in 25 border districts where trafficking in children is rampant. A national task force to combat child trafficking was formed under this project with NGO collaboration.[2] Another initiative under the Women's Ministry is looking at empowerment and protection of women and children in especially difficult circumstances, including street children and trafficked children.

Concerns: However, some of the concerns that NGO groups in Bangladesh are raising are that, though laws against trafficking exist, their implementation remains weak. Although the new laws have increased penalties, their application has certain technical problems which are in the process of being identified. There is scope for misapplication and harassment of innocent persons. The law-enforcing authorities and the judiciary need to be better sensitized about the issues involved. There is a need for stronger action against members of law-enforcing authorities, who are themselves involved in trafficking. Regional cooperation is essential to coordinate legal and administrative measures and procedures. Information needs to be shared and extradition of offenders allowed. Victims are sometimes charged with prostitution or immoral behaviour and put in jail. The repatriation of Bangladeshi women trafficked abroad needs to be facilitated.

INDIA

Till very recently the Government of India's emphasis was primarily on internal trafficking; it is only recently that the issue of cross-border trafficking and the need for regional engagement has been acknowledged.

Political Commitment: The Department of Women and Child Development (DWCD), has instituted the Central Advisory Committee on Child Prostitution, which was set up as per the directives of the Supreme Court of India (fall out of the Vishal Jeet vs Union of India case). The Secretary, DWCD regularly holds meeting of the Central Advisory Committee where state representatives are asked to report back on the action taken in each state on the implementation of the National Plan of Action to combat trafficking and commercial exploitation of women and children.

In September 2001 the Government of India launched a scheme called 'Swadhar' for women in difficult circumstances. The objective of the scheme is to provide shelter and care to women without social and economic support; counselling and emotional support; legal and clinical support; and rehabilitation through education and skill upgradation.

Involvement of Independent Autonomous Ombudspersons/ Commissions: The National Human Rights Commission (NHRC) has identified trafficking as a priority issue for itself and it has been looking at it from the human rights perspective. As a part of this commitment and prioritization NHRC undertook a national level action research to understand the status and dimension of trafficking in women and children in India. This is the first intensive research of its kind and is now being looked upon as a baseline study on the issue for India

Strengthening of Legislative Instruments/Acts: The major legal framework addressing trafficking is the Immoral Trafficking (Prevention) Act (ITPA) of 1956, which is based on the 1949 UN Convention. Prostitution is not illegal in India but soliciting and exploiting prostitution are considered offences. In 1986 amendments were made to ITPA to shift presumption of guilt onto the accused cases where minors in brothels were found to be sexually abused after medical examination. The government is further seeking to amend ITPA in order to increase penalties and place greater criminal culpability against the trafficker and ensure speedy relief to the victims. ITPA is supplemented by provision of the Indian Penal Code, 1860, which includes offences such as abduction, wrongful confinement, slavery and forced labour and sexual offences. In addition, the new version of the Juvenile Justice Act is also relevant to the issue of trafficking.

Efforts are on to further amend ITPA and it is proposed that Section 8 which makes soliciting an offence be deleted. This would be a welcome amendment, as it would move away from re-victimizing the women who may have been trafficked into prostitution. The amendment is waiting to be tabled in the parliament after receiving concurrence of the states and Union Cabinet's approval.

However, the manner in which ITPA is implemented leaves much to be desired. The UN Special Rapporteur noted that governments and NGOs claim that 80 per cent of the cases registered under ITPA are for soliciting. Thus, the person who is being arrested and booked is the victim. On the other hand, the number of cases filed against the traffickers is marginal.

As per Section 13 (4) of the ITPA the government is supposed to appoint a Special Police Officer (Trafficking Police Officer) for dealing with offences under this Act. The government has notified the Central Bureau of Investigation (CBI) that personnel of and above the rank of Inspectors would act as the "Trafficking Police Officers" for the whole of India. The CBI is yet to respond to this notification. However, the CBI has set up a "missing person's cell" in its office in Delhi.

Given the recent spate in different government actions to address the issue, there are still major gaps that need to be addressed. The coordination between different law enforcement agencies is one such area. There is an urgent need to understand the socio-economic dimensions that create supply sites within the country along with the economic compulsions that define the demand sites. The new partnership between the NGOs and the government agencies that has emerged needs to be further strengthened.

A very positive development has been the growth and strengthening of NGO networks and coalitions across the country and the region. These networks have formed both at the state as well at the national level. This has given impetus to the lobbying and advocacy work that the NGOs had been doing with the government machinery.

Nepal

Political Commitment: Nepal developed a National Policy and Plan of Action (NPA) to combat trafficking in women and children in 1998, which was approved by the cabinet in July 1999. The government, as a part of the NPA, has carried out various consultations and awareness generation programmes.

Strengthening of Legislative Instruments/Acts: The Human Trafficking (Control) Act, 1986 is the present active law under which trafficking is being addressed. The government has drafted a new Bill on trafficking of human beings. The Bill has broadened the definition of trafficking and also proposes to impose additional punishment to person who trafficks his own wife or his/her near relatives, women or child under his/her protection. However, the dissolution of parliament and the changed political process in Nepal has thwarted the passage of the Bill.

Institutional and Programmatic Mechanisms to Address Trafficking: The Nepal government is an active partner in the "Joint Initiative Against Trafficking" which is a project being implemented jointly by the MWCSW government of Nepal and the UN agencies. The project is being coordinated by UNDP and UNIFEM is an active partner in this. The overall objective of the project is to reduce trafficking by redressing the gender inequities and discriminatory practices that make women and children vulnerable to being trafficked. The strategy uses an umbrella approach that build upon the initiatives of the UN Task Force on Trafficking allowing donors and UN agencies to pool resources for implementation of the components envisaged.

SRI LANKA

In Sri Lanka the dimensions of trafficking are different from the rest of South Asia. Here, the issue is more about internal trafficking from rural to urban centres and is primarily focusing on children forced into domestic servitude. Another critical concern in Sri Lanka is that of paedophile sex tourism. In Sri Lanka, unlike the other South Asian countries, majority of the child prostitutes are boys. Though there are instances of large number of outmigration by women to the Middle East, primarily with the intention of working as maids or lower level staff in industries/offices, the extent of trafficking under such circumstances is not clearly documented.

Political Commitment: Sri Lanka discussed the first draft of the National Plan of Action to Combat Trafficking of Children in 2001. The process of national consultation has begun with broad-based participation with key stakeholders from the government and civil society. The first consultation was held on 27 March 2001 under the patronage of the Attorney General of Sri Lanka. The Sri Lankan government is collaborating with ILO/IPEC to build national capacity to address trafficking in children. The National Plan of Action to Combat Trafficking of Children has been finalized.

Institutional and Programmatic Mechanisms to Address Trafficking: The government of Sri Lanka has set up the National Child Protection Authority (NCPA) to address the growing menace of child trafficking and abuse. The NCPA carries out investigative work on paedophilia and other form of child sexual abuse and trafficking. It provides the necessary support to the law-enforcement agencies in their prosecution work.

Strengthening of Legislative Instruments/Acts: Sri Lankan government, in order to deal with this problem, has made certain very stringent laws on the exploitation of children, making paedophilia a non-bailable offense, with the maximum penalty of 20 years in prison, and victims entitled to compensation. In 1996, the government raised the age of trafficked children to 16, and made prison sentences, ranging from 10 to 20 years, mandatory for sex offenders. The NCPA was set up to deal with the problem of child sexual abuse and paedophilia. In a recent sentencing the court gave a convicted paedophile 34 years of imprisonment, which sent out the message about the law-enforcement agencies serious concern in dealing with the problem.

Though Sri Lanka has ratified many international conventions on children and many legal reforms have taken place, the processes and avenues for holistic rehabilitation and reintegration are limited. The priorities, according to NCPA, are to improve facilities and training of service providers. There is also a need to study the extent of trafficking in women through the process of outmigration, if any.

PAKISTAN

The official recognition to the issue of both cross-border and internal trafficking has today become important in Pakistan. Pakistan is used as a transit point on account of its strategic geographical location for trafficking from South Asia to other global regions. Added to this, a substantive number of women, children and men are trafficked from Pakistan to the Middle East and other locations. Apart from inter-border trafficking, there is also inter-provincial trafficking within Pakistan; this involves rural to urban migration and transportation of persons for motives that are common with inter-country trafficking. There are increasing number of documented cases of Pakistani children being trafficked to the Middle East for the purpose of jockeying.

Political Commitment: Pakistan has developed the National Policy and Plan of Action against Child Sexual Abuse and Exploitation with the joint efforts of the National Commission for Child Welfare and Development (NCCWD), the Child Rights and Abuse Committee of the Pakistan Pediatric Association (PPA), and other NGO groups. The National Plan of Action has three distinct components: prevention, protection, and recovery and rehabilitation.

Endorsement of International Treaties and Conventions: Pakistan has signed the Optional Protocols on Convention on the Rights of the Child (CRC) regarding Sale of Children, Child Prostitution and Pornography and the Involvement of Children in Armed Conflict in 2001 and the ILO Convention 182 on the worst forms of child labour, including trafficking. It is also a signatory to the SAARC Convention on Trafficking. Pakistan has also ratified the Stockholm Declaration and Agenda for Action against Commercial Sexual Exploitation of Children.

Strengthening of Legislations/Acts: On the legislative side Pakistan has recently introduced the Human Trafficking Ordinance, which is looking at combating different forms of trafficking. However, like the rest of South Asia, it is the implementation of the laws that need to be strengthened

NGO and civil society groups in Pakistan have addressed the issues of Child Sexual Abuse (CSA) and Child Sexual Exploitation

(CSE). There has been a lot of work by civil society organizations on the issue of trafficking – both cross-border as well as internal. Its prime focus is on research and information dissemination pertaining to cross-border trafficking and providing legal aid to victims of trafficking. Organizations in collaboration with the government have also set up help lines for women and children.

Concerns: While some initial work to address the problem has started in Pakistan, the nature of interventions has been very limiting. Many parents are fully aware of the fact that their children are being sold either for illicit purposes, or in the case of camel jockeys, are being herded into a job that endangers their lives. Unfortunately, there are no laws under which the authorities can penalize these parents. Centralization of information regarding trafficking cases and child repatriation is an important and emerging need. NGOs feel that countries that share a border or the countries of origin, transit and destination of trafficking should consider establishing bilateral or multilateral agreements to define the terms and procedures of cooperation.

Resolving the Definitional Impasse and Moving Forward in South Asia

In South Asia, in the last few years, a series of consultative processes and dialogue between different stakeholders and support agencies have taken place to arrive at an "operational definition" of trafficking. This has led to the general acceptance of a process-centric understanding of trafficking. This new and evolving understanding stated below was endorsed by many at the 'Consultative Meeting on Anti-Trafficking Programs in South Asia' in September, 2001 at Kathmandu:

> "Trafficking comprises a dynamic process consisting of four stages: pre-movement, movement, exploitation and post-exploitation. Interventions are specific to each stage of the process. To be effective, interventions must be context specific and respond to physical, emotional, educational, and social needs of vulnerable groups or rescued victims, and must address the legal prosecution of the trafficker."

The scope and extent of initiatives addressing trafficking at the micro, meso and macro levels are quite multi-pronged and have added to expanding the conceptual understanding defining trafficking. Some of the present-day socio-economic issues and challenges that have a bearing on the problem of trafficking are as follows:

- A large global labour force, with little or no legal safety and precautionary measures, has been thrown up with the opening of the global markets and the processes of globalization. This has increased the vulnerabilities of people and opened them up to exploitation by the entire nexus of those making a profit out of trafficking.
- Trafficking is today seen and understood more as an exploitative process in a continuum of events and conditions, and not as a one-off, exploitative situation.
- What this means in programmatic terms is that initiatives aimed at prevention or reduction of trafficking should deal not just with the actual act of trafficking, but recognize and address the causal factors, and more critically, address the conditions and circumstances accompanying/preceding the act.
- It is important to deal with issues of gender, age, class and caste dimensions, which have very clear roles to play in defining vulnerabilities.
- Economic aspects like poverty, lack of opportunities, and breakdown of livelihood options are also factors, which need to be addressed, but have to be situated within the contextual reality of harm, which has different impacts on gender, age, caste and class.
- The line between legal migration for better livelihood options as against illegal migration bordering on trafficking and movement for trafficking per se, is getting more and more blurred. There have been growing indications by grassroots

groups that this concern needs to be addressed by anti-trafficking programmes.

Global Processes Impacting on South Asia

The positive action by governments has been prompted by some larger regional and international initiatives as well which have impacted in giving the issue of trafficking greater visibility and attention.

In the year 2000 the then UN Special Rapporteur on Trafficking, Dr. Radhika Coomaraswamy visited South Asia for an assessment of the problem and evaluate the response of state and non-state partners to combat the problem. Her visit was followed by a report on the status of the problem in South Asia along with recommendations for action, which was forwarded to all governments and later tabled in the UN General Assembly. It further prompted all governments to take serious note of the issue and put certain things in perspective:

- that trafficking was both an across-border and intra-country issue;
- that trafficking was not just limited to prostitution alone, though the sex industry was the largest 'demand sector' for trafficked women and children;
- that economic disparities within borders as well as across borders created vulnerabilities towards trafficking;
- that extensive community participation and advocacy were crucial to addressing trafficking; and
- that bilateral collaboration is critical towards addressing cross-border trafficking.

The fact that the process of her reporting was consultative and therefore her recommendations were taken cognizance of by different governments in the region is significant.

The adoption of the United Nations Convention Against Transnational Organized Crime in November 2000, along with two optional protocols by which countries would undertake in-depth measures to combat smuggling of migrants and the trafficking in women and children, was a significant move. The protocol to prevent, suppress and punish trafficking in persons, especially women and children is the first attempt to address trafficking in persons in a comprehensive manner based on the expanded understanding of the term "trafficking" and its multiple dimensions. The protocol applies to the prevention and combating of trafficking as well as to the protection of and assistance for victims and cooperation among state parties.

But, the general criticism against the protocol is that no methodological guidelines are included for making clear distinctions between trafficking and migrations or trafficking and prostitution. Thus, the general perception that trafficking is synonymous with migration and/or prostitution remains unchallenged.[3]

The adoption by the SAARC of the Convention on 'Prevention of Trafficking in Women and Children for Prostitution' has been a critical event. Though the Convention is limited in its definitional understanding of the problem, however, its importance lies in the fact that for the first time there is a regional treaty addressing trafficking. This in effect is an official acceptance of the regional nature of the problem and creates an important opening for dealing with the problem from within the formal structures of governance.

The Convention, though has its limitations, defines trafficking within the limited scope of prostitution. It also fails to specifically address the differential needs and rights of children. Though the Convention is a regional instrument, yet it holds back from laying out specific actionable process for regional or bilateral collaboration to combat trafficking.

Another international development has been the Trafficking in Persons (TIP) Report that has been brought out by the Government of United States of America following the Bill on Trafficking adopted by the US Senate in 2000. The report is based on the assessment of government and civil society action in each country to combat trafficking. It places different countries in different tiers depending on the action their governments have taken to combat the problem of trafficking. The report also talks of applying non-humanitarian sanctions on countries that have not taken adequate action to combat this problem. It would be interesting to see how far this monitoring mechanism being instituted by the US government is actually able to influence other governments to take action to combat the problem of human trafficking.

The US State Department's report on trafficking has also been criticized by the Women's Rights Division of Human Rights Watch (HRW) for concentrating primarily on trafficking for "sexual exploitation" to the exclusion of trafficking into other forms of forced labour.[4]

Despite the limitations of the international and regional treaties and conventions, it is true that these have contributed in pushing the anti-trafficking agenda and getting it the much-needed political attention. However, having said that, it is also important to note that specific and targeted national and regional level action has still to go a long way before we can claim to be effectively in control of the situation.

The New Age Dilemmas: Migration and Trafficking

In the contemporary reality of South Asia, women and young girls are the new migrants and the new workforce. Decline in job opportunities associated with traditional male migrations for employment, together with increasing insecurity of food and sustainable livelihoods, have pushed women and girls into assuming key roles as income earners for the families. Therefore, increasingly larger numbers of women, girls and young people are migrating in search of gainful employment to labour markets in urban centres of their own or neighbouring countries. But, this fast emerging new age workforce with its clear gender identity is greatly limited by its lack of access to information and resources because of inherent gender inequities. This makes them extremely vulnerable to exploitation as they tend to move into unsafe/illegal channels of mobility because of lack of resource and information. This in turn pushes them further into situations where legal and social protection becomes completely inaccessible.

In recent years, the emerging profile of a trafficked person is one of a young female migrant. Regular, legal and safe migration channels are getting more stringent the world over, due to increased perception of security threats and greater polarization between the developed and the developing worlds. It is subtext with increasing unemployment, break down of existing livelihood options due to economic and political instability, and change in trade regimes affecting existing employment patterns in the economically less developed countries and the growing demand for cheap labour in high growth countries. This has given rise to a growing market for irregular migration processes and trafficking is an outcome of this mismatch between demand and supply conditions in the global market.

In order to understand the interlinkages between migration and trafficking, some fundamental factors need to be grasped. Understanding this interlinkage is critical to any policy, legal or other programmatic intervention on trafficking. However, often, the tendency to draw an oversimplistic assumption of migration being the same as trafficking leads to ineffective and faulty legislation and programs.[5]

In South Asia migration has been a common phenomenon, which has been accelerated more today by the economic order that has come along with rapid globalization and liberalization. Movement of migrants of rural and urban poor in search of livelihood to distant unknown cities is capitalized by the traffickers/procurers. The widespread assumption that most trafficking incidents start with kidnapping and coercion is far from true and has been validated by many recent researches on this issue. Most trafficking starts as a migration experience, which could be legal or illegal, and is for economic (employment) or social (marriage) reasons. It may have elements of deception in it from the beginning but the process of force and coercion possibly comes into play after the initial first steps towards migration have taken.

However, there is a fundamental difference in migration and trafficking. While movement is central to both migration and trafficking and this commonality between the two builds a complex relationship. Radhika Coomaraswamy states that trafficking is distinguished from migration by a coerced transport and coerced end practices. Sometimes, the element of coerced movement is found to be absent especially in the case of the bonded labour system where men, women and children may be exploited in their own place of origin without having to cross geographical borders. The issue of consent in physical movement brings to the fore the problem of distinguishing between an exploited migrant and a trafficked person. Trafficked people do not have the opportunity of informed consent with respect to the experiences they undergo. Cases of exploited migrants are offences in themselves but they do not become the cases of trafficking. However, the majority of trafficked people will be exploited migrants. The decisive factor in distinguishing between the two will be the nature of consent. The intention of the agency is determined by the information made available at the start of the journey while the circumstances they find themselves to be in at the end of the journey may be very different from what was intended. A difficult and complex situation arises when migrants agree to work and accept exploitative relations, perceiving they are "better off than if they had stayed home".[6]

It is imperative that the issue of trafficking in women and children be considered within the larger spectrum of issues within labour migration. Trafficking is not opposed to migration but an aspect of it. Case histories collected by Therese Blanchet in "Beyond Boundaries" show that the experience of being trafficked often initiates a migrant career. Lured, deceived, cheated, deprived of freedom and/or income, compelled to engage in work against their will, women (and children) who are trafficked painfully learn and acquire skills useful to their survival. In an adverse situation the incentive to learn can be very strong. After being trafficked, life goes on with the need to earn, tackle risks and manage in an environment offering poor protection. There is usually no return to a pre-trafficked situation and that the outcome of being trafficked very seldom leads to rehabilitation in a rescue home.[7]

In this age of globalization, most countries of the world are engaged, to varying degrees, in process of substantial economic reforms. These include the adoption of market economies, trade liberalization, and privatization, new rules of international investment and new labour regimes, as well as new forms of international cooperation and trade agreements. The move to more competitive markets is likely to increase disparity between and within nations, providing the stimulus for rapidly increased migration. With labour not enjoying similar freedom of movement to capital, much of this migration is "illegal" or irregular, placing migrants in a highly vulnerable position and leading to exploitation and trafficking.[8]

Research and policy interventions on migration till very recently did not address gender as an analytical category. This exclusion of "women" was based on the assumption that women are too traditional and culture-bound to migrate or that they migrate only as family followers to associational migrants for family reunification. With the changing face of migration and its gendered contour, women are moving not only as members of families but as independent persons for a variety of reasons. Acting voluntarily to migrate has been recently recognized as a measure and indicator of women's empowerment by gender and development experts as well as the World Bank. It is argued that women are traditionally and notionally assigned the sphere of the private and domestic realm and excluded from the public world of travel and trades due to their historical disadvantage arising out of the sexual division of labour. In the context of this notional confinement, when women seek to improve their existing situation, then, this is to be viewed as an exercise of agency. It has also been acknowledged that exposure and increased ability to negotiate structures of power in the public world amounts to women's empowerment through enhancing their awareness and negotiating skills.[9]

The condition under which migration occurs determines whether a woman or girl will feel empowered or victimized at the end of this process. If she migrates consensually within or across borders into a situation of work or personal arrangement of which she had full knowledge, then, she has succeeded in exercising her agency and right to freedom of mobility with a positive outcome. If, on the other hand, a woman's need or wish to migrate is facilitated through the use of coercion, abuse or deception and the entire chain of events, from recruitment and transport to the end purpose, is exploitative, then, the woman has been trafficked. As states elsewhere by the author, "trafficking is the process of transforming an agent into a victim within the context of migration. It is an outcome of migration and one of its most heinous forms. The equation between trafficking and migration is such that all trafficked women and girls are migrants as well but all migrants are not trafficked".[10]

In the existing anti-trafficking legal intervention and initiatives, persons affected by trafficking, especially women and girls, are not only disempowered but also often criminalized and further victimized. While certain positive welfare measures for care and support are included in some of the action plans, yet at the very heart of the matter what is visible is not an empowering or rights-protective approach. The problem arises from combination of genuine lack of clarity and confusion on the issue, but at the very deep core there lies a moralistic bias which obfuscates the issue and prevents the formulation of strategies which will genuinely place the interest of the persons affected by trafficking at the centre, and promote their right to mobility, to livelihood and to their autonomy. So persistence and singular is the conflation of trafficking with prostitution, that measure for the prevention of trafficking to all other sites and for all other purposes are more or less ignored in most of the anti-trafficking laws in the region. This conflation stems again, it seems, from a moralistic preoccupation with prostitution. In the recent past, anti-trafficking advocates in the region have been repeatedly drawing the attention of agencies of the governments to the need to address trafficking for other purposes as well but thus far, little concrete measures have been considered.[11]

Gender Dimensions of Movement Arising out of Social and Economic Exclusion and Marginalization

It is difficult to understand as to why anybody would want to stay in exploitative situations. To get the fuller picture of trafficking and migration nexus, one has to visit the victim's situations before trafficking or taking a decision to migrate. Simplistically, it is defined as push and pull factors beyond individual's choice that impels one into the stream shaped by both macro and micro economics. One's vulnerability is very much shaped by where one stands in relation to macro economic development and social hierarchy. Mostly, the trafficking victims are usually those who are in disadvantaged position in both.

The most commonly identified push factor is poverty. However, poverty needs to be unpacked in terms of economic and social exclusion and marginalization based on gender, ethnicity and caste. This makes women the least powerful and the most vulnerable and puts them into highly abusive and exploitative situations. People migrate all the time for various reasons like personal and professional development. Usually they are middle class professionals, semi-skilled, unskilled and low skilled workers. However, the chances of migration turning into trafficking are higher for those who are at the bottom level in terms of skills, who also happens to be poor. Women and children form a large group of poor unskilled labour due to systemic gender and social discrimination against them.

Recently, the most composite assessment of poverty called human poverty angle confirms that women are indeed poorer in most societies when it comes to parameters like education and health as a result of biased resource allocation. There are reasons to believe that gender-based inequalities in education, health and nutrition, labour and other markets are likely to increase the overall level of poverty. About 70 per cent of the world's poor happen to be women not by an accident but by the systematic gender discrimination in all fields. It is truer in South Asian context because of strong patriarchy, a gender-biased superstructure that places women in deprived position in terms of resources and power. According to the 1991 Census of India, a large number of women migrants were agricultural labourers (44.1%) and cultivators (37.6%), and only 3.2 per cent women were occupied in household industries and 15.1 per cent in other activities. The trend holds up for other South Asian countries too. The gender gap as reflects in low literacy rates, estimated earned income, etc., in turn, affects the decision-making power of women, forming a two-way cycle of poverty and discrimination. Human Development Reports indicate that there is considerable gender gap resulting in feminization of poverty. It is supported by the fact that female-headed households are poorer than male-headed households. It is true for all the countries in South Asia that a greater percentage of female-headed households fall below poverty line. It should also be borne in mind that women's poverty is more severe than men's because of low human capital and lack of access to resources at the same time.

Poverty in South Asia is characterized by social exclusion based on gender, ethnicity and caste. These characteristics of social exclusion are reinforced by tradition and are institutionalized in areas such as politics, education, health and access to development resources. Gender-based discrimination is institutionalized in family and community. The low status of women is perpetuated with the help of these institutions. Women are made to believe that they are helpless without the protection of men and societies not having defined roles of women beyond family put them in vulnerable situation if they break free from the families to be easily tapped by the traffickers. Abuse of authority is even more complicated issue where family members turn into traffickers or become factors propelling trafficking. The South Asian perception of home being safest haven mirrors the laws that distinguish private from public when it comes to domestic abuses. Moreover, with such a low literacy rate, women generally constitute a mass that is unaware of their rights. This is aggravated by harmful social practices like dowry, sex-selective abortion, stigmatization of widow etc. which reinforces the idea that girls are liability to their families. The economic contribution of the woman remains invisible resulting in further discrimination.

The pull factor comes from the fact that there has been an increased demand for trafficked labour coming from a wide range of sectors topped by commercial sex workers. Needless to say that there is a growing demand for trafficked labour in factories where a trafficked person becomes debt bonded to factory owners or coerced into work under slave-like conditions. South Asia has become a centre for low cost, labour intensive, manufacturing operations. This has been further aided by the globalization policies attracting more factories to come in resulting in fierce competition among the companies. Cut-throat competition has led to cut down on the production, which in turn has decreased labour cost.

Labour migration satisfies demands for labour at all levels of the economic sector, while trafficking supplies mainly to the unorganized and exploitative sectors of the economy. It has been realized that the majority of the 'victims' were trafficked into commercial sexual exploitation, domestic work, rag picking, begging and other unskilled jobs. The nature, terms and conditions of work in these sectors give them little hope of voluntary and legitimate recruitment in the local labour force. Some might be lucky but many fall into the trap of traffickers.

Conclusion

It is critical to understand that the problem of trafficking cannot be solved in isolation and migration cannot be understood without looking at the dynamics of trafficking. A holistic response to the problem also recognizes that there are limitations within the enforcement paradigm in responding to issues of trafficking which is propelled by strong forces of demand and supply, arising out of economic and social compulsions and realities.

In looking at the relationship between globalization, migration and trafficking, lessons can perhaps be drawn from the harm minimization approach, which has been a feature of the global response to HIV. Such an approach would recognize that, under current global conditions, migration (regular or irregular) is usually a rationale human response to the situation in which people find themselves. It would recognize that (women, men, boys and girls) people will continue to migrate in search of better opportunities, whether they be socio-economic or for reasons of human security. There is need to educate people on the dangers and realities of irregular migration, including information that would allow migrants (men, women, boys and girls) to protect themselves from abuse (and gender-based violence). The recent response by governments is South Asia to address trafficking by clamping down on people's legitimate right to migrate and move in search of better economic and social options needs to be revised, as the aim should be to promote safe migration and improve law enforcement rather than curtail movement of people. There is also need to promote increased understanding and tolerance among both sending and receiving communities; and, finally give consideration to how might we find a place for a meaningful voice for trafficked people in the discourse.[12]

Trafficking is today seen and understood more as an exploitative process in a continuum of events and conditions, and not as a one-off, exploitative situation. What this means in programmatic terms is that initiatives aimed at prevention or reduction of trafficking should deal not just with the actual act of trafficking, but also recognize and address the causal factors, and more critically, the conditions and circumstances accompanying/preceding the act. It is important to deal with issues of gender, age, class and caste dimensions, which have very clear roles to play in defining vulnerabilities. Economic aspects like poverty, lack of opportunities, and breakdown of livelihood options are also factors, which need to be addressed, but have to be situated within the contextual reality of harm, which has different impacts on gender, age, caste and class. The line between legal migration for better livelihood options as against illegal migration bordering on trafficking and movement for trafficking, per se, is getting more and more blurred. There have been growing indications by grassroots groups that this concern needs to be addressed by anti-trafficking programmes.

Most of the solution would need to look at long-term approaches. The challenge is of moving from the broad picture to the specifics: from the general to the particular. There is also need for adopting a human rights approach – moving away from a service delivery approach – to see that women's rights are not violated and that they are promoted.

There is also need for a paradigm shift in the approach to trafficking of women and girls. Programmatic and conceptual approach needs to shift from a moralistic or traditional protection model under the umbrella of criminal law to a genuine human rights model. The core objective should be to ensure a commitment towards empowering the survivors and getting them to move away from the construct of victimhood to being acknowledged as autonomous human beings capable of acting in their own best interest.

Annexure 1

Recent studies in India, Nepal and Bangladesh have shown clear statistics that a large number of women, who are trafficked, are largely lured/duped by the possibility of a better life – both economic and social – across borders.

The UNIFEM–NHRC study in India interviewed approximately 500 survivors in the age group of 16-35 and 68 per cent of these trafficked survivors stated that they were lured with the option of improved economic status and 16 per cent were lured or duped with the option of marriage.

In Nepal, the study by IIDS referred to the WOREC documentation of male trafficked survivors in the age group of 12-18 years in which 66 per cent identified severe economic deprivation at home as a reason for their being trafficked into exploitative and slave like labour.

The SARI/Q supported a large-scale service programme in 2001-2003 in collaboration with an NGO called STOP. Nearly 300 girls were rescued through this initiative from brothels and urban and rural slum areas. Of the rescued girls close to 64 per cent got trafficked given the lure of better economic status since deprivation both economic and social were very acute at home. About 18 per cent were duped with the option of marriage.

Annexure 2
Trafficking of Girls to Punjab and Haryana

Hindustan Times 26/12/03 (Chandigarh Edition)
Shocking level of girl trafficking

IANS
Rewari (Haryana), December 25

TRAFFICKING in girls from states like Jharkhand, Assam and West Bengal has assumed alarming proportions in Punjab and Haryana. Girls are being traded for less than the price of a buffalo, say police officials.

People are scared to speak, but some confide that the price for a girl ranges between Rs 5,000 and Rs 15,000, depending on her age and the number of times she has been bought and sold.

Roshanara, from Dhubri in Assam, was sold three times before she was finally rescued. Mohsina, also from Dhubri, was repeatedly raped till the police rescued her from the local mafia in June. She is now pregnant. There were at least 5,000 girls from Assam and West Bengal who are confined in households in Faridabad, Gurgaon and Rewari.

"Women are treated as a commodity. This is primarily due to abject poverty and social approval," a police official said. "In fact, the police are yet to fully understand the gravity of the situation," the officer admitted.

Another reason is the discrepancy in the sex ratio in Haryana and Punjab, which forces men to "procure" women from outside. While Haryana has 861 women for 1,000 men, in Punjab the figure is even lower at 768 women for 1,000 men.

Remaining unmarried is a social taboo in these patriarchal societies, where men are discarded for marriage if they do not marry at a young age. This forces families to "buy" brides. In fact, most of the Assamese and Bengali girls in Rewari were married to men in their 40s.

What has emerged as a new trend in the last decade or so is the "dependence" of villages and districts on particular regions in states. If girls to Haryana come from Assam and Bengal, trafficking to Punjab involves a network spanning Bengal, Jharkhand and Orissa.

The girls are initially lured by agents to venture out of their native places with the prospects of jobs. The police alleged at least two gangs belonging to Bhind village and Fatehpur village in Hoshiarpur district are involved in trafficking tribal girls.

According to the police, on every Saturday, about 15-20 tribal girls from Jharkhand arrive at the Phillaur railway station in Nawanshahr by the Mori Express. Some girls have been married and lead happy lives though. Like 20-year-old Pranati Das, from Assam, who was brought by her husband Pappu Singh for Rs. 10,000. And does not repent it.

Annexure 3

Source: http://www.iom.int/DOCUMENTS/PUBLICATION/EN/tm_23.pdf

Trafficking Flows in South Asia

From	*To*	*Type*	*Scale*
Nepal	India	Sex industry	5,000–7,000 women and girls a year
Bangladesh	India	Sex industry	Of 500,000 prostitutes in India it is estimated that 13,500 are Bangladeshi
Bangladesh	Pakistan	Sex industry	4,500 women and children a year (around 200,000 in 10 years)
Bangladesh	Middle East		200,000 women and children over the last 20 years (1980-2000), 3397 children I n the last 10 years (11683 were boys) – (1990-2000)
Sri Lanka	Internal	Children: begging, labour, sex industry, soldiers	Affects ca. 100,000 children in Sri Lanka under the age of 16
Sri Lanka		Unclear, some sex industry, domestic	2,000–3,000 children per year

http://www.ilo.org/public/english/region/asro/newdelhi/ipec/responses/

Country	*Internal trafficking*	*Cross-border trafficking*
Bangladesh	Data not available	13,220 children smuggled out of the country between 1990 and 1995
India	Data not available	12,000–12,500 women and children trafficked every year into the country from neighboring states for the sex trade
Nepal	Data not available	12,000 girls trafficked every year from Nepal and across borders
Pakistan	100,000 women and children	200,000 women and children trafficked from Bangladesh to Pakistan between 1990 and 2000 More than 19,000 boys aged 2–11 have been trafficked as camel jockeys from Pakistan to the Middle East
Sri Lanka	5,000	Sporadic incidences

http://www.catwinternational.org/factbook/Pakistan.php

- There have been 1 million Bangladeshi and more than 200,000 Burmese women trafficked to Karachi, Pakistan.
- 200,000 Bangladeshi women were trafficked to Pakistan in the last ten years, continuing at the rate of 200-400 women monthly.

NOTES

1. CATW – Asia Pacific, Trafficking in Women and Prostitution in the Asia Pacific.
2. Five Years after Stockholm: ECPAT report on the implementation of the agenda for action at the First World Congress CSEC in Stockholm.
3. Towards the Construction of an Empowered Subject: Human Rights Analysis of Anti-trafficking Legal Interventions and Trends in South Asia 2001 – Jyoti Sanghera (Technical Paper: Consultative Meeting on Anti-Trafficking Programs in South Asia).
4. Human Rights Watch's response to the US trafficking report (website http://www.hrw.org).
5. From Risks to Rights: Migration, trafficking of women and girls and their vulnerability to HIV/AIDS in South Asia: A Regional Strategic Framework; UNDP Regional Project – Jyoti Sanghera.
6. Radhika Coomaraswamy, Addendun Mission to Bangladesh, Nepal and India on the Issue of Trafficking in Women and Girls: Report of the UN Special Rapporteur on Violence Against Women and Its Causes and Consequences, 2000.
7. Beyond Boundaries, Therese Blanchet, 2002.
8. Marshal, P., Paper at the Globalization Workshop in Kuala Lumpur, 8-10 May 2001.
9. From Risks to Rights, op. cit.
10. Ibid.
11. Radhika Coomaraswamy, op. cit.
12. Marshal, P., op. cit.

12

Dimensions of Gender Development in South Asia Based on Human Development Indicators

Preet Rustagi

This paper highlights the significance of development indicators in the context of South Asian women and their scope in addressing issues of gender concern. The importance of a broad conceptual framework that accounts for the gender ideologies prevalent in the South Asian region as a base, within which the quantitative indicators are to be analyzed and evaluated, is presented through a discussion of issues of concern for women in South Asia.

Women as a category for analysis brings up the issue of heterogeneity vs. homogeneity (Stromquist, 1998). This assumes greater importance in the context of South Asia – a region comprising different sovereign nations, with their sets of diverse socio-cultural and ethnic populations, with a range of religious faiths, legal frames, economic and political forces – all of which impact upon the lives of women in the region. Within these diversities, the region stands together on a number of counts and the women of South Asia, too, face similar conditions on various fronts.

South Asia is a highly populated, agriculture dependent, income poor and identified as the most deprived region in the world (HDSA, 1997). The region is also recognized as a "patriarch belt" (Caldwell, 1982). The women in South Asia are subordinated to men in a kin-ordered social structure (Mathema, 1998), have low status, little or no access to property and land[1] (Bardhan, 1986) and suffer from non-recognition of their work which is largely unpaid.

Religious and cultural practices, based on a strong patriarchal ideology prevalent in the region, curtail women's mobility, and prevent them from utilizing opportunities to enhance capabilities. They often face discrimination in spheres of education, nutrition, health, work and political participation in most of the South Asian countries. This is in spite of the equality among men and women granted for in their respective constitutions.

Over three decades now, the goals of gender equality and empowerment of women have been gaining acceptance internationally as well as nationally and a range of efforts are on to work towards attaining these. Some of the prominent international efforts began in 1975 with the first World Conference in Mexico. The fourth World Conference in Beijing in 1995 was a hallmark, when the international communities accepted the need for a strong gender perspective in all areas of development planning and implementation. More recently, the eight Millennium Development Goals[2] (MDGs), specified in the 2000 millennium summit of the United Nations (UN), is another global initiative, which recognizes the centrality of gender equality and empowerment for achieving all other seven goals as well.

By far, the most acclaimed global endeavour in the area of indicators as a tool for measuring human and gender development began in the 1990s with the United Nations Development Programme (UNDP) Human Development Reports (HDRs). The calculation of composite indices presented as a replacement of the reigning economic measure of Gross Domestic Product (GDP) had a remarkable impact that helped popularize the conceptual framework for human development, wherein the well-being of people was central.

What all these endeavours have enabled with the quantification through development indicators is a healthy process of stocktaking, monitoring and evaluation. This paper elaborates on the measures evolved by HDRs and presents their findings for South Asia. However, there are limitations of these composite indices which demand perusal of individual indicators for identification of priority concerns in each of the South Asian countries, especially in the context of women.

These aspects are dealt with in this paper under three sections. The first section deals with the evolution of concepts like human development and gender development, scope and relevance of indicators in general and that of composite indices such as Human Development Index (HDI), Gender-related Development Index (GDI), Gender Empowerment Measure (GEM), and so on. The discussion will also cover the spread of HDRs from global to regional and national levels. The positive impact of these endeavours as well as lacunae will be addressed.

The second section will deal with the situation of women in South Asia to illustrate what indicators are relevant for, how quantification of this kind can aid the monitoring process as well as point out the structural and institutional dimensions which challenge quantification. Diverse dimensions are dealt with to bring out the gender ideologies prevalent in South Asia that create hurdles to women's development. These are issues relating to work, education, health, survival, political participation and violence, which cover a wide spectrum of the discrimination and biases faced by women.

Finally, in the last section, some concluding remarks are made which touch upon the issue of data gaps and how they affect any indicator-based approach to tackle the problems facing women in general and in the South Asian region in particular.

I

Evolution of Concepts

Conceptualization of ideas like human development, which forms the basis for creation of indicators from available statistical information, has occupied the interests of many researchers through the

20th century. The realization that income growth does not automatically translate into human well-being came to be noticed prominently after the world wars. The presence of human miseries, grave levels of deprivations and lack of freedoms brought home the realization that the traditional measure of Gross Domestic Product (GDP)-based national income is an inadequate indicator for welfare.

Various agencies, organizations and individuals, such as the United Nations, Food and Agricultural Organisation (FAO), Organisation for Economic Cooperation and Development (OECD), UN Research Institute for Social Development (UNRISD), World Bank, and so on, made efforts to evolve an alternative economic measure to replace the one representing income – the GDP. The focus of these attempts were oriented towards calculating an appropriate measure, which took into account social concerns of any country's development, such as individual security, social adjustment, political participation, freedom, justice, peace and harmony, in addition to health, literacy, employment, income, consumption and so on (UN, 1954, 1961; FAO, 1949; OECD, 1976; UNESCO, 1981; UNRISD, 1968; Baster, 1972; Lisk, 1979; McGranahan, et al., 1972; Sen, 1987).

To conceptualize aspects of living standards and be able to measure them posed many philosophical as well as statistical problems (Moser, 1973; Morris, 1979). Since the search was for one single indicator that could replace GDP, most agencies arrived at the conclusion that no single indicator that could serve a similar purpose was feasible (UN, 1954). Efforts to work towards creating a composite index by combining a set of identified crucial variables were ongoing through this period. Most of these too, proved, largely abortive (OECD, 1976).

The first composite index propounded in 1979 by Morris D. Morris settled for using three out of 100 indicators that were being considered to form the Physical Quality of Life Index (PQLI). This measure was limited for poor countries and focussed on meeting the most basic needs of people. The three components included finally were life expectancy, infant mortality and literacy (also see

Morris and McAlphin, 1982; Larson and Wilford, 1979 for a critique).

The efforts made through the latter half of the 20th century generated substantial interest in aspects of social and human well-being. However, by far, the most poignant impact was made by the human development concept propounded by the UNDP whose flagship was the composite index – Human Development Index (HDI).

While the earlier endeavours have a role in the evolution, the conceptualization of human and gender development is associated with the UNDP and the Human Development Reports (HDRs) that have come to be viewed as a culmination of these efforts. The flagships of these reports, viz., the composite indices Human Development Index (HDI) and subsequently Gender-related Development Index (GDI), presented as the much-awaited replacement to the income measure, have a major role in its popularity and global acceptance.

The Human Development Report defines the basic objective of development as enlarging people's choices. This is sought through striving for equality of opportunities for all people in society, sustainability of such opportunities from one generation to the next and empowerment of people so that they participate in – and benefit from – development processes (UNDP, different years from 1990 onwards). Conceptually broad, this frame is, indeed, well defined. The endeavour is to face the challenge of translating the human development concern from a concept into reality.

With each year, the HDR focuses on specific aspects (see Table 1) and has also created many more indices. The first index measured by UNDP in the HDR (1990) is the HDI. The HDRs over the years have admitted that the concept of human development is much broader than the measure of HDI. Admittedly, the "HDI is not a substitute for the fuller treatment of the richness of the concerns of the human development perspective" (HDR, 1998).

To come up with a comprehensive measure is a daunting task and in fact, impossible, given the fact that many vital dimensions of human development are non-quantifiable. The HDI measures average achievement in three basic dimensions of human development – a long and healthy life, knowledge and a decent standard of living. Simply stated, the HDI is an average of life expectancy index, educational attainment index and adjusted real GDP per capita index. This measure was used to draw attention to the issues concerning human development which it has managed to do to a large extent.

Table 1
Themes of Human Development Reports

Year	*Theme*
1990	Concept and Measurement of Human Development
1991	Financing Human Development
1992	Global Dimensions of Human Development
1993	People's Participation
1994	New Dimensions of Human Security
1995	Gender and Human Development
1996	Economic Growth and Human Development
1997	Human Development to Eradicate Poverty
1998	Consumption for Human Development
1999	Globalization with a Human Face
2000	Human Rights and Human Development
2001	Making New Technologies Work for Human Development
2002	Deepening Democracy in a Fragmented World
2003	Millennium Development Goals: A Compact among Nations to End Human Poverty

Source: UNDP (Various Years 1990-2003).

Over the years, the HDR sought to enrich the concept, analyze one specific aspect of human development critically and develop more elegant measures of well-being. Among the many indices introduced in the HDR, some have become annual features, while some others have been discarded for want of data and feasibility of calculating across countries (the Human Freedom Index is one such measure). Among the ones that have gained popularity and widespread acceptance, despite the significant share of critique and debates these have generated, are the HDI,

Gender-related Development Index (GDI), Gender Empowerment Measure (GEM) and Human Poverty Index (HPI-1 for developing countries and HPI-2 for selected, OECD countries).

Each of these indices are based on a set of chosen indicators. The HPI-1 designed for developing countries considers the same three dimensions through four identified indicators. As opposed to the HDI, which measures the overall progress in a country in achieving human development, the HPI reflects the distribution of progress and measures the backlog of deprivations that still exists. HPI-1 is based on the probability at birth of not surviving to age 40, adult illiteracy rate and deprivation in overall economic provisioning – public and private – reflected by the percentage of population without sustainable access to an improved water source and percentage of children under five years who are underweight.

HPI-2 devised as a measure of human poverty in industrial countries, since human deprivation varies with social and economic conditions of a community, is also based on four indicators. Their probability at birth of not surviving to age 60, percentage of adults lacking literacy skills, percentage of people living below the poverty line and long-term unemployment rate.

The GDI and GEM were the two new indices floated by the HDR (1995) which coincided with other international events that focused or sought to draw specific attention to women's issues. The GDI captures the inequalities in achievements between women and men in the same three dimensions as considered in the HDI. This measure viewed along with HDI reflects the extent of gender equity. The greater the gender disparity in basic human development, the lower will be the GDI compared to HDI for any country.

The GEM exposes inequality in opportunities in selected areas – the participation of women in economic and political life and decision-making. The components of this measure are the percentage of women in parliament, among administrators, managers, professional and technical workers, and women's earned income share as a percentage of men's.

In the context of the efforts being made to bring gender issues at the centre stage, the GDI and GEM proved important tools to establish the prevalence of gender inequality across the world. With the measurement of the indices, the HDRs emphasized the significance of mitigating these disparities as critical for overall development (HDR, 1995).

As stated earlier, while the concepts gained wider acceptance and generated extensive debates, the indices devised by the HDRs have received substantial criticism (Kelley, 1991; Krishnaji, 1997; Hirway and Mahadevia, 1996; among others). There is widespread acknowledgement of the fact that composite indices such as GDI and GEM cannot be taken as complete measures of gender equality and women's empowerment, as many facets of equity and empowerment, such as security, mobility, dignity, autonomy, access to resources, cannot be adequately represented by proxy measures (Gurumurthy, 1998; HDSA, 2000).

Within the limited purpose served by these indices, the process of assigning ranks to the nations on the basis of their index values introduced a means of deriving a comparative picture. A simultaneous parallel effort to make nations responsible and involve them in these processes through participation in and preparation of the national HDRs ensued.

Indicators created out of variables for which data is available lie at the core of any measurement or quantification (whether of the UNDP's composite indices or individual/single type). The importance of indicators is manifold. They provide information, enable analysis and comparison. These aid the process of planning, intervention, evaluation and monitoring. By stressing on the need for indicators (as is being effectively done by the UN and its agencies through what is termed as the 'human development revolution' by some), the aspects which are not adequately captured by statistics are identified.

The identification of data gaps thus enables the process of generating the required information which has its benefits for the overall betterment of all beings. Intertwining the processes of planning with development indicators thus facilitates mechanisms of setting objectives that are quantifiable, measurable and time-bound. The HDR (2003) highlights that 135 countries have used country-owned processes to produce more than 450 national and regional HDRs. These processes have generated very useful disaggregated data along gender, ethnic, age, race, geographic and other lines which have aided deeper analysis of country-specific situation and causes of inequality and poverty.

Among the other important parallel processes are the global action plans initiated post-Beijing ever since the fourth World Conference when the world community accepted the need for a strong gender perspective in all areas of development planning and implementation. The Beijing Platform for Action (BPFA) became the base document to measure progress on gender justice and women's empowerment (UNIFEM, 2003a). The BPFA identified 12 critical areas[3] of concern for women's advancement.

Ever since Beijing, National Plans of Action have been drafted and the process of review initiated in all the South Asian countries with the exception of Bhutan.[4] This review process monitors progress and identifies priority focus areas for action. It also reveals areas that have data gaps and where disaggregated information needs to be generated. Specific regional focus is also pursued in these endeavours. United Nations Development Fund for Women (UNIFEM) South Asia Regional Office (SARO) is one agency which initiated a mechanism of ministerial level biennial regional reviews. Four such review meetings have been held in India (1996), Nepal (1998), Maldives (2000) and Bhutan (2003) (UNIFEM, 2003a).

Another process, which supports the development of indicators to track progress, is the adoption of the UN Millennium Declaration and setting of the eight Millennium Development Goals (MDGs). All these processes are working in tandem towards a set of common objectives. The HDR (2003), which focuses on the MDGs, is one good example of the synergistic approach being followed.

The acceptance of HDRs and the healthy debates on human development that have been generated by these endeavours globally, regionally, nationally and at sub-national level forms a significant contribution. By far the strongest criticisms or controversies have arisen in the context of the methodology adopted for measurement of development, specifically the formation of the composite indices.

Since the HDI and other indices club together three dimensions, the weights assigned in the technical formation to each variable and the overwhelming tilt of the index to the income indicator have been among the prominent objections raised (Kelley, 1991; Djikstra and Hanmer, 1997; Bardhan and Klassen, 1999). Also, the choice of variables to reflect human or gender development as well as gender empowerment as adopted by UNDP HDRs have formed another serious segment of the controversial debates (Hirway and Mahadevia, 1996; Mehta, 1996; Viswanathan, 2001).

Regional Human Development Reports for South Asia

South Asia[5] consists of seven nations – India, Pakistan, Bangladesh, Sri Lanka, Nepal, Bhutan and Maldives. The total population of the region is estimated to be 1,326 million in 2000. The number of women to every 100 men in the population is 94, which is 3 points lower than the sex ratio calculated for developing countries as a whole (HDSA, 2000). The South Asian region, as compared to developing countries, has a lower level of urbanization, with less than one-third of South Asian population inhabiting urban areas.

The founder of HDRs, Mahbub-ul-Haq after seven reports in 1997 prepared the first South Asian regional report titled "Human Development for South Asia" (HDSA). This report focused on various dimensions of human development to highlight the region's deprivation levels as being among the worst in the world. Nearly 40 per cent of the world's poor and almost 46 per cent of the world's illiterate population inhabit South Asia, making it the poorest and most illiterate region in the world. Half of its children are malnourished, which is worse than the situation of Sub-Saharan Africa (where malnourishment is prevalent among 30%).

The HDSA, 1997 reveals that human deprivation levels are among the highest with 260 million people lacking access to even rudimentary health facilities, 337 million people lack safe drinking water, 830 million have no access to basic sanitation facilities and over 400 million go hungry every day.

This first regional report introduced yet another index called the Human Deprivation Measure (HDM). Presented as an improvement over the income poverty measure, the HDM sought to capture many other forms of deprivation. This index too was viewed as a measure that can remind policy makers which human capabilities are lacking in a society, among which population groups, and what specific steps need to be taken to integrate the poor into the mainstream of the country's economic, social and political life.

This inclusion of the deprived by enhancing human capabilities cannot be attained with the budgetary allocations for social sectors of health, education and so on being low, while the share of defence spending is very high. South Asia is among the most militarized regions in the world with two of the largest armies. Even a small country of 1,190 coral islands – Maldives – allocates a high share of its GDP for military expenditure (4.9% in 2000) as compared to its expenditure on health (which is lower at 3.7% in 1998) (HDSA, 2000).

Table 2

Human and Gender Development Indices for South Asia: 1993-97

Country/ Region	*HDI*			*GDI*			*GEM*		
	1993	*1997*	*2003*	*1993*	*1997*	*2003*	*1993*	*1997*	*2003*
India	0.436	0.545	0.590	0.410	0.525	0.574	0.235	0.240	NA
Pakistan	0.442	0.508	0.499	0.383	0.472	0.469	0.165	0.176	0.414
Bangladesh	0.365	0.440	0.502	0.336	0.428	0.495	0.291	0.304	0.218
Nepal	0.332	0.463	0.499	0.308	0.441	0.479	NA	NA	NA
Sri Lanka	0.698	0.721	0.730	0.699	0.712	0.726	0.306	0.321	0.272
Bhutan	0.307	0.459	0.511	NA	0.444	NA	NA	NA	NA
Maldives	0.610	0.716	0.751	0.599	0.711	NA	0.324	0.342	NA
South Asia weighted average	0.432	0.532	0.582	0.402	0.511	NA	0.233	0.236	NA
Developing Countries	0.563	0.637	0.655	0.530	0.630	NA	0.351	–	NA

Source: HDSA, 1997 and 2000; HDR 2003.

The composite indices – HDI, GDI and GEM – calculated by UNDP HDRs, reveal an improvement in values for all South Asian countries over 1993 to 1997. Sri Lanka and Maldives are the two nations which portray medium human development levels. In 2003, Maldives performance surpasses the HDI value of Sri Lanka (see Table 2).

The gender development levels in the region are second lowest in the world being just better than the Arab countries. However, the GEM values are the lowest (HDSA, 2000). In 2003, the human and gender development levels for Pakistan as calculated through HDI and GDI values shows a decline. This is the only instance of a decline in the region as seen in Table 2. The GEM values, however, have increased substantially for Pakistan. This is probably due to the higher share of women in parliament, which is partly an outcome of the one-third women's reservations policy introduced after the period when parliament was suspended (2000-02).

Ever since the 1997 report, every year, thematic reports were published. The 2000 HDSA focused on the theme titled gender question. It sought to address the issue of why women have to bear a disproportionately higher share of the burden of this deprivation that is prevalent in South Asia. The report elaborated on the region's tradition-bound, patriarchal systems and how these affect women's lives and the issue of women's invisibility in economic and political spheres. There were suggestions made on how women's capabilities can be enhanced and what institutional mechanisms are needed to bridge the prevalent gender gaps in South Asia.

In the following section, the study focuses on some of the dimensions of women's development in the context of South Asia, highlighting the low status of women and how this affects the recognition of their work, their survival, education, health, political participation and the violence they face.

II

Dimensions of Women's Development in South Asia

This section discusses some of the key concerns facing women in South Asia, such as the non-recognition of their economic contribution and work, issues of their survival, discrimination faced in educational and health spheres and violence against them. Despite the wide disparities among the countries in the region, these concerns are relevant for the women inhabiting therein due to the strong patriarchal ideologies and low socio-economic status assigned to women.

The South Asian region consists of three countries with relatively large populations, with India containing more than one-fifth of all humanity, while another two countries – Maldives and Bhutan – are fairly small in comparison. In terms of religious faiths, Pakistan, Bangladesh and Maldives have declared Islam as the state religion, while Nepal is by constitution a Hindu State. India, with all its diversities, which includes people following different religious faiths, is a secular state. Sri Lanka and Bhutan, despite their ethnic multiplicities, are largely followers of Buddhism.

Ethnic and religious conflicts occur almost throughout the region, with the exception of Maldives and Bhutan. Maldives is by far the most homogeneous state with a single religion and one language. Bhutan has managed its ethnic interests through the constitutional power structure of combining monarchy with a two-thirds share of people elected representatives. The region boasts of two long-standing democracies and one recently established, including one of the largest democracies in the world. On the flip side, it is also host to two of the largest armies in the world making it the most militarized region. Violence against women in the context of rising ethnic conflicts and religious fundamentalism has worsening impact on the security levels in the region, vitiating the environment to the detriment and loss of many lives and livelihoods.

The interaction between religious and cultural beliefs and practices varies across the countries in the region, especially in the ways in which it manifests in gender relations across communities. The communities themselves differ in terms of geography, ecology and predominant systems of livelihoods, each with their own influence on accepted gender roles and relations (HDSA, 2000). For instance, Buddhism as practised in Bhutan is different from Sri

Lankan Buddhism. Similarly, Islam has found different modes of expression in different parts of Bangladesh, Pakistan, India, Sri Lanka and the Maldives. The practices in legal sphere which include personal laws based on customary practices, many of which are not codified, are often biased heavily against women (Mathema, 1998; UNIFEM, 2003b).

An analysis of the situation of women in South Asia has to acknowledge these diversities and heterogeneities and then address factors that transcend class, religion, culture and locality. The subordinate status of women affects every sphere of their lives.

Most South Asian countries are agrarian economies. The participation and contribution of women to their economies is substantial but unrecognized and undervalued. The low economic 'worth' of women compounds their poor socio-cultural status stemming from prevalent patriarchal thinking. The discussion on the dimensions covered in this section includes women's work, survival, health, education, political participation and violence. The information made available through the HDRs and HDSA through collation of a range of data sources from the countries of South Asia over the years forms the basis for analysis.

WOMEN'S WORK

As stated above, the discrimination faced by women in the economic sphere reinforces their low status as their contribution goes unrecognized and remains undervalued. Women in South Asia, which is a predominantly agricultural and tradition-bound region, participate in economic activities and contribute their labour actively. Yet, due to the nature of their work, which is intertwined with household activities at times and is often unpaid, on the one hand, and the flawed definition of economic activity, on the other hand, women's economic participation remains statistically invisible.

The role played by women in the care sector – activities – predominantly their reproductive work, bearing, rearing, nurturing children and household maintenance – falls outside the national accounting systems followed by different countries. While these activities are crucial for household members' well-being and effective participation in different spheres – economic, social and political – they continue to remain non-economic activities, which are not considered for direct contribution to national incomes. By virtue of women performing these roles, which are statistically not counted as economic and hence not monetarily valued, women's roles and their contribution are assigned low status. This forms the major bone of contention for women's studies scholars and activists of the women's movements who are fighting for women's equality and rights.

Women's contribution in the activities that are recognized by definition as economic activities also remains unrecognized and non-enumerated. This is due to cultural and traditional values which constrain recognition of women's economic participation. In the South Asian countries, the historical gender roles, spaces and stereotypes of the 'public' male breadwinner (provider) and 'private' female care-giver are espoused even under changing situations. This is due to the association of household status with women's 'non-work'. However the circumstances of women having to offer their labour in the paid market work spheres under extreme economic stress and poverty does not really alter her private status.

In addition is the nature of women's work, with dominance of domestic work, where it is often difficult to separate production for self-consumption from production for sale. Thus, a vast magnitude of women's home-based work remains unreported and unaccounted. This is true of the share of women workers involved in informal sector activities, or as unpaid family labour (which includes helpers in manufacturing and in self-employed activities such as trading) as well.

The majority of South Asian women work in the informal sector or as unpaid family helpers. Among the economically active women workers in India, 96 per cent are in the unorganized sector. In Nepal, 75.3 per cent are self-employed and 28 per cent are unpaid family members. In Pakistan, 65 per cent of the female labour force that is officially enumerated are in the informal sector. The percentage of women earning a living in the informal sector in Bangladesh in 1995-96 was 75 per cent (HDSA, 2000).

As the limitations of enumeration of women's work in standard national accounting statistics are increasingly being recognized, there have been efforts to prepare satellite accounts which can capture women's work through alternative methods such as time use surveys (Acharya, 2000). Nepal among the South Asian countries has pioneered in the preparation of such statistics. India has also undertaken a pilot survey (Hirway, 2002; CSO, 2000). Other efforts to access women's economic participation and the time spent in various activities across South Asia have been in the form of micro studies (Elson and Evers, 1996; Jain and Chand, 1982, to name a few). HDSA, (2000) based on some observations suggests that South Asian women work for 10 to 12 hours per day, which is 2 to 4 hours more than men's work.

Despite the conceptual, methodological and definitional flaws, statistics on women's work from the respective national data sources reveal nearly one-third participation of women in the labour force. In South Asia, Maldives and Pakistan are the two countries where female percentage of labour force is relatively lower, while in Bangladesh and Nepal the share of women labour force is higher compared to other countries in the region (see Table 3).

Table 3

Sectoral Distribution of Women Labour Force in South Asia

Country	*Percentage Labour Force in*			*Percentage of Female Workers*
	Agriculture	*Industry*	*Services*	
India	62	11	27	32
Pakistan	47	20	33	27
Bangladesh	59	13	28	42
Nepal	93	1	6	40
Sri Lanka	49	21	30	36
Bhutan	92	3	5	32
Maldives	25	32	43	22

Source: HDSA, 1997, 2000.

The region, as a whole, has been witnessing rising levels of women's economic participation over the years. The factors that have aided or influenced these trends differ from country to country. Nevertheless, the characteristics of women's labour, in terms of the nature of tasks undertaken and the wages earned, remain by and large unchanged. Majority of the women are undertaking manual, non-mechanized, low or unpaid tasks. Even among those entering the paid labour market, face gender discrimination in access to jobs, and gender inequalities in pay and job security.

An overwhelming majority of economically active women in Nepal and India work in agriculture (see Table 4). In Sri Lanka, where agriculture is the main life-supporting sector for rural populations, women are involved extensively in the plantation sector. Tasks of plucking tea, tapping of rubber and processing of coir fibre are undertaken by Sri Lankan women (Weerahewa and Ariyawardana, 2003).

Table 4

Sectoral Employment in South Asia by Sex

(in %)

Country	*Sex**	*Agriculture*	*Industry*	*Service*
Bangladesh (1996)	Male	53.9	19.2	26.8
	Female	41.7	27.8	30.5
India (1994)	Male	58.3	16.5	25.2
	Female	78.0	10.9	11.1
Nepal (1996)	Male	78.9	4.9	13.2
	Female	93.7	1.4	4.5
Pakistan (1997)	Male	40.7	20.2	39.0
	Female	66.4	10.6	23.2
Sri Lanka (1995)	Male	35.4	28.2	36.4
	Female	41.5	30.8	27.7

*For each country male figures are percentages of male labour force and female figures are percentages of female labour force.

Source: Respective labour force surveys of the countries; cited in HDSA, 2000.

Rural women in South Asia participate in crop farming, animal husbandry and a host of off-farm activities. A substantial amount of time is spent in looking after livestock, from rearing to protecting animals, collecting fodder and water, collecting eggs, milking, ensuring the health of animals, poultry, etc.

By and large, among the secondary sector activities of industry, manufacturing and so on, women's enumeration is low as seen in Table 4. Sri Lanka and Bangladesh have relatively higher share of women's employment in the secondary sector. Sri Lanka began its phase of trade liberalization and export-oriented growth as early as in 1977. The nature of these industries and the additional labour demand generated therein facilitated entry of women workers. However, in a large majority of these occupations, the working conditions are poor and workers are exploited and underpaid. Bangladesh, comparatively speaking, has recently embarked on industry-led growth policies, specially in such areas as garments. While this thrust has led to South Asia becoming one of the world's largest exporters of textiles (with India, Sri Lanka and Bangladesh), the work and pay conditions are no better than sweat shops.

The discriminatory wages paid to women workers is a common factor emerging from studies in South Asian countries (Acharya, 2000; Atapattu, 2000; Mahmud, 2000; Mehta, 2000). Women workers are demanded for their docility, lower probability of organizing or fighting for better wages and work conditions. The patriarchal norms that are prevalent make it easier to manage women as workers.

Women's participation, although increasing in South Asia, still accounts for the smallest percentage of formal sector employment. Even in the formal jobs, women occupy the lower rungs of clerical and low-skilled occupations. The lower levels of literacy and skill/training among women in South Asia only add to their woes.

Women are often occupied in community, social and personal services. In India, 57 per cent of women in formal sector fall in this employment category, while the corresponding figure for Bangladesh is 59 per cent (see Table 4). Sri Lanka, given the better educational levels of women, displays a far more even distribution of females in formal sector employment. Nevertheless, even here, greater numbers of females are employed in unskilled jobs

(UNIFEM, 2003a; HDSA, 2000). To encourage women's participation, some of the South Asian countries have introduced policies of reservation in government jobs. In Bangladesh, 10 to 15 per cent and in Pakistan, 20 per cent government jobs are reserved for women.

Thus, to sum up the discussion on women's work and economic participation, it can be stated that the overall lower status, low literacy and skill levels, lack of access or control over land, property and other resources curtail women from effectively participating and deriving benefits from the contribution they make.

Survival Issues

The strong presence of traditional values and perceptions in South Asia, wherein the role and status of women are assigned lower significance, reflects in the demographic balance as well. As opposed to the global sex ratio of 106 women per 100 men, South Asia is one of the few regions (other than China and parts of the Arab world) where the proportion of women are lower – only 94 women per 100 men in the population.

Table 5

Survival Indicators for South Asia

2003 HDI Rank	*Country/ Region*	*Sex Ratio (females per 100 males)*	*Female Life Expectancy at Birth*	*Female Child Mortality Rate*	*Female to Male Child Mortality Rate*
86	Maldives	93	66	80	1.51
99	Sri Lanka	102	76	20	0.91
127	India	94	64	97	1.18
136	Bhutan	98	64	94	0.96
139	Bangladesh	95	61	116	1.09
143	Nepal	100	59	124	1.13
144	Pakistan	92	60	104	0.96
	South Asia	94	–	99	1.14

Source: HDSA, 2000; HDR, 2003.

Relatively balanced sex ratios are recorded for Sri Lanka and Nepal while Pakistan, India and Maldives have lower proportion of females in their populations (see Table 5). In India, where the sex ratios have been declining, especially among the younger age cohorts, practices of female infanticide and foeticide to prevent the birth of girls have been noted in some parts of the country (see George et al., 1992; Agnihotri, 2000, among many others). The introduction and ease of access to pre-natal screening methods, such as ultrasonography and amniocentesus technologies, which can help detect the sex of the foetus, are being used to selectively abort female foetuses (Patel, 1997; Dasgupta, 1987). Efforts to prevent and discourage such practices have begun, for instance, India has enacted a law criminalizing such acts.

Examinations of the causes leading to such demographic imbalances ever since these trends were observed in South Asian countries have exposed the strong son preference traits. The declining trend of sex ratios witnessed despite reduction in mortality rates have led researchers to examine other variables such as sex ratios at birth, gender differentials in nutrition and extent of gender variations in mortality rates among populations belonging to different age cohorts (see UN, 1998; Bhat, 2002; Krishnaji and James, 2002; Waldron, 1998). Linkages have been examined in many of the South Asian countries between fertility rates, contraceptive use, abortion and sex preference even in Nepal and Bangladesh where the imbalance is not so pronounced (Arnold, 2001; Karki, 1992; Leone et al., 2003; Bairagi, 2001, among others).

The reasons for son preference stem from patrilineal and religious structures that lay emphasis on the role and significance of male offsprings. Most ritual functions in the family are undertaken by sons. Even, despite law, property transfers are made in favour of sons, who, as is believed, carry the name of the household. Having one or more sons in every household is therefore considered almost essential. In the context of declining fertility rates and smaller family size becoming desirable, the pressure to give births to male offsprings further worsens the condition of women's health and status.

Frequent child bearing and the exposure of women's bodies to a host of tests take a toll on their health. Since women conceive and give birth, and if a son is not born, this becomes a cause for violence, abuse and torture against them. Even when girls are born, they are discriminated against in a number of ways (UN, 1998; Miller, 1981; UN Secretariat, 1988). Neglect and lack of adequate care in feeding girls, and looking after their nutrition and health, are noted in a number of studies revealing the gender discriminatory practices in South Asia. These are mostly outcomes of the lower status assigned to women (Basu, 1992).

The efforts being made by the respective governments and other concerned agencies have resulted in improvements in life expectancy and reduction of mortality rates in all the South Asian countries over the quarter century from 1975 to 2000 (HDR, 2003). Yet, as compared to male child mortality rates, the female child mortality rates are higher revealing excess female mortality among under-5 age groups. The female to male ratio is above 1 in four countries, viz., Maldives, India, Nepal and Bangladesh. By far the best performance among the survival indicators is witnessed in the case of Sri Lanka (see Table 5).

Consideration of three survival dimensions using sex ratios, child mortality and life expectancy display discrepancies in ordering of different countries. Nepal has a more balanced sex ratio, but the worst life expectancy and child mortality rates among females. This is one instance to highlight the significance of considering individual indicators to identify where policy intervention will be needed in any country.

Health Concerns

The overall lower status of women in South Asia influences their health status too. Factors, such as lack of access to resources, poor decision-making power or control, low recognition of their work, that is, low economic worth, and their social position as subservient to males or other household members, put their health requirements on to low priority. In fact, often, these health needs are not realized or articulated by the women themselves. Their low self-esteem and their socialization into 'non-entities' prevent them from such articulation.

The emphasis laid on women's marriage reiterates the stress on their reproductive roles, undermining all other spheres of human development. In South Asian countries, marriages are traditionally carried out at early ages with little choice being given to women. The governments of most South Asian countries are actively working towards preventing child marriages and pushing the minimum age at marriage up for girls. Bangladesh, India and Bhutan have stipulated the legal minimum age at marriage at 18 years. Yet, many marriages are occurring before girls attain the legal minimum age statutorily fixed.

Early marriage along with young age pregnancies compounded by poor health and economic poverty puts undue stress on the women's bodies. A majority of South Asian pregnant women suffer from anaemia (see Table 6). The total fertility rate (TFR) has been declining over the last three decades, but still continues to be quite high in Maldives, Pakistan, Bhutan and Nepal. The most significant decline in TFR is witnessed for Bangladesh, India and Sri Lanka (see Table 6).

Table 6

Some Health Indicators for South Asia

Country/ Region	*Total Fertility Rate*		*% of Pregnant Women with Anaemia*	*% of Birth Attended by Skilled Personnel*	*Health Expenditure as % of GDP*	
	1970-75	*2000-2005*			*Public*	*Private*
Maldives	7.0	5.3	62	70	6.3	1.3
Sri Lanka	4.1	2.0	60	97	1.8	1.9
India	5.4	3.0	72	43	0.9	4.0
Bhutan	5.9	5.0	73	15	3.7	0.4
Bangladesh	6.2	3.5	58	12	1.5	2.6
Nepal	5.8	4.3	75	11	1.6	3.6
Pakistan	6.3	5.1	45	20	0.9	3.2
South Asia	5.6	3.3	–	36	–	–

Source: HDR, 2003; HDSA, 2000.

Maternal mortality rates are quite high in the region (HDSA, 2000). The probability of women not surviving childbirth is further aggravated by a large proportion of them having non-institutional deliveries, unaided by skilled personnel. Only 36 per cent of South Asian babies are born with the assistance of skilled personnel (see Table 6). In Sri Lanka and Maldives, the situation is relatively better compared to other South Asian countries.

The cultural basis of women's status and their perception of low self-worth in the tradition-bound South Asian countries also results in discriminatory practices beginning from basic nutrition to accessing health care. The lack of adequate public health services acts as a constraint for women to access such services (Baru, 2003; Gopalan and Shiva, 2000).

Public health expenditure as percentage of GDP is relatively higher in Maldives and Bhutan, whereas the private sector proportion exceeds public health expenditure in all other countries of the region (see Table 6). However, this allocation alone is inadequate in understanding how such money is spent and what is the nature of impact on health in general and of women specifically.

Given the levels of poverty in South Asia, the accessibility of private paid health services among women is likely to be limited, since their needs are not considered to be important. There is very often excessive concentration on reproductive health to the utter neglect of other health concerns of women in government policies (see Qadeer, 1998; Datta, 2003). Other areas, which have not been researched adequately and lack data, are women's mental health, sexuality and so on.

EDUCATION

The importance of education for human development as well as women's empowerment as a core dimension is gaining widespread acceptance, even in South Asia. Sri Lanka and Maldives are among the best performing countries in the region with regard to female literacy rates. However, the gender biases at higher educational levels, in professional courses or in non-traditional subjects, are visible even among these countries (HDSA, 2000).

The adult literacy rate (ALR) for the population above 15 years has been improving over the years. Even, over the last decade from 1990 to 2001, ALR has increased from 48 to 56 (see Table 7). However, this rate is low compared to even developing countries, where it was 75 per cent in 2001. The literacy rate for youth (refers to population in the age cohort of 15-24 years) in all South Asian countries shows signs of positive trends, reflecting inter-generational improvements. In South Asia, the youth literacy rate is 71 for 2001.

Table 7

Adult and Youth Literacy Rates for South Asia, 1990 and 2001

Country/Region	*Adult Literacy Rate (15 years and above) (%)*		*Youth Literacy Rate (15-24 years) (%)*	
	1990	*2001*	*1990*	*2001*
Maldives	94.8	97.0	98.1	99.1
Sri Lanka	86.7	91.9	95.1	96.9
India	49.3	58.0	64.3	73.3
Bhutan	–	–	–	–
Bangladesh	34.2	40.6	42.0	49.1
Nepal	30.4	42.9	46.6	61.6
Pakistan	35.4	44.0	47.4	57.8
South Asia	47.7	56.3	61.7	70.6
Developing Countries	67.2	74.5	81.1	84.8

Source: HDR, 2003.

There is a definite improvement in literacy levels among females across South Asian countries. Some countries have achieved remarkable literacy levels among females as seen in Maldives and Sri Lanka. Gender disparity levels, both in literacy and enrolment ratios, are negligible in these two countries (see Table 8). Gender gaps in literacy are high in Nepal and Pakistan, with India following next.

Table 8
Adult Literacy Rate and Gross Enrolment Ratio by Gender

Country	*Adult Literacy Rate*		*Gender Gap*	*Gross Enrolment Ratio*	
	Female	*Male*		*Female*	*Male*
Maldives	96.9	97.1	0.2	79	78
Sri Lanka	89.3	94.5	5.2	64	63
India	46.4	69.0	22.6	49	63
Bangladesh	30.8	49.9	19.1	54	54
Nepal	25.2	60.5	35.3	57	70
Pakistan	28.8	58.2	29.4	27	45

Source: HDR, 2003; gap calculated from Cols. 1 and 2.

The statistics which pose a cause for concern in South Asian context is the large proportion of women among illiterates. The tradition-based stereotypes and role demarcation for women are strongly prevalent in most South Asian countries. Given the social ordering along patrilineal-patrilocal families, women are married out and investing in their education is not perceived as a priority. Among resource constrained households, often, educational cost is strategically borne for the male child while depriving the girl sibling (Khan, 1993). The role of women is associated with their reproductive functions, to the detriment of their own – personal and educational – development as a human being. These attitudes and perceptions based on socio-cultural and economic factors constitute the demand side constraints to women's education.

On the supply side, factors such as inadequate investment, lack of infrastructure, schools, teachers (especially female teachers), and so on reflect the state's commitment and impinge on the levels of accessability. In most of the countries of South Asia, average years of schooling are quite low – 6 years for girls and 8 years for boys.

In an effort to improve this situation, a number of countries in the region have stressed upon free and compulsory primary education and put emphasis on enrolment and retention of girls in schools. Various incentive schemes, such as scholarships for girls, free school meals (in India, Bangladesh and Nepal) and separate schools for girls in each Thana (Bangladesh), have been operational (HDSA, 2000). Efforts have also been made to increase female teachers in schools. The National Plan of Action (NPA), prepared by all South Asian countries, has facilitated a process of fixing targets that are time-bound, and help in monitoring and evaluation processes. The commitment is there, but more locally devised strategies are required to address specific problems in the sphere of educational attainment among girls.

POLITICAL PARTICIPATION

The region of South Asia has reported the largest number of women leaders who have been heads of the nation (e.g., Indira Gandhi, Shaikh Hasina, Benazir Bhutto, Srimavo Bandaranaike and Chandrika Kumaratunga). Despite the visible levels of women at the higher echelons of governance, the overall public participation of women remains low for the region (see Table 9). There is no data available on female membership of most political parties and only few of them are given tickets to stand for elections.

Table 9

Percentage of Women Participating in Governance Structures

Parliamentary Seats	7
Cabinet Members	9
Judiciary	6
Civil Servants	9
Local Government	20

Source: HDSA, 2000.

Various South Asian governments – Bangladesh, Pakistan and India – have reserved seats for women to increase their political participation in institutions of local governance. This policy has clearly assisted women's participation, which would have been denied given the deep-rooted patriarchal traditions wherein men wield power.

The experience of the Indian amendment to its constitution reserving one-third seats for women in its local governance structures generated tremendous interest in the other countries of the region. In 1997, both Nepal and Bangladesh introduced women's reservation in local bodies. While it was 20 per cent in Nepal, in the case of Bangladesh it was one-third seats in all four tiers of local government. In Pakistan also, one-third seats are reserved in local bodies, which is visible in the current figures of women's political participation.

In India, as elsewhere, there is substantial propaganda against such reservation on the pretext of misuse (Buch, 2000; ISS, different years). Women also face backlash in the form of violence often since they are seen as altering the power equations and challenging the status quo.

Table 10

Women in Parliament

Country/Region	*Women (%)*
Maldives	6.0
Sri Lanka	4.4
India	9.3
Bhutan	9.3
Bangladesh	2.0
Nepal	7.9
Pakistan	20.6

Source: HDR, 2003.

VIOLENCE

Violence against women assumes various forms – physical, sexual, psychological and emotional. All forms of discrimination against women, which are biased and treat women unequally, are forms of violence. The Convention on Elimination of All Forms of Discrimination against Women (CEDAW) is a central legally binding international agreement regarding women's rights which all South Asian states have ratified. However, there are reservations expressed by India, Pakistan, Maldives and Bangladesh (UNIFEM, 2003a).

There are various culture-specific forms of violence that persist in South Asia such as dowry-related violence, honour killings, acid throwing, forced temple prostitution, witch hunting, marriage of girls to Quran, sati, and so on (UNIFEM, 2003b). As these crimes assume significant proportions, special legislations are enacted in the respective countries to impose sanctions for the guilty.

However, there is very little systematic statistical information or data collection that is available for national level except in case of India where police record based data on cases registered is published by government agencies annually (CWDS, 2002). Even, in such data, there are limitations as women do not always report the violence they face, given the social stigma and poor recognition associated with it (Panda, 2003).

In the absence of data and uniform definitional classifications, comparisons across countries are ruled out, suggesting undifferentiated approaches to rectify the situation as more appropriate, rather than having blanket solutions under these circumstances.

III
Concluding Remarks

The most significant pointer to be noted in the context of indicator-based analysis of South Asian women is related to the data aspects. First, not all the issues that are critical to understand women's status are quantifiable. Second, among those that can be quantified, data is not available for many, such as work, violence, income, autonomy, etc. Third, apart from absence of gender disaggregated data, there is lack of uniformity in the concepts, definitions and data categories employed in different countries and by different sources of data. Fourth, there are time gaps in the provision of data. All sources do not follow similarity in periodicity of generating data on any given dimension. Therefore, comparison across countries and trend analysis is not always feasible. These are the gaps in data that pose problems for indicator-based analysis in a regional context, especially for women.

The focus on quantitative and qualitative dimensions of human as well as gender development as initiated by UNDP HDRs is useful for facilitating the awareness on these lacunae. This can aid in beginning work to fill these gaps and also make policy makers as well as other stakeholders join in this endeavour.

Overall, these processes have facilitated stocktaking, goal setting, monitoring and evaluating progress in the status of women.

The availability of data on South Asian countries from UNDP HDRs and the HDSA with all its problems and gaps made such as an exercise of looking at the situation of South Asian women feasible. Alternatively, the disparities would create many hurdles in considering the critical dimensions facing women of this region.

NOTES

1. Only among few of the communities in the region where matriliny is practised, women have control over land and economic property through inheritance; for instance, in Bhutan, 80 per cent of the population follows matriliny. Similarly, parts of Kerala and northeast region in India also follow matrilineal property transfers.
2. The eight MDGs are: eradicate extreme poverty and hunger; achieve universal primary education; promote gender equality and empower women; reduce child mortality; improve mental health; combat HIV/AIDs, malaria and other diseases; ensure environmental sustainability; and develop a global partnership for development.
3. The 12 critical areas of concern mentioned in the PFA are Women and Poverty; Education and Training for Women; Women and Health; Violence against Women; Women in Armed Conflict, Women in the Economy; Women in Power and Decision making; Institutional Mechanisms for the Advancement of Women; Human Rights of Women; Women and the Media; Women and the Environment; and the Girl Child.
4. The basis for Bhutan not preparing an NPA was the official belief that gender discrimination does not exist in the country (HDSA, 2000). However, the Bhutanese government has incorporated the BPFA into the Ninth Plan, committing itself to bringing women into mainstream development processes.
5. As defined by the Human Development of South Asia reports, excluding Afghanistan and Iran. The seven nations included are also members of the South Asian Association for Regional Cooperation (SAARC).

REFERENCES

Acharya, Meena, 2000, 'Women and the Economy in Nepal', Background Paper for the HDSA, 2000.

Agnihotri, S.B., 2000, *Sex Ratio Patterns in the Indian Population: A Fresh Exploration,* New Delhi: Sage.

Arnold, Fred, 2001, 'Son Preference in South Asia', in Sathar and Phillips (eds.), *Fertility Transition in South Asia*, pp. 281-99.

Atapattu, Danny, 2000, 'Women and the Economy in Sri Lanka', Background Paper for HDSA, 2000.

Bairagi, Radheshyam, 2001, 'Effects of Sex Preference on Contraceptive Use: Abortion and Fertility in Matlab, Bangladesh', *International Family Planning Perspectives,* 27(3): 137-43.

Bardhan, K. and S. Klassen, 1999, 'UNDP's Gender-Related Indices: A Critical Review', *World Development*, 27: 985-1010.

Bardhan, Kalpana, 1986, 'Women: Work, Welfare, and Status: Forces of Tradition and Change in India', *South Asia Bulletin*, 6(1): 3-16.

Baru, Rama V., 2003, 'Privatisation of Health Services: A South Asian Perspective', *Economic and Political Weekly,* 38(42): 4433-37.

Baster, N., 1972, 'Development Indicators: An Introduction' in N. Baster (ed.), *Measuring Development,* London: Frank Cass, pp. 1-20.

Basu, A.M., 1992, *Culture, the Status of Women and Demographic Behaviour,* Oxford: Clarendon Press.

Bhat, P.N. Mari, 2002, 'On the Trail of 'Missing' Indian Females – I: Search for Clues and II: Illusion and Reality', *Economic and Political Weekly,* 37(51-52): 5105-18, 5244-63.

Buch, Nirmala, 2000, *Women's Experience in New Panchayats: The Emerging Leadership of Rural Women*, Occasional Paper No. 35, New Delhi: Centre for Women's Development Studies.

Caldwell, John, 1982, *Theory of Fertility Decline*, London: Academic Press.

Clark, Alice, 1987, 'Social Demography of Excess Female Mortality in India: New Directions', *Economic and Political Weekly,* 22(17): WS 12-21.

CSO, 2000, *Report of the Time Use Survey,* Ministry of Statistics and Programme Implementation, New Delhi: Government of India.

CWDS, 2002, *Crime Against Women: Bondage and Beyond: Revelation of Data,* New Delhi: Centre for Women's Development Studies.

Dasgupta, Monica, 1987, 'Selective Discrimination Against Female Children in Rural Punjab, India', *Population and Development Review,* 13(1): 77-99.

Datta, Anindita, 2003, 'Articulation of an Integrated Women's Health Policy Using the Life Cycle Approach', *Indian Journal of Gender Studies,* 10(1): 25-43.

Dijkstra, A.G. and L.C. Hanmer, 1997, 'Measuring Socio-Economic Gender Inequality: Towards an Alternative to the UNDP Gender Related Development Index', ISS *Working Paper Series No. 251,* The Hague, July.

Elson, D. and B. Evers, 1996, *Gender Aware Country Economic Report: Pakistan,* University of Manchester: GENECON Unit.

FAO, 1949, *Essential of Rural Welfare*, FAO Agricultural Studies No. 27, Rome: FAO.

George, Sabu, Rajarathram Abel and B.D. Miller, 1992, 'Female Infanticide in Rural South India', *Economic and Political Weekly,* 27(22): 1153-56.

Gopalan, Sarla and Mira Shiva, 2000, *National Profile on Women, Health and Development,* Voluntary Health Association of India compiled for WHO, August.

Gurumurthy, Anita, 1998, *Women's Rights and Status: Questions of Analysis and Measurement,* Gender in Development, Monograph Series No. 7, UNDP: April.

HDSA (1997-2002), *Human Development in South Asia*, Mahbub ul Haq Human Development Centre, Karachi: Oxford University Press.

Hirway, Indira and Darshini Mahadevia, 1996, 'Critique of Gender Development Index: Towards an Alternative', *Economic and Political Weekly,* 31(43):WS87-WS96.

Hirway, Indira, 2002, 'Indian Experiences in Time Use Survey', paper presented at the national Seminar on Applications of Time Use Statistics, 8-9 October, organized by CSO and UNIFEM, New Delhi.

ISS, 1995-2001, *Women and Political Empowerment* Series, New Delhi: Institute of Social Science.

Jain, D. and Malini Chand, 1982, 'Time Allocation Study: Its Methodological Implications', ISST Report. Technical Seminar on *Women's Work and Employment,* 9-11 April.

Karki, Y.B., 1992, 'Sex Ratio in Nepal', *Economic Journal of Nepal,* 15(1): 30-37.

Kelley, A.C., 1991, 'The Human Development Index: Handle with Care', *Population and Development Review,* 17(2): 315-24.

Khan, Shahrukh R., 1993, 'South Asia' in Elizabeth M. King and M. Anne Hill (eds.), *Women's Education in Developing Countries: Barriers,*

Benefits and Policies, Baltimore: John Hopkins University Press for the World Bank, pp. 211-46.

Krishnaji, N., 1997, 'Human Development Index: A Critique', *Economic and Political Weekly,* 32(35): 2202-05.

Krishnaji, N. and K.S. James, 2002, 'Gender Differentials in Adult Mortality with Notes and Rural-Urban Contrasts', *Economic and Political Weekly,* 37(46): 4633-37.

Larson, B.A. and W.T. Wilford, 1979, 'The Physical Quality of Life Index: A Useful Social Indicator?', *World Development,* Vol. 7, No. 6, pp. 581-84.

Leone, Tiziana, Zoe Mathews and Gianpiero Dalla Zuanna, 2003, "Impact and Determinants of Sex Preference in Nepal", *International Family Planning Perspectives,* 29(2): 69-75.

Lisk, F., 1979, 'Indicators of Basic Needs-Oriented Development Planning', *Labour and Society*, Vol. 4, No. 3.

Mathema, Madhuri, 1998, 'Women in South Asia: Pakistan, Bangladesh, and Nepal' in Stromquist (ed.).

Mahmud, Simeen, 2000, 'Women and the Economy in Bangladesh', Background Paper for HDSA 2000.

McGranahan, D.V., C. Richard-Proust, M.V. Sovani and M. Subramanian, 1972, *Contents and Measurement of Socio-Economic Development,* New York: Praeger.

Mehta, Aasha Kapur, 1996, 'Recasting Indices for Developing Countries: A Gender Empowerment Measure', *Economic and Political Weekly*, October 26.

Mehta, Aasha Kapur, 2000, 'Women and the Economy in India', Background Paper for HDSA, 2000.

Miller, Barbara D., 1981, *The Endangered Sex: Neglect of Female Children in Rural North India,* Ithaca and London: Cornell University Press.

Morris, D.M. and Michelle B. McAlphin, 1982, *Measuring the Condition of India's Poor: The Physical Quality of Life Index,* New Delhi: Promilla and Co.

Morris, M.D., 1979, *Measuring the Condition of the World's Poor,* New York: Pergamon.

Moser, C., 1973, 'Social Indicators: Systems, Methods and Problems', *The Review of Income and Wealth,* Vol. 19, No. 2, pp. 133-41.

OECD, 1976, *Measuring Social Well-Being: A Progress Report on the Development of Social Indicators,* Paris: Organization for Economic Cooperation and Development.

Panda, P.K., 2003, *Rights-Based Strategies in the Prevention of Domestic Violence,* Working Paper 344, Trivandrum: Centre for Development Studies.

Patel, Vibhuti, 1997, 'Technology in Service of Female Foeticide', *Humanscape,* 4(7): 19-20.

Qadeer, Imrana, 1998, 'Reproductive Health: A Public Health Perspective', *Economic and Political Weekly,* 33(41): 2675-84.

Sathar, Zeba Ayesha and James F. Phillips (eds.), 2001, *Fertility Transition in South Asia,* New York: Oxford University Press.

Sen, A., 1987, *The Standard of Living,* Tanner Lectures, Cambridge: Clare Hall.

Stromquist, Nelly P. (ed.), 1998, *Women in the Third World: An Encyclopedia of Contemporary Issues,* Garland Publishing, New York and London.

UN, 1954, *Report on International Definition and Measurement of Standards and Levels of Living,* New York: United Nations.

—, 1961, *International Definition and Measurement of Levels of Living: An Interim Guide*, New York: United Nations.

—, 1998, *Too Young To Die: Genes or Gender?,* Department of Economic and Social Affairs, Population Division, New York: United Nations.

UN Secretariat, 1988, 'Sex Differentials in Survivorship in the Developing World: Levels, Regional Patterns and Demographic Determinants', *Population Bulletin of the UN,* 25: 51-64.

UNDP, 1990-2003, *Human Development Report,* United Nations Development Programme, New Delhi: Oxford University Press.

UNESCO, 1981, 'Women and Development: Indicators of their Changing Role', *Socio-Economic Studies*, 3, Paris: UNESCO.

UNRISD, 1970, *Contents and Measurement of Socio-Economic Development,* Geneva: UNRISD.

Viswanathan, Renuka, 2001, 'Development, Empowerment and Domestic Violence: Karnataka Experience', *Economic and Political Weekly,* 36 (24): 2173-77.

Waldron, Ingrid, 1998, 'Sex Differences in Infant and Early Childhood Mortality: Major Causes of Death and Possible Biological Causes', in UN, *Too Young to Die: Genes or Gender,* New York: United Nations, pp. 64-83.

Weerahewa, Jeevika and Anoma Ariyawardana, 2003, 'Impact of the WTO on Women Workers in Sri Lanka, in Jha, Veena (ed.), *Trade, Globalisation and Gender: Evidence from South Asia,* UNIFEM in Collaboration with UNCTAD, New Delhi: UNIFEM.

13

Reproductive Health of Women in South Asia

Sheela Saravanan

The economic and social conditions of the South Asian countries are similar. They have low-income economies, with not very pronounced economic growth, predominantly rural population with high rates of unemployment and illiteracy. There is a persistence of strong son preference. Maternal mortality rates remain high, with very less facilities provided for safe deliveries. The general situation reflects inadequate health infrastructure and lack of qualitative services provided to the people. Given the similar socio-economic conditions of these countries, there exists profound differences between countries and substantial variation within cultural zones, especially in terms of demographic characteristics and general reproductive health situation. Since the ICPD,[1] many of the countries have tried to bring about changes in their respective population policies. Some have succeeded to bring about changes whereas some have faced failures or a much slower improvement. Sri Lanka stands out as an exception, reflecting positive indicators of safe motherhood, adequate facilities and better quality of life among the people. Recently, Bangladesh has also shown remarkable and rapid changes in the pattern of fertility and contraception.

This paper tries to explore the situation of reproductive health in the five South Asian countries (Bangladesh, India, Nepal, Pakistan and Sri Lanka) and tries to answer some questions on what went wrong in some of the countries and what can be learnt from the success stories. In this context, it provides an overview of selected aspects of the reproductive and sexual health of women in these countries including age at marriage, fertility and contraception and maternal health.

AGE AT MARRIAGE

A very important aspect of adolescent reproductive health is the timing of marriage. Age at marriage is linked with educational opportunities for girls and early childbearing. Ten years ago women were marrying earlier (18-21 yrs) and consequently having an average of more births (4-6) during their lifetime. Today, the women are marrying at a later age (19-22 years) and the average number of births is also reducing (3-5). However, as an exception, the mean age of marriage for women in Nepal has reduced further between 1991 and 2000 (18 to 17 years). Sri Lanka is an exception with girls marrying much later (24-25 years). Table 1 below presents the mean age at marriage for selected countries in South Asia:

Table 1

Female Mean Age at Marriage

Country	*1991-92*	*1997-98*
Bangladesh	18.1	20.2
India	19.5	19.7
Nepal	18.1	17.1
Pakistan	20.5	22.1
Sri Lanka	24.4 (1981)	25.5 (1994)

Sources: 1. Bangladesh: www.bbsgov.org/, Table 2.8.
2. India: National Family Health Survey-2 (1998-99), p. 21.
3. Nepal: www.mope.gov.np/status/popstat/popstatuseng.htm, Table 22.
4. Pakistan: Pakistan Demographic Survey, 1999 and 2000.
5. Sri Lanka: Jayweera, Swarna (2000), p. 72.

Shaikh (1997) examines the positive effects of rising age at marriage that would contribute to the health of mothers and children and the rate of population growth. However, in Pakistan, the rising age at marriage does not seem to have made a major impact either on the use of contraceptives or on fertility rates. Almost 50 per cent of the girls in Nepal and Bangladesh were married in the adolescent age group (15-19) in 1991 and this has not reduced very much in 1998 as summarized below in Table 2:

Table 2

Women Married in Age Group (15-19 years)

Country	*Women Married (%)*	
Bangladesh	49.0 (1991)	42.0 (1997)
India	35.3 (1991)	24.7 (1995-96)
Nepal	47.0 (1991)	44.0 (1996)
Pakistan	29.4 (1981)	21.6 (1998)
Sri Lanka	7.3 (1987)	7.1 (1993)

Sources: 1. Bangladesh: www.bbsgov.org/, Table 2.10.
2. India: 1991, Census of India, Manpower Profile, IAMR, 2001, p. 274.
3. Nepal: www.mope.gov.np/status/popstat/chapter3.html Table 20, CBS - 1995, MOH – 1997.
4. Pakistan: Siddiqui, Rehana et al. (2001), p. 30.
5. Sri Lanka: Jayweera, Swarna (2000), Table 3.5.

Sri Lanka has been successful in increasing the age at marriage by providing better education facilities and relatively high status to women. Adult literacy rate among women is 88 per cent and girls have access to free education upto university level. As a result, there has been an increase in the age of marriage – to 25 in 1994 – and women are better able to take advantage of family planning and maternal health services.

Abeykoon (1996), in a data analysis of the age of marriage and contraceptive use, indicates that these two variables have to a large extent contributed to the fertility decline in Sri Lanka. The female mean age at marriage has increased to 25+; similarly, the contraceptive prevalence has increased from 32 per cent in 1975 to 66 per cent in 2001. In turn, the fertility rate has steadily declined.

Increasing the age at marriage alone is not sufficient to bring about improvements in the usage of contraceptives, fertility rates or in the reproductive health of women. There is a need for an integrated approach, including family planning, education and health departments.

FERTILITY AND CONTRACEPTION

As Table 3 shows, fertility rates vary widely across countries in the region. Nepal and Pakistan have total fertility rates close to 5. India and Bangladesh have a fertility rate of about 3 and Sri Lanka has the lowest fertility rate at 2. Sri Lanka is the only country among the five countries under study that has completed the transition to replacement-level fertility.[2] The decline began in the 1950s, largely as a result of a rise in the age at marriage (especially of females), and subsequently through a fall in marital fertility as a result of increased contraceptive use (De Silva, 1994).

Table 3
Total Fertility Rate

Country	*1991*	*2000*
Bangladesh	4.6	3.7
India	3.9	3.1
Nepal	5.2	4.7
Pakistan	6.0	5.3
Sri Lanka	2.6	2.1

Source: www.childinfo.org/eddb/maternal/database1.htm (UNICEF Global Database)

Women in Bangladesh and India presently are having an average of three children. However, there has been a rapid fertility decline in Bangladesh since the early 1980s. This contrasts sharply with the much steadier change that has occurred in India. There was initial scepticism about the magnitude of fertility in Bangladesh given its limited socio-economic development. This has now been swept aside by evidence from Demographic and Health Surveys in the 1990s showing increasing use of modern methods of contraception, with contraceptive prevalence rates above 50 per cent (Leele, 1999). According to Ahmad (1991), the fertility decline in Bangladesh is due in part to a rise in the age at marriage and the adoption of modern contraceptives. This, in turn, has been attributed to a successful family planning programme and the involvement of NGOs in the programme. However, the socio-economic conditions which elsewhere in the developing world are associated with fertility decline have not improved significantly in Bangladesh: adult literacy, infant mortality rate, life expectation at birth, female labour force participation and others (Chen, 1991).

By contrast, fertility levels in Pakistan and Nepal remain high, with women bearing an average of five children during their lifetime. Key factors in the maintenance of high fertility in both countries appear to be the neglect of women's education and their general low status, together with large unmet need for reproductive health services: a significant proportion of sexually active women want to avoid or postpone pregnancy, but do not use contraception. The family planning programme of Pakistan has a long history, however it has been conspicuous by its lack of impact and it contrasts sharply with the successful programme of Bangladesh,[3] which has been able to overcome traditional barriers. The programme in Pakistan has suffered from a lack of consistent political support and policy focus, coupled with a weak social enabling environment, including insufficient resource allocation (Leele, 1999).

Fertility levels of urban women is lower than for rural women in the countries. An average Indian or Bangladeshi woman residing in a rural area would give birth to one more child when compared to her urban counterpart, while in case of Pakistan the difference is more than one child.

Table 4

Contraceptive Prevalence Rate

Country	*CPR*	*Year*	*CPR*	*Year*
Bangladesh	40	1991	54	1997
India	41	1993	48	1999
Nepal	23	1991	39	1996
Pakistan	12	1991	24	1997
Sri Lanka	62	1987	66	1993

Source: 2001, www.unicef.org/statis/Country_1Page14.htm

The contraceptive prevalence rate in Sri Lanka is well ahead (62%) than the neighbouring countries and is steadily rising in the last decade to 66 per cent. Bangladesh has caught up and even gone ahead of India now, where contraceptive prevalence rate is currently around 50 per cent. Both Nepal (39%) and Pakistan (24%) remain well below these levels, consistent with their high fertility (see Table 4).

Table 5

Married Women Using Specific Methods of Contraceptives

(in %)

	Bangladesh	*India*	*Nepal*	*Pakistan*
Any method	53.8	48.2	39.3	23.9
Any modern method	43.4	42.8	35.4	16.9
Pill	23.0	2.1	1.6	1.6
IUD	1.2	1.6	0.4	3.4
Condom	4.3	3.1	2.9	4.2
Injectables	7.2	-	8.4	1.4
Implants/Norplants	0.5	-	0.6	-
Female sterilization	6.7	34.2	15.0	6.0
Male sterilization	0.5	1.9	6.3	-
Foam/Jelly	-	-	-	-
Any traditional method	10.3	5.0	3.9	7.0
Rhythm/Safe period, abstinence	5.4	3.0	1.1	1.9
Withdrawal	4.0	2.0	2.6	4.6
Folk methods	-	-	0.3	-
Other methods	0.9	0.4	-	0.8
Not using any method	46.2	51.8	60.7	76.1

Sources: 1. Bangladesh: Bangladesh Demographic and Health Survey, 1999-2000, p. 51.
2. India: NFHS 2, 1998-99, Table 5.3, p. 131.
3. Nepal: NFHS, Table 5.2, p. 69.
4. Pakistan: Zeba Sathar, 1998, p. 8, Table 3, Ref: Pakistan Fertility and Family Planning Survey (1996-97).

The South Asian Family Planning Programmes have traditionally placed more emphasis on long-term and permanent measures of family planning, particularly female sterilization. This is clearly evident from the data of the currently married women using specific methods of contraceptives (see Table 5). Female sterilization dominates contraceptive use in India, accounting for 75 per cent of current contraceptive prevalence. Similarly, in Nepal and Pakistan, a major proportion (around 40%) of the contraceptive use is in the form of female sterilization. However, in contrast, more than half of the women using contraceptives in Bangladesh are using pills and 13 per cent are using injectables.

In Nepal too, about one-fourth of the women using contraceptives are using injectables. Bangladesh seems to be emphasizing more on methods that require lesser follow-ups with acceptors and are logistically convenient to deliver. Differences in contraceptive methods used may be due to the availability in the country concerned than a reflection of user preferences. Methods, such as Norplant, are either not available or not easily accessible in Bangladesh, India and Sri Lanka. The common factor in the five countries is the almost negligible use of male methods of contraception, such as condoms and male sterilization.

Table 6

Unmet Need and Total Demand for Family Planning, 2000-01

Country	*Unmet Need*	*Total Demand*
Bangladesh	15.3	70.8
India	15.8	64.0
Nepal	27.8	67.1
Pakistan	33.0	-

Sources: 1. Bangladesh: Bangladesh Demographic and Health Survey, 1999-2000, p. 91.
2. India: National Family Health Survey 2, 1998-99, Table 5.23.
3. Nepal: Nepal Demographic and Health Survey, 2001, p. 120
4. Pakistan: Pakistan Reproductive Health and Family Planning Survey, 2000-01.

Fertility rates have been declining and contraceptive use has been increasing in South Asia, nevertheless many women who want to stop having children or to delay their next both are not using contraceptives. As shown in Table 6, 15.8 per cent of the currently married in India have an unmet need for family planning. If all the women who say that they want to space or limit their births were to use family planning, the contraceptive prevalence rate would increase from 48 per cent to 64 per cent of currently married women. Young women deserve special consideration because unmet need is highest among them. One-third of the currently married women in Pakistan and more than a quarter of them in Nepal want to space or limit children and are not using contraceptives.

To conclude, the decline in fertility rate in Bangladesh and Sri Lanka has been due to the increased contraceptive use and a rise in the age at marriage. The additional factor has been the successful family planning programme and the involvement in the non-governmental organizations in the programme. In Sri Lanka, the status of women has also had an impact on the fertility decline. In contrast, India and Pakistan are facing the hurdles of lack of policy focus, and inadequate facilities provided by the programme.

To be more effective, it is important that family planning programmes should respond to the need of individuals, promote sustainability and, much more than in the past, take into account gender perspectives, including male involvement and encourage young women to use contraceptives to space children.

Maternal Health

Maternal health includes illness and complications related to pregnancy and childbirth, effecting maternal health and the children born to them. The complications and illness during pregnancy and childbirth could be due to poor maternal health or due to inadequacy or underutilization of the available maternal health care services.

Apart from the physical existence of medical facilities, there are certain cultural restrictions of woman's personal freedom that limit dramatically her access to health care. Women's mobility under these circumstances is severely restricted. Having male doctors and health care workers limit women's ability to avail to these services. Male dominance in sexual relations and use of contraceptives leave women with little control over their pregnancies and childbirth.

MATERNAL HEALTH SERVICES

Women are most in need of skilled care during delivery and the immediate post-partum period. Millions of women do not have access[4] to good quality health services during pregnancy and child-birth – especially women, who are poor, not educated or living in rural areas.

Insufficient maternal care during pregnancy and delivery is largely responsible for the high rate of maternal mortality and infant deaths that occur just before or during delivery or in the first week of life. During the pregnancy, regular contact with a doctor, nurse or midwife allows health personnel to manage the pregnancy; immunize the mother-to-be against tetanus to protect her and her infant; promote good nutrition, hygiene and rest; and detect potential complications making it advisable to give birth in a health facility equipped to handle high-risk deliveries and aftercare (UNICEF, 2000). The WHO recommends a minimum of four antenatal visits. Doctors, midwives or nurses with the midwifery skills should supervise labour and delivery. They would handle normal deliveries safely and recognize the onset of complications beyond their capacity to handle, referring the mother for emergency care to better-equipped medical institutions.

Maternal health services have a potentially important role to play in the improvement of reproductive health. There is little doubt that access to skilled assistance and well-equipped health institutions during delivery can reduce maternal mortality and morbidity and improve pregnancy outcomes (Bhatia and John Clelend, 1995: 142). Antenatal care (ANC) programmes reduce maternal morbidity and mortality directly through detection and treatment of pregnancy-related illness, or indirectly through detection of women at increased risk of complications of delivery and ensuring that they be delivered in a suitably equipped facility (Acharya, 1995: S41). The effectiveness of antenatal programmes can however be directly related to the quality of care, access and its coverage. Statistical analysis, based on NFHS 1 and 2, reveals that even after controlling for other factors, mothers who received antenatal check-ups are two to five times more likely to give birth in a medical institution than mothers who did not receive any antenatal check-up (Sugathan et al., 2001).

PRE-NATAL CARE

In Nepal and Bangladesh, relatively few women use maternal health services during pregnancies. According to Nepal Family Health Survey (NFHS), 51 per cent of the women do not receive any prenatal care during pregnancy. In addition, most children are delivered at home with the help of a trained traditional birth attendant or family members. Similarly, less than a quarter of the women in Bangladesh and Pakistan have trained assistance during delivery. Only Sri Lanka, as an exception, has 94 per cent of the births attended by trained health personnel as indicated below in Table 7:

Table 7

Pregnant Women Going for Pre-natal Check-ups

Country	*Women (%)*	*Year*
Bangladesh	37.0	2001
India	65.4	1998-99
Nepal	49.1	2001
Pakistan	51.0	2000-01
Sri Lanka	98.0	1996

Sources: 1. Bangladesh: Bangladesh Demographic and Health Survey, 1999-2000, p. 112.
2. India: National Family Health Survey (NFHS-2), (1998-99) India, p. 283.
3. Nepal: Nepal Demographic and Health Survey (2001), p. 142.
4. Pakistan: www.mopw.gov.pk/census11.htm
5. Sri Lanka: WHO, Women of South East Asia: A Health Profile (2000), p. 268.

ASSISTANCE DURING DELIVERY

The situation with regard to assistance during delivery is a cause of serious concern. In Nepal, the situation is appalling with only 13 per cent of the births assisted by health professionals and only 9 per cent delivered with health facilities. Only one-fourth of the births in Bangladesh and Pakistan are attended by skilled health personnel (see Table 8).

Table 8

Percentage of Births Attended by Skilled Health Personnel

Country	*Trained Assistance**	*Untrained/no Assistance***	*Year*
Bangladesh	22	78	2001
India	42	58	98-99
Nepal	13	87	2000
Pakistan	20	80	98-99
Sri Lanka	94	6	1993

Notes: * Trained Assistance: Government Doctor, Other Doctor, and Other Government Nurse/Midwife

** Untrained Assistance: Other Nurse/Midwife, and Other (Friends/Relatives)

Sources: 1. Bangladesh: Bangladesh Demographic and Health Survey, 1999-2000, p. 118.

2. India: National Family Health Survey (NFHS-2) (1998-99) India, p. 299.
3. Nepal: Nepal Demographic and Health Survey (2001), p. 150
4. Pakistan and Sri Lanka: www.childinfo.org/eddb/maternal/database1.htm

Sri Lanka is one country that stands out as an exception. Though about a third of Sri Lankans live below the national poverty line, the maternal mortality rate at 60 per 1,00,000 live births is among the lowest in the developing world. Trained birth attendants (TBAs) assist over 90 per cent of the deliveries in Sri Lanka and 90 per cent take place at a place having facility for the same, with a referral system in place to ensure transport to one of 45 hospitals if complications occur.

Despite an increase in the number of health facilities offering delivery services in Nepal, use of health facilities during deliveries is still minimal among most Nepalese women. About 55 per cent of the births in Nepal are assisted by relatives, friends and other non-health personnel, 23 per cent by TBAs and 9 per cent without any help. TBAs, whether trained or untrained, can neither predict nor cope with serious complications.

PLACE OF DELIVERY

Over 90 per cent of births in Nepal and Bangladesh are delivered at home, while only 8 per cent are delivered at health centres. The utilization of postnatal care is also very low in Nepal. Only 12 per cent of women receive postnatal care from a health professional (UNICEF, 1996; DHS, 1996). Some reasons for the low utilization of maternal health services are a result of the poor quality, unavailability and inaccessibility of services. However, the underutilization of maternal health services in Nepal is partly due to the poor provision of services.

Table 9
Place of Delivery

Country	*At Home*	*Health Centre*	*Others*
Bangladesh	91.6	7.9	0.4
India	65	34	1
Nepal	89	9	2
Pakistan	77	23	-

Sources: 1. Bangladesh: Bangladesh Demographic and Health Survey, 1999-2000, p. 117.
2. India: National Family Health Survey (NFHS-2), (1998-99) India, p. 295.
3. Nepal: Nepal Demographic and Health Survey (2001), p. 148.
4. Pakistan: 2001 www.mopw.gov.pk/census13.htm

In a multivariate analysis of women's status, household structure and the use of maternal health services in Nepal using NFHS (1996) data, it was found that education[5] plays an important role in enhancing the use of maternal services. Employment had a negative impact on the use of maternal services. Women living in households with poor economic status and in nuclear families have significantly less chances of using the maternal health care services in Nepal (Matsumura, 2001: 26).

MATERNAL MORTALITY

The magnitude of women's reproductive health problems in India is reflected in the number of deaths related to pregnancy and childbirth – the most direct indicator of reproductive health care. Nepal's maternity mortality rate is the highest at 407 per 1,00,000 live births, followed by India (see Table 10). India's maternal mortality ratio – 407 per 1,00,000 live births (CSO, 2000) – is fifty times higher than that of many developed countries and six times higher than that of neighbouring Sri Lanka. In India, maternity-related complications are leading causes of death and disability among women during their reproductive years. The major causes of these deaths have been identified as haemorrhage (both ante- and post-partum), toxaemia (hypertension during pregnancy), anaemia, obstructed labour, puerperal sepsis (infections after delivery) and unsafe abortion. WHO and UNICEF estimate that women face a one in 37 risk of dying from pregnancy or childbirth during their lifetime. By contrast, European women have a one in 1,400 risk of dying from these causes. Globally, one out of four women who die from maternity-related complications reside in India (WHO, UNICEF, 1998). The vast majority of these deaths are preventable. Most births in India take place outside health centres (65%) and only 42 per cent are attended by skilled health personnel.

Table 10
Maternal Mortality Ratio

Country	*MMR*	*Year*	*Source*	*MMR*	*Year*	*Source*
Bangladesh	432	1996	(1)	350	1997	(4)
India	420	1992-93	(1)	407	1998	(5)
Nepal	-	-	-	539	1990-96	(6)
Pakistan	500	1993	(2)	340	1996	(2)
Sri Lanka	40	1991	(3)	20	1995	(3)
Sri Lanka	-	-	-	60	2001	(7)

Sources: 1. WHO, Women of South East Asia: A Health Profile (2000), pp. 239, 255.
2. Siddiqui, Rehana et al. (2001), p. 32
3. www.lk/census/Documents/Sub/Motality.htm
4. www.bangladeshgov.org/mop/ndb/data_sheet/intex.htm
5. CSO, Women and Men in Indi, (2000), p. 28.
6. www.mope.gov.np/status/popstat/popstatuseng.htm (ch 4, Table 26).
7. www.unicef.org/statis/Country_1Page157.html

High maternal mortality rate in South Asia is an indication of a poor quality of reproductive health services, including family planning, particularly in rural areas. Significant proportions of mothers give birth without the presence of a skilled birth attendant, and are out of reach of emergency care facilities to deal with obstetric complications.

It is necessary at this point to know why certain countries have shown positive trends of reproductive health and why others have slowed down. Is there anything we could learn from each other's experience? In the next section, we will throw some light on this aspect by undertaking a review of the status of reproductive health in five South Asian countries under the present study.

Reproductive Health: A Review of the Status in the Five South Asian Countries

Bangladesh

Bangladesh has managed to achieve a steep decline in fertility in spite of its unremarkable socio-economic development in the past decade. Researchers have attributed this decline in the total fertility rate (TFR) to increased use of contraception, which in turn has been credited to a strong and successful family planning programme among several other factors in the country.

Since independence, the Bangladesh government has attempted to strengthen the national family planning programme through increased allocation of resources for family planning activities, extended use of the multi-sectoral approach, use of mass media campaigns and promotion of increased participation of voluntary and private agencies in the national population programme. In addition, the family planning programme has been extended to include field workers, Family Welfare Assistants (FWAs) who are trained to provide at the doorstep family planning services and information on modern contraceptive methods. Logistic regression analysis by Shahid Ullah and Rashid Kamal of Bangladesh Fertility Survey (BFS), 1989 proves that frequency of visits of family planning workers is significantly and positively related to current use of contraceptive methods.

Strong government commitment has been successful in maintaining the momentum and motivation of the family planning programme. Barriers to its implementation especially in a society in which many women live under conditions of *purdah,*[6] have been lowered by providing women with family planning services where they are most convenient for the user. Most couples live within five miles of a service delivery point and a network of village workers also visit women and men in their homes. Pills and condoms are available free through the village workers and subsidised pills and condoms are available through the commercial sector. In addition, societal and cultural barriers to use have been minimized by the active inclusion of community and religious leaders by the family planning programme (Mc Eachran, 2001).

However, there were other external positive elements that helped the programme to proceed in the right direction. Firstly, in 1975, the International Centre for Diarrhoeal Disease Research (ICDDR), Bangladesh[7] used the test area in Matlab Thana, south of Dhaka, to study family planning interventions and experiments. This study proved that with the increase in quality of services delivered, contraceptive prevalence rose and fertility fell. In 1983, this study area was extended to other parts of Bangladesh with the same results (Robinson, 2001).

The second favourable factor was the existence of several NGOs in the rural scenario of Bangladesh. Apart from the hundreds of NGOs working directly in the area of family planning and MCH programmes, organizations like Bangladesh Rural Advancement Committee (BRAC) and Grameen Bank which had a large coverage also started including family welfare and other social welfare components in their programmes. Kamal and others have mentioned Grameen Bank, BRAC and Swanirvor among the NGOs as being successful in promoting the use of modern methods of contraceptives.

As noted by Robinson (2001), the concerted NGO and donor programme efforts to empower women probably resulted in a more favourable environment for family planning. The government though reluctantly was willing to learn from the NGOs. The international community was allowed to play an important role in providing financial as well as technical support. This acted as an added force for change and for a critical review of the programme (Robinson, 2000).

Due to many factors put together, there was a substantial effect on the fertility and contraceptive rates in Bangladesh. The use of contraception rose dramatically from 9.6 per cent in 1985 to 54 per cent in 2001. TFR decreased from 7 in 1989 to about 4 in 2000. However, the existing programmes need to be strengthened further to reduce the unmet need, which is presently 20 per cent. The dominance of pills, used as contraceptive, needs to be examined in terms of its sustenance of contraceptive use.

Whether the societal and cultural barriers have really been minimized in Bangladesh has to be studied further. Questions like how is power equilibrium changing within the household with more women now using contraceptives, especially in the given religious context of Bangladesh. The sudden increase of contraceptive use has to be assessed at the family level, whether the changes in contraceptive use and fertility levels have brought about any changes within the households.

India

India is the first independent country in the world to adopt a policy of reducing population growth through a government-sponsored national family programme, as called for in the First Five-Year Plan (1951-56). The programme has since then gone through a lot of changes in order to influence the reproductive behaviour of the population and increase the number of acceptors of various family planning methods. However, the pace of fertility decline has been relatively slow.

Initially, the main objective of the programme was on providing education and counselling on child and marriage, as it was felt that the root cause of ill-health among women was narrowly spaced pregnancies and births, aggravated by marriage at a very early age.

After the 1961 census, and the crisis of rising population being evident, the focus shifted from improving health of women and children to halting the rise in population growth. Family planning centres were expanded and new depots for contraceptive distribution were set up. Annual targets were fixed for acceptors of different types of contraceptives, and sterilization, mainly tubectomy, became the most common method. Incentive for acceptors was also introduced.

The family planning programme in India continues to emphasize on terminal methods (particularly sterilization). In the recent times, even young women are opting for tubectomy as a form of contraceptive. It is important to include younger couples but for the temporary methods of contraceptives for birth spacing and eventually to stop child bearing. The quality of services, information and follow-up services is poor in India. Most people here know about sterilization and IUDs, but knowledge about other methods is poor.

Target setting became a routine approach to streamline the Indian family planning programme from the mid-1960s. The personnel recruited for this were not trained and equipped to deal with such sensitive areas as individual family life. So, the kind of pressure applied by these people was very crude, lacking the human touch. The problem was further compounded by the incentives and sanctions offered by state governments to their staff for fulfilling quotas. This resulted in over-reporting performance and a tendency to pressurize the people, which at times resulted in unethical practices. This created a negative image of the family planning programmes and also gave rise to misconceptions about certain methods among the people.

There was sharp criticism raised on the monetary incentives and women-centred methods of contraceptives. There was further reorientation of the programme. In 1975, Integrated Child Development Services (ICDS) came into existence, which aim at strengthening community-based initiatives through improved linkages with the health system. Targeted to reach mothers and children of disadvantaged groups and those living in remote areas, the ICDS programme provides children, pregnant women and lactating mothers with nutritional supplements, imparts pre-school education to children in the age group 2-5 years through anganwadi[8] workers and enhances immunization coverage of pregnant women and children.

After International Conference on Population and Development (ICPD, in Cairo), a new approach – the National Reproductive and Child Health Programme – was launched in 1997 to encourage smaller families by helping clients meet their own health and family planning goals. Instead of birth control, this approach seeks to provide a full range of maternal and child health services. This programme aimed towards reduction of child mortality by providing immunization against vaccine preventable diseases, and reduction in maternal mortality by providing essential emergency obstetric care.

The National Population Policy (NPP), 2000 is a further step towards promotion of women's empowerment. Fortunately, it seems to be attempting to move in a more humane direction. Often, policies are made without appropriate provision for its smooth functioning at the grassroots level. But, NPP, 2000 is an ambitious policy and it has to be seen whether it can provide appropriate training and necessary supply of equipment and staff to achieve the targets.

The plan of NPP, 2000 to reward panchayats and zilla parishads (local government bodies at village and district levels) for exemplary performance has no safeguards built in to prevent ground-level coercion of poor women (or men) towards unwanted and/or unsafe sterilizations, intra-uterine device (IUD) insertions or other methods (Sen, 2000).

Although adolescents find a place in the population policy, there is only a mention in the context of their health and a holistic approach to their development is absent. Given below are some of the important models used till date to improve maternal health in India. This will be followed by the policy implications for India, some of which have already been mentioned in NPP, 2000.

Selected Models of Increasing Access to Maternal Care in India

It is important to look at the different approaches and rationale of the existing approaches to understand why this study is important. Certain approaches prescribed by WHO are accepted world wide, however, there are locally adopted approaches like the community-based approach using self-help groups, Information, Education and Communication (IEC) and partnership models evolved through experiential learning.

The aim of maternal, including antenatal, care is to produce a healthy mother and baby at the end of the pregnancy by:

- preventing and treating pregnancy-related morbidity, such as hypertension of pregnancy, anaemia, malaria, tetanus, and STDs; and
- detecting women at increased risk of complications of delivery.

There are various approaches that are adopted to achieve these goals and the major ones are given below:

(a) *High-risk Approach/Registration Approach*: Another aim of ANC to produce a healthy mother and baby, to detect risk factors that will predict obstetric emergencies, has proved to be a false hope. The predictability of maternal outcomes based on these risk factors has been shown by many studies to be extremely low (McDonald, 1996). Risk prediction wrongly identifies many women as being at risk who go on to have normal deliveries, with considerable cost implications for both the health system and the women who want to comply with advice to deliver in hospital, especially when they are poor. It also wrongly identifies any women as being low risk who subsequently develop complications, offering them a false sense of security and contributing to late health care seeking. Of the five main causes of maternal mortality, only hypertension is detectable during pregnancy: none of the others can be predicted or prevented through ANC (Gerein et al., 2003).

In the 1970s and 1980s the Indian government emphasized on high-risk approach for improving maternal and child health. Now, it is becoming clear that given the epidemiology of maternal mortality, preventing complications during birth or predicting who will develop them is not possible in majority of the cases and there is a shift from the high-risk approach to registering every pregnancy. The National Population Policy, 2000 states that ANM should be responsible and accountable for registering every pregnancy and childbirth in her jurisdiction, and for providing universal antenatal and postnatal services.

However, adequate support in terms of facilities and amenities are not given to the ANMs, which would affect their productivity. Apart from this responsibility, the ANM is expected to perform a large number of diverse preventive and curative functions such as motivation for family planning, immunization, conducting deliveries, and treatment for childhood illnesses. The additional burden of identifying every pregnant woman and registering them would not be successful as a strategy for improving women's access to antenatal care unless they is given the appropriate amenities and facilities to do so. ANM is expected to reside in the sub-centre village and remain available round the clock. However, a study conducted by Indian Council of Medical Research in 1997 in 23 districts of the country showed that only 57 per cent of all ANMs stayed at the sub-centre village, while the rest commuted to their place of work (ICMR, 1997).

ANMs also have the responsibility of child immunization, family planning and others. Not to mention that the ANMs are low paid and their job satisfaction level is low. Despite the government's own assertions about doing away with a target-oriented approach and opting for better maternal and child health care, the emphasis on female sterilization is very much in place. It is very unlikely that ANMs would give importance to antenatal care during her village visits.

(b) *Emergency Obstetric Care (EOC) Approach*: The World Summit for Children in 1990 included pledge made by head of states from over 70 countries to reduce maternal mortality. India took up the challenge and started a programme to ensure that the services needed to accomplish this purpose are available, accessible and utilized. The Child Survival and Safe Motherhood (CSSM) programme in India incorporates ongoing activities in women's health and family planning, but adds the crucial component of emergency care to cope with obstetric complications. Since preventive efforts have little impact on maternal mortality rates, timely treatment of obstetric complications is significant in reducing maternal deaths (Nirupam and Yuster, 1995).

The key to preventing deaths, once a woman becomes pregnant, is access to emergency care needed to treat these complications. Access includes not only availability of services, but also the knowledge to recognize problems, and the ability to reach the facility in time. Mortality reduction depends largely on assuring the availability, access and utilization of health facilities equipped to provide EOC. This includes ensuring that communities are educated to recognize complications and willing and able to transport patients to these facilities.

A study in ten districts drawn from ten major states in India reveals not only a low institutional birth rate but, more importantly, that few women with complications ever reach facilities. Clearly, efforts are needed at the periphery to ensure that they and their families can recognize the danger signs of obstetric complications, know when and where to go, and are willing and able to reach an appropriate health facility (Nirupam and Yuster, 1995).

(c) *Information Education Communication (IEC) Approach*: The National Population Policy, 2000 makes a reference to education with special reference to schools and that health must be integrated from the schools itself. However, there is no mention on how this would be operationalized. There is a mention of utilization of radio and television as a media and use of public leaders and film stars to spread the message of small family norm, female literacy, delayed marriages for women, fewer babies, healthier babies, child immunization, and so on. This further emphasizes the government focus on family planning and child immunization. It also states about funding Nagar Palikas, panchayats, NGOs and community based organizations for interactive and participatory IEC activities. The plan was also to utilize dairy co-operatives, the public distribution system, and other established networks like the LIC at the district and sub-district levels for IEC and for distribution of contraceptives and basic medicines to target infant/childhood diarrhoea, anaemia and malnutrition among adolescent girls and pregnant mothers. This, the plan mentions, will widen the outreach and coverage. It will definitely widen the coverage however it is doubtful whether there would be any positive outcomes in terms of outreach. On the whole, the IEC and counselling are weak and not integrated with service delivery.

A recent framework for improving maternal care has been presented with the following components (Gerein et al., 2003). The approach lists a plan that the ANC workers should help the pregnant women from their first visit onwards:

- Prepare a simple and inexpensive clean birth kit.
- Know the signs and symptoms of complications during pregnancy and labour and post-partum which require professional care at a health facility.
- Know where to go for expert care, and how to get there.
- Have a transport plan – know which transport they can use, how to find transport at night.
- Have a plan for saving money in the vent of an emergency.
- Have identified a person to accompany them to hospital in the event of an emergency, preferably their birth attendant and a family member.

This framework is very much in the lines of the study objectives and World Health Organization (WHO) prescriptions of required number of visits for antenatal care.

Fundamental questions about the effectiveness of the standard approach to ANC and its effectiveness and efficiency in improving maternal health prompted a recent study by WHO in 2001.

How many ANC visits are required? A systematic review of randomized trials concluded that a lower number of visits were as effective as a higher number, in terms of clinical outcomes and satisfaction, with lower provider and consumer costs (Carroli et al., 2001). A trial of ANC in four countries in different stages of development has shown that maternal and child outcomes (eclampsia, maternal mortality, low birth weight, urinary tract infections, post-partum anaemia, hospital admission and treatment) were no different for women who had a median of five ANC visits, compared to women with a median of eight visits (Villar et al., 2001).

The WHO has recently proposed a new approach to ANC, focusing on the components known to be effective, including a stress on ensuring that all women understand why they need to have skilled attendance for their delivery, and how they are able o access obstetric care for emergencies. This involves an emphasis on communication; however, the programme in India has been weak in communication.

(d) *Community-based Approach*: The National Population, Policy 2000 suggests that village self-help groups would be organized to provide basic services for reproductive and child health. Combining with the ongoing ICDS ANMs would be members of these self-help groups. The policy claims that this would facilitate dissemination of integrated reproductive and child health services at village and household levels. The services would include registration of births, deaths, marriages and pregnancies, weighing of children under five years, preventive care for fever, injections, diarrhoea, nutritional supplements and advocacy and enrolment of children in schools.

(e) *Developing Health Partnerships*: Women are targeted by ANC programmes because of their reproductive role, but in the South Asian context their voices are not heard in community decisions about health, and they are even more rarely involved in influencing the planning and management of local health services. At the most basic level, they may need permission and money from their husband or family to access health care. Hence, there is a realization for more involvement of men and decision-makers in ANC and reproductive health. A new approach to antenatal care suggests making use of existing family and community support systems, and developing partnerships beyond the health services to help women prepare for safe pregnancies and deliveries (Gerein et al., 2003).

Though awareness is important but it has not been given special emphasis in implementation in India. Women who did not have antenatal check-ups were asked why they did not do so. For almost three-fourths of the births to mothers who did not have any antenatal check-ups, mothers did not consider having a check-up to be necessary (60%) or customary (4%) or were not allowed by their families to do so (9%). Costs account for another 15 per cent of cases and lack of knowledge, distance, and lack of transport account for the majority of the remaining reasons. Studies have found that there is little awareness and that most maternal deaths could be avoided if the woman had received proper and timely advice towards the end of their pregnancy and during immediate postnatal period; they had received better care at home; their families (especially decision-makers in the families) had known of the danger signs in pregnancy and childbirth; and adequately equipped and managed referral centres had existed (Ramakrishna et al., 2000; Maitra, 2001). These results suggest the need to inform mothers and decision-makers within the families about the availability and benefits of antenatal check-ups to help women seek proper health care.

Findings of all the above studies point out to the fact that awareness among women regarding the usefulness of health care seeking is low and there is a need to improve this knowledge among women and other decision-makers in the society. Some of the policy implications that are relevant to India are presented in the section that follows:

Policy Implications for India

Services through PHCs: Reproductive health information and health services must be accessible through primary health care systems to all individuals. Such care should include, family planning counselling, information, education, communication and services; education and services for prenatal care, safe delivery and postnatal care, especially breastfeeding and infant and women's health care; prevention and treatment of infertility; abortion, treatment of reproductive tract infections, sexually transmitted diseases including HIV/AIDS and other reproductive conditions; and information, education and counselling on human sexuality, reproductive health and responsible parenthood (NCAER, 2001). This service is especially required in the context that the women neither have the time or money to travel long distances for information or care.

PHC's hours of operation frequently conflict with women's work schedule, and the inconvenient location of PHCs have made them inaccessible to most of the women.

Improve referral services: One of the weaknesses of the PHCs is that they have a very poor referral hospitals or Community Health Centres (CHCs) at the taluka level. Emergency obstetric care is life saving for certain complicated childbirths. Unimpeded flow of services to any pregnant woman at any time should be made available. Often doctors are not available at the centres or their post is vacant.

Awareness generation among users: Experiences of our neighbouring countries have proved that improvement in awareness can play a major role in bringing about changes in reproductive health. Provision of simple, useful information by local health workers can be crucial.

Training of health workers: Skilled and competent attendants as well as efficient managers and administrators are indispensable to the efficient functioning of the entire health system. The workers in the PHCs and sub-centres need to be fully equipped in knowledge of all the issues related to reproductive health. They need to be trained in inter-communication skills and capacity building. One of the main criticisms of the programme personnel is that they are insensitive to the needs of the people.

Maternal health: The most critical intervention for safe motherhood is to ensure that a competent health worker with midwifery skills is present at every birth and transport is available to a referral facility for obstetric care in case of emergency. This may be supplemented with awareness generation regarding the danger signs during delivery, educate people on giving immediate and proper help in obstetric emergencies, conduct safe motherhood campaigns for village leaders, women's groups, families and adolescents, train traditional birth attendants and field health care providers on pregnancy care, safe delivery practices and care after delivery, improve quality of emergency obstetric care, and increase women's decision-making power in the family and community by educating them.

According to a survey conducted by the Population Council, the post-partum period is the riskiest period with 62 per cent of all the deaths occurring then. The families of the deceased reported massive bleeding and high fever as the main complications. About 73 per cent of the deaths took place at home and had not sought treatment. Poor roads and transportation posed a great barrier to seeking health care. Results showed that most maternal deaths might not have happened if the women had received proper and timely advice towards the end of their pregnancy and during immediate postnatal period, had received better care at home, their families had known of the danger signs in pregnancy and childbirth, and adequately equipped and managed referral centres had existed (Kuhu, 2001: 3).

Inter-sectoral approach: Inter- and intra-departmental coordination should be promoted to achieve an overall improvement in the quality of life. Apart from information regarding their own health, women are also seeking information for other members of the family, including their children. The Education/Health/ Nutrition and Child Department should work hand in hand to achieve these welfare-oriented changes in the society. Health services should be linked with programmes on employment generation and food security. For instance, self-help groups and self-employment programmes can include simple health awareness like first aid, nutrition, and other information on immunization.

This inter-departmental coordination will help to bring about a decline in infant mortality through the prevention of neo-natal tetanus, immunization of children and use of homemade treatments for diarrhoea. The health sector could also improve the present situation of occurrence of birth in institutions and basic improvement in the quality of life (achieved through improvements in literacy, status of women and infant mortality, and a reduction in the level of poverty).

The NPP, 2000[9] has recognized the importance of taking inter-sectoral approach. However, a strong institutional mechanism than the one suggested by the policy is needed, together with a clear and time-bound mandate to evolve workable procedures and operational guidelines to ensure that such coordination among departments and ministries actually occurs (Sen, 2000).

Focus on welfare-oriented targets: Family planning programmes in India need to be focused at achieving some welfare-oriented targets rather than a certain number of contraceptive acceptors. It is important that family planning programmes utilize mass media and person-to-person communication channels using local personalities who have known to make a difference in the people. National family planning programmes should aim at all married fecund women, irrespective of their age and the number of children ever born. Male responsibility is still being viewed by the programme as a need to encourage men to use condoms rather than supporting gender equality, and women's reproductive and sexual health and rights.

Partnerships/linkages between governmental, non-governmental and private health providers: Lessons need to be learnt from Bangladesh where an integrated attempt by the family welfare workers and NGO efforts put together has made a difference. The government, non-government and private services can strengthen mutually by this partnership. For example, a 'dai' can strengthen her role in the community if she can successfully refer her clients to the government and private services. Similarly, the implementation of government services can strengthened by linking them with NGOs and local village workers.

NEPAL

Nepal has the highest maternal mortality in the selected countries in South Asia. Of the estimated 9,27,000 pregnancies that take place in Nepal every year, 40 per cent are considered to be highly risky for both the mother and the child (UNICEF, 1996). Frequent pregnancies and inadequate nourishment of women during pregnancy increase the risks to expectant mothers. Thus, maternal health services, such as prenatal care, skilled assistance during delivery and postnatal care, along with adequately equipped health institutions, play a major role in the reduction of maternal mortality and morbidity.

The need for family planning was recognized as early as 1958, when a private organization – the Nepal Family Planning Association – was established in Kathmandu. In 1968, a semi-autonomous organization (Nepal Family Planning and Maternal Child Health Board – FP/MCH) was established to formulate and implement family planning policy and programmes. Under the FP/MCH, family planning services were offered mainly through the existing maternal and child health clinics. The Fifth Five-Year Development Plan (1975-1980) extended family planning services through a system of outreach workers. In 1978, the FP/MCW was upgraded, becoming the National Commission of Population. A large number of family planning workers, mostly women workers, have been trained and recruited including physicians, nurses and paramedics. In 1989, the Commission offered family planning services in 52 of Nepal's 75 districts. Such services were provided by three means: stationary services, mobile facilities and door-to-door campaigns. The stationary services were provided through the health posts, health centres and hospitals. At least two full-time workers, apart from the staff, were assigned to deliver family planning and maternal and child health services. However, it has been reported that most health and family planning workers in rural health posts were rarely found in their assigned units. As a result, the availability of such services in rural areas remained poor.

The mobile services were a product of necessity given the remoteness of much of the population and the lack of local family planning services, or easy accessibility to such a facility. These mainly stressed on permanent sterilization. Since then, two committees were formed and dissolved and finally in 1996, a National Population Committee was established. Overall, the 20-year trend of the Nepal population programme has favoured integrated programmes through short-term gains of family planning adoption and long-term changes in values surrounding family size, support for education and employment programmes that raise women's status and lower infant mortality, and the launching of population-related programmes through agriculture, forestry, urbanization, manpower and employment, education, women's development, and community development agencies. The integrated strategy has paid off, as there have been positive changes in the last four decades. The problems of the Nepal family planning programme are mainly on the institutional and operational levels and not on policy as the UNFPA mission report remarked that the national population strategy is an appropriate guide for population activities.

Pakistan

In response to concern about rapid growth, Pakistan was one of the first countries to frame a national policy in the 1960s, with a programme of family planning services, however the programme appeared to have had scant impact on the total fertility rate which continued to be at the level of 6-7 births per woman throughout the 1970s and 1980s and the population growth rate approached 3 per cent per annum.

Some of the reasons for the failure of the programme have been the inconsistency in political support for family planning. Since the third family planning programme (1965-70) a comprehensive national family planning programme was designed as an integral part of overall development strategy. The scheme drawn up for this period emphasized that family planning was essentially an administrative, not a clinical, programme (Hakim and Miller, 2001). The scheme operated mostly through the existing political and administrative structures in provinces, districts, thanas and villages by attaching family planning staff at each level, or by adding family planning to their functions on a part-time basis. Covering the entire nation the scheme made an effort mainly to distribute conventional contraceptives through village midwives (dais) and other local agents. Even, this programme had no major effect on the contraceptive prevalence rates (Robinson, 2001).

In 1970, a new strategy, the Continuos Motivation System (CMS) was introduced with dais being replaced by a team of men and women working in pairs as field motivators. However, all the criteria required for the pair working as field workers proved impossible to implement. In 1975, another new strategy in favour of a multi-sectoral approach was implemented through Family Welfare Centres (FWCs) as well as health outlets of governmental and non-governmental agencies. However, this resulted in inadequate coverage of family planning services. The programme moved hands from Ministry of Health to Ministry of Planning and Development.

This failure of different models as well as fluctuating political motivation resulted in negative consequences of staff morale and management problems of the programme itself. According to Hakim and Miller (2001), only the CMS, given time and suitable modification, might have succeeded. Over and above there has been resistance to the family planning programme in the name of religion and ideology. On the other hand, several other factors also resulted in a higher demand for children.

However, there is evidence of a change in the reproductive behaviour in the 1990s. There has been a decline in fertility and increase in the contraceptive prevalence rate during this period.

Underlying this development has been an increase in the demand of family planning as a result of the economic and social changes that occurred in the late 1970s and 1980s (Hakim and Miller, 2001). The macro-economic trends have led to widespread economic distress at the household level and social changes that have diluted the influence of extended kin and resulted in greater husband-wife convergence in reproductive decision-making. The more direct causes of declining fertility are a crystallization of existing desires and a reduction in the social, cultural and psychic costs of contraception. Improvements in family planning services (their density and quality) have contributed little to the onset of fertility decline but could be decisive in sustaining the decline over the next decade. Other obstacles to contraceptive use, including fear of health side effects and perceptions that husbands are opposed, must also be overcome in order for contraceptive practice to become more widespread and the decline in fertility to continue. Over the long term, progression to replacement level fertility will require a substantial decline in the demand for children and a simultaneous fulfilment of unmet demand for family planning. The ideal family size was between 3.5 and actual fertility was about 5.3 in 1996-97 pointing out that there is a substantial percentage of unmet need for family planning in Pakistan. However, it is clear that the process of reproductive change has begun.

During the past decade, though the programme enjoyed full political support and commitment, yet it lacked backing from the community. The community-based approach could not be fully materialized due to religious, social and cultural norms of the society. Low literacy rate, particularly among womenfolk, happened to be another major impediment in the way of programme success.

SRI LANKA

Sweden and Norway in the mid-17th century, the US in the early 1900s, Sri Lanka and the state of Kerala (India) in the late 1800s and Malaysia in the late 1940s – all decided to institute measures to prevent maternal deaths. There are lessons that we could learn from each of their experience.

Sri Lanka has experienced transitions in major demographic phenomena and it is now at the very important stage of the fertility transition where it seems to be heading even below replacement level fertility.[10] Many researchers have indicated that up to 1970 marriage postponement in Sri Lanka was responsible for about 60 per cent of the fertility decline, but after 1970 the main contributing factor in the fertility decline was the control of fertility within marriage (De Silva, 1994).

After a new government came to power in 1977, it relied heavily on population information, education and communication (IEC) programmes and implemented such activities with view to developing a favourable social climate for the acceptance of family planning. At the same time, more and more resources were devoted to contraceptive service delivery, particularly voluntary sterilization, by introducing incentives for service providers as well as acceptors of sterilization. After 1979, there was a considerable increase in the number of sterilizations among married couples. Some argue that that the most plausible explanation for this rapid increase was the introduction of a cash incentive of 100 rupees in 1980 with subsequent increase in the payment to acceptors (De Silva, 1994).

The level of contraceptive use among Sri Lankan women increased rapidly in the period following 1970. There was increasing awareness of contraception not only for the purpose of ceasing childbearing but also for the spacing of births. The level of contraceptive use increased from 32 per cent in 1975 to 62 per cent in 1987 and further to 66 per cent in 1993. The use of modern contraceptives is a relatively recent development. In the 1975 Sri Lanka Fertility Survey among the current users of contraception, 59 per cent were relying on modern methods; in both the 1987 SLDHS[11] and 1993 SLDHS, the corresponding estimates were 66 per cent only. This clearly implies that a large proportion of users in Sri Lanka are still relying on traditional methods. At present, among the current users, just over one-third rely on traditional methods (De Silva, 1994).

Sri Lanka's success in preventing maternal deaths has been achieved by the government's commitment to improve education and health care. Over 93 per cent of the people today have access to basic health care. Health services are provided free of charge – although over 50 per cent of the people use the private sector – and a few people are more than 1.4 km from the nearest health centre. Maternal and child health services are available at community level as part of integrated reproductive health services. About 60 per cent of married women using contraceptives have also helped reduce maternal deaths.

Conclusion

The impressive changes in Sri Lanka have been attributed to the government's commitment towards improving educational and health situation and providing for the resources required in the country to make these changes possible. However, examples of Bangladesh, Tamil Nadu and Andhra Pradesh in India tell a different story. They are worse off in terms of socio-economic factors but have managed to attain better levels of contraceptive use and fertility. Political will and government commitment have played a major role in these examples.

Andhra Pradesh has a low literacy rate, however its fertility rate has improved in the last decade. In Andhra Pradesh, the self-help group, DWCRA has been a central element in the state's community mobilization. These groups forming of women from the socio-economically weaker sections also discuss health/ sanitation and family planning apart from helping women to earn additional income.

In Bangladesh this change has been attributed to the success of grassroots workers involved with the government programmes as well as the NGOs like BRCA and BRDB, which also promote self-help groups with millions of beneficiaries. It can thus be inferred that literacy in the form of awareness is what makes the difference in the people's behaviour pattern. Mere increase in the number of literates is insufficient; it has to be supplemented with adequate awareness generation. This has to be supported by a strong commitment of the government programmes, adequate investment and political will. A lesson to be learnt from Sri Lanka is that social changes are a possibility even in low-income economies if adequate investments are made in the social service sector and with a strong commitment.

Bangladesh is now viewed as an emerging success story with its low income economy and improving fertility and contraception indicators. The changes in the pattern of fertility and contraception in Bangladesh have again been attributed to government's commitment, NGOs efforts, and willingness of the government to learn from NGOs' efforts.

The concept of diffusion explains the changes that take place in spite of little or no change in the socio-economic indicators. The essence of diffusion argument is that of an innovation that spreads from person to person and region to region. This is generally from a core area to a periphery. Closer to the context of individual community interaction mentioned by Bongaarts and Watkins (1996), that although the decision on number of children and

Attendance during Delivery
Percentage of Births Attended by Skilled Health Professionals, 1998-2001

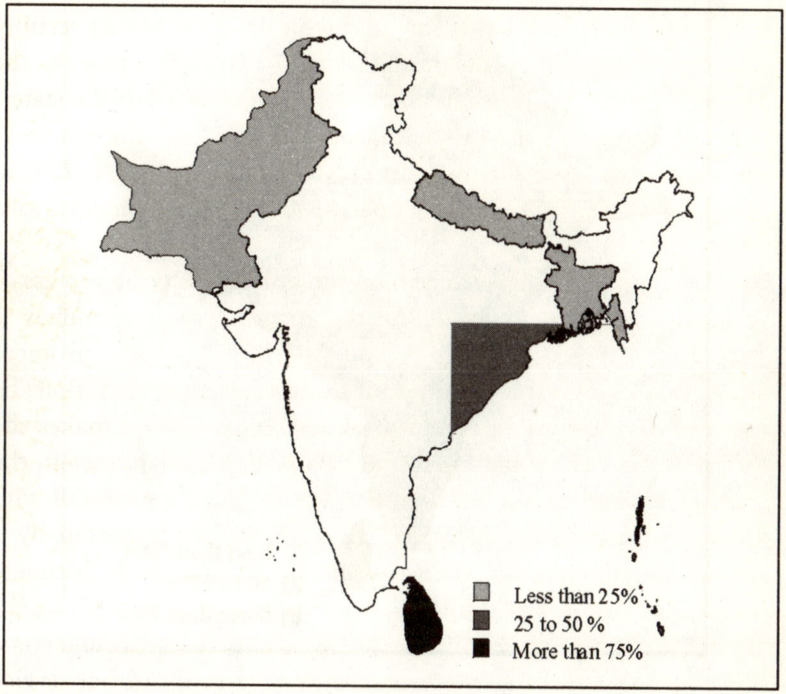

contraceptive use is purely private, these are also shaped by the interaction one has with the community. Bongaarts and Watkins (1996) observed that social influence was critical factor in maintaining high fertility in many societies. In India and Bangladesh this social influence for women to take progressive decisions has been being part of self-help groups. This brings us to the inference that if the social response is conducive women are more likely to take progressive decisions about fertility and contraceptive use. This also makes it evident that geographical area has an influence on the reproductive behaviour of people. This concept can be explored further with the help of Geographical Information System (GIS) by identifying the core areas of change and its spread in the surrounding geographical area.

Percentage of Pregnant Women going for Prenatal Check-ups, 1996-2000

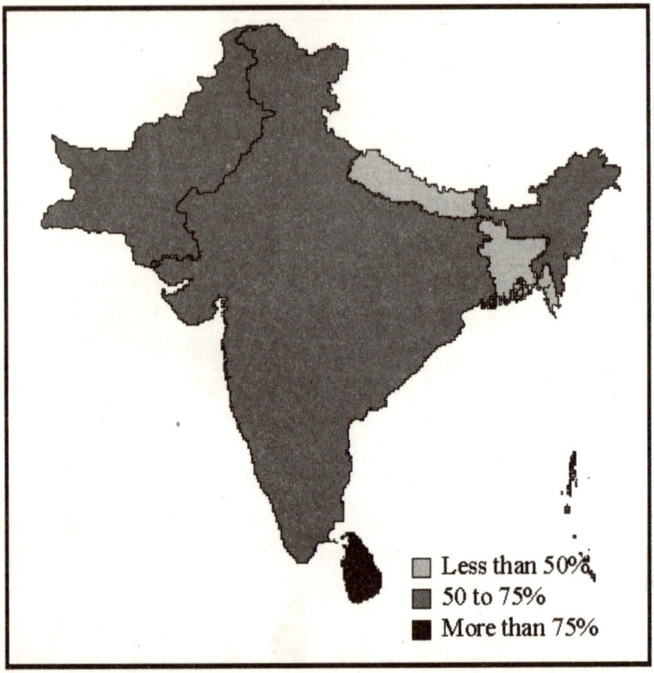

Education forms an important component of measures to improve women's reproductive health mainly because women who take to secondary schooling are less likely to go into childbirth during adolescent years. An equally important component is to create awareness by giving accurate information and non-judgmental and accessible services to help them avoid unwanted pregnancies, care for their health and take advantage of education and other opportunities. Improving participation of women in education alone will not necessarily improve the reproductive health choices and decisions they make.

The belief that increased schooling for women will automatically bring about women's advancement is common and somewhat unexamined. It is often assumed that it is lack of schooling that has been holding women back. The education system is very closely

Maternal Mortality Rate

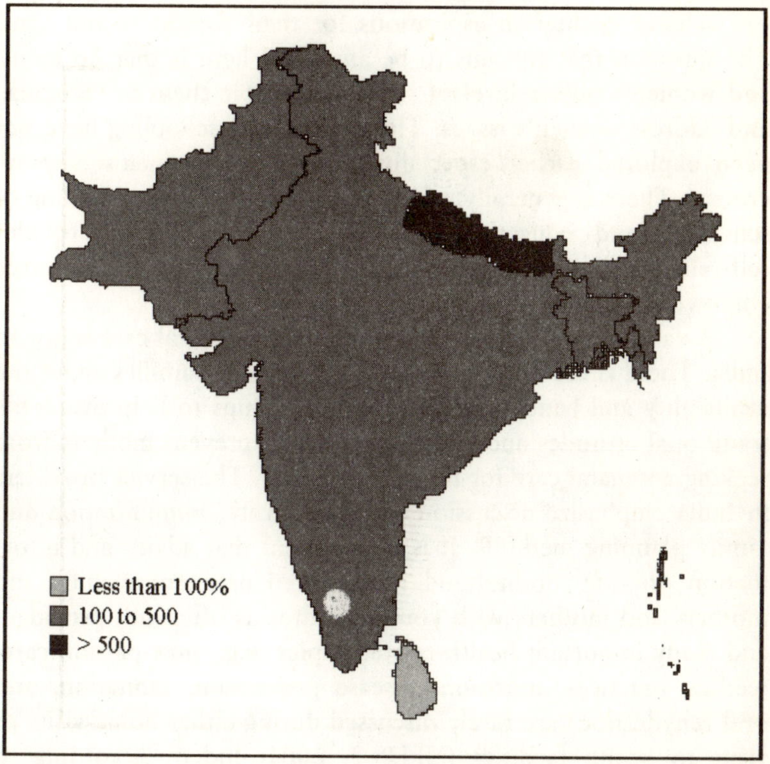

linked to this social system; firstly, women who marry young are withdrawn from schools. Secondly, the parents' decision to send girls to school is surrounded in gender bias. The school curriculum and attitude of teachers may reinforce the existing gender bias in the society. Schools are generally patriarchal establishments, which are grounded in the values and rules of patriarchal society. Pupils are schooled to conform, and to do as they are told. In other words, girls are taught to accept patriarchal authority. Females are schooled to accept the 'naturalness' of male domination and to accept success on male terms (Longwe, 1999). This also stands for men's schooling, they are taught to dominate and consider themselves superior in terms of decision-making and that women are good in working as subordinates under their instructions. Little is known whether girls and boys educated under these conditions can achieve egalitarian aspirations for their daughters and sons. The question that remains to be answered here is that do men's and women's higher level of schooling enable them to recognize and address women's issues. These aspects of schooling have not been explored earlier especially in terms of women's empowerment. There is generally a mix-up between the understanding of schooling and education. Schooling in South Asia provides self-reliance whereas education goes a step further towards empowerment.

Awareness regarding the usefulness of antenatal care is low in India. There is the need to inform mothers and families about the availability and benefits of antenatal check-ups to help overcome traditional attitudes and other hurdles that prevent mothers from seeking antenatal care for their pregnancies. The service providers in India emphasize discussion about childcare, immunization and family planning methods. It is also evident that advice and information on safe motherhood practices to pregnant women and mothers and mothers with young children is often not provided, and many important health-related topics (e.g., post-partum care, feeding practices, nutrition, disease prevention, sanitation, and oral rehydration) are rarely discussed during either home visits or visits to health facilities (NFHS-2, 2001, India). According to NFHS-2 data, antenatal, delivery and post-partum care is hardly discussed by the health workers in India.

Client-provider[12] interaction is another vital factor that affects the access to maternal health care and needs to be explored in a systematic manner. Not enough is known about the client-provider interaction in the study area, except for a few questions on quality of care that were included in NFHS-2, India 1998-99. Studying client-provider interaction may revolutionize how programmes are conceptualized. It involves listening to the voices of those who matter most – the people for whom services are provided and those who work on the frontline: the field worker and the service provider at the clinic or community level. Ignorance of client-provider interaction is ignorance of the centerpiece of programmes, not just of one small piece in a large jigsaw puzzle.

The other question that remains to be answered is that why many of the mothers with emergencies never reach the hospital in some of these countries? It is because they may not have been warned about how to identify emergencies and what should be done in case there is one. Studies show that people are searching for information and plan during that life and death situation. What if they are provided a safe birth information and plan of action before hand? A plan that consists of their knowledge and expert knowledge put together. Will it make a difference if villages in these countries had a safe birth plan, which people could access to if required and improvise according to their experiences? What if each panchayat is given a responsibility to prepare a safe birth plan with the help of health providers (private and public) and the people and this plan is communicated to the people?

NOTES

1. The ICPD stands for the International Conference on Population and Development held in Cairo in 1994.
   Reproductive health, as defined by the World Health Organization and adopted by the Programme of Action of International Conference on Population and Development (ICPD), is "...a state of complete physical, mental and social well-being and not merely the absence of disease or infirmity, in all matters relating to the reproductive system and to its functions and processes. Reproductive health therefore implies that people are able to have a satisfying and safe sex life and that they have the capability to reproduce and the freedom to decide if, when and how often to do so" (WHO, 2000: 75).
2. Replacement level fertility implies a total fertility rate usually between 2.1 and 2.2 children per woman, depending on a country's level of mortality (De Silva, 1994).
3. Details have been given when the case of Bangladesh has been mentioned separately later.

4. Access means that services are available and within reach of women who need them. Good quality services require that health care providers have adequate clinical skills and are sensitive to women's needs; that facilities have necessary equipment and supplies; that referral systems function well to ensure that women with complications get essential treatment.
5. Education may enhance female autonomy and woman's ability to make decisions regarding her own health and it addition; it also increases the knowledge of modern health care thus increasing demand for these services.
6. Covering the skin completely with cloth so that no part is exposed is the *purdah* system.
7. Even before independence a major international epidemiological research Centre, which was then called Pakistan SEATO Cholera Research Laboratory, existed in Dhaka. This laboratory operated an epidemiological surveillance area in Matlab Thana (rural area south of Dhaka) collecting birth, death and morbidity data.
8. Anganwadi workers are those working in the crèche or day care centres for very young children. Anganwadi also runs a kindergarden programme and provides afternoon meals for children.
9. The National Population Policy, 2000 (NPP, 2000)
10. Replacement level fertility implies a total fertility rate usually between 2.1 and 2.2 children per woman, depending on a country's level of mortality. Since the infant mortality rate of Sri Lanka is at a very low level (19 per 1,000 live births in 1990), its replacement level fertility is defined as an average of 2.1 children per woman.
11. SLDHS (Sri Lanka Demographic and Health Survey).
12. Client here means the women accessing the health services and provider means the health care service providers.

References

Abeykoon, A.T.P.L, 1996, "Demographic Implications of Health Care in Sri Lanka", *Asia-Pacific Journal*, Vol. 2 (2), pp. 47-58.

Acharya, S., 1995, "How effective is antenatal care to promote maternal and neonatal health?" *International Journal of Gynecology and Obstetrics*, Vol. 50, Sup. 2, pp. S35-S42.

Ahmad, Alia, 1991, *Women and Fertility in Bangladesh*, Sage Publications, New Delhi.

Amin Ruhul, Chowdhury, Asraf U. Ahmed, Robert, B. Hill and M. Kabir, 1993, "Reproductive Change in Bangladesh: Evidence from Recent Data", *Asia-Pacific Population Journal*, Vol. 8(4), pp. 39-58.

Anandalakshmy, P.N., Talwar, P.P., Buckshee, K., and Hingorani, V., 1993, "Demographic and Social Economic and Medical Factors Affecting Maternal Mortality: An Indian Experience", *The Journal of Family Welfare*, Vol. 39(3), pp. 1-4.

Ansari, Gopalakrishnan V., 1994, "Determinants of Contraceptive Use in Kerala: The Case of Son/Daughter Preference", *The Journal of Family Welfare*, Vol. 40(3), pp. 19-25.

Bhatia, J.C. and John Cleland, 1995, "Determinants of Maternal Care in a Region of South India", *Health Transition Review*, Vol. 5, pp. 127-42.

Carroli, G., Villar, J., Piaggio G., Khan-Neelofur D., Gulmezoglu M., Mugford M., Lumbiganon P., Farnot U. and Bersgio P., "WHO systematic review of randomised controlled trials of routine antenatal care", *Lancet 2001*, 357(9268): 1565-70.

Central Statistical Organization, 2000, *Women and Men in India*, Ministry of Statistics and Programme Implementation, India.

Chatterjee, Mirai and Usha Parekh, 2000, "Gender Equity and Population Policies", *Health Watch Update*, Issue 12, pp. 2-3.

Chen, Marty, 1991, "Poverty, Women's Status and Fertility", *Economic and Political Weekly*, Vol. 26(52).

De Silva, W. Indralal, 1994, "Ahead of Target: Achievement of Replacement Level Fertility in Sri Lanka Before the Year 2000", *Asia-Pacific Population Journal*, Vol. 9(4), pp. 3-22.

—, 1997, "The Ireland of Asia: Trends in Marriage Timing in Sri Lanka", *Asia-Pacific Population Journal*, Vol. 12(2), pp. 3-24.

Dev, S. Mahendra, 2002, "Causes of Fertility Decline in India and Bangladesh: Role of Community", *Economic and Political Weekly*, October 26.

Dissanayake, Lakshman, 1996, "Relative Impact of Starting, Spacing and Stopping Fertility Behaviour in Sri Lanka", *The Journal of Family Welfare*, Vol. 42(3), pp. 1-7.

"Fertility and Contraceptive Prevalence Rates 1974-75 to 2000-01", www.mopw.gov.pk/pdindex.htm

Gerein, N., Mayhew, S., Lubben, M., "A framework for a new approach to antenatal care", *International Journal of Gynecology and Obstetrics*, Vol. 80, pp. 175-82.

Government of India, 1997, *Women in India: A Statistical Profile*, Department of Women and Child Development, Ministry of Human Resource Development, Government of India.

Hakim, Abdul and Peter C. Miller, 2001, "Family Planning in Pakistan: A Turning Point", in Zeba Ayesha Sathar and James F. Phillips (eds.), *Fertility Transition in South Asia*, Oxford University Press, New York, pp. 135-57.

International Institute for Population Sciences (IIPS), 2000, National Family Health Survey 1998-99. IIPS, Mumbai and ORC Macro, Calverton, Maryland USA.

Islam, Mazharul M. and Mamun Mahmud, 1996, "Marriage Patterns and Some Issues Related to Adolescent Marriage in Bangladesh", *Asia-Pacific Population Journal,* Vol. 11(3), pp. 27-42.

Jain, Anrudh, 2001, "Population Policy Implications of the 1994 International Conference on Population and Development (ICPD)", in Zeba Ayesha Sathar and James F. Phillips (eds.), *Fertility Transition in South Asia*, Oxford University Press, New York, pp. 135-57.

Jayweera, Swarna, 2000, "Major Conventional Indicators in Sri Lanka", Centre for Women's Research, co-ordinated by ISST, India and submitted to IDRC, Canada.

Kamal, Nashid and Andrew Slogget, 1996, "The Effect of Female Family Planning Workers on the Use of Modern Contraception in Bangladesh", *Asia-Pacific Population Journal*, Vol. 11(3), pp. 15-26.

Karkal, Malini, 1996, "Reproductive Health and Women: A Review of Literature", *Radical Journal and Health*, Vol. 2(1), pp. 54-67.

Khuda, Barkat-e-, John C. Caldwell, Bruce K. Caldwell, Indrni Pieris, Pat Caldwell and Shameen Ahmed, 2001, "Determinants of the Fertility Transition in Bangladesh", in Zeba Ayesha Sathar and James F. Phillips (eds.), *Fertility Transition in South Asia*, Oxford University Press, New York, pp. 364-85.

Khuda, Barkat-e-, Nikhil Chndra Roy and Dewan Md. Mizanur Rahman, 1999, "Unmet Contraceptive Need in Bangladesh: Evidence from the 1993/94 and 1996/97", Demographic and Health Surveys, *Asia-Pacific Population Journal*, Vol. 14(2), pp. 37-51.

Leete, Richard, Iqbal Alam, 1999, "Asia's Demographic Miracle: 50 Years of Unprecedented Change", *Asia-Pacific Population Journal*, Vol. 14(4), pp. 9-20.

Longwe, S.H., 1998, "Education for Women's Empowerment or Schooling for Women's Subordination?", *Gender and Development*, July, Vol. 6 # 2, pp. 19-26.

Maitra, Kuhu, 2001, "Priority actions for safe motherhood: What are the challenges?" *Health for the Millions*, 27(3): 7-8.

Maternal and Child Health Care in India, NSS 52nd Round, July 1995–June 1996 (1998), National Sample Survey Organization, Department of Statistics, India, December.

Matsumura, Masaki and Bina Gubhaju, 2001, "Women's Status, Household Structure and the Utilisation of Maternal Health Services in Nepal", *Asia Pacific Population Journal*, Vol. 16 (1), March.

Mc Eachran, Juliet, 2001, "Trends in Fertility and Contraceptive Use in Bangladesh", in Zeba Ayesha Sathar and James F. Phillips (eds.), *Fertility Transition in South Asia*, Oxford University Press, New York, pp. 158-74.

Ministry of Health (Nepal), New ERA, and ORC macro, 2002, Nepal Demographic and Health Survey 2001. Calverton, Maryland, USA: Family Health Division, Ministry of Health; New ERA; and ORC Macro.

Ministry of Population and Environment, 1997, Status of Population–Nepal, Nepal.

Ministry of Population and Environment, 2000, "The State of Population, Nepal 2000", Nepal. www.mope.gov.np/status/popstat/popstatus eng.htm

Mosse, Julia Cleves, Cassels, Andrew, 1996, "Reproductive and Child Health in India: A Health Systems Development Agenda", *Social Change*, Vol. 26(3-4), pp. 6-13.

National Council of Applied Economic Research, 2001, "Concurrent Evaluation of Integrated Child Development Services – National Report", Gupta, D.B., Anil Gumber, V.S. Saravanan, Poushali Majumdar, Ramamani Sundar, Rajesh Jaiswal, Dalip Kumar, S.K. Bathla and P. Srivatsan, June 2001.

National Institute of Population Research and Training Dhakha, Bangladesh and ORC Macro, Calverton, Maryland (2001) Bangladesh Maternal Health Services and Maternal Mortality Survey, Preliminary Report, USA.

Nirupam, S., and Yuster, E.A., 1995, "Emergency obstetric care: measuring availability and monitoring progress", *International Journal of Gynecology and Obstetrics*, Vol. 50 Suppl. 2, pp. S79-S88.

Ramakrishna, Jayashree, Saraswathy Ganapathy, Zoë Matthews, Shanti Mahendra and Asha Kilaru, 2000, "Health, Illness and Care in the Obstetric Period: A Prospective Study of Women in Rural Karnataka". Paper presented at the Reproductive Health in India: New Evidence and Issues, Tata Management Training Centre, Pune, Maharashtra, India, February 28 to March 1.

Rishyasringa, Bhanwar, 2000, "Social Policy and Reproductive Health", in Shireen J. Jejeebhoy (ed.), *Women's Reproductive Health in India*, Rawat Publications, Jaipur and New Delhi, pp. 419-45.

Robinson, Warren C., 2001, "Common Beginnings but Different Outcomes: The Family Planning Programmes of Pakistan and Bangladesh", in Zeba Ayesha Sathar and James F. Phillips (eds.), *Fertility Transition in South Asia*, Oxford University Press, New York, pp. 347-63.

Shaikh, Kashem, 1997, "Recent Changes in Marriage Patterns in Rural Bangladesh", *Asia-Pacific Journal*, Vol. 12(3), pp. 31-48.

Siddiqui, Rehana, Shahnaz Hamid, G. Yasin, Soomro, Rizwana Siddiqui and Naeem Akhtar, 2001, "Gender Dimension of the Impact of Macroeconomic Policies: A Case Study of Pakistan", Pakistan Institute of Development Economics, submitted to IDRC, Canada.

Sugathan, K.S., Vinod Mishra and Robert D. Retherford, 2001, "Promoting Institutional Deliveries in Rural India: The Role of Antenatal-Care Services", National Family Health Survey Subject Reports, No. 20, December.

Ullah, Md. Shahid and Nitai Chakraborty, 1993, "Factors Affecting the Use of Contraception in Bangladesh: A Multivariate Analysis", *Asia-Pacific Population Journal*, Vol. 8(3), pp. 19-30.

United Nations, Economic and Social Commission for Asia and the Pacific, 1995, *Women in Pakistan: A Country Profile*.

Villar, J., Ba'aqeel H., Piaggio G., Lumbiganon P., Belizan J.M., Farnot U., "WHO antenatal care randomised control trial for the evaluation of a new model of routene antenatal care", *Lancet 2001*, 357(9268): 1551-64.

World Health Organization, 2000, Women of South East Asia: A Health Profile, Regional Office for South East Asia, New Delhi, India.

www.bbs.gov.org (Bangladesh Bureau of Statistics, 1991, 1998) accessed in February 2003.

www.childinfo.org/eddb/maternal/database1.htm accessed in February 2003.

www.mope.gov.np/population/(ministry of Population and Environment, Nepal Population Report 2002 accessed in February 2003.

www.pap.org.pk/PopulationPak.htm (accessed in June 2003).

www.statistics.gov.lk/abstract/(Statistical Abstract 2002) Department of Census and Statistics (DCS), Sri Lanka (accessed in February 2003).

www.unfpa.org/news/features/(accessed in February 2003).

www.unicef.org/statis/(accessed in February 2003).

Zeba, Sathar, Cynthia B. Lloyd, Cem Mete, Minhanj Ul Haque, 2000, "Schooling Opportunities for Girls as a Stimulus for Fertility Change in Rural Pakistan", Population Council, No. 143.

Zodgekar, Arvind V., 1996, "Family Welfare Programme and Population Stabilization Strategies in India", *Asia-Pacific Population Journal*, Vol. 11(1), pp. 3-24.

Zohir, Salma Chaudhuri, Sharifa Begum and Abul Basher, 2001, "Changes in Conventional Indicators During Adjustment in Bangladesh", Bangladesh Institute of Development Studies, submitted to IDRC, Canada.

14

Persisting Structures, Ideological Manoeuvres and Everyday Challenges

Reflections on Women's Movements in South Asia

Uma Chakravarti

Like all hesitant beginnings, let me also start with an anecdote: a few months ago I met up with an old student of mine from the early seventies whom I hadn't seen since then. She was now a very successful freelance photographer and I was seeking her help in identifying visuals for an illustrated history of early India. I was very clear that I wasn't going to produce one more book with the biases of most history writers and this was going to be my opportunity to insert women and other marginalized groups now into a visual account of the ancient past. As I tried to tell her some of my concerns she began to get a sense of what we may call my ideological 'slant' and broke into the conversation with a casual question, "Are you one of those strident feminists?" "Yes," I said equally casually, but quite unashamedly, "I am a feminist – just a feminist," and we went on with the rest of our conversation on the same note as before. There is a point to this story that has a bearing on the women's movement in South Asia, in fact across the globe in varying degrees. A feminist is 'strident' whether the word is actually used or not. In South Asia there is an additional baggage that feminism carries and that is the association with the West. Later I will have occasion to dwell in more detail with this issue. For the moment it is enough to note the irony of the passing comment of my student: in some ways she was the exact opposite of me as a girl, I'd had to struggle to make my choices, my generation and the next had struggled to create spaces for women and it was our struggles that had made it possible for my student to live the life that she did and make the choices that she made and yet she was not only delinking her life from the struggles of other women but, by implication, trivializing the very basis of those struggles. I hope that by the end of the book she will better understand the terms that she used so casually to put me into a pigeonhole in her view of the world. At the end of the millennium we are still dealing with our being pigeonholed, even if we have made an impact, which we certainly have in every country of South Asia.

There are other kinds of pigeonholes we in South Asia have to confront. Apart from the economic exploitation and political domination that colonialism entails, it is the psychological and cultural consequences that are particularly significant for women. Cultural nationalism is a highly emotive way of binding together a subject people still living under colonial rule; in South Asia it was the bedrock of the movements for independence. The East-West dichotomy was especially applicable to women's status where the 'liberation' of the western woman, standing here for rampant individualism and the inability to be nurturing, was contrasted with the unique capacity of the women of the East to sacrifice themselves for the good of others. Built into a powerful trope this model of womanhood made it difficult to articulate women's interests or to recognize the material basis of patriarchies operative in the East, as also in the west requiring a women's movement across the globe. Thus, while the woman's question was an important part of cultural nationalism, making social reform pertaining to women a highly contested and explosive terrain, no transformation of unequal gender relations or even addressing the problem in any sustained manner was possible till the end of colonialism. The continuing anxieties about identities of nations/peoples of the new nation-states in relation to women however still make it difficult to lay the ghost of the East-West dichotomy to rest; it is most persistently rehearsed to brand the women's movements of South Asia as derivatives of, and oriented towards, the west by its opponents. The western stigma not only has an emotive power in a post-colonial society, but it also has the power to deflect from fundamental issues women are raising. It will be my effort throughout this essay to demonstrate the very specific location of the movements in this region to the social and political contexts here making clear that the west derived label is both without substance and, in fact, a way of denying the material basis of women's subordination – a convenient escape route for those who are implicated in reproducing the inequalities of gender.

I

Across South Asia women's movements originated roughly in the seventies more or less a quarter of a century after these nation-states came into existence. In essence this 'moment' had a broader social context than recognizing inequalities of gender but was in fact closely linked to a crisis of state power. In the late sixties and early seventies a series of movements punctured the complacencies of the political elites; the unrest was rooted in the failure of the political system to what in colloquial parlance is called deliver the goods as far as the expectations of its huge populations of deprived groups were concerned. The structural crisis resulted in a leftward shift in oppositional politics as peasants, tribals, workers, dalits, students and women protested the state's failure on virtually every front. Though exacerbated by colonial rule many of these social contradictions originated in our own home-grown material and social arrangements and were problems of the *longue duree* on the subcontinent. There were two ways in which the women's movement was organically linked to this political context: women were as materially affected as men by the economic crisis so they were an intrinsic part and in some cases even the largest component of a movement as in Shahada in India; at the same time, women activists drawn from the middle class as well as peasant and tribal women found that the gender question was not being addressed within the otherwise democratic and often radical movements that they were part of. Early manifestations of the need for organizing as women did not fully develop immediately in India because of the imposition of the Emergency by the state, an unsuccessful means by which the state attempted to surmount the political crisis. But, by the late seventies, several aspects of women's oppression – some old and others gross manifestations of the deeply gendered way in which economic processes were being experienced by sections of the population – provided the context for the birth of the autonomous women's movement. Thereafter, a broad coalition of women's groups – some linked to political parties and others constituting autonomous women's groups – mobilized opinion and launched struggles on various issues around 'atrocities' – a catch-all term for particular forms of violence against women.[1]

The focal point of a nation-wide campaign, in some ways heralding what has come to be loosely referred to as the women's movement in India, was the outrageously biased judgment on the rape of a young, low status, tribal woman called Mathura in a police station while in custody. The specific circumstances of this starting point are important to note as a significant feature of women's movements in South Asia: whatever the nature and extent of interaction between women in South Asia and women in other parts of the world (not just the West) and regardless of our mutual collaboration in how we conceptualize the woman's question, it is the reality of the specific forms of oppression that women in our regions suffer that have crucially shaped the interventions of women in resisting these oppressions. The relationship between class, gender and state was evident in the judgment where the patriarchal workings of two separate arms of the state – the police and the law – meshed together to draw attention to custodial rape and the specific forms that patriarchal power can take in a Third World country. A similar case earlier on in Hyderabad had been an issue around which civil rights groups, women's groups and political parties had agitated to demand that the accused policemen be prosecuted but now a nation-wide campaign was launched to address the biases of the law; whatever some uncritical practitioners of postmodernism might now argue about the futility of engaging with the law the legal basis of patriarchy and the biases of the judicial system have been closely linked to the women's movements in South Asia. In many cases struggles over the law have literally triggered off the women's movement in certain regions and cities as in Pakistan over the Hudood ordinances and in Rajasthan in India over 'sati'. It is perhaps time to remind ourselves that whether we launch struggles to change the law or not, we cannot ignore it – it is all around us and will continue to operate on us whether we want it to or not. It is often literally a matter of life and death in some cases, so there is no question of abdicating it as field of struggle.

The women's movement of the late seventies and early eighties placed the women's question in a new perspective and the working towards a just order was conceptualized in radically different terms. The enormity of the discrimination women faced and their essential homelessness, the denial of basic constitutional and human rights, their experience of violence and the cultural practices under which their subordination was inivisibilized – all began to coalesce around an incipient feminist consciousness and this provided the backdrop to the emergence of the women's movements. A range of strategies were used by the movement from interventions in the law to protest marches against acts of violence on women, to street plays staged at public places; a most subversive use of humour in street theatre was a hilarious play women in Lahore created about the Hudood provision that the testimony of two women would equal that of one man.[2] The movement spread rapidly across many towns, especially since a spate of dowry murders in North India drew stark attention to what went on 'inside the family'. With individual variations broadly this was the experience in other parts of the sub-continent too. Further, across South Asia, whatever the nature and degree of economic and social changes that had occurred, marriage, sexuality and reproduction had remained a central concern for these societies. Community control over the sexuality of women had not eroded and has remained a major source of violence against women with the explicit sanction of the community; women's lack of autonomy, choice and agency are sharply tested here. While the women's movement has intervened to help individual women in India and in Pakistan, and integrated such issues in their analysis of patriarchies, there has been no other way in which this crucial area of control has been addressed.

Although the urban women's movement gained the greatest visibility, partly because of the urban bias of the press, movements were taking place in different contexts and social locations. I shall briefly analyze two movements in India to outline the kinds of issues that were being addressed and the distinctive responses each generated for certain insights they provide, and their links with other contests in the future: the Chipko movement of hill women of the Himalayan region against deforestation and the Bodh Gaya movement of landless peasants in central Bihar.[3]

The Chipko movement of the hill regions of Uttar Pradesh, which is now internationally known because it embodies the eco-feminist perspective and has been written about extensively, drew its strength from a traditional form of resistance, which was put to telling effect in the mid-seventies, primarily by women, in saving timber forests in the region from being felled. The word 'chipko' originates from a particular form of non-violent action developed by hill women in the 19th century who would embrace (chipko) the trees to prevent them from being felled. The Gandhian aspect of the movement was very notable as the movement had originated in a region where the Sarvodaya workers had a long-standing presence and the struggle had been in gestation over a period of 13 years. This laid the foundations for the spontaneous response of Gaura Devi and other women in the village of Feni. When the contractor's men arrived to cut down the trees they were spotted by a little girl who immediately informed Gaura Devi, a middle aged widow of the village. Arriving with a group of other women at the felling spot, Gaura Devi pushed herself forward in front of the gun of one of the contractor's men and challenged him to shoot her down before he touched the trees. Comparing the forest with her mother's home she and other women faced the contractor's men squarely and forced them to retreat. This started off the Chipko movement, which spread in the region and has become a symbol for those who are critical of a type of development which is destroying the ecological balance of the region, wherever that may be. The slogans of the Chipko movement were, "soil, water and vegetation are the basis of life," and "the forest is our home, we will not let it be cut down". The understanding of the ecological question of women in the Chipko movement did not come to them from scientific research but sprang from their daily experience and struggle to survive.

Following the first expression of resistance by women in the Chipko movement they also had to confront the cash-hungry men of their own community, who could not care less if the forests were destroyed while their women had to walk for many more miles to collect their daily load of fuel and fodder. The women had also to face the wrath of the village patriarchal organization, since political power within the village has been in the hands of men despite the near total burden the women carry in sustaining the economy. However, it does not appear that the women, who had successfully resisted compliance with the wishes of their menfolk carried the movement further and tried to alter the structure of traditional gender relations in the area.

Gender relations came in more directly in the anti-liquor campaign in neighbouring areas. The targets of women's action here were the liquor shops set up in the region which women perceived as adding to oppression against them by their menfolk. But it was the state and the contractors, through whom the state was seeking to collect its revenues, that were the primary targets of the women's mobilization. Their own men, who were complicit in a system in which it was women who paid the price of 'development' and enhanced revenue for the state – entailing greater physical hardship on the one hand and depleted family resources and physical violence on the other, remained more or less unchallenged in terms of understanding the relationship between the state, class and patriarchies as they operated within the household. Further, in both the Chipko movement focussing on ecological issues, and the anti-liquor campaign focussing on state revenue policies, there was widespread 'social' support including the support of sections of the bureaucracy and a number of men from civil society; the movements were not perceived as interrogating or upsetting existing gender relationships. While they challenged the power of vested interests, they drew their legitimacy from the Gandhian framework into which they had easily fitted. The movement had also built on traditional 'feminine' characteristics of nurturance, of being better equipped to resist passively, and of using moral rather than physical strength to resist their opponents. It is not surprising therefore that even a forest department official had conceded that the Chipko movement was 'patriotically' motivated in terms of its ideals.

It is in the Bodh Gaya movement that one can discern a less unambiguous confrontation with unequal gender relations by women within the larger context of oppressive relations while also drawing upon Gandhian political strategy. This makes the movement one of the most creative explorations of class and gender issues as two aspects of the structure of oppressive relations in India. The fact that the movement was directed against the mahant of Bodh Gaya because it identified the head of a religious institution as the oppressor, something that would be impossible in today's political climate given over to a violent display of street power to defend religious power, is also significant. Women who participated in the movement did so both as agricultural labourers demanding fair wages, and later land rights; in this they struggled along with their menfolk. But, the women in the struggle also demanded that they be recognized as individuals in their own right, not merely as wives of their husbands. Thus, they demanded that title deeds be given to them as distinct from those given to their husbands so that they had independent access to the means of production; and thirdly they demanded to be treated with dignity by their own husbands. To that end they launched struggles against drunkenness and wife battering, using social ostracism and collective resistance as powerful weapons against the offenders. Children played an important part in both struggles: against their fathers by publicising their misdeeds and in the larger social struggle by acting as buffers in the resistance against the greater coercive strength of the landowner, lying down in the field to prevent ploughing by his men. Questions of non-violence were debated in the face of violence unleashed on the movement; could non-violence also be militant? The struggle continued after the people (as articulated by a woman activist) vowed that they would take revenge "for every drop of blood that has been shed, not by spilling blood but by reaping the crop from the land, by making that land ours, which till yesterday was watered with our sweat and has now been watered with our blood".

While sharing the oppression of their menfolk in relation to the mahant the women also took up the oppression within the home, conceptualizing the gender inequality vividly despite the complacency of the male activists who were convinced that things would improve once socio-economic changes were achieved. Earlier, there had been struggles between the men and women activists around who would have primacy in creating theory with the women activists refusing to concede the monopoly of creating theoretical formulations to the men. These struggles at the level of activists and the grassroots actors led to some of the most colourful formulations on the links between class power and patriarchal power. One woman agricultural labourer argued:

> If these men who are today landless beat up their wives so badly, merely using the power derived from being men, then tomorrow when they get the land will they not become relatively more powerful? Will they not be even more cruel to women? If they establish relationships based on justice and equality, will this not strengthen them in their struggle against the mahant?[4]

When the land came to be distributed among the landless initially it went only to the men. The women were outraged and demanded that they be treated as individuals in their own right who had worked the land as much as the men and not as appendages of the men. They effectively rebutted their own men about how little they did on the land. Since the men had dismissed their labour, they devised a system of points about the different kinds of labour performed on the land between ploughing the crops and reaping them. When the points were arranged, every one could see that women did more than men, not less than them, despite being barred from touching the plough. Then began the task of convincing the district officer who held the view that land in India had to go to the head of the household who was a man and not a woman. Finally, after much persistence, the women won the battle and received little plots in their own names. Many years later, one of the women activists of the struggle movingly recalled the significance of that moment for a dalit woman of Bodh Gaya, as she stepped onto her own piece of land and looked up at the little patch of the sky above it – both of which were hers in her own right. It is not surprising that the women have held on to the land much more tenaciously than their men have.

The experience of women in the Bodh Gaya struggle is significant for the way in which patriarchy was recognized within the larger context of social relations and was treated as an integral part of the collective oppression they faced. Women had to face the repression let loose by the mahant and his henchmen and simultaneously take on the opposition of their own menfolk, often taking on physical assaults. In terms of conceptualizing their own subordination, they had moved radically forward – a feature that was missing in the Chipko movement with which it shared a basically similar though more militant approach in terms of following the principle of non-violence for their political struggles. The movement of the women of Bodh Gaya has been one of the most creative applications of feminism seen in recent years in India. It is particularly notable because while ecological movements have considerable legitimacy, especially because women are not perceived as behaving in an unfeminine way, women's struggle for higher wages or something like land rights is much more unsettling and hardly has the same legitimacy. But, in the context of postcolonial India where women's real oppression was addressed in all its manifestations for the first time by the women's movements across the country, the Bodh Gaya movement stands out for its very indigenous roots, economic and social, and its equally indigenous political strategies. At the same time, it unambiguously rejected the traditional model of womanhood, built on the nurturing and sacrificing 'Indian' woman, and demanded dignity and rights for themselves as individuals

Both the Chipko and Bodh Gaya struggles not only point to the range of issues around women that were being addressed by movements but also to the intermeshing of material and cultural factors and the centrality of questions of survival. The movements drew attention to the continuing failure of the state to even partially fulfil the aspirations of the people. By the mid-eighties in India a second phase of the crisis of governance was manifesting itself. This time round a rightward shift in politics introduced a new dimension into the women's movement. Similar shifts with similar links between political crises, manipulation of religious identities and its impact on the women's movements at a different point of time hold for other countries of South Asia too. It is the experience of the region that as nation-states experience a crisis of the legitimacy of the state and political instability they move into a more sharply nationalist or religion based nationalist position immediately affecting women adversely. This was most starkly demonstrated in the Hudood ordinances brought in by General Zia ul Haque in Pakistan but it happened in less direct but nonetheless damaging ways in other parts of the sub-continent.

II

A cynical manipulation of religious or ethnic identities within the larger framework of a stagnant economy, competition for scarce economic resources and political control has the potential to turn violent. In India, the mobilization of the Hindus as Hindus meant that other religious minorities began to feel insecure with sporadic riots breaking out in many cities some fairly severe. It was widely believed that the police were often complicit in the riots and failed to protect all citizens equally. At this point, the Shah Bano judgment was pronounced resulting among other serious things in an internal crisis within the women's movement. The crucial question that arose then was "do women constitute a homogeneous category with the same oppressions and material interests?" Can women be abstracted from the larger communities and affiliations that they share with the men of their communities? These questions were certainly not unique to the movement in India and were being posed across the globe along lines of ethnic or racial divisions. It continues to be a question we are still trying to address in terms of how to understand women's identities and interests, according to their specific social and political locations, while still maintaining the possibility and need for a way of incorporating them in a women's movement that can link up in a larger struggle for an end to gender-based inequality. What was distinctive was the arena in which these issues created divisions: the legal rights of women. The issues remain unresolved and continue to generate a debate in India.

Apart from fracturing women into the category majority/minority other fractures have also surfaced along rural-urban, and upper caste-dalit. These too have led to looking for strategies and conceptualizations to overcome genuine differences without getting locked into identity based blocks or creating a hierarchy of oppressions such that joint struggles cannot be undertaken. By far the most serious challenges have come from the majoritarian defence of cultural identity, hinging on oppressive practices for women. This is now a real battleground between feminists and right-wing religious forces across South Asia but I shall focus on one 'event' around which women mobilized, as well as the reactions to their campaigns from the point of view of my argument here: the campaign against 'sati' in India.

The issue of sati has certain features which are notable. Claiming a right to preserve tradition or return to it now was the majority community through right-wing mobilization, a means by which a political group was seeking to consolidate its own position in a unstable political situation. In the Shah Bano controversy it was a beleaguered minority community pegging its right to cultural autonomy through a defence of the sanctity of the personal law regardless of its unequal gender implications. In the context of sati as well as the Hudood ordinances in Pakistan the same claim was being made more aggressively and more dangerously by the majority and again it was women who had to bear the burden of this demand. In the case of sati the women's campaign was fiercely countered by the Rajput community which claimed that the practice of sati was an intrinsic and fundamental part of their tradition and it was then extended by certain priests to the entire

Hindu community. The most significant dimension of this entire controversy for me were two features: the first was that unlike the Shah Bano controversy the women's movement was not internally divided on the issue; and second, the tradition argument forwarded by the defenders of the practice of sati was replayed in a most sinister way by certain male intellectuals in terms of that old dichotomy of 'real' Indian women versus westernized feminists: feminists were not authentic and were out of sync with their culture. Further, an attack on practices however oppressive they might be for women could be legitimate only if it was mounted from within the tradition, said the high priest of indigenism, an intellectual, not an activist we must note, with a huge following in the West.[5] On that criteria he regarded a radical reformist swami as having a right to speak but middle class educated urban women like me even though I was born in very conventional Indian home had none – never mind if our voices were completely in sync with huge numbers of urban and rural women from the state in which the sati had taken place. Feminists were by definition western, products of a colonial mentality, deracinated and so condemned to perpetual silence. The slide from valorizing Chipko over Bodh Gaya, from women who are nurturing and act on behalf of the community using indigenous forms of protest to a full scale attack on women who mobilize against oppressive 'traditional' practices of communities was not only complete but it was also showing up an unexpected conjunction of indigenism and cultural fundamentalism. The indigenist position on the sati controversy has to date been the most serious attack on the women's movement from outside its own ranks. It has also been the most unwarranted.

Among the most distressing aspects of the rightward shift of politics and religious majoritarianism from the late eighties and early nineties in India is the complicity of women in the often violent mobilization by a combine of fascist religious majoritarian groups against different minorities. Women in these formations have displayed agency in aggressively reiterating their material interests as a class or caste making for the most painful recognition that all women are not among the oppressed, they can be as anti-democratic or violent as their men are. By taking recourse to the powerful slogans of the women's movement, they can and have confused people both within the women's movement and others outside it. Although this is not the only kind of mobilization of women to be happening, this new mobilization has been more visible in some senses because it is so unacceptable to the women's movement. Since right-wing mobilization works within the framework of settled ideological positions, alongside 'tradition', 'culture' and patriarchal structures and does not require taking stands that question existing hierarchies of gender and class it can appear to be a more successful mobilization of women than those by groups working for more democratic ends. Looking back we can see that the first political crisis took the politics of the people leftward and energized the women's movement whereas the second stage of the crisis of governance has witnessed a rightward shift of politics fracturing and creating conceptual problems for the women's movement in India. The only positive dimension of the surfacing of such questions is that we are now in the process of acquiring a deeper level of understanding of the complexities of gender relations

III

The women's movement in India, like other movements for transformation of social relations, is perforce a movement that has to react to events or social pressures rather than work things out at its own pace; consequently even before we can deal with one set of problems in our societies we are overtaken by others. Something along these lines is happening currently. While the right-wing political formations have now captured state power bringing in new complexities India has since the early nineties entered a phase of economic reforms in consonance with global economic developments. Caught in a vortex of mounting external debt and under pressure from the World Bank and IMF structural adjustment, liberalization and privatization were the key elements through which development would finally arrive. By now we have been globalized as it were for almost a decade and we can see some of its consequences unfolding: the state has abdicated whatever little role it was playing in education and health care and retreated quite happily under IMF and World Bank conditionalities, a euphemism for their diktat, to its grossest and minimalist function of policing its people – in my common-sense critique of the new economic policy in discussions with others of my class who welcomed the new world order I would ask, "What is your notion of the state? Is it to be just the army and the police now?" That is exactly what the new state in India now is. I must strongly stress that globalization, liberalization and the market have different implications for Third World countries than they have for countries of the First World where social welfare schemes had mediated, to an extent, the depredations of capitalism and the market. Western feminists may now have to fight to retain them but we had not even started on the road to welfare and we have already abandoned such schemes, even at the notional or rhetorical level.

Unfortunately, globalization has in the public debate been virtually denuded of its economic implications and reduced to a cultural phenomenon as far as concern for its impact goes. Typically, such concern returns us to the familiar terrain of cultural nationalism where women in particular have become the icons of cultural inviolability. While global capital, i.e., western capital, is welcome by all sections of the governing elite, including the right-wing religious majoritarian formations, resistance is confined to the cultural sphere. I shall return to this point later: for the moment there are other dimensions to current economic processes which impact gender and need to be briefly outlined before I try and conclude.

I am now going to selectively take up the proliferation of NGOs (non-governmental organizations) to focus on the intersections of globalization and the women's movements through the transformation of many of the autonomous women's groups into NGOs. As a phenomenon, this has been happening even before the formal processes of globalization were encountered in India; in Pakistan and especially Bangladesh this linkage has a long presence as a consequence of international policy since the days of the latter's liberation. Notions of development operating in the First World as solutions for problems of the Third World with a specific focus on gender empowerment – for what it has never been clear –

were initially routed through the state in the mid-eighties in India. One such programme, the Women's Development Programme, reached a crisis point by the late eighties as the contradictions within the programme between the rhetoric and substance of empowerment became acute. It is now one of the biggest embarrassments of the women's movement. One of the lessons it has provided is that the state's, and the international funders, notions of development are very different from those of feminists and grassroots activists of the *sathin programme*. Far from being empowered, the programme has shown how powerless the *sathins* were at the hands of the state and developmentalists. Many women who had collaborated with the state in the programme and others who had been its targets now believe that both international agencies and the Indian state are only interested in women's empowerment for the limited purpose of population control, i.e., women need to gain a small measure of autonomy over their own lives from feudal and family control to make the family planning programmes successful.[6] The experience has sharpened the dilemmas of the women's movement about the nature of collaboration that is possible between the women's movement and the state as far as a transformation in gender relations is concerned. More acute in some senses are the dilemmas of autonomous women's groups (AWGs); the NGOization of many of these groups over the last fifteen years and their reliance on foreign funds from development agencies is raising questions of how autonomous they really are and how far they can go in achieving their earlier goals. A sharp critique of the NGOization of social movements has charged the NGOs of having paved the way for the entry of global capital. This does place an enormous responsibility on those sections of the AWGs, which have been NGOized to do some serious thinking about their strategies for battling patriarchies within a larger goal of creating an egalitarian society within their own nation-states and between nation-states.

There are other aspects to globalization and its more direct impact on all women which require the attention of the women's movement. Briefly these are some dimensions that have begun to be understood by feminists. Among the wider implications of globalization documented for Third World economies is the deleterious effect it has on the food security systems as production of food crops give way to the production of exportable non-food crops. The increasing difficulty of getting food can have a disastrous effect on women's domestic lives and further erode their social position. The consequences of the Structural Adjustment Programme (SAP) suggest that unemployment and retrenchment of workers – both male and female – is increasing women's vulnerability. As the state rolls back its minimalist social welfare programmes compounding problems of illiteracy, poverty, medical and health care it is setting up the home once again as a servicing institution where women's labour will provide the buffer against the depredations of the market. Further structural deformations of the environment, damage to subsistence production and the transfer of natural resources to which women and the poor had access, to multinationals constitutes a serious threat to livelihood. While multinationals dump hazardous reproductive devices with no concern for health but have an enormous interest in women's appearance the burgeoning beauty industry clothes and cosmetics, new relations are being made between consumption pleasure and culturally specific forms of femininity. Miss World contest here. The East-West dichotomy, played up by the right-wing as also the protection of national culture which some women have articulated, cannot capture these complex relations. The emphasis on the need for family values from right-wing quarters in the face of what is projected selectively as an unrelated cultural assault from the West is a culturalism that can comfortably serve the material interests of global capital.

Globalization has also altered the face of the state and the faces of exploitation are getting more remote and less easy to identify and therefore to confront. The state is retreating not only from its earlier reformist paradigm but also since the indigenous family under globalization is being made part of the protected sphere of culture even a recognition of oppressions within the family are becoming harder in the new environment.[7] Rights for women are already under attack from the very right-wing groups that have colluded to bring in the global capital.

Concluding Observations

Before post-colonial nation-states, whose problems of gender did not begin with their colonization, could address their *longue duree* contradictions given their history of colonization a new remote control imperialism, i.e., global capital and global capitalist culture are impacting these societies in crucial ways. Given that under colonialism the cultural crisis had resulted in pushing under the carpet certain structural contradictions, especially those of gender as in the case of the age of consent hysteria, and given the tendency to treat gender inequality as a secondary problem by nationalists under the new threat of cultural invasion generated by globalization, cultural independence will and has already begun to hinge on the uniqueness of the Indian woman and the uniqueness of Indian family arrangements as portrayed recently in the all-time hit film – *Hum Aapke Hain Kaun*. The film had all the elements of the economic shifts and the cultural articulations of the contemporary moment: a Hindu family that has multi-national business connections, is pious in its *Rambhakti* and closely knit, modern in its business orientation but traditional in its family values, where it is natural that women and younger brothers can sacrifice their love for the greater good of the family. Right-wing critiques of globalization have already been denuded of economic content and solely pegged on culture. Once more real issues of food, livelihood, health and the vulnerability of women under oppressive structures of patriarchies are being deflected in the name of protecting culture (all of which were so evident in the controversy around the filming of *Water*). The challenge before the women's movement is to disassemble globalization into its different segments and the distinctive ways it is working in order to determine which elements they must add to their list of things to struggle against. Perhaps, the women's movement is uniquely placed to address the complexities of the current economic and social contradictions. It is the only movement today that encompasses, and links, such issues as work, wages, environment, ecology, civil rights, sexual oppression, violence, political representation, caste, class, unequal allocation of basic resources, health, militarism, and individual and social relationships. This is true not only of South Asia but also of the women's movement globally. The women's movement therefore has the vibrancy to speak and mobilize on behalf of and in conjunction with other marginalized groups – the poor, the elderly and the disprivileged.

The real challenge before the women's movement in India today is that it should not only take up gender inequalities in the family, in the community, and in the state, but also inequalities along other lines. Following globalization the need to take up social welfare has become imperative; in the current tensions in South Asia militarization and nuclearization are major drags on budgetary allocations and have a direct bearing on women and the poor. In Pakistan and Sri Lanka the women's movement has addressed the problems of militarization and its impact on women but we in India are yet to do so. We also need to mobilize for democratically arrived upon development strategies and against policies determined by global centres of power with their counterparts in our state structures. In this the only kind of globalization that is acceptable to the women's movements in South Asia is the support and solidarity we can extend to our respective struggles across the globe, in the East and in the West, in the North and in the South – however we want to categorize ourselves. The global culture that is welcome is the culture of resistance. In this the First World women's movements and the Third World women's movements can find and have found common ground; that women's movements and perhaps only women's movements can do this, rising above narrow nationalisms and opposing material interests is borne out by the examples of the Women's Action Forum, a major constituent of the women's movement in Pakistan, which apologized to Bangladeshi women for the happenings in 1972, or as an all women group from India visited Lahore in March 2000. They were all committed to non-nuclearization, reduced military expenditure, and the resolving of all disputes through dialogue at a time when officials, politicians and the military establishments in India and Pakistan were growling at each other. As we enter the new millennium, the women's movement has a major responsibility for revisioning the world. This is different kind of globalization – a global responsibility to struggle for a less oppressive world.

NOTES

1. This paper draws from my own participation in campaigns which were part of the women's movement and recollections of those I was unable to participate in. It is also based on my reading about the women's movements during the last two decades. References will be provided only when I specifically use the works of other scholars or those who have written about specific movements.
2. For the last three years I have been a visiting faculty member of the Institute of Women's Studies, Lahore. My understanding of the women's movement in Pakistan is based on numerous discussions, formal and informal, with women active in the movement. I watched the farce on the Hudood ordinances at the formal inauguration of the Institute in February 1998. The setting up of the Institute in Lahore itself is a tribute to the women's movements in South Asia as it draws students and faculty from all over South Asia, regardless of the official relations between the countries of the region. During these visits I have also had access to a large number of publications dealing with the women's movements in Pakistan, some of which are cited in the additional bibliography, provided below.
3. The discussion in this section is based on Vimla Bahugana, 'The Chipko Movement,' and Govind Kelkar and Chetna Gala, 'The Bodh Gaya Land Struggle,' in Ilina Sen (ed.), *A Space Within the Struggle*, Delhi, Kali for Women, 1990 and Gopa Joshi and Sunderlal Bahugana, 'Protecting the Sources of Community Life,' and Manimala, 'Zamin Kenkar? Jote Onkar', in Madhu Kishwar and Ruth Vanita (eds.), *In Search of Answers*, London, Zed Books, 1984.
4. Govind Kelkar and Chetna Gala, 'The Bodh Gaya Land Struggle,' op. cit., p. 100.

5. I am referring to Ashish Nandi's attack on feminists in his newspaper articles during the Roop Kanwar sati controversy.
6. These observations are based on presentations made by Arti Sawney and Kiran Dubey on the *sathin* movement at seminars on the Indian women's movement(s) in Patna in 1995 and Miranda House, Delhi in 1999.
7. Kumkum Sangari and Uma Chakravarti, 'Introduction,' in *From Myths to Markets: Essays on Gender*, Shimla, Indian Institute of Advanced Study, 1999.

Index